PROSE MODELS

third edition

third edition prose models

gerald levin
the university of akron

 HARCOURT BRACE JOVANOVICH, INC.
new york   chicago   san francisco   atlanta

ISBN: 0-15-572277-8

Library of Congress Catalog Card Number: 74-14293

Printed in the United States of America

PREFACE

The purpose of the Third Edition remains that of the first and second editions: to introduce students to rhetorical and logical ideas in prose composition through the analysis of prose models. The selections are both models of good writing and interesting discussions of important ideas.

The book progresses from part to whole. It begins with such topics as emphasis, coordination and subordination of ideas, and climax in the paragraph and the sentence, and moves to their use in the whole essay. In this way students are encouraged to think about the rhetoric and logic of the essay through close analysis of models followed by the writing of paragraphs and sentences. The sections are developed cumulatively, building on earlier definitions and discussions and providing a continuity for class use that is difficult with books that present a random collection of illustrative selections. But each section is self-contained so that sections can be taught in different order whenever that seems desirable.

Discussions of rhetorical and logical topics follow the first selection under each topic, preceding the questions. For this Third Edition, many of the discussions have been expanded or revised. As in the earlier editions, the principles of logical analysis are explained thoroughly, but in easy-to-understand terms. The discussions may of course be assigned separately. Wherever possible the writing assignments are based on the rhetorical or logical topics as well as on the ideas of the various selections.

Over half the selections are new to this edition, representing a careful balance of the contemporary and the classic. The number of complete essays or sections of books complete in themselves has been increased to thirty-five. The essays on language now include George Orwell's "Politics and the English Language"; I have selected it because Orwell's indictment of much political writing is now classic and is especially pertinent to American political life in the 'seventies. New to the book also are essays on ecology, television news programs, minority stereotypes in America, and civil disobedience. The Third Edition also contains a new section on persuasive writing, with essays by Archibald Cox, Vine Deloria, Jr., and Bayard Rustin.

Ideas introduced in the shorter selections that open the book
are often developed at greater length or from other points of view
in the essays in Part Two. Among these topics are the world of
the child, the problems of adolescence, the kinds of education,
attitudes toward sports and war, the relation of humankind to
nature, and the nature and influence of the media. A thematic
table of contents at the back of the book groups the selections for
quick reference and illustrates this continuity of ideas from the
short, paragraph-length models to the complete essay. The final
section on the interpretation of evidence discusses feminist issues; as in the previous editions, this section introduces the documented paper.

Again I wish to thank Forrest Read for suggestions and cor-
rections in the original manuscript. Alan Hart, The University of
Akron, read the first draft of the discussion of logic and made
valuable comments on it. I also wish to thank the following people who made helpful suggestions for this revision: Mary Alice
DeHaven, Dale Doepke, Julia A. Hull, Bruce Holland, David L.
Jones, Walter Lehrman, Alice MacDonald, Ruth Messenger, Sally
Slocum, James Switzer, Cathryn Taliaferro, and Arlene Toth, all
of The University of Akron; Elmer Ericson and Elray L. Peder-
son, Weber State College; Ruth R. Cox, Scottsdale Community
College; Elizabeth M. Guiney, North Hennepin State Junior College; John F. Fleischauer, Columbus College; Ronald Fort, Tar-
rant County Junior College; John T. Hatley, Phoenix College; Sylvia Huete, Dillard University; Jonathan Lawson, St. Cloud State
College; Robert B. Lyons, Queens College; O. B. Moor, Jr., Lake-
land Community College; Eleanor M. Stewart, San Diego City
College; and Joseph H. Wessling, Xavier University. My wife,
Lillian Levin, and Elizabeth and Sylvia Levin, helped me in preparing the manuscript. Eben Ludlow, Dorothy Mott, and Lee
Shenkman of Harcourt Brace Jovanovich were, as always, immensely encouraging and helpful.

GERALD LEVIN

CONTENTS

the elements of the essay

THE
PARAGRAPH

TOPIC SENTENCE

Peter Fleming
THE END OF THE WORLD

[1] The other day a great many people in Rome became suddenly and inexplicably convinced that the world was going to end at midnight on Monday; the Vatican had to issue a statement saying "there is nothing to warrant the present panic." [2] When I read about this I began to wonder how, if the British nation knew for a fact that the world was going to end in twenty-four hours' time, it would spend those hours. [3] I suppose that most people, including many who had not done such a thing for years, would go to church. [4] What else would happen? [5] Except for midwives, stockmen, B.B.C. announcers, the crews of ships at sea and keepers in zoological gardens, hardly anybody would have any reason to do any work. [6] If the Government recommended a "business as usual" policy, would it work? [7] There wouldn't be much point in the shops or the banks staying open, since money and goods would be valueless; and the schools (which in Rome were poorly attended on Monday) might just as well be closed. [8] It would, on the other hand, be a pity to cancel cricket fixtures. [9] Cricket is one of the few forms of human activity which would not be robbed, both for players and spectators, of all meaning and all interest by the fact that the world was about to end; it would still be worth hitting a six or holding a catch, when designing a cathedral or assassinating a tyrant had become completely pointless acts. [10] But I suspect that most people would spend an anxious, frustrated and probably rather boring day, irked by remembrance of all the things they had always wanted to do and by the realization that, if it was not too late, it was either impossible or useless to do them now.

DISCUSSION: TOPIC SENTENCE

Fleming's paragraph is an essay in miniature, but most paragraphs do not stand alone. Later in this book we will study the ways paragraphs

THE END OF THE WORLD: From *My Aunt's Rhinoceros,* by Peter Fleming. © 1956 by Peter Fleming. Reprinted by permission of Simon and Schuster, Inc., and Rupert Hart-Davis Ltd.

are connected; we will begin with ways that single paragraphs are organized to distinguish the main idea or thesis of the paragraph from subordinate ideas.

The topic sentence is exactly what the term suggests: a statement of the subject, or topic, of the paragraph. The topic sentence may be reduced to a single word, as in these opening sentences of a Dickens novel:

> London. Michaelmas Term lately over, and the Lord Chancellor sitting in Lincoln's Inn Hall. Implacable November weather. As much mud in the streets, as if the waters had but newly retired from the face of the earth. . . .—*Bleak House*

Or it may be a general statement that will be developed in specific ways:

> The question of ruins is interesting.—Mary McCarthy, "One Touch of Nature"

Or it may be a specific idea:

> Individual combat between champions goes back to the very beginnings of knighthood in the Dark Ages.—Crane Brinton, *A History of Western Morals*

Whatever form it takes, the topic sentence introduces an idea, a consideration, a question to be examined or answered in the paragraph: Why do ruins fascinate people? Why is individual combat basic to knighthood? This topic idea may be repeated in the course of the paragraph or restated at the end through the details of the discussion. The topic sentence of the following paragraph is a general statement of the subject; the concluding sentence restates the topic idea, explaining it fully:

> There is something depressing about French eighteenth-century literature, especially that of the latter half of the century *[topic sentence]*. All those sprightly memoirs and risky stories and sentimental effusions constitute, perhaps, the dreariest body of literature we know, once we do know it. The French are essentially critics of life, rather than creators of life. And when the life itself runs rather thin, as it did in the eighteenth century, and the criticism rattles all the faster, it just leaves one feeling wretched *[topic sentence restated]*.—D. H. Lawrence, "The Good Man"

Occasionally the paragraph will open with a transitional sentence linking it to the previous paragraph or serving as a lead-in to the topic sentence. Another paragraph by Brinton opens:

> At the outset we run into a difficulty that can be no more than acknowledged. The Middle Ages regarded both the knight and the

saint as complementary facets of a single ideal, the Christian; both were needed servants of God and of His order on earth.—*A History of Western Morals*

The first sentence warns that a problem will be examined but not solved in the discussion; the second sentence states the topic idea. The topic idea, it should be noted, may or may not be the most important idea or thesis of the paragraph. In some paragraphs, the topic sentence appears toward the middle or at the end; a series of details leads to it.

QUESTIONS

1. Does sentence 1 or sentence 2 in Fleming's paragraph state the topic idea of the paragraph? How are the sentences related to each other?
2. Does Fleming reach a specific conclusion or thesis about people, or does he instead present a series of random observations relating to his topic?
3. Which sentences in the paragraph are transitional, connecting ideas rather than stating them?
4. The following paragraph from a short story describing a young war veteran might have opened with a statement of the controlling idea. Provide a topic sentence for the paragraph:

   In the evening he practised on his clarinet, strolled down town, read and went to bed. He was still a hero to his two young sisters. His mother would have given him breakfast in bed if he had wanted it. She often came in when he was in bed and asked him to tell her about the war, but her attention always wandered. His father was non-committal.—Ernest Hemingway, "Soldier's Home"

WRITING ASSIGNMENT

Write a paragraph on other forms of human activity that, in your opinion, would be robbed of all meaning if the end of the world were imminent. Begin with a topic sentence that states why they would be.

TOPIC SENTENCE

Anthony Bailey
THE DUTCH SENSE OF PRIVACY

¹ To me, being by myself means being in a room alone. ² The Dutch, like children in big families, can be by themselves in a room with six other people, or on a canal bank lined with people fishing almost shoulder to shoulder. ³ Stand on any street corner in Amsterdam at five-thirty in the evening and watch the phalanxes of bicycles go by—a sight not quite what it used to be but still impressive enough. ⁴ If you pick at random one serenely pedalling individual from the thick, staggered formation, you see that he isn't really looking at the city, the street, or the bicyclists around him. ⁵ He seems aware only of a small portion of space, a bubble within which he and his bike exist, with a few spare inches outside his knuckles on the handlebars, his twirling feet, his steady shoulders. ⁶ He is secure within this space, which encloses him and moves with him, the way energy moves through water, giving an appearance of fast forward motion to a wave. ⁷ Then the traffic light has changed, he is gone, and others have whirled up to the junction, jousting with each other in a remote, impersonal way, ignoring an interloping car or a sputtering *brommer*. ⁸ On any face—the face of a girl, the face of a dignified gentleman wearing a hat—you may glimpse the most private of smiles. ⁹ Pedalling homeward, they have their own thoughts as their wheels revolve and as cars and trams and *brommers* assail them from four, or even six, directions, the man on the right, whatever his vehicle, having the right of way, which he—sometimes with more courage than sense—always takes, their reflexes operating splendidly though their minds are elsewhere. ¹⁰ These Amsterdam rush-hour bicycle riders always fascinate me. ¹¹ They are a wonder, like salmon going upstream, demonstrating, as they do, that in the most crowded places a human being can go on being himself, can become even more himself.

THE DUTCH SENSE OF PRIVACY: From *The Light in Holland*, by Anthony Bailey. Copyright © 1970 by Anthony Bailey. Reprinted by permission of Alfred A. Knopf, Inc. Originally appeared in *The New Yorker*. Selection title by editor.

1. ... is the topic idea of the paragraph—what it means to be alone or what it means to be alone in Holland? Is the focus of sentence 11 on the first or the second of these concerns?
2. Bailey develops his topic idea through "one serenely pedalling individual" (sentence 4) and other cyclists he observed (sentence 8). Do sentences 8 and 9 make new points or illustrate other qualities—or could they be omitted without reducing the thought of the paragraph?

WRITING ASSIGNMENTS

In a single paragraph explain what being alone means to you—and illustrate from your observations of other people. You may want to choose your examples from a single area of experience, as Bailey does, or you may choose from a wide range of experiences.

In a single paragraph develop an observation you have made about persons your age—perhaps their attitude toward the privacy of others—and substantiate it with a series of brief examples. State your observation early in the paragraph and restate it at the end.

Hal Borland
THE EFFECT OF AUTUMN

[1] The strange thing is that Autumn, especially on a wooded ridge, changes the relationship of time and distance. [2] The days shorten, and at the same time they increase in height and breadth. [3] It is almost as though there were a fixed ratio that keeps the days in balance. [4] The leaves begin to fall and the eye begins to reach. [5] New vistas open. [6] I saw those vistas opening that morning, there on the ridge, and my eye could see brand-new horizons. [7] Not exactly new, of course, since they have been there since this earth assumed its present shape; but they seemed new that morning because they were newly seen after weeks and months when they were hidden. [8] And I know that tonight I can

THE EFFECT OF AUTUMN: From *Countryman: A Summary of Belief*, by Hal Borland. Copyright © 1957, 1958, 1961, 1962, 1963, 1964 and 1965 by Hal Borland. Reprinted by permission of J. B. Lippincott Company. Selection title by editor.

look up from my dooryard, through the branches of the big sugar maples, and see the constellations of Pegasus and Andromeda. [9] They, too, have been there a long time, but I couldn't see them from the dooryard all Summer.

QUESTIONS

1. Sentence 1 states the topic idea of the paragraph: the relationship between time and distance. Sentences 2–4 illustrate the relationship. How is it dealt with or illustrated in the remainder of the paragraph?
2. How does the author illustrate the height and the breadth of autumn days?

WRITING ASSIGNMENTS

Develop an idea relating to the effect of another season of the year and illustrate from your personal experience.

Develop one of the following statements or phrases through illustration:

a. He had been kicked in the Head by a Mule when young and believed everything he read in the Sunday Papers.—George Ade, *The Slim Girl*
b. All the modern inconveniences.—Mark Twain, *Life on the Mississippi*
c. Courage is resistance to fear, mastery of fear—not absence of fear.—Mark Twain, *Pudd'nhead Wilson*
d. The victor belongs to the spoils.—F. Scott Fitzgerald, *The Beautiful and the Damned*

MAIN AND SUBORDINATE IDEAS

Edwin Way Teale
COUNTRY SUPERSTITIONS

[1] In the folklore of the country, numerous superstitions relate to winter weather. [2] Back-country farmers examine their corn husks—the thicker the husk, the colder the winter. [3] They watch the acorn crop—the more acorns, the more severe the season. [4] They observe where white-faced hornets place their paper nests—the higher they are, the deeper will be the snow. [5] They examine the size and shape and color of the spleens of butchered hogs for clues to the severity of the season. [6] They keep track of the blooming of dogwood in the spring—the more abundant the blooms, the more bitter the cold in January. [7] When chipmunks carry their tails high and squirrels have heavier fur and mice come into country houses early in the fall, the superstitious gird themselves for a long, hard winter. [8] Without any scientific basis, a wider-than-usual black band on a woolly-bear caterpillar is accepted as a sign that winter will arrive early and stay late. [9] Even the way a cat sits beside the stove carries its message to the credulous. [10] According to a belief once widely held in the Ozarks, a cat sitting with its tail to the fire indicates very cold weather is on the way.

DISCUSSION: MAIN AND SUBORDINATE IDEAS

The topic idea may be the thesis or main idea of the paragraph, and a series of subordinate ideas may illustrate or modify it. In this kind of paragraph the main idea may be distinguished from the subordinate ones by repeating or restating it, by using it in a pivotal position to or-

COUNTRY SUPERSTITIONS: From *Wandering Through Winter*, by Edwin Way Teale (New York: Dodd, Mead and Company, 1966). Reprinted by permission of the publisher. Selection title by editor.

ganize or connect the subordinate ideas, or by building the paragraph to a statement of it. In organizing paragraphs, it is useful to keep in mind that the beginning and ending are the most emphatic parts. We said earlier that paragraphs frequently open with the main idea, or with a statement of the general subject, and may end with a restatement of it—a way of giving the idea additional emphasis. Transitional words and phrases may be needed to clarify the relation of ideas. When a series of ideas equal in importance (coordinate ideas) develops the main idea, parallel construction makes formal transitions unnecessary:

> The democratic system cannot be operated without effective opposition. For, in making the great experiment of governing people by consent rather than by coercion, it is not sufficient that the party in power should have a majority. It is just as necessary that the party in power should never outrage the minority. *That means that* it must listen to the minority and be moved by the criticisms of the minority. *That means that* its measures must take account of the minority's objections, and that in administering measures it must remember that the minority may become the majority.—Walter Lippmann, *The Indispensable Opposition* (Italics added—Ed.)

Some paragraphs state an idea and restate it at the end in different words, sometimes without illustration. These final sentences restate an idea, developing its implications in the course of the restatement:

> Actually, we who engage in nonviolent direct action are not the creators of tension. We merely bring to the surface the hidden tension that is already alive. We bring it out in the open, where it can be seen and dealt with. Like a boil that can never be cured so long as it is covered up but must be opened with all its ugliness to the natural medicines of air and light, injustice must be exposed, with all the tension its exposure creates, to the light of human conscience and the air of national opinion before it can be cured.—Martin Luther King, Jr., "Letter from Birmingham Jail"

QUESTIONS

1. Sentence 1 in Teale's paragraph—the topic sentence—states the main idea; sentences 2–10 are subordinate and develop the main idea. Sentences 2–6 are parallel in construction. Do they express ideas equal in importance?
2. Are the ideas in sentences 7–10 equal in importance to those in 2–6, even though the sentences differ in construction? In other words, are the ten or more superstitions described in the paragraph of equal importance in developing the topic idea?

WRITING ASSIGNMENT

Present and illustrate a generalization about superstitions, or a single superstition, held by educated people. State the generalization as your topic sentence and restate it after illustrating it.

Gene Weltfish
THE PAWNEE UNIVERSE

¹ There is no simple formula for describing the intricate logic of the Pawnee people's lives. ² One thing is clear—that no one is caught within the social code. ³ Against the backdrop of his natural environment, each individual stands as his own person. ⁴ The Old World design for the human personality does not apply to this New World Man. ⁵ The Pawnee child was born into a community from the beginning, and he never acquired the notion that he was closed in "within four walls." ⁶ He was literally trained to feel that the world around him was his home— *kahuraru,* the universe, meaning literally the inside land, and that his house was a small model of it. ⁷ The infinite cosmos was his constant source of strength and his ultimate progenitor, and there was no reason why he should hesitate to set out alone and explore the wide world, even though years should pass before he returned. ⁸ Not only was he not confined within four walls but he was not closed in with a permanent group of people. ⁹ The special concern of his mother did not mean that he was so closely embedded with her emotionally that he was not able to move about.

¹ In its very essence, the Pawnee outlook on reality differs from our own. ² For us the material aspect is primary. ³ On a second level of discourse, we place observed events; on a third level, which we count still less sure, is the "human factor"; and finally furthest removed from solid reality is the realm of ideas. ⁴ In the Pawnee estimate of the world around him, the primary level of reality is thought. ⁵ In our own story of creation, the deity

THE PAWNEE UNIVERSE: From *The Lost Universe* by Gene Weltfish, © 1965 Basic Books, Inc., Publishers, New York. From Chapters 4 and 2. Selection title by editor.

shaped man out of clay, but the Pawnee deity—Vault-of-the-Heavens—began the process of creation with thoughts and so created the universe and the stars, and they in turn were to create man in their own image. [6] When a Pawnee individual wanted to organize his life goals, he looked within himself in his thinking and was blessed by Heaven with a vision. [7] In the Pawnee context, the *thinking* man was the essential human being. [8] The universe continued its seasonal round only when man willed it through his thought of Heaven and its creative power. [9] In creating man, Heaven had also created the moving force of the universe. [10] In this order of things, events were an adjunct of *human* ongoing, and all the nonliving things were a fluid manifestation of the universal life process. [11] A thing manufactured was a manifestation of a very personal skill, and a thing used was equally personal. [12] The skill of the priest who kept the universe in motion and that of the arrowshaft maker had an analogous quality which was inherent in the person himself, and both were considered as dedicated public professions. [13] For both living and nonliving things in the time of the creation, there were always two storms—one to build the empty structure and one for its continuity. [14] This estimate of the nature of reality is almost the complete reverse of our own and is one of the many ways in which the Pawnee outlook contrasts rather sharply with ours.

QUESTIONS

1. The first paragraph consists of increasingly specific statements: sentence 1, the most general statement of the paragraph, is transitional and introduces the topic idea in sentence 2. Does sentence 3 restate the topic idea or introduce a new one?
2. If we think of a subordinate idea as one that *explains,* sentence 4 is obviously subordinate to sentences 2 and 3 in the first paragraph. How is sentence 4 explained in the remainder of the paragraph?
3. The first paragraph may be mapped (as in the familiar sentence outline) by arranging the sentences (in reduced form or reworded) to indicate *levels* of subordination:
   1 No simple formula can describe the intricate logic of Pawnee life.
      2 *No one is caught within the social code.*
      3 Each individual stands as his own person.
         4 The Old World design does not apply to this New World man.
            5 The Pawnee child never came to feel he was enclosed by four walls.

6   He felt that the world around him was his home.

7   The infinite cosmos was his source of strength and progenitor.

There was no reason to hesitate about exploring the whole world.

8   The Pawnee child was not closed in with a permanent group of people.

9   He did not feel embedded emotionally by his mother.

Each statement at a reduced level is subordinate to that immediately above it. Sentences 2 and 3 are coordinate ideas—of equal importance in developing sentence 1. What indication is there in the original paragraph that sentences 5 and 8 are also coordinate—equal in importance in developing sentence 4?

4. The second paragraph develops the topic idea through one block of ideas dealing with the New World view of reality and a second block of ideas dealing chiefly with the Pawnee (there is brief reference to the New World view in sentence 5). The two blocks develop the topic idea—the main idea of the paragraph—presented in sentence 1. Which sentences in the second block of ideas (from sentence 4 to the end of the paragraph) illustrate general statements about the Pawnee view of reality?

WRITING ASSIGNMENT

Using the second paragraph as a model of organization, contrast two views of a single experience—perhaps a child's and the mother's view of his or her room, or the student's and the teacher's view of the classroom. Comment on what is seen and what is thought.

UNITY

Robert Louis Stevenson
EXTREME BUSYNESS

¹ Extreme *busyness*, whether at school or college, kirk or market, is a symptom of deficient vitality; and a faculty for idleness implies a catholic appetite and a strong sense of personal identity. ² There is a sort of dead-alive, hackneyed people about, who are scarcely conscious of living except in the exercise of some conventional occupation. ³ Bring these fellows into the country, or set them aboard ship, and you will see how they pine for their desk or their study. ⁴ They have no curiosity; they cannot give themselves over to random provocations; they do not take pleasure in the exercise of their faculties for its own sake; and unless Necessity lays about them with a stick, they will even stand still. ⁵ It is no good speaking to such folk: they *cannot* be idle, their nature is not generous enough; and they pass those hours in a sort of coma, which are not dedicated to furious moiling in the gold-mill. ⁶ When they do not require to go to the office, when they are not hungry and have no mind to drink, the whole breathing world is a blank to them. ⁷ If they have to wait an hour or so for a train, they fall into a stupid trance with their eyes open. ⁸ To see them, you would suppose there was nothing to look at and no one to speak with; you would imagine they were paralyzed or alienated; and yet very possibly they are hard workers in their own way, and have good eyesight for a flaw in a deed or a turn of the market. ⁹ They have been to school and college, but all the time they had their eye on the medal; they have gone about in the world and mixed with clever people, but all the time they were thinking of their own affairs. ¹⁰ As if a man's soul were not too small to begin with, they have dwarfed and narrowed theirs by a life of all work and no play; until here they are at forty, with a listless attention, a mind vacant of all material of amusement, and not one thought to rub against another, while

EXTREME BUSYNESS: From "An Apology for Idlers" in *Virginibus Puerisque*, by Robert Louis Stevenson, published by Charles Scribner's Sons. Selection title by editor.

they wait for the train. [11] Before he was breeched, he might have clambered on the boxes; when he was twenty, he would have stared at the girls; but now the pipe is smoked out, the snuff-box empty, and my gentleman sits bolt upright upon a bench, with lamentable eyes. [12] This does not appeal to me as being Success in Life.

DISCUSSION: UNITY

The sentences of a paragraph should connect to a central idea. If their connection to the central idea and to one another is not immediately clear to the reader, such means to clarity as transitions and parallel sentence construction may be needed. In seeking to be clear and also convincing and interesting, the writer must keep his audience in mind. One kind of organization may be a good way of reaching one particular audience but not another. For example, with schoolchildren it may be best, in explaining a complex idea like nuclear energy, to move from details to a general statement of the idea; schoolchildren would surely find a presentation that began with general statements and definitions difficult to understand. The choices open to the writer are sometimes restricted by his subject matter: an account of the discovery of the planet Neptune would mainly be chronological.

The order in which the writer presents his ideas, then, may be determined not only by the requirements of exposition but by considerations of what will be the most effective presentation—in short, by *rhetorical* considerations. He may decide that he will best be understood if he proceeds chronologically, or from the least to the most interesting or important of his ideas, or from the general to the specific, or from the simple to the complex. The paragraph or the essay he writes will be unified if he deals with one idea at a time, without shifting abruptly from one idea to another, and he should always have clearly in mind the reason for proceeding as he does.

The accomplished writer often makes these choices unconsciously; indeed, he may develop a style of organization—a manner of organizing ideas that recurs in many of the paragraphs, a manner determined by his personal preferences and ways of looking at experience as well as by his habits of thought (perhaps his habit of moving from general statements to specific examples—or the reverse).

QUESTIONS

1. This complex paragraph of Stevenson's is concerned with causes of extreme busyness—"deficient vitality" and a lack of generosity—and with the consequences of these traits. Stevenson deals with one

cause at a time, illustrating it before proceeding to the next. How is
the transition made to the lack of generosity as a cause, in sentence
5?
2. How is the transition made to the consequences of these qualities of
   character, toward the end of the paragraph?
3. Does Stevenson state or imply that a lack of generosity is the *outcome* of "deficient vitality"—that the busy person is too lacking in
   vitality to be generous in his attitude toward life? If your answer to
   this question is "no," can you account for the order of ideas in sentences 1–9?

WRITING ASSIGNMENTS

Stevenson might have illustrated, then explained extreme busyness; or
explained, then illustrated, without dividing his statement of the
causes; or focused on consequences, instead of considering both causes
and consequences. Rewrite the paragraph, organizing it in another way,
substituting examples, and perhaps adding your own ideas.

Write a paragraph on extreme idleness, illustrating and discussing
causes and consequences. Be ready to account for and justify your
order of ideas.

Mary McCarthy
UNCLE MYERS

[1] And here was another strange thing about Myers. [2] He not
only did nothing for a living but he appeared to have no history.
[3] He came from Elkhart, Indiana, but beyond this fact nobody
seemed to know anything about him—not even how he had met
my aunt Margaret. [4] Reconstructed from his conversation, a picture of Elkhart emerged for us that showed it as a flat place consisting chiefly of ball parks, poolrooms, and hardware stores.
[5] Aunt Margaret came from Chicago, which consisted of the
Loop, Marshall Field's, assorted priests and monsignors, and the
black-and-white problem. [6] How had these two worlds impinged? [7] Where our family spoke freely of its relations, real and

UNCLE MYERS: From "Tin Butterfly," copyright, 1951, by Mary McCarthy. Reprinted from her
volume *Memories of a Catholic Girlhood* by permission of Harcourt Brace Jovanovich, Inc.
Selection title by editor.

imaginary, Myers spoke of no one, not even a parent. [8] At the
very beginning, when my father's old touring car, which had
been shipped on, still remained in our garage, Myers had certain
seedy cronies whom he took riding in it or who simply sat in it
in our driveway, as if anchored in a houseboat; but when the car
went, they went or were banished. [9] Uncle Myers and Aunt
Margaret had no friends, no couples with whom they exchanged
visits—only a middle-aged, black-haired, small, emaciated
woman with a German name and a yellowed skin whom we were
taken to see one afternoon because she was dying of cancer.
[10] This protracted death had the aspect of a public execution,
which was doubtless why Myers took us to it; that is, it was a
spectacle and it was free, and it inspired restlessness and depression. [11] Myers was the perfect type of rootless municipalized man
who finds his pleasures in the handouts or overflow of an industrial civilization. [12] He enjoyed standing on a curbstone, watching
parades, the more nondescript the better, the Labor Day parade
being his favorite, and next to that a military parade, followed by
the commercial parades with floats and girls dressed in costumes;
he would even go to Lake Calhoun or Lake Harriet for doll-car-
riage parades and competitions of children dressed as Indians.
[13] He liked bandstands, band concerts, public parks devoid of
grass; sky writing attracted him; he was quick to hear of a de-
partment-store demonstration where colored bubbles were
blown, advertising a soap, to the tune of "I'm Forever Blowing
Bubbles," sung by a mellifluous soprano. [14] He collected coupons
and tinfoil, bundles of newspaper for the old rag-and-bone man
(thus interfering seriously with our school paper drives), free
samples of cheese at Donaldson's, free tickets given out by a
neighborhood movie house to the first installment of a serial—in
all the years we lived with him, we never saw a full-length movie
but only those truncated beginnings. [15] He was also fond of
streetcar rides (could the system have been municipally owned?),
soldiers' monuments, cemeteries, big, coarse flowers like cannas
and cockscombs set in beds by city gardeners. [16] Museums did
not appeal to him, though we did go one night with a large
crowd to see Marshal Foch on the steps of the Art Institute. [17] He
was always weighing himself on penny weighing machines.
[18] He seldom left the house except on one of these purposeless
errands, or else to go to a ball game, by himself. [19] In the winter,
he spent the days at home in the den, or in the kitchen, making

candy. [20] He often had enormous tin trays of decorated fondants cooling in the cellar, which leads my brother Kevin to think today that at one time in Myers' life he must have been a pastry cook or a confectioner. [21] He also liked to fashion those little figures made of pipe cleaners that were just then coming in as favors in the better candy shops, but Myers used *old* pipe cleaners, stained yellow and brown. [22] The bonbons, with their pecan or almond topping, that he laid out in such perfect rows were for his own use; we were permitted to watch him set them out, but never—and my brother Kevin confirms this—did we taste a single one.

QUESTIONS

1. At the beginning of the paragraph Mary McCarthy discusses Uncle Myers's history and proceeds to his friendships and his interests. What are these interests?
2. Why is the information about the pipe cleaners and the candy saved for the end of the paragraph? How would the impression of Uncle Myers have been altered if the paragraph ended instead with the details of his cronies and his collections?
3. The paragraph is unified because Mary McCarthy discusses one thing at a time, without returning to earlier considerations. What is the principle of order in the paragraph?
4. How does the detail about the candy help to reveal Mary McCarthy's attitude toward Uncle Myers? Are her value judgments stated or implied?

WRITING ASSIGNMENT

Build a paragraph around a central impression of an unusual person, selecting details from different areas of experiences that develop this impression. Do not state your opinion of the person directly; let your details reveal it.

TRANSITIONS

George Orwell
THE ARMY PARADE-STEP

¹ One rapid but fairly sure guide to the social atmosphere of a country is the parade-step of its army. ² A military parade is really a kind of ritual dance, something like a ballet, expressing a certain philosophy of life. ³ The goose-step, for instance, is one of the most horrible sights in the world, far more terrifying than a dive-bomber. ⁴ It is simply an affirmation of naked power; contained in it, quite consciously and intentionally, is the vision of a boot crashing down on a face. ⁵ Its ugliness is part of its essence, for what it is saying is "Yes, I *am* ugly, and you daren't laugh at me," like the bully who makes faces at his victim. ⁶ Why is the goose-step not used in England? ⁷ There are, heaven knows, plenty of army officers who would be only too glad to introduce some such thing. ⁸ It is not used because the people in the street would laugh. ⁹ Beyond a certain point, military display is only possible in countries where the common people dare not laugh at the army. ¹⁰ The Italians adopted the goose-step at about the time when Italy passed definitely under German control, and, as one would expect, they do it less well than the Germans. ¹¹ The Vichy government, had it survived, was bound to introduce a stiffer parade-ground discipline into what was left of the French army. ¹² In the British army the drill is rigid and complicated, full of memories of the eighteenth century, but without definite swagger; the march is merely a formalized walk. ¹³ It belongs to a society which is ruled by the sword, no doubt, but a sword which must never be taken out of the scabbard.

DISCUSSION: TRANSITIONS

In Mary McCarthy's paragraph on Uncle Myers, transitions within and between blocks of ideas are made chiefly through parallel phrases:

THE ARMY PARADE-STEP: From "England Your England" in *Such, Such Were the Joys* by George Orwell. Reprinted by permission of Harcourt Brace Jovanovich, Inc. Also by permission of A. M. Heath & Company, Ltd. for Mrs. Sonia Brownell Orwell and Secker & Warburg. Selection title by editor.

Sentence 12: *He enjoyed* standing on a curbstone . . .
Sentence 13: *He liked* bandstands, band concerts . . .
Sentence 14: *He collected* coupons and tinfoil . . .
Sentence 15: *He was also fond* of streetcar rides . . .

She depends on a single transitional question ("How had these two worlds impinged?") and on very few formal transitional words and phrases ("also") that specify the relationship of ideas.

These relationships are numerous and in other pieces of writing are indicated by the following transitional words:

qualification: however, nonetheless, nevertheless
comparison: similarly, in the same way
contrast: by contrast, on the one hand, on the other hand
illustration: for example, thus
consequence: thus, as a result, consequently, therefore
concession: admittedly
explanation: thus
amplification: moreover, furthermore
emphasis: indeed
summation: all in all, in summary, in conclusion

Such formal transitions are a kind of punctuation, needed only when the relationships between ideas (and other relationships) are not immediately clear to the reader. Where they are unneeded they become deadwood and overweigh the paragraph. Within sentences, punctuation can usually provide a clear enough connective: a colon indicates that an expansion of the previous idea or an explanation or illustration of it follows; a semicolon, that the connected ideas are equal in importance or closely related. Where transitions are made formally, they are best kept brief and unobtrusive. In the paragraph as in the whole essay, coherence must be the chief consideration governing their use: the reader should be able to discover the logical relation of ideas without difficulty.

QUESTIONS

1. Which words or phrases in Orwell's paragraph are transitional? Which could be omitted without loss of clarity?
2. What sentence is wholly transitional—indicating the connection between ideas rather than stating them?
3. Are any of the formal transitions superfluous—that is, is the connection between ideas clear without them?
4. What is the function of the topic sentence—to indicate what is to be discussed or to state the main idea? How does it indicate the way ideas will be organized?

WRITING ASSIGNMENT

Write a paragraph discussing what you consider to be a "fairly sure guide to the social atmosphere" of an educational institution. You may wish to compare two schools—perhaps your high school and your college—to develop your generalization. Underline your transitional words, phrases, and sentences to determine whether they are clear, precise, and necessary. Where the connection between ideas is unclear, you may need formal transitions.

Bruno Bettelheim
THE HITLER SALUTE

1.   What was true of the inner responses of Germans to the concentration camps was also true for their overall reaction to total mass control. But in the Hitler state it was always more than fear for one's life that made it impossible to remain inwardly opposed to the system. Every nonconformist was subject to many contradictions. To cite the obvious dilemma: He could expose himself as a dissenter and thus invite persecution, or he could profess faith in something he not only did not believe, but hated and despised.

2.   So the unwilling subject of the mass state had to begin to trick himself, to look for excuses and subterfuges. But in so doing he lost exactly the self respect he was trying to maintain. An example of the way this works may be seen in the Hitler salute. The salute was deliberately introduced so that everywhere—in the beer garden, the railroad, the place of work, and on the street—it would be easy to recognize anyone who hung on to the old "democratic" forms of greeting his friends.

3.   To Hitler's followers, giving the salute was an expression of self assertion, of power. Each time a loyal subject performed it, his sense of well-being shot up. For an opponent of the regime it worked exactly opposite. Every time he had to greet somebody in public he had an experience that shook and weakened his integration. More specifically, if the situation forced him to salute,

THE HITLER SALUTE: Reprinted with permission of Macmillan Publishing Co., Inc. from *The Informed Heart* by Bruno Bettelheim. Copyright © The Free Press.

he immediately felt a traitor to his deepest convictions. So he had to pretend to himself that it did not count. Or to put it another way: he could not change his action—he *had* to give the Hitler salute. Since one's integration rests on acting in accord with one's beliefs, the only easy way to retain his integration was to change his beliefs. Things were made simpler by the fact that in most of us there is a great desire to conform. Everyone knows how hard it is to be deviant with even a casual acquaintance we meet on the street; it is infinitely more so when being different puts one's very life in danger. Thus many times a day the anti-Nazi had either to become a martyr or abandon self respect.

4.   I once spoke with a young German psychologist who was a child at the beginning of the Hitler regime. Her father was a strong opponent of the Nazi movement and she felt as he did. But life went on and she had to go to school. At school she had to swear allegiance to the Führer, to give the Hitler salute repeatedly. For a long time she mentally crossed her fingers. She told herself that the oath and salute didn't count because she didn't mean them. But each time it became more difficult to hang on to her self respect and still keep up the pretense, until finally she gave up her mental reservation and swore allegiance like anybody else.

5.   While this development was still going on, a parallel process was taking place in her inner relation to her father. At first his morality had given the girl strength to go on without wavering in her convictions. But as time went on, she felt herself more and more projected into a most difficult conflict. First she had sided with the father and simply resented the state that forced such a conflict on her. But eventually there came a time when she blamed her father for being the source of her difficulties. Once this happened, she also began to resent her father's values. But values we resent can no longer give us strength, nor can they motivate us strongly. So after this point in her inner development, the father's values which had fortified her resistance became weaker and weaker and what had once been an asset became a liability.

6.   If a parent asks too much of us, we often end up complying even less than we might have done otherwise. By this time it was no longer a conflict between her and the Hitler state, with her father firmly on her side; the conflict was now within her, and her father could no longer support her because he was now a

separate party in the conflict. Until she began to waver she took pride in his moral support; after that because she felt shame at her own behavior, he appeared to her as a critical figure, critical of her for doubting, for wishing to give in. So at the moment of indecision when she most needed to feel that her father respected her, he seemed to be pulling her still further apart. Here, then, is another example of how the personality splits under the impact of the coercive state if the individual tries to resist.

7.   What was true for the Hitler salute was of course true for all other features of the regime. The inescapable power of the total state rests exactly on this: not only that it reaches the minutest and most private life activities of the individual, but more, that it splits the inner person if he resists.

8.   To use another experience out of this young woman's student days: While attending *Gymnasium*, the girls in her school were asked to take a census of the population one day. To refrain from taking part would again have meant risking the well-being of herself and her family. Moreover, the request seemed innocuous enough. But in taking the census she suddenly found herself having to ask for private details from a Jewish family. She realized that these Jews saw her as a symbol of the regime and hated her. She resented this, and then realized that she was feeling just as the regime wanted her to: resentful of Jews. She also hated herself for helping to exterminate Jews. Certainly she hated the regime that forced the predicament on her, but she hated herself even more.

9.   And the total state finds almost daily tasks that each subject must perform or risk destruction. Most persons, in fulfilling these requirements, start out hating the system that forces them, but then end up hating themselves more. Moreover, the regime can stand their hatred, but they cannot endure the self hate, which is so destructive to integration.

QUESTIONS

1. The first sentence of paragraph 1 is transitional. The second and third sentences state the topic idea or subject of the nine paragraphs—but not the point Bettelheim wishes to make: the conclusion that he draws from his analysis of the behavior of the "unwilling subject:" that is, the *thesis* of the nine paragraphs. Where is this conclusion first stated?

2. If you wished to group the nine paragraphs into larger paragraphs representing blocks of ideas, which paragraphs would form such blocks? Would transitions be needed within these larger paragraphs—or would the connection of ideas be clear?
3. One kind of effective transition between paragraphs is reference to a preceding idea. Which paragraphs depend on this kind of transition?
4. To what extent does Bettelheim depend on formal transitions between paragraphs? Note the use of *moreover* in paragraphs 8 and 9. Could this formal transition be deleted without disturbing the sense of coherence?
5. Which sentences in paragraph 3 open with a formal transition? Could any of these be deleted without disturbing the clarity of the paragraph?
6. What purpose do the semicolons in paragraph 6 and the colons in paragraph 8 serve?
7. What is the purpose of paragraph 9—to restate the thesis or to draw new (and less important) conclusions from the analysis?

WRITING ASSIGNMENT

Orwell and Bettelheim are concerned in different ways with the psychology and power of totalitarian regimes. Comment on these differences and use your analysis to draw a conclusion about them.

CLIMAX

Lytton Strachey
QUEEN VICTORIA AT THE END
OF HER LIFE

¹ She gave orders that nothing should be thrown away—and nothing was. ² There, in drawer after drawer, in wardrobe after

QUEEN VICTORIA AT THE END OF HER LIFE: From *Queen Victoria* by Lytton Strachey, copyright, 1921, by Harcourt Brace Jovanovich, Inc.; renewed, 1949, by James Strachey. Reprinted by permission of the publishers. Selection title by editor.

wardrobe, reposed the dresses of seventy years. [3] But not only the dresses—the furs and the mantles and subsidiary frills and the muffs and the parasols and the bonnets—all were ranged in chronological order, dated and complete. [4] A great cupboard was devoted to the dolls; in the china room at Windsor a special table held the mugs of her childhood, and her children's mugs as well. [5] Mementoes of the past surrounded her in serried accumulations. [6] In every room the tables were powdered thick with the photographs of relatives; their portraits, revealing them at all ages, covered the walls; their figures, in solid marble, rose up from pedestals, or gleamed from brackets in the form of gold and silver statuettes. [7] The dead, in every shape—in minatures, in porcelain, in enormous life-size oil-paintings—were perpetually about her. [8] John Brown stood upon her writing-table in solid gold. * [9] Her favorite horses and dogs, endowed with a new durability, crowded round her footsteps. [10] Sharp, in silver gilt, dominated the dinner table; Boy and Boz lay together among unfading flowers, in bronze. [11] And it was not enough that each particle of the past should be given the stability of metal or of marble: the whole collection, in its arrangement, no less than its entity, should be immutably fixed. [12] There might be additions, but there might never be alterations. [13] No chintz might change, no carpet, no curtain, be replaced by another; or, if long use at last made it necessary, the stuffs and the patterns must be so identically reproduced that the keenest eye might not detect the difference. [14] No new picture could be hung upon the walls at Windsor, for those already there had been put in their places by Albert, whose decisions were eternal. [15] So, indeed, were Victoria's. [16] To ensure that they should be the aid of the camera was called in. [17] Every single article in the Queen's possession was photographed from several points of view. [18] These photographs were submitted to Her Majesty, and when, after careful inspection, she had approved of them, they were placed in a series of albums, richly bound. [19] Then, opposite each photograph, an entry was made, indicating the number of the article, the number of the room in which it was kept, its exact position in the room and all its principal characteristics. [20] The fate of every object which had undergone this process was henceforth irrevocably sealed. [21] The whole multitude, once and for all, took up its

* John Brown (1826–1883) was the Scottish attendant to Victoria's husband, Albert, and after the death of the Prince in 1861, to the Queen herself. [Ed.]

steadfast station. [22] And Victoria, with a gigantic volume or two of the endless catalogue always beside her, to look through, to ponder upon, to expatiate over, could feel, with a double contentment, that the transitoriness of this world had been arrested by the amplitude of her might.

DISCUSSION: CLIMAX

A sense of climax is found in a paragraph when one idea seems to anticipate another and when the concluding idea is given weight as it completes the sequence of thought. There is a natural order of climax in certain sentences and paragraphs, as in Julius Caesar's "I came, I saw, I conquered." It must not be thought, however, that this sense of rising importance is inherent in all such sequences. Compare the following sentences from a paragraph by Stephen Crane:

> The crest of each of these waves was a hill, from the top of which the men surveyed, for a moment, a broad tumultuous expanse, shining and wind-driven. It was probably splendid. It was probably glorious, this play of the free sea, wild with lights of emerald and white and amber.—The Open Boat

> The crest of each of these waves was a hill, from the top of which the men surveyed, for a moment, a broad tumultuous expanse, shining and wind-driven. It was probably glorious, this play of the free sea, wild with lights of emerald and white and amber. It was probably splendid.

Reversing the concluding sentences in no way lessens the sense of climax; the short four-word sentence is as effective as Crane's nineteen-word sentence in achieving a sense of climax. The terminal position—a position of natural emphasis in English sentences—is in part responsible for the effect. In short, the writer is free to make one idea seem more important by virtue of the position he gives it. A series of ideas, facts, or events thus can be arranged so that each succeeding one seems more significant or forceful than the preceding and the final one the most significant or forceful of all.

QUESTIONS

1. Strachey develops and illustrates several ideas in the paragraph: he states in sentence 2 that Queen Victoria saved the dresses of seventy years; in sentence 3, that she saved her furs and bonnets as well as other articles of clothing—and had them arranged and dated chronologically. How does the transition between these sentences help to

suggest that Strachey is moving from one surprising, perhaps astonishing, fact to an even more astonishing one?
2. Compare sentences 11 and 12 with those that follow. How does Strachey indicate that he is building the paragraph to even more astonishing details?
3. How do the details and ideas of the paragraph anticipate the final sentence? What in that final sentence contributes to the sense of climax?
4. What traits of Queen Victoria does Strachey illuminate? What is the dominant trait, and how does Strachey indicate that it is the dominant one?

WRITING ASSIGNMENT

Write a character sketch of a contemporary political figure, centering on a dominant trait and presenting related traits. Present the latter in order of increasing importance as illustrations of the dominant trait.

Katherine Anne Porter
THE BULLFIGHT

1.   I took to the bullfights with my Mexican and Indian friends. I sat with them in the cafés where the bullfighters appeared; more than once went at two o'clock in the morning with a crowd to see the bulls brought into the city; I visited the corral back of the ring where they could be seen before the corrida. Always, of course, I was in the company of impassioned adorers of the sport, with their special vocabulary and mannerisms and contempt for all others who did not belong to their charmed and chosen cult. Quite literally there were those among them I never heard speak of anything else; and I heard then all that can be said—the topic is limited, after all, like any other—in love and praise of bullfighting. But it can be tiresome, too. And I did not really live in that world, so narrow and so trivial, so cruel and so unconscious; I was a mere visitor. There was something deeply,

THE BULLFIGHT: Excerpted from "St. Augustine and the Bullfight," by Katherine Anne Porter. Originally published in *Mademoiselle* as "Adventure in Living." Copyright 1955 by Katherine Anne Porter. Reprinted by arrangement with the publisher Delacorte Press/Seymour Lawrence. Selection title by editor.

irreparably wrong with my being there at all, something against the grain of my life; except for this (and here was the falseness I had finally to uncover): I loved the spectacle of the bullfights, I was drunk on it, I was in a strange, wild dream from which I did not want to be awakened. I was now drawn irresistibly to the bullring as before I had been drawn to the race tracks and the polo fields at home. But this had death in it, and it was the death in it that I loved. . . . And I was bitterly ashamed of this evil in me, and believed it to be in me only—no one had fallen so far into cruelty as this! These bullfight buffs I truly believed did not know what they were doing—but I did, and I knew better because I had once known better; so that spiritual pride got in and did its deadly work, too. How could I face the cold fact that at heart I was just a killer, like any other, that some deep corner of my soul consented not just willingly but with rapture? I still clung obstinately to my flattering view of myself as a unique case, as a humane, blood-avoiding civilized being, somehow a fallen angel, perhaps? Just the same, what was I doing there? And why was I beginning secretly to abhor Shelley as if he had done me a great injury, when in fact he had done me the terrible and dangerous favor of helping me to find myself out?

2.   In the meantime I was reading St. Augustine; and if Shelley had helped me find myself out, St. Augustine helped me find myself again. I read for the first time then his story of a friend of his, a young man from the provinces who came to Rome and was taken up by the gang of clever, wellborn young hoodlums Augustine then ran with; and this young man, also wellborn but severely brought up, refused to go with the crowd to the gladiatorial combat; he was opposed to them on the simple grounds that they were cruel and criminal. His friends naturally ridiculed such dowdy sentiments; they nagged him slyly, bedeviled him openly, and, of course, finally some part of him consented—but only to a degree. He would go with them, he said, but he would not watch the games. And he did not, until the time for the first slaughter, when the howling of the crowd brought him to his feet, staring: and afterward he was more bloodthirsty than any.

3.   Why, of course: oh, it might be a commonplace of human nature, it might be it could happen to anyone! I longed to be free of my uniqueness, to be a fellow-sinner at least with someone: I could not bear my guilt alone—and here was this

student, this boy at Rome in the fourth century, somebody I felt I knew well on sight, who had been weak enough to be led into adventure but strong enough to turn it into experience. For no matter how we both attempted to deceive ourselves, our acts had all the earmarks of adventure: violence of motive, events taking place at top speed, at sustained intensity, under powerful stimulus and a willful seeking for pure sensation; willful, I say, because I was not kidnapped and forced, after all, nor was that young friend of St. Augustine's. We both proceeded under the power of our own weakness. When the time came to kill the splendid black and white bull, I who had pitied him when he first came into the ring stood straining on tiptoe to see everything, yet almost blinded with excitement, and crying out when the crowd roared, and kissing Shelley on the cheekbone when he shook my elbow and shouted in the voice of one justified: "Didn't I tell you? Didn't I?"

QUESTIONS

1. Notice that the three paragraphs end with a focus on similar ideas. What are these ideas, and how does this focus contribute to a sense of climax in the whole selection? Is the sense of climax greater at the end of the final paragraph?
2. How many blocks of ideas does paragraph 1 contain, and how is this division of ideas marked? Would the paragraph be more effective divided into two or more paragraphs?
3. How does the discussion explain how St. Augustine helped the writer find herself again, whereas Shelley helped her find herself out?
4. To what extent does the writer depend on formal transitions to indicate rising excitement? To what extent does her punctuation convey excitement?

WRITING ASSIGNMENT

Write two or three paragraphs describing and analyzing an exciting experience about which you had mixed feelings at the time. In one of the paragraphs arrange the sentences in climactic order.

POINT OF VIEW

Geoffrey Moorhouse
CALCUTTA

1.   When the international and jet-propelled traveller disembarks at Dum Dum he finds, if he has come by the right airline, that a highly polished limousine awaits his pleasure. It will be 6.30 or thereabouts in the morning, and the atmosphere will already be faintly sticky with heat and so unmistakably sweetened with a compound of mainly vegetable odours that the visitor can almost taste it. He need fear no discomfort at this stage, however, for he is to be transported into the city in air-conditioned splendour behind delicately tinted windows. From this smooth and relaxing position he can begin to observe how the other half of humanity lives. From the outset he notices some things which are reassuringly familiar. Along the first mile of this wide and tarmacadamed airport road are spaced the very same collection of gaudy hoardings that signal the way in and out of Heathrow or J. F. Kennedy or Fiumicino; 'Try a Little VC-10derness', says one —and some untidy idiot seems to have thrown up a collection of chicken coops in the shade of BOAC. Beside these homely reference points, however, the peculiarities of India are to be seen. The road is bordered by ditches and ponds, all brimming with water, in which women even at this hour are flogging garments clean, in which men are taking the first bath of the day. Beyond the spindle-elegant sodium lights, with buzzards and vultures perched on top, stand thickets of bamboo-and-thatch huts among avenues of palm. Along a canal, a large black barge top-heavy with hay is being poled inches at a time through a mass of pretty but choking mauve water hyacinth. And in the distance, lurking on the horizon, a range of tall factory chimneys is beginning to smoke.

2.   Calcutta is announced with a pothole or two. Then a bus

is overtaken, such a vehicle as the traveller has never seen before; its bodywork is battered with a thousand dents, as though an army of commuters had once tried to kick it to bits, and it is not only crammed with people, it has a score or so hanging off the platform and around the back like a cluster of grapes. It is lumbering and steaming into a suburban wasteland, stippled with blocks of dilapidated flats; and maybe Bishop Heber's imagery was not so far-fetched after all, for these are not at all unlike some of the homes for the workers you can see in Moscow today, though there they are not coloured pink and they certainly haven't been decorated with the hammer and sickle in crude whitewash on the walls.* Swiftly, the outer Calcutta of these revolutionary symbols now coagulates into the inner Calcutta which is unlike anywhere else on earth. The limousine now lurches and rolls, for there are too many potholes to avoid. It rocks down cobblestoned roads lined with high factory walls which have an air of South Lancashire about them. It begins to thread its way through traffic along thoroughfares that have something of Bishopsgate or Holborn in their buildings.

3.   It is the traffic that makes it all unique. A traffic in trams grinding round corners, a traffic in approximately London buses whose radiators seem ready to burst, in gypsy-green lorries with 'Ta-ta and By-by' and other slogans painted on the back, in taxis swerving all over the road with much blowing of horns, in rickshaws springing unexpectedly out of sidestreets, in bullock carts swaying ponderously along to the impediment of everyone, in sacred Brahmani cows and bulls nonchalantly strolling down the middle of the tram-tracks munching breakfast as they go. A traffic, too, in people who are hanging on to all forms of public transport, who are squatting cross-legged upon the counters of their shops, who are darting in and out of the roadways between the vehicles, who are staggering under enormous loads, who are walking briskly with briefcases, who are lying like dead things on the pavements, who are drenching themselves with muddy water in the gutters, who are arguing, laughing, gesticulating, defecating, and who are sometimes just standing still as though wondering what to do. There never were so many people in a city at seven o'clock in the morning. Patiently the driver of the limousine steers his passage between and around them, while

* Reginald Heber (1783–1826), who became bishop of Calcutta in 1823, compared the city to Moscow. He commented also on the large Greek-style houses and its hospitality.

they pause in mid-stride to let him through, or leap to get out of his way, or stare at him blankly, or curse him roundly, or occasionally spit in the path of his highly polished Cadillac. Presently, and quite remarkably, he comes to the end of the journey without collision and deposits the traveller and his luggage upon the pavement in front of an hotel. And here, the traveller has his first encounter with a beggar. He had better make the best of it, for beggary is to be with him until the end of his days in Calcutta.

DISCUSSION: POINT OF VIEW

When we ask about the point of view of a piece of writing, we are asking about the physical angle of vision (the place from which the observation is made) or the dominant mood or attitude (the mental state of the observer). Our question assumes that the writer is disposed to notice some things and not others as a result of an attitude, prejudice, or expectation; this disposition may become habitual—illustrated by the tendency of certain film directors to show their characters mainly in close-up or in long shots. We know that none of us is likely to notice the same details when returning to a place visited earlier: our mood and feelings—so important to what we perceive, as all photographers know—alter from moment to moment. The French artist Cézanne painted Mont Sainte-Victoire many times, and each time in a different light or perspective. No photographer is able to duplicate a landscape, even if he returns to it in the same season at the same time of day and stands in precisely the same place.

In some paragraphs both the angle of vision and the mental state of the observer will be specified; in other paragraphs the selection of detail will suggest both. Shifting the angle of vision or moving abruptly into another mood without preparing the reader causes confusion in some pieces of writing.

QUESTIONS

1. The traveler to India might see Calcutta for the first time from a taxi or bus rather than from "a highly polished limousine." What, if anything, is gained by showing the city from Moorhouse's angle of vision?

2. The reference to the "very same collection of gaudy hoardings" leading in and out of Heathrow, J. F. Kennedy, and Fiumicino (the international airports of London, New York, and Rome respectively) suggests that the traveler will at first think he is in a familiar world. Is Moorhouse showing that, as the limousine moves from the outskirts

to the inner city, the traveler is moving from a familiar world to an unfamiliar one, or from the ordinary to the extraordinary, or from the beautiful to the ugly? What accounts for the selection of detail?

3. How does Moorhouse show why the inner city is "unlike anywhere else on earth"?

4. How does Moorhouse establish not only the mental state of the typical traveler at the end of his journey to the hotel but also his own attitude toward Calcutta?

5. The reference to Bishopsgate and Holborn indicates that Moorhouse is writing with a British audience in mind, people familiar with the architecture of these areas of London. What other statements call for knowledge of this kind? Do phrases like "the canyons of New York" or "the maze of Los Angeles" convey more information to a greater number of readers—British and American? What phrases of this kind do you habitually use about American cities or towns? Do you think they should be avoided in descriptive writing?

WRITING ASSIGNMENT

Use Moorhouse's description of Calcutta as a model for a description of a section of a college town or your hometown. You may wish to portray the town or city as seen from a limousine or Volkswagen, but be careful to make the angle of vision contribute to the overall impression and the revelation of an attitude. Do not specify this attitude; let your selection of details reveal it.

Virginia Woolf
THE ECLIPSE

1.   Never was there a stranger purpose than that which brought us together that June night in Euston Railway Station. We were come to see the dawn. Trains like ours were starting all over England at that very moment to see the dawn. All noses were pointing north. When for a moment we halted in the depths of the country, there were the pale yellow lights of motor cars also pointing north. There was no sleep, no fixity in England that night. All were on the roads; all were travelling north. All were

THE ECLIPSE: From *The Captain's Death Bed and Other Essays* by Virginia Woolf, copyright, 1950, by Harcourt Brace Jovanovich, Inc. and reprinted with their permission and the permission of the author's literary estate and the Hogarth Press. Selection title by editor.

thinking of the dawn. As the night wore on, the sky, which was the object of so many million thoughts, assumed greater substance and prominence than usual. The consciousness of the whitish soft canopy above us increased in weight as the hours passed. When in chill early morning we were turned out on a Yorkshire roadside, our senses had orientated themselves differently from usual. We were no longer in the same relation to people, houses, and trees; we were related to the whole world. We had come, not to lodge in the bedroom of an inn; we were come for a few hours of disembodied intercourse with the sky.

2.   Everything was very pale. The river was pale and the fields, brimming with grasses and tasselled flowers which should have been red, had no colour in them, but lay there whispering and waving round colourless farmhouses. Now the farmhouse door would open, and out would step to join the procession the farmer and his family in their Sunday clothes, neat, dark and silent as if they were going uphill to church; or sometimes women merely leant on the window-sills of the upper rooms watching the procession pass with amused contempt, it appeared—they have come such hundreds of miles, and for what? they seemed to say—in complete silence. We had an odd sense of keeping an appointment with an actor of such vast proportions that he would come silently and be everywhere.

3.   By the time we were at the meeting-place, on a high fell where the hills stretched their limbs out over the flowing brown moorland below, we had put on too—though we were cold and with our feet stood in red bog water were likely to be still colder, though some of us were squatted on mackintoshes among cups and plates, eating, and others were fantastically accoutred and none were at their best—still we had put on a certain dignity. Rather, perhaps, we had put off the little badges and signs of individuality. We were strung out against the sky in outline and had the look of statues standing prominent on the ridge of the world. We were very, very old; we were men and women of the primeval world come to salute the dawn. So the worshippers at Stonehenge must have looked among tussocks of grass and boulders of rock. Suddenly, from the motor car of some Yorkshire squire, there bounded four large, lean, red dogs, hounds of the ancient world, hunting dogs, they seemed, leaping with their noses close to the ground on the track of boar or deer. Meanwhile, the sun was rising. A cloud glowed as a white shade

glows when the light is slowly turned up behind it. Golden wedge-shaped streamers fell from it and marked the trees in the valley green and the villages blue-brown. In the sky behind us there swam white islands in pale blue lakes. The sky was open and free there, but in front of us a soft snowbank had massed itself. Yet, as we looked, we saw it proving worn and thin in patches. The gold momentarily increased, melting the whiteness to a fiery gauze, and this grew frailer and frailer till, for one instant, we saw the sun in full splendour. Then there was a pause, a moment of suspense, like that which precedes a race. The starter held his watch in his hand, counting the seconds. Now they were off.

4.   The sun had to race through the clouds and to reach the goal, which was a thin transparency to the right, before the sacred seconds were up. He started. The clouds flung every obstacle in his way. They clung, they impeded. He dashed through them. He could be felt, flashing and flying when he was invisible. His speed was tremendous. Here he was out and bright; now he was under and lost. But always one felt him flying and thrusting through the murk to his goal. For one second he emerged and showed himself to us through our glasses, a hollowed sun, a crescent sun. Finally, he went under for his last effort. Now he was completely blotted out. The moments passed. Watches were held in hand after hand. The sacred twenty-four seconds were begun. Unless he could win through before the last one was over, he was lost. Still one felt him tearing and racing behind the clouds to win free; but the clouds held him. They spread; they thickened; they slackened; they muffled his speed. Of the twenty-four seconds only five remained, and still he was obscured. And, as the fatal seconds passed, and we realized that the sun was being defeated, had now, indeed lost the race, all the colour began to go from the moor. The blue turned to purple; the white became livid as at the approach of a violent but windless storm. Pink faces went green, and it became colder than ever. This was the defeat of the sun, then, and this was all, so we thought, turning in disappointment from the dull cloud blanket in front of us to the moors behind. They were livid, they were purple; but suddenly one became aware that something more was about to happen; something unexpected, awful, unavoidable. The shadow growing darker and darker over the moor was like the heeling over of a boat, which, instead of righting itself at

the critical moment, turns a little further and then a little further on its side; and suddenly capsizes. So the light turned and heeled over and went out. This was the end. The flesh and blood of the world was dead; only the skeleton was left. It hung beneath us, a frail shell; brown; dead; withered. Then, with some trifling movement, this profound obeisance of the light, this stooping down and abasement of all splendour was over. Lightly, on the other side of the world, up it rose; it sprang up as if the one movement, after a second's tremendous pause, completed the other, and the light which had died here rose again elsewhere. Never was there such a sense of rejuvenescence and recovery. All the convalescences and respites of life seemed rolled into one. Yet, at first, so light and frail and strange the colour was, sprinkled rainbow-like in a hoop of colour, that it seemed as if the earth could never live decked out in such frail tints. It hung beneath us, like a cage, like a hoop, like a globe of glass. It might be blown out; it might be stove in. But steadily and surely our relief broadened and our confidence established itself as the great paint-brush washed in woods dark on the valley, and massed hills blue above them. The world became more and more solid; it became populous; it became a place where an infinite number of farmhouses, of villages, of railway lines have lodgement; until the whole fabric of civilization was modelled and moulded. But still the memory endured that the earth we stand on is made of colour; colour can be blown out; and then we stand on a dead leaf; and we who tread the earth securely now have seen it dead.

QUESTIONS

1. How does Virginia Woolf reveal her mental point of view in paragraph 1 through her comments on the trains and automobiles pointing north? Who are the "we" of the paragraph?
2. How does paragraph 2 establish an angle of vision? Does this angle of vision shift in the course of the passage?
3. How specific is the writer about what she expected to see? Does she suggest these expectations without stating them?
4. What is the purpose of the reference to Stonehenge in paragraph 3?
5. How is the detail of paragraph 4 organized?
6. What is the significance of the conclusion that "the whole fabric of civilization was modelled and moulded"?

WRITING ASSIGNMENT

Compare this account of the eclipse with Virginia Woolf's earlier version in *A Writer's Diary*. Specify the differences in point of view and detail.

Winston S. Churchill
MY FIRST INTRODUCTION TO THE CLASSICS

The school my parents had selected for my education was one of the most fashionable and expensive in the country. It modelled itself upon Eton and aimed at being prepaiatory for that Public School above all others. It was supposed to be the very last thing in schools. Only ten boys in a class; electric light (then a wonder); a swimming pond; spacious football and cricket grounds; two or three school treats, or 'expeditions' as they were called, every term; the masters all M.A.'s in gowns and mortar-boards; a chapel of its own; no hampers allowed; everything provided by the authorities. It was a dark November afternoon when we arrived at this establishment. We had tea with the Headmaster, with whom my mother conversed in the most easy manner. I was preoccupied with the fear of spilling my cup and so making 'a bad start.' I was also miserable at the idea of being left alone among all these strangers in this great, fierce, formidable place. After all I was only seven, and I had been so happy in my nursery with all my toys. I had such wonderful toys: a real steam engine, a magic lantern, and a collection of soldiers already nearly a thousand strong. Now it was to be all lessons. Seven or eight hours of lessons every day except half-holidays, and football or cricket in addition.

When the last sound of my mother's departing wheels had died away, the Headmaster invited me to hand over any money I had in my possession. I produced my three half-crowns which were duly entered in a book, and I was told that from time to time there would be a 'shop' at the school with all sorts of things

MY FIRST INTRODUCTION TO THE CLASSICS: Reprinted by permission of The Hamlyn Publishing Group Limited and Charles Scribner's Sons from *My Early Life* by Winston S. Churchill. Copyright 1930 Charles Scribner's Sons. Selection title by editor.

which one would like to have, and that I could choose what I liked up to the limit of the seven and sixpence. Then we quitted the Headmaster's parlour and the comfortable private side of the house, and entered the more bleak apartments reserved for the instruction and accommodation of the pupils. I was taken into a Form Room and told to sit at a desk. All the other boys were out of doors, and I was alone with the Form Master. He produced a thin greeny-brown-covered book filled with words in different types of print.

'You have never done any Latin before, have you?' he said.

'No, sir.'

'This is a Latin grammar.' He opened it at a well-thumbed page. 'You must learn this,' he said, pointing to a number of words in a frame of lines. 'I will come back in half an hour and see what you know.'

Behold me then on a gloomy evening, with an aching heart, seated in front of the First Declension.

Mensa	a table
Mensa	O table
Mensam	a table
Mensae	of a table
Mensae	to or for a table
Mensa	by, with or from a table

What on earth did it mean? Where was the sense of it? It seemed absolute rigmarole to me. However, there was one thing I could always do: I could learn by heart. And I thereupon proceeded, as far as my private sorrows would allow, to memorise the acrostic-looking task which had been set me.

In due course the Master returned.

'Have you learnt it?' he asked.

'I think I can *say* it, sir,' I replied; and I gabbled it off.

He seemed so satisfied with this that I was emboldened to ask a question.

'What does it mean, sir?'

'It means what it says. Mensa, a table. Mensa is a noun of the First Declension. There are five declensions. You have learnt the singular of the First Declension.'

'But,' I repeated, 'what does it mean?'

'Mensa means a table,' he answered.

'Then why does mensa also mean O table,' I enquired, 'and what does O table mean?'

'Mensa, O table, is the vocative case,' he replied.

'But why O table?' I persisted in genuine curiosity.

'O table,—you would use that in addressing a table, in invoking a table.' And then seeing he was not carrying me with him, 'You would use it in speaking to a table.'

'But I never do,' I blurted out in honest amazement.

'If you are impertinent, you will be punished, and punished, let me tell you, very severely,' was his conclusive rejoinder.

QUESTIONS

1. The episode narrated, Churchill states in his autobiography, was "my first introduction to the classics." The selection of details—and in particular the concluding conversation with the Form Master—reveals his attitude not only toward the preparatory school but toward a conception of education. What is that conception? What details indicate that Churchill is not concerned merely with the misery of a seven-year-old boy left by his parents with strangers?
2. How does the arrangement of details in the sentence beginning "Only ten boys in a class" help to reveal Churchill's attitude toward the preparatory school? Would the implication of the sentence be changed if it ended with the first two or three characteristics named?
3. The Form Master is directly characterized through his responses to the boy's questions. Is the Headmaster characterized at all?
4. Churchill establishes a physical angle of vision through his setting of the episode. How does he establish his mental state?

WRITING ASSIGNMENT

Write a carefully organized paragraph on one of the following topics. Indicate a point of view and create a single dominant impression.
a. the first day at high school
b. the first day in a college classroom
c. a visit to an asylum or prison
d. an appearance in a courtroom on a traffic charge
e. a first view of a military barracks

DEFINITION

Jeremy Bernstein
SKIING AS A CHILD

1.   I first took up skiing as a child of ten or so, in the late nineteen-thirties. Rochester, New York, where I grew up, had, and still does have, heavy, severe winters, and winter sports, especially ice-skating, were exceedingly popular. I soon found out that I had weak ankles, so ice-skating was a disaster for me; hence the skis. With the aid of a Boy Scout pamphlet, a small group of us attempted to teach ourselves skiing on a broad slope in Ellison Park, near where we lived. Lifts were unknown to us, and our ski equipment was such that the user of the oldest ski yet to be discovered—the ski was found in Hoting, Sweden, and is about forty-five hundred years old—would have felt himself in familiar territory among us. ("Ski" is the Norwegian word for "snowshoe," and the Hoting ski essentially resembles a snowshoe; there are, however, Scandinavian skis over two thousand years old with turned-up, pointed tips which resemble the modern version.) We had wooden skis—mainly hickory—with a groove carved in the bottom along the axis of the ski; this groove, which produced a small raised line in the middle of each ski track, was supposed to make the skis more stable. A rule of the day was that skis, whatever the skier's proficiency, should be one's height plus the length of an outstretched arm. Some of the more mechanical-minded among us tacked metal strips along the sides of our ski bottoms. These helped to preserve the wood from abrasion—without them our skis would have been chipped away after a season or so—and they also helped in controlling descents when the terrain was icy, for they could be edged into the ice. Waxing these wooden skis was a ritual that all but approached high alchemy. Waxes came in every color and variety, and were to be applied in layers with cheesecloth whenever the snow conditions warranted—whenever the snow was wet or sticky. (As I

SKIING AS A CHILD: From "Le Poids Sur Le Ski Aval." Reprinted by permission; © 1974 The New Yorker Magazine, Inc. Selection title by editor.

recall, the first wax I used was my mother's floor wax—a limited success.) We spent hours in basements happily applying and scraping off wax.

2.   The attachment of skis to the feet evolved some-what during those years. At first, there had been a system of leather straps that more or less tied the boot to the ski. One put the toe of the boot in an open iron wedge, buckled the straps over the boot, and hoped for the best. Sometime in the early thirties, the cable binding was introduced. The old toe wedge remained, but the back of the boot had a groove carved in it, and through this groove went a metal cable—spring-wound—that wedged one's foot into the toe iron. These cables had three or four possible tensions, depending on how they were adjusted. (There was a gadget in front of the binding into which the cable could be set, in various positions. One then tightened the cable by pulling forward on a lever.) In adjusting the cable tension, one was faced with an unpleasant choice: either to attach the ski so loosely that it would fall off at the slightest movement of the foot or to attach it so tightly that it could never come off and there would inevitably be a tangle of skis and feet when one fell. It is a miracle that none of us broke a leg or an ankle with this ar-rangement, which was extremely dangerous, but, then, children are rarely hurt in ski falls. Our ski boots were leather hiking boots with the soles modified—cut square by the manufac-turer—to fit into the toe iron and with the groove cut into the heel for the cable. The system worked about as well with ordi-nary hiking boots, or even with gym shoes. Ski poles were made of light bamboo, and each pole had a large wheel of leather near the bottom. Special ski clothes were unknown to us.

DISCUSSION: DEFINITION

So far we have been concerned with organizing the paragraph so that it communicates ideas effectively. In this and succeeding sections we will be concerned with important ways by which ideas can be developed and analyzed.

Definition is the most fundamental of these ways, for readers must know the meaning of strange words or those of special importance to the discussion. How complete the definition is and what kind is used depends on how much specific information the reader needs. The au-

thor of the following passage has been describing Carrie Nation's encounters with Kansas bartenders:

> The symbol of their authority was the bung starter, a handy tool for
> cooling hot skulls, which was beginning to take its revered place in
> informal brawling alongside the shillelagh and brass knucks.
> —Robert Lewis Taylor, *Vessel of Wrath*

The bung starter is defined through its use; Taylor might have described it completely by giving details of its construction. Whether or
not the reader misses this information depends on how necessary the
full details are to understanding what happens.

Perhaps the simplest kind of definition is to point to objects or activities covered by a term without characterizing them: in a historical museum I might simply point to an object and tell you it is called a bung
starter. Sometimes this is the only kind of definition possible. Though
the writer of the following passage does explore the nature of mathematics, he raises a question about the difficulty of definition:

> The logical way to begin is to describe what mathematics is and what
> mathematicians do. But this is probably impossible. Almost cer-
> tainly, any two mathematicians would disagree in significant ways if
> they were asked to give such a description. . . . It can be said that
> mathematics is whatever mathematicians are doing. This sounds cir-
> cular, and in some respects it is. But there is never any doubt about
> who is and who is not a creative mathematician, so all that is
> required is to keep track of the activities of these few men. A
> stronger case can be made for the assertion that mathematics is in
> large part the discovery and study of analogies.—Alfred Adler, *Math-
> ematics and Creativity*

But usually we want to know the characteristics of an object or activity—or at least know as much as can be indicated. To inform us of
these characteristics, the writer may begin with the original meaning of
the word—that is, with its etymology. For example, he may tell us that
mathematics derives from a Greek word that meant "disposed to
learn." His purpose is to shed light on current meanings—why, for example, mathematicians may define their activity as the discovery of new
realities—or relate the word to other, less familiar words of the same
root or base. The purpose of etymological definition is usually not to
indicate that the word must be used in its original sense; however, the
writer may wish to argue that the original meaning of the word be restored and present meanings discarded.

Most definitions are concerned with current meanings and are said
to be either denotative or connotative. *Denotative* definition points to

or singles out an object; it identifies the class of objects to which the word belongs [*genus*], then distinguishes the word from other members of the class [*specific difference*]. The genus may be exceedingly broad or exceedingly narrow:

> **hero** A man [*genus*] distinguished for exceptional courage, fortitude, or bold enterprise, especially in time of war or danger [*specific difference*]
> **hero** *U.S.* A sandwich [*genus*] made with a loaf of bread cut lengthwise [*specific difference*]—*Standard College Dictionary*

This kind of definition is possible with words with describable properties; it is not possible with a word so broad that it can be cited as a genus. It is impossible to cite a genus for the word *thing* broader than the word itself or describe its properties; to define the word, the dictionary usually lists synonyms: *inanimate object, matter, concern,* and so on.

Connotative definition presents ideas and impressions, the emotional aura that has come to be associated with an object or activity, but does not distinguish it from all objects and activities. The word *rose* has a precise denotation and a range of connotations, as in the expression "a rosy future." [1] Though *inexpensive* and *cheap* generally mean low in price, *cheap* usually carries the implication of poor quality or contemptibility. *Inexpensive* is an emotionally neutral word; *cheap* is usually not. The same is true of *soiled* and *filthy*. Certain words may lack a precise denotation and are used to convey rather loose connotative meanings; few people will agree precisely on the meaning of *cute* and may point to a "cute" dress or "cute" girl to be sure they are understood.

Stipulative definition proposes a new word to describe something in a new way or to name a newly discovered phenomenon; occasionally an older word may be stipulated for the purpose. *Quasar* came into use in the 1960s to distinguish newly discovered quasi-stellar sources of light, which were thought by some astronomers to be at the outer reaches of space. The value of stipulative definition depends on its proven accuracy as a description of the phenomenon: the stipulation that *quasar* be defined in the way indicated may be rejected if the astronomers prove these mysterious sources of light to be closer to our solar system than some have thought. A wholly new word may then be

[1] Logicians object, and rightly, that the popular distinction between denotation and connotation is inconsistent, since qualities associated with a word may be intrinsic and therefore considered denotative. We speak loosely of a connotative difference between the words *heavy* and *weighty*—the first connotes greater than average weight; the second, actual rather than relative weight—but in fact these meanings are intrinsic to the word. In formal logic denotation refers to the sum of objects to which the word extends (people we designate as heroic); connotation, to the sum of characteristics and qualities these objects contain. Emotive meanings are matters of *subjective* connotation.

stipulated to discard misleading connotations. Indeed Fred Hoyle recently proposed a redefinition of *quasar* to account for "two quite different classes of objects which have hitherto been associated together as 'quasars.'"[1]

Theoretical definition proposes an adequate description of reality and a theory about it—that is, an account of its true nature. Einstein's formulations of gravity and of the space-time continuum, in the General and Special Theory of Relativity, were theoretical definitions. New theoretical models of the universe have recently been formulated on the basis of so-called antimatter.[2] Philosophical discussions on the nature of beauty and truth and justice are theoretical also.

Precising definitions fix meanings that are indefinite, have come to overlap, or have become confused in usage. Recent Supreme Court decisions on obscenity and pornography have involved precising definitions.

QUESTIONS

1. The formal dictionary definition of *ski* is as follows:

   One of a pair of wooden or metal runners about 5 to 7 feet long and 3½ inches wide, with turned-up points, attached to the feet and used in sliding over snow, especially on slopes.—*Standard College Dictionary*

   How formal the definition in expository or informal writing is depends on how necessary this information is and on the complexity of the object or substance. How much of the formal definition above is included in Bernstein's discussion of the skis he used in childhood?
2. What purpose does the etymological definition of *ski* serve? Is Bernstein indicating that the original meaning of the word has changed since it came into existence?
3. Bernstein defines a number of objects as a way of indicating the difficulty he experienced as a child. How do these definitions help to suggest these difficulties?
4. Give the genus and the specific differences of the dictionary definitions of the following words: cucumber, geography, sun, proof, laurel, exile, hasp, inch, barn, jackal. For which of the words is the genus extremely general? Could a more restricted one have been provided?
5. In formal definition a word must not be used to define itself (for ex-

[1] Fred Hoyle, *From Stonehenge to Modern Cosmology* (San Francisco: W. H. Freeman and Company, 1972), p. 91.

[2] Hannes Alfven, *Worlds-Antiworlds* (San Francisco: W. H. Freeman and Company, 1966), pp. 87–103.

ample: Logic is the science of logical thinking) and the specific difference must not exclude essential characteristics (for example: An automobile is a four-wheeled vehicle). Use your desk dictionary to determine whether the following formal definitions are complete and uncircular:

a. A republic is a political union in which citizens qualified to vote are supreme.
b. Democracy is government by the people.
c. A constitutional monarchy is a government in which monarchical rule is constitutionally limited.
d. Oligarchy is government by a few.
e. Fascism is a system of government in which political opposition is prohibited and often ruthlessly suppressed.
f. Communism is an economic system in which there is common ownership of the means of production and distribution.
g. Capitalism is an economic system in which the means of production and distribution are operated for profit.

WRITING ASSIGNMENTS

Write an account of a childhood sport, defining two or three pieces of equipment necessary to it. Introduce your definition as a way of commenting on the difficulties or challenge or enjoyment presented by the sport.

Use the *Oxford English Dictionary* and other reference books to investigate the etymology and properties of one of the following and write an account of the word:
a. gyroscope
b. cotton gin
c. alcohol
d. telescope

Use the *Oxford English Dictionary* and other reference books to show how the etymology of a word like *puritan* or *humorous*—and the use of the word in texts of earlier centuries—sheds light on current meanings. Indicate the extent to which original meanings of the word have been retained in current usage.

Russel Nye
BLUEGRASS AND COUNTRY MUSIC

1.   The increasing sophistication and commercialization of country music evoked a counteraction from portions of its original audience. "Bluegrass," which emerged in the thirties, was a deliberate return to country music's rural, Southern folk-song roots, best exemplified in the recordings made by Bill Monroe and His Blue Grass Boys in 1945. Earl Scruggs of North Carolina, who played for Monroe, joined Lester Flatt of Tennessee in 1948 to form The Foggy Mountain Boys, followed by the Stanley Brothers, The Carter Family, The Clinch Mountain Boys, and others, about forty major bluegrass groups in all.

2.   Unlike country, which is guitar-based, bluegrass is banjo-based, a descendant of the nineteenth-century string bands, built about nonelectrified bass, rhythm guitar, fiddle, banjo, dobro, and mandolin, though some groups have occasionally added drums, harmonica, or accordion, much to the disapproval of the purists. Bluegrass music is light and fast, instrumental rather than vocal, usually in three-part or duet harmony with seldom more than five chord changes in a song. It is built on a four-line verse, in simple 2/4 or 4/4 time for vocal music and a fast 4/4 for instrumentals.

3.   Close to their folk origins, bluegrass lyrics tend to be traditional. The Foggy Mountain Boys' most popular album, for example, featured tunes like "Heaven," "Mama's and Daddy's Little Girl," "Big Black Train," "Old Folks," and "Goin' Home." Though bluegrass records rarely sold in the "top twenty" class, they have maintained a steady nationwide market, since they represent the Southern white's protest against urbanization and commercialization—a quiet musical protest against the move to Detroit or Chicago to look for work—and furnish him with some sense of cultural roots wherever he lives.

4.   Country music in fully developed form uses the standard thirty-two–bar song form (occasionally a twelve-bar blues) with the usual "blues" chord order. It does not ordinarily use flatted blues notes, nor does it emphasize syncopation. Its instrumenta-

tion is usually nonamplified guitar, steel guitar, violin, accordion, and string bass (sometimes piano and drums), emphasizing a strong one and three beat in 4/4 time. The country vocal style is consciously nasal, with an exaggerated Southern or Southwestern accent; older country singers may slip into falsetto, yodel, or quaver, though younger ones tend to avoid both nasality and dialect. Since the narrative element in country lyrics is important, vocalists are practically a necessity for any band.

QUESTIONS

1. Must the lyrics of bluegrass be accounted for in the definition of this kind of music? How complete a lexical definition does Nye give us?
2. Using the details that Nye gives us, what lexical definition of country music would you write?
3. How does Nye's history of bluegrass and country music serve the function of etymological definition?
4. Nye's definition of bluegrass and country music is essentially denotative. To what extent is he concerned with their connotations?

WRITING ASSIGNMENTS

Analyze the lyrics of two or three pieces of country music to distinguish it from other kinds of popular American music. Explain why the lyrics you choose to analyze are characteristic of country music.

Write a definition comparable to Nye's of a type of rock music or popular vocal music. Comment on the significance of the lyrics in understanding this type of music.

Investigate the origins of American musical comedy—for example, a show by Rodgers and Hammerstein—and that of a closely related type of musical entertainment—a Viennese operetta, a Gilbert and Sullivan operetta, an American folk opera (*Porgy and Bess, The Ballad of Baby Doe*), a rock opera (*Tommy*)—for the purpose of defining and distinguishing between them.

Marcia Seligson
THE AMERICAN WEDDING

1.   Every culture, in every time throughout history, has commemorated the transition of a human being from one state in life to another. Birth, the emergence into manhood, graduation from school at various levels, birthdays, marriage, death—each of these outstanding steps is acknowledged by a ceremony of some sort, always public, the guests in effect becoming witnesses to the statement of life's ongoingness, of the natural order of history. To insure the special significance of the rite of passage, its apartness from any other event of the day, these rituals usually require pageantry, costumed adornment, and are accompanied by gift-bearing and feasting. We wear black to funerals, bring presents to christenings and birthday parties, get loaded at wakes, eat ourselves sick at bar mitzvahs. Birth, marriage and death, to be sure, are the most elemental and major steps, and as there is only one of those ritual commemorations for which we are *actually*, fully present, the wedding becomes, for mankind, its most vital rite of passage. And for this reason it is anchored at the very core of civilization.

2.   For the rites of passage the ceremony itself is organic to the society for which the individual is being groomed, in his journey from one state to the next. In African hunting societies, for example, a boy at puberty is thrown naked into the jungle and required to kill a lion. His value as a man will be judged by how successful he can be in meeting the demands of his culture. In America, newlyweds are being prepared for their roles in a consumer society, so it is surely appropriate that all of the dynamics of wedding hoo-hah testify to these commercial, mercantile terms. Gifts are purchased not only by the "witnesses" but by bride for groom, groom for bride, bride for attendants, attendants for bride. Prenuptial parties, bachelor dinners, showers. The ever-mushrooming splash and flash circusness of the wedding itself. The American wedding is a ritual event of ferocious, gluttonous consuming, a debauch of intensified buying, never again to be repeated in the life of an American couple.

QUESTIONS

1. The first paragraph defines *rite of passage* denotatively; the second
   paragraph defines the American wedding stipulatively—that is, it
   proposes to define the wedding as something more than a marital
   union. How does this stipulative definition serve as a theoretical
   one—proposing a theory of social reality?
2. What is the principle of order in the first paragraph? Is the second
   paragraph developed in the same way?

WRITING ASSIGNMENT

Describe a ceremony of high-school or college life—June graduation,
the class play, the senior dance, Founder's Day—and discuss the extent
to which it is "organic" to the society of the institution.

Joseph Wood Krutch
THE MEANING OF "NORMAL"

1.   The words we choose to define or suggest what we believe to be important facts exert a very powerful influence upon
civilization. A mere name can persuade us to approve or disap-
prove, as it does, for example, when we describe certain attitudes
as "cynical" on the one hand or "realistic" on the other. No one
wants to be "unrealistic" and no one wants to be "snarling."
Therefore his attitude toward the thing described may very well
depend upon which designation is current among his contemporaries; and the less critical his mind, the more influential the
most commonly used vocabulary will be.
2.   It is for this reason that, even as a mere verbal confusion,
the use of "normal" to designate what ought to be called
"average" is of tremendous importance and serves not only to indicate but actually to reinforce the belief that average ability, re-
finement, intellectuality, or even virtue is an ideal to be aimed at.
Since we cannot do anything to the purpose until we think
straight and since we cannot think straight without properly de-

THE MEANING OF "NORMAL": From *Human Nature and the Human Condition*, by Joseph Wood
Krutch. Copyright © 1959 by Joseph Wood Krutch. Reprinted by permission of Random
House, Inc. Selection title by editor.

fined words it may be that the very first step toward an emancipation from the tyranny of "conformity" should be the attempt to substitute for "normal," as commonly used, a genuine synonym for "average."

3.   Fortunately, such a genuine and familiar synonym does exist. That which is "average" is also properly described as "mediocre." And if we were accustomed to call the average man, not "the common man" or still less "the normal man," but "the mediocre man" we should not be so easily hypnotized into believing that mediocrity is an ideal to be aimed at.

4.   A second step in the same direction would be to return to the word "normal" its original meaning. According to the Shorter Oxford Dictionary it derives from the Latin "norma," which has been Anglicized as "norm" and is, in turn, thus defined: "A rule or authoritative standard."

5.   The adjective "normative" is not commonly misused— no doubt because it is not part of that "vocabulary of the average man" by which educators now set so much store. It still generally means "establishing a norm or standard." But "normal" seldom means, as it should, "corresponding to the standard by which a thing is to be judged." If it did, "a normal man" would again mean, not what the average man *is* but what, in its fullest significance, the word "man" should imply, even "what a man *ought* to be." And that is a very different thing from the "average" or "mediocre" man whom we have so perversely accustomed ourselves to regard as most worthy of admiration.

6.   Only by defining and then attempting to reach up toward the "normal" as properly defined can a democratic society save itself from those defects which the enemies of democracy have always maintained were the necessary consequences of such a society. Until "preparation for life" rather than "familiarity with the best that has been thought and said" became the aim of education every schoolboy knew that Emerson had bid us hitch our wagons to a star. We now hitch them to a mediocrity instead.

7.   Unless, then, normal is a useless and confusing synonym for average it should mean what the word normative suggests, namely, a *concept of what ought to be* rather than a *description of what is*.

8.   It should mean what at times it has meant—the fullest possible realization of what the human being is capable of—the

complete, not the aborted human being. It is an *entelechy,* not a mean; something excellent, not something mediocre; something rare, not common; not what the majority are, but what few, if any, actually measure up to.

9.   Where, it will be asked, do we get this norm, upon what basis does it rest? Upon the answer to that question depends what a civilization will be like and especially in what direction it will move. At various times religion, philosophy, law, and custom have contributed to it in varying degrees. When none of these is available poetry and literature may do so. But unless we can say in one way or another, "I have some idea of what men ought to be as well as some knowledge of what they are," then civilization is lost.

QUESTIONS

1. Krutch's definition of *normal* is a precising definition. He is not stipulating a *new* meaning for the word; instead, he is seeking to make an uncommon meaning its common meaning. How does Krutch try to persuade us of the need for this other definition?

2. How does Krutch account for the present differences in the connotations of *normative* and *normal*—which derive from the same word? Does he state or imply why *normal* came to mean *average?*

3. Can the meaning of *entelechy* be determined from its context? What help does the etymology of the word provide?

4. Use the synonym listings in your dictionary to determine the *exact* difference in meaning between the following pairs of words and write sentences using ten of the italicized words to reflect their precise dictionary meanings:
   a. *essential* and necessary
   b. *perturbed* and agitated
   c. *infuse* and inculcate
   d. root and *inception*
   e. dogma and *tenet*
   f. *predict* and prophesy
   g. *mimic* and mock
   h. sinister and *portentous*
   i. fortitude and *forbearance*
   j. phase and *facet*
   k. agent and *factor*
   l. recumbent and *prone*
   m. prostrate and *supine*
   n. adroit and *deft*

o. *dextrous* and handy
p. blended and *mingled*
q. merged and *coalesced*

WRITING ASSIGNMENTS

Define one of the following words by indicating what it is not as well as what it is. Comment on the significance of its etymology
a. tolerance
b. contempt
c. contraband
d. impeachment

Discuss the different meanings—denotative and connotative—of one of the following words, illustrating these meanings by your use of them:
a. silly
b. proper
c. average
d. reasonable

Geoffrey Gorer
THE SISSY

This concept of being a sissy is a key concept for the understanding of American character; it has no exact parallel in any other society. It has nowadays become a term of opprobrium which can be applied to anyone, regardless of age or sex; although it is analogous to some English terms of opprobrium (e.g. milksop, cry-baby, nancy, mother's darling) it is more than any of them. Schematically, it means showing more dependence or fear or lack of initiative or passivity than is suitable for the occasion. It can be applied to a gambler hesitant about risking his money, to a mother overanxious about the pain her child may suffer at the hands of a surgeon, to a boy shy about asking a popular girl for a "date," to stage fright, to overt apprehension about a visit to the dentist, to a little girl crying because her doll is

THE SISSY: Reprinted from *The American People*, Rev. Ed., by Geoffrey Gorer. By permission of W. W. Norton & Company, Inc. and David Higham Associates Ltd. Copyright 1948 by Geoffrey Gorer. Revised Edition Copyright © 1964 by Geoffrey Gorer. Selection title by editor.

broken, just as well as to occasions which directly elicit courage
or initiative or independence and which may be responded to
more or less adequately. It is the overriding fear of all American
parents that their child will turn into a sissy; it is the overriding
fear of all Americans from the moment that they can understand
language that they may be taken for a sissy; and a very great deal
of American speech and activity, so often misinterpreted by non-
Americans, is designed solely to avert this damning judgment.
Particularly self-confident Americans may say "I guess I'm just a
sissy . . ." when they feel quite sure that they are not. When
applied to adult males (but only in that case) the term also implies sexual passivity.

QUESTIONS

1. Is Gorer's definition of *sissy* denotative or connotative—or both?
   Would Gorer expect to find agreement among Americans on the
   meaning of the word?
2. How has he sought to convey the nuance of the word to non-
   American readers?

WRITING ASSIGNMENTS

Discuss a current word like *cute*, whose meanings are chiefly connotative. Base your analysis of these meanings on your experience and use
of the word.

Develop by definition a paragraph on one of the following:
a. flag-waving
b. Monday-morning–quarterbacking
c. nagging
d. needling
e. buck-passing

DIVISION AND CLASSIFICATION

Marshall McLuhan
HOT AND COLD MEDIA

[1] There is a basic principle that distinguishes a hot medium like radio from a cool one like the telephone, or a hot medium like the movie from a cool one like TV. [2] A hot medium is one that extends one single sense in "high definition." [3] High definition is the state of being well filled with data. [4] A photograph is, visually, "high definition." [5] A cartoon is "low definition," simply because very little visual information is provided. [6] Telephone is a cool medium, or one of low definition, because the ear is given a meager amount of information. [7] And speech is a cool medium of low definition, because so little is given and so much has to be filled in by the listener. [8] On the other hand, hot media do not leave so much to be filled in or completed by the audience. [9] Hot media are, therefore, low in participation, and cool media are high in participation or completion by the audience. [10] Naturally, therefore, a hot medium like radio has very different effects on the user from a cool medium like the telephone.

DISCUSSION: DIVISION AND CLASSIFICATION

Any group or class or abstract idea (oranges, automobiles, discipline, injustice) can be divided or subdivided. There are usually a number of ways to do so. Oranges may be divided according to their size or their use or their country of origin (American, Israeli, Spanish oranges, and so on), and any one of the subdivisions (American oranges) may in turn be divided according to another principle: American oranges may be divided according to their size or their use or their state of origin (Florida, Texas, California oranges, and so on). The choice of a principle of division depends on the purpose of the analysis. The writer of the following paragraph first states the purpose of his analysis, then divides and subdivides:

purpose of analysis

principle of division: types according to constituent material

principle of subdivision

For the investigator of meteorites the basic challenge is deducing the history of the meteorites from a bewildering abundance of evidence. The richness of the problem is indicated by the sheer variety of types of meteorite. The two main classes are the stony meteorites and the iron meteorites. The stony meteorites consist mainly of silicates, with an admixture of nickel and iron. The iron meteorites consist mainly of nickel and iron in various proportions. A smaller class is the stony-iron meteorites, which are intermediate in composition between the other two. Stony meteorites are in turn divided into two groups: the chondrites and the achondrites, according to whether or not they contain chondrules, spherical aggregates of iron-magnesium silicate. Within each group there are further subdivisions based on mineralogical and chemical composition.—I. R. Cameron, "Meteorites and Cosmic Radiation"

The following points about division should be kept in mind:
1. The group or class being divided may be broad (automobiles) or restricted (Fords).
2. Each division or subdivision must be consistent—that is, worked out according to a single principle exclusively (model name, engine size, place of manufacture, kind of transmission, and so on).
3. Each division should be as exhaustive as knowledge permits, if the division claims to be complete (all engine sizes should be mentioned). If the division is not meant to be complete, the writer should so indicate in stating the purpose of his analysis.

Classification is the opposite of division. Two or more persons, objects, actions, or ideas may be placed in a single class (saws and hammers are tools; Pintos and Vegas are economy cars; Washington, Madison, and Jefferson were early presidents of the United States); or a person, an action, an object, or an idea may be placed in a class (Florida oranges are American oranges), and that class in a broader or more encompassing one (American oranges, like Israeli and Spanish oranges, are citrus fruit). Anything can be classified in numerous ways: a particular automobile may be discussed as a vehicle of transportation, an air pollutant, a badge of social status, an item in the family budget, and so on.

QUESTIONS

1. Media might have been divided according to the agency of transmission (the air waves, print, and so forth). By what "basic principle" does McLuhan divide media? Does he state this principle directly?
2. How do the words *hot* and *cold* help to explain the qualities McLuhan is distinguishing? Are these words synonymous with *high* and *low*, which are used in the "definition" of photographs and cartoons?
3. McLuhan's discussion of media constitutes a theoretical definition as well as a stipulative one. What new meanings of words is he stipulating, and what theory about communication is he proposing?

WRITING ASSIGNMENT

Develop the concluding sentence of the paragraph on the basis of your personal experience. Define "hot" and "cold" media in your own words.

John Holt
KINDS OF DISCIPLINE

1.   The word "discipline" has more and more important meanings than just this. A child, in growing up, may meet and learn from three different kinds of disciplines. The first and most important is what we might call the Discipline of Nature or of Reality. When he is trying to do something real, if he does the wrong thing or doesn't do the right one, he doesn't get the result he wants. If he doesn't pile one block right on top of another, or tries to build on a slanting surface, his tower falls down. If he hits the wrong key, he hears the wrong note. If he doesn't hit the nail squarely on the head, it bends, and he has to pull it out and start with another. If he doesn't measure properly what he is try-

KINDS OF DISCIPLINE: From *Freedom and Beyond* by John Holt, copyright © 1972 by John Holt. Reprinted by permission of the publisher, E. P. Dutton & Co., Inc. Selection title by editor.

ing to build, it won't open, close, fit, stand up, fly, float, whistle, or do whatever he wants it to do. If he closes his eyes when he swings, he doesn't hit the ball. A child meets this kind of discipline every time he tries to *do* something, which is why it is so important in school to give children more chances to do things, instead of just reading or listening to someone talk (or pretending to). This discipline is a great teacher. The learner never has to wait long for his answer; it usually comes quickly, often instantly. Also it is clear, and very often points toward the needed correction; from what happened he can not only see that what he did was wrong, but also why, and what he needs to do instead. Finally, and most important, the giver of the answer, call it Nature, is impersonal, impartial, and indifferent. She does not give opinions, or make judgments; she cannot be wheedled, bullied, or fooled; she does not get angry or disappointed; she does not praise or blame; she does not remember past failures or hold grudges; with her one always gets a fresh start, this time is the one that counts.

2.   The next discipline we might call the Discipline of Culture, of Society, of What People Really Do. Man is a social, a cultural animal. Children sense around them this culture, this network of agreements, customs, habits, and rules binding the adults together. They want to understand it and be a part of it. They watch very carefully what people around them are doing and want to do the same. They want to do right, unless they become convinced they can't do right. Thus children rarely misbehave seriously in church, but sit as quietly as they can. The example of all those grownups is contagious. Some mysterious ritual is going on, and children, who like rituals, want to be part of it. In the same way, the little children that I see at concerts or operas, though they may fidget a little, or perhaps take a nap now and then, rarely make any disturbance. With all those grownups sitting there, neither moving nor talking, it is the most natural thing in the world to imitate them. Children who live among adults who are habitually courteous to each other, and to them, will soon learn to be courteous. Children who live surrounded by people who speak a certain way will speak that way, however much we may try to tell them that speaking that way is bad or wrong.

3.   The third discipline is the one most people mean when they speak of discipline—the Discipline of Superior Force, of sergeant to private, of "you do what I tell you or I'll make you

wish you had." There is bound to be some of this in a child's life. Living as we do surrounded by things that can hurt children, or that children can hurt, we cannot avoid it. We can't afford to let a small child find out from experience the danger of playing in a busy street, or of fooling with the pots on the top of a stove, or of eating up the pills in the medicine cabinet. So, along with other precautions, we say to him, "Don't play in the street, or touch things on the stove, or go into the medicine cabinet, or I'll punish you." Between him and the danger too great for him to imagine we put a lesser danger, but one he can imagine and maybe therefore want to avoid. He can have no idea of what it would be like to be hit by a car, but he can imagine being shouted at, or spanked, or sent to his room. He avoids these substitutes for the greater danger until he can understand it and avoid it for its own sake. But we ought to use this discipline only when it is necessary to protect the life, health, safety, or well-being of people or other living creatures, or to prevent destruction of things that people care about. We ought not to assume too long, as we usually do, that a child cannot understand the real nature of the danger from which we want to protect him. The sooner he avoids the danger, not to escape our punishment, but as a matter of good sense, the better. He can learn that faster than we think. In Mexico, for example, where people drive their cars with a good deal of spirit, I saw many children no older than five or four walking unattended on the streets. They understood about cars, they knew what to do. A child whose life is full of the threat and fear of punishment is locked into babyhood. There is no way for him to grow up, to learn to take responsibility for his life and acts. Most important of all, we should not assume that having to yield to the threat of our superior force is good for the child's character. It is never good for *anyone's* character. To bow to superior force makes us feel impotent and cowardly for not having had the strength or courage to resist. Worse, it makes us resentful and vengeful. We can hardly wait to make someone pay for our humiliation, yield to us as we were once made to yield. No, if we cannot always avoid using the Discipline of Superior Force, we should at least use it as seldom as we can.

4.   There are places where all three disciplines overlap. Any very demanding human activity combines in it the disciplines of Superior Force, of Culture, and of Nature. The novice will be told, "Do it this way, never mind asking why, just do it that way, that is the way we always do it." But it probably *is* just the

way they always do it, and usually for the very good reason that it is a way that has been found to work. Think, for example, of ballet training. The student in a class is told to do this exercise, or that; to stand so; to do this or that with his head, arms, shoulders, abdomen, hips, legs, feet. He is constantly corrected. There is no argument. But behind these seemingly autocratic demands by the teacher lie many decades of custom and tradition, and behind that, the necessities of dancing itself. You cannot make the moves of classical ballet unless over many years you have acquired, and renewed every day, the needed strength and suppleness in scores of muscles and joints. Nor can you do the difficult motions, making them look easy, unless you have learned hundreds of easier ones first. Dance teachers may not always agree on all the details of teaching these strengths and skills. But no novice could learn them all by himself. You could not go for a night or two to watch the ballet and then, without any other knowledge at all, teach yourself how to do it. In the same way, you would be unlikely to learn any complicated and difficult human activity without drawing heavily on the experience of those who know it better. But the point is that the authority of these experts or teachers stems from, grows out of their greater competence and experience, the fact that what they do *works*, not the fact that they happen to be the teacher and as such have the power to kick a student out of the class. And the further point is that children are always and everywhere attracted to that competence, and ready and eager to submit themselves to a discipline that grows out of it. We hear constantly that children will never do anything unless compelled to by bribes or threats. But in their private lives, or in extracurricular activities in school, in sports, music, drama, art, running a newspaper, and so on, they often submit themselves willingly and wholeheartedly to very intense disciplines, simply because they want to learn to do a given thing well. Our Little-Napoleon football coaches, of whom we have too many and hear far too much, blind us to the fact that millions of children work hard every year getting better at sports and games without coaches barking and yelling at them.

QUESTIONS

1. Does Holt divide discipline according to source or to the uses of discipline in education—or according to another principle?

2. Holt states in paragraph 4 that the kinds of discipline distinguished overlap. Does he show that they nevertheless remain distinct?
3. The principle of division might have been the *effects* of discipline on the personality of the young person. To what extent is Holt concerned with effects in the course of his discussion?
4. What other principles of division might be employed in a discussion of discipline and to what purpose?

WRITING ASSIGNMENTS

Divide discipline according to a different principle from that of Holt. Make your divisions exclusive of one another and indicate how exhaustive you think they are.

Write an essay on fools or lies or advertisements, developing the topic by division. If you divide by more than one principle, keep each breakdown and discussion separate and consistent.

Jacob Brackman
THE PUT-ON

1.   Though there are suddenly many more of them, conversational put-ons are related to old-fashioned joshing and kidding, or to the sort of joke that Southerners call "funning" and Englishmen call "taking a mickey out of" someone. Not unlike the put-on, these older cousins depend upon a certain gullibility in the victim. They are like April-fool gags, perpetrated deadpan to get the victim to believe something that isn't so. Miniature hoaxes, their raison d'être is the surprise revelation of truth ("I was only kidding" or "It was just a gag") and laughter at the fall guy's credulity. Naturally, there were, and still are, habitual kidders or practical jokers. But the object of kidding, as of hoaxing, is always manifest: to *pass off* untruth as truth just for the fun of it. Ideally, there's no doubt in anyone's mind. At first, the victim

THE PUT-ON: From *The Put-On* by Jacob Brackman, published by Henry Regnery Company, 1971. Text copyright © 1967, 1971 by Jacob Brackman. Originally published in *The New Yorker* in slightly different form. By permission of Bantam Books, Inc. Selection title by editor.

believes the false to be true, whereas the kidder knows the truth. Then, the gulling accomplished, the kidder lets the victim know he's been taken for a ride. This payoff is the kidder's goal. With kidding and other hoax-derived precedents, the perpetrator smooths the rug out, has you stand on it, and then suddenly yanks it out from under you.

2.   The put-on is more like one of those irregularly moving platforms at an amusement park. The victim must constantly struggle to maintain his balance, constantly awkward, even (perhaps especially) when the floor *stops* moving for an instant; i.e., a "straight" moment, which makes the victim feel he has been paranoid. As he readjusts himself to this vision, the floor, so to speak, starts moving again. If conversation with a kidder is spiced by bosh, conversation with a put-on artist is a process of escalating confusion and distrust. He doesn't deal in isolated little tricks; rather, he has developed a pervasive style of relating to others that perpetually casts what he says into doubt. The put-on is an *open-end* form. That is to say, it is rarely climaxed by having the "truth" set straight—when a truth, indeed, exists. "Straight" discussion, when one of the participants is putting the others on, is soon subverted and eventually sabotaged by uncertainty. His intentions, and his opinions, remain cloudy.

3.   We remember the kidder as a good-natured, teasing sort—that moment when he rendered his victim absurd was quickly dissipated in the general laughter that followed. The put-on artist draws out that derisive moment; the gull has time to reflect (What's he up to? . . . He's trying to make a monkey out of me. . . . How should I respond?), and the joke's latent malice wells close to the surface. As the put-on pursues its course (at times while the subject matter shifts), it becomes clear that the victim is the butt of a generalized ridicule. Occasionally, a victim will try to explain away his confusion by assuming that the put-on artist is "just being ironical"—that he really means precisely the reverse of everything he says. This interpretation is hardly more helpful than taking put-ons at face value. Irony properly suggests the *opposite* of what is explicitly stated, by means of peripheral clues—tone of voice, accompanying gestures, stylistic exaggeration, or previous familiarity with the ironist's real opinions. Thus, for "Brutus is an honorable man" we understand "Brutus is a traitor." Irony is unsuccessful when misunderstood. But the put-on, inherently, *cannot* be understood.

QUESTIONS

1. Conversational put-ons, old-fashioned joshing and kidding, "funning," and the English "taking a mickey out of" are classified at the beginning of the first paragraph. What is the general classification?
2. How is the difference between the put-on and other forms of hoaxing explained? What does Brackman mean by "an *open-end* form"?
3. How do the *intentions* of the put-on artist differ from those of other hoaxers? What is the chief intention of the ironist?
4. Why is it inherent in the put-on that it *"cannot* be understood"?

WRITING ASSIGNMENT

Categorize the style of comedy of two contemporary satirists or the style of music of two contemporary rock groups (for example, by analyzing their attitudes toward their audiences or the subjects of their material).

COMPARISON AND CONTRAST

Jonathan Swift
A MEDITATION UPON A BROOMSTICK
According to the Style and Manner of the
Honourable Robert Boyle's Meditations

1.   This single stick, which you now behold ingloriously lying in that neglected corner, I once knew in a flourishing state in a forest; it was full of sap, full of leaves, and full of boughs; but now, in vain does the busy art of man pretend to vie with nature, by tying that withered bundle of twigs to its sapless trunk; 'tis now, at best, but the reverse of what it was, a tree turned upside down, the branches on the earth, and the root in the air; 'tis now handled by every dirty wench, condemned to do

her drudgery, and, by a capricious kind of fate, destined to make other things clean, and be nasty itself: at length, worn to the stumps in the service of the maids, it is either thrown out of doors, or condemned to the last use of kindling a fire. When I beheld this, I sighed, and said within myself, Surely man is a broomstick! Nature sent him into the world strong and lusty, in a thriving condition, wearing his own hair on his head, the proper branches of this reasoning vegetable, until the axe of intemperance has lopped off his green boughs, and left him a withered trunk: he then flies to art, and puts on a periwig, valuing himself upon an unnatural bundle of hairs (all covered with powder) that never grew on his head; but now, should this our broomstick pretend to enter the scene, proud of those birchen spoils it never bore, and all covered with dust, though the sweepings of the finest lady's chamber, we should be apt to ridicule and despise its vanity. Partial judges that we are of our own excellencies, and other men's defaults!

2.   But a broomstick, perhaps, you will say, is an emblem of a tree standing on its head; and pray what is man, but a topsy-turvy creature, his animal faculties perpetually mounted on his rational, his head where his heels should be, grovelling on the earth! and yet, with all his faults, he sets up to be a universal reformer and corrector of abuses, a remover of grievances, rakes into every slut's corner of Nature, bringing hidden corruption to the light, and raises a mighty dust where there was none before; sharing deeply all the while in the very same pollutions he pretends to sweep away: his last days are spent in slavery to women, and generally the least deserving, till, worn out to the stumps, like his brother besom, he is either kicked out of doors, or made use of to kindle flames for others to warm themselves by.

DISCUSSION: COMPARISON AND CONTRAST

Two or more people, objects, actions, or ideas may be compared and contrasted for the purpose of arriving at a relative estimate or evaluation:

> If Socrates was as innocent as this at the age of seventy, it may be imagined how innocent Joan was at the age of seventeen. Now Socrates was a man of argument, operating slowly and peacefully on men's minds, whereas Joan was a woman of action, operating with

impetuous violence on their bodies. That, no doubt, is why the contemporaries of Socrates endured him so long, and why Joan was destroyed before she was fully grown. But both of them combined terrifying ability with a frankness, personal modesty, and benevolence which made the furious dislike to which they fell victims absolutely unreasonable, and therefore inapprehensible by themselves.
—George Bernard Shaw, Preface to *St. Joan*

The opening comparison tells us something important through the differences in Socrates's and Joan's ages and ways of operating on minds and bodies; the concluding sentence moves to similarities between them. The evaluation of both Socrates and Joan is made *through* the comparison and contrast; light is shed on both of them, not on one only.

In general, comparison is concerned with resemblance, contrast with difference (however, comparison is sometimes used to mean a concern with resemblance and difference). When comparison and contrast occur in the same passage, they must be carefully distinguished to avoid confusing the reader. They can, of course, be combined with other methods of analysis: important terms may be defined before being compared; or comparison and contrast may serve to define these terms.

QUESTIONS

1. In the first paragraph of his mock imitation of Robert Boyle's Meditations, Swift is concerned with resemblances between man and broom. What are these, and what point does the comparison establish? How does a man come to resemble a broom?
2. How is the comparison extended in the second paragraph and used to make a new point?
3. Explain how the comparison makes it possible for Swift, in a humorous way, to say more about man than he would be able to say if he had merely described man's condition.

WRITING ASSIGNMENT

Compare a man to some common object. Use the comparison to arrive at a relative evaluation and to make a definite point.

S. S. Wilson
CYCLING AND WALKING

1.   The reason for the high energy efficiency of cycling compared with walking appears to lie mainly in the mode of action of
the muscles. Whereas a machine only performs mechanical work
when a force moves through a distance, muscles consume energy
when they are in tension but not moving (doing what is sometimes called "isometric" work). A man standing still maintains
his upright posture by means of a complicated system of bones
in compression and muscles in tension. Hence merely standing
consumes energy. Similarly, in performing movements with no
external forces, as in shadowboxing, muscular energy is con-
sumed because of the alternate acceleration and deceleration of
the hands and arms, although no mechanical work is done
against any outside agency.
2.   In walking the leg muscles must not only support the
rest of the body in an erect posture but also raise and lower the
entire body as well as accelerate and decelerate the lower limbs.
All these actions consume energy without doing any useful external work. Walking uphill requires that additional work be done
against gravity. Apart from these ways of consuming energy,
every time the foot strikes the ground some energy is lost, as
evidenced by the wear of footpaths, shoes and socks. The swinging of the arms and legs also causes wear and loss of energy by
chafing.
3.   Contrast this with the cyclist, who first of all saves energy by sitting, thus relieving his leg muscles of their supporting
function and accompanying energy consumption. The only recip-
rocating parts of his body are his knees and thighs; his feet rotate
smoothly at a constant speed and the rest of his body is still.
Even the acceleration and deceleration of his legs are achieved ef-
ficiently, since the strongest muscles are used almost exclusively;
the rising leg does not have to be lifted but is raised by the
downward thrust of the other leg. The back muscles must be
used to support the trunk, but the arms can also help to do this,
resulting (in the normal cycling attitude) in a little residual strain
on the hands and arms.

QUESTIONS

1. The author first compares standing still to shadowboxing to explain "the mode of action of the muscles." What are the points of similarity, and what does the comparison show? (The phrase *compared to* usually means that similarities will be indicated; *compared with*, that differences will be indicated.)
2. How is walking similar to and different from standing still, and what does the comparison show? Could the discussion of standing still and shadowboxing have been omitted without loss to the main contrast between cycling and walking?
3. What are the points of dissimilarity between walking and cycling?
4. The comparison of standing still with shadowboxing provides a relative estimate of these activities for the purpose of illustration. What is the purpose of the relative estimate provided by the contrast between cycling and walking?

WRITING ASSIGNMENT

Compare and contrast one of the following pairs of activities to arrive at a relative estimate of them and to make a point:

a. softball and hardball
b. football and touch football
c. jogging and running
d. tennis and badminton
e. checkers and chess

Hannah Arendt
THE CONCENTRATION-CAMP INMATE

Forced labor as a punishment is limited as to time and intensity. The convict retains his rights over his body; he is not absolutely tortured and he is not absolutely dominated. Banishment banishes only from one part of the world to another part of the world, also inhabited by human beings; it does not exclude from the human world altogether. Throughout history slavery has been an institution within a social order; slaves were not, like concentration-camp inmates, withdrawn from the sight and

THE CONCENTRATION-CAMP INMATE: From *Origins of Totalitarianism* new edition by Hannah Arendt. Copyright 1951. © 1958, 1966 by Hannah Arendt. Reprinted by permission of Harcourt Brace Jovanovich; Inc. Selection title by editor.

hence the protection of their fellow-men; as instruments of labor they had a definite price and as property a definite value. The concentration-camp inmate has no price, because he can always be replaced; nobody knows to whom he belongs, because he is never seen. From the point of view of normal society he is absolutely superfluous, although in times of acute labor shortage, as in Russia and in Germany during the war, he is used for work.

QUESTIONS

1. Hannah Arendt might simply have described the typical existence of the concentration-camp inmate. Instead she defines that existence through contrast with other forms of imprisonment and servitude: through a relative estimate. What is the advantage of this procedure—defining by means of contrast—over other methods?
2. What accounts for the order of ideas? Are they presented in the order of their importance?

WRITING ASSIGNMENT

Make a list of significant similarities and differences between one of the following pairs and use it to write a paragraph. Use your comparison and contrast to arrive at a relative estimate—which is better or worse?—and to make a definite point.
a. streetcar or bus nuisance and back-seat driver
b. silent bore and talkative bore
c. classroom leech and dormitory leech
d. expectations of high-school English teachers and expectations of college English teachers

ANALOGY

Fred Hoyle
THE EXPANDING UNIVERSE

1.   The degree to which the background material has to be
compressed to form a galaxy is not at all comparable with the
tremendous compression necessary to produce a star.* This you
can see by thinking of a model in which our Galaxy is represented by a 50-cent piece. Then the blob of background material
out of which our Galaxy condensed would be only about a yard
in diameter. This incidentally is the right way to think about the
Universe as a whole. If in your mind's eye you take the average
galaxy to be about the size of a bee—a small bee, a honeybee, not
a bumblebee—our Galaxy would be roughly represented in
shape and size by the 50-cent piece, and the average spacing of
the galaxies would be about two yards, and the range of tele-
scopic vision about a mile. So sit back and imagine a swarm of
bees spaced about two yards apart and stretching away from you
in all directions for a distance of about a mile. Now for each
honeybee substitute the vast bulk of a galaxy and you have an
idea of the Universe that has been revealed by the large American telescopes.

2.   . . . Perhaps you've noticed that a whistle from an approaching train has a higher pitch, and from a receding train a
lower pitch, than a similar whistle from a stationary train. Light
emitted by a moving source has the same property. The pitch of
the light is lowered, or as we usually say reddened, if the source
is moving away from us. Now we observe that the light from the

THE EXPANDING UNIVERSE: From pp. 111–12, 114–16 in *The Nature of the Universe*, Revised
Edition by Fred Hoyle. Copyright © 1950, 1960 by Fred Hoyle. Reprinted by permission of
Harper & Row, Publishers, Inc. Also by permission of Basil Blackwell, Publisher. Selection
title by editor.

* This background material is the thin, interstellar gas out of which, Hoyle speculates, clouds
and, eventually, stars condensed. Its total amount "exceeds about a hundredfold the combined quantity of material in all the galaxies put together." [Ed.]

galaxies is reddened, and the degree of reddening increases proportionately with the distance of a galaxy. The natural explanation of this is that the galaxies are rushing away from each other at enormous speeds, which for the most distant galaxies that we can see with the biggest telescopes become comparable with the speed of light itself.

3.   My nonmathematical friends often tell me that they find it difficult to picture this expansion. Short of using a lot of mathematics I cannot do better than use the analogy of a balloon with a large number of dots marked on its surface. If the balloon is blown up, the distances between the dots increase in the same way as the distances between the galaxies. Here I should give a warning that this analogy must not be taken too strictly. There are several important respects in which it is definitely misleading. For example, the dots on the surface of a balloon would themselves increase in size as the balloon was being blown up. This is not the case for the galaxies, for their internal gravitational fields are sufficiently strong to prevent any such expansion. A further weakness of our analogy is that the surface of an ordinary balloon is two dimensional—that is to say, the points of its surface can be described by two co-ordinates; for example, by latitude and longitude. In the case of the Universe we must think of the surface as possessing a third dimension. This is not as difficult as it may sound. We are all familiar with pictures in perspective—pictures in which artists have represented three-dimensional scenes on two-dimensional canvases. So it is not really a difficult conception to imagine the three dimensions of space as being confined to the surface of a balloon. But then what does the radius of the balloon represent, and what does it mean to say that the balloon is being blown up? The answer to this is that the radius of the balloon is a measure of time, and the passage of time has the effect of blowing up the balloon. This will give you a very rough, but useful, idea of the sort of theory investigated by the mathematician.

4.   The balloon analogy brings out a very important point. It shows we must not imagine that we are situated at the center of the Universe, just because we see all the galaxies to be moving away from us. For, whichever dot you care to choose on the surface of the balloon, you will find that the other dots all move away from it. In other words, whichever galaxy you happen to be in, the other galaxies will appear to be receding from you.

DISCUSSION: ANALOGY

Illustrative analogy is a special kind of example, a comparison between two different things or activities for the purpose of explanation: a child growing like a tender plant and needing sun, water, and a receptive soil as well as proper care from a skilled gardener. Because the two things or activities share a number of qualities, the comparison may be point by point. But, of course, there are differences also, and if there is danger that the analogy may be carried too far (the child is not so tender that it needs full protection from the hazards of living), the writer may indicate these differences to limit the inferences that may be drawn. He has chosen the analogy for the sake of vivid illustration and nothing more. As we shall see, analogy is often used in argument: a child *should* be fully protected from various hazards because he or she is a tender plant. The argument will stand or fall depending on how convinced we are of the similarities and of the unimportance of the differences.

QUESTIONS

1. The advantage of comparing galaxies and bees derives from their re-markably different sizes. Size can be absolute in mathematical terms, but imagined only in *relative* terms—through familiar objects such as Hoyle employs. Given the characteristics of the galaxies in the discussion, why are bees more appropriate to the analogy than berries thrown into the air—objects of roughly the same size as bees?
2. Why are moving trains appropriate in explaining the "red shift"? What other objects might have been employed in the analogy?
3. Hoyle considers at length the dissimilarities between the dots on the balloon, the balloon itself, and the phenomena compared to these. Why is this consideration of dissimilarities necessary? What does the balloon represent?
4. In another discussion of the same phenomena, Hoyle analogizes "a raisin cake baking in an oven" to the expansion of the galaxies. In what ways would the raisin cake be analogous?

WRITING ASSIGNMENT

Explain a phenomenon with which you are familiar—for example, condensation or stereophonic or quadriphonic sound—by the use of analogy.

John Henry Newman
USEFUL EDUCATION

1.   This is the obvious answer which may be made to those
who urge upon us the claims of Utility in our plans of Education;
but I am not going to leave the subject here: I mean to take a
wider view of it.* Let us take "useful," as Locke takes it, in its
proper and popular sense, and then we enter upon a large field of
thought, to which I cannot do justice in one Discourse, though
today's is all the space that I can give to it. I say, let us take
"useful" to mean, not what is simply good, but what *tends* to
good, or is the *instrument* of good; and in this sense also, Gentlemen, I will show you how a liberal education is truly and fully a
useful, though it be not a professional, education. "Good" indeed means one thing, and "useful" means another; but I lay it
down as a principle, which will save us a great deal of anxiety,
that, though the useful is not always good, the good is always
useful. Good is not only good, but reproductive of good; this is
one of its attributes; nothing is excellent, beautiful, perfect, desirable for its own sake, but it overflows, and spreads the likeness of itself all around it. Good is prolific; it is not only good to
the eye, but to the taste; it not only attracts us, but it communicates itself; it excites first our admiration and love, then our
desire and our gratitude, and that, in proportion to its intense-
ness and fullness in particular instances. A great good will impart
great good. If then the intellect is so excellent a portion of us, and
its cultivation so excellent, it is not only beautiful, perfect, admirable, and noble in itself, but in a true and high sense it must be
useful to the possessor and to all around him; not useful in any
low, mechanical, mercantile sense, but as diffusing good, or as a
blessing, or a gift, or power, or a treasure, first to the owner,

USEFUL EDUCATION: From *The Idea of a University* (1852), Discourse VII. Selection title by editor.

* Newman is answering critics of classical education who had been arguing that it developed
the feelings and imagination, but not the intellect. John Locke asked in *Some Thoughts Concerning Education* (1693): "Could it be believed, unless we have everywhere amongst us examples of it, that a child should be forced to learn the rudiments of a language which he is
never to use in the course of life that he is designed to, and neglect all the while the writing a
good hand, and casting accounts, which are of great advantage in all conditions of life, and to
most trades indispensably necessary?" Newman's "obvious answer" is "Whether youths are
to be taught Latin or verse-making will depend on the *fact*, whether these studies tend to
mental culture. . . ." [Ed.]

then through him to the world. I say then, if a liberal education be good, it must necessarily be useful too.

2.   You will see what I mean by the parallel of bodily health. Health is a good in itself, though nothing came of it, and is especially worth seeking and cherishing; yet, after all, the blessings which attend its presence are so great, while they are so close to it and so redound back upon it and encircle it, that we never think of it except as useful as well as good, and praise and prize it for what it does, as well as for what it is, though at the same time we cannot point out any definite and distinct work or production which it can be said to effect. And so as regards intellectual culture, I am far from denying utility in this large sense as the end of Education, when I lay it down, that the culture of the intellect is a good in itself and its own end; I do not exclude from the idea of intellectual culture what it cannot but be, from the very nature of things; I only deny that we must be able to point out, before we have any right to call it useful, some art, or business, or profession, or trade, or work, as resulting from it, and as its real and complete end. The parallel is exact: As the body may be sacrificed to some manual or other toil, whether moderate or oppressive, so may the intellect be devoted to some specific profession; and I do not call *this* the culture of the intellect. Again, as some member or organ of the body may be inordinately used and developed, so may memory, or imagination, or the reasoning faculty; and *this* again is not intellectual culture. On the other hand, as the body may be tended, cherished, and exercised with a simple view to its general health, so may the intellect also be generally exercised in order to its perfect state; and this *is* its cultivation.

3.   Again, as health ought to precede labor of the body, and as a man in health can do what an unhealthy man cannot do, and as of his health the properties are strength, energy, agility, graceful carriage and action, manual dexterity, and endurance of fatigue, so in like manner general culture of mind is the best aid to professional and scientific study, and educated men can do what illiterate cannot; and the man who has learned to think and to reason and to compare and to discriminate and to analyze, who has refined his taste, and formed his judgment, and sharpened his mental vision, will not indeed at once be a lawyer, or a pleader, or an orator, or a statesman, or a physician, or a good landlord, or a man of business, or a soldier, or an engineer, or a

chemist, or a geologist, or an antiquarian, but he will be placed in that state of intellect in which he can take up any one of the sciences or callings I have referred to, or any other for which he has a taste or special talent, with an ease, a grace, a versatility, and a success, to which another is a stranger. In this sense then, and as yet I have said but a very few words on a large subject, mental culture is emphatically *useful*.

QUESTIONS

1. In these paragraphs Newman argues against "the claims of Utility"— that is, against the claim that education must serve immediate, practical needs and prepare the student for a particular career. (Newman did believe, however, that university education might do so, but that its primary aim was as he describes it here.) In paragraph 1 he prepares the ground for the discussion by defining *good* and *useful*. How does he define them and establish a necessary relation between them?
2. In paragraphs 2 and 3 how does Newman argue by analogy that "if a liberal education be good, it must necessarily be useful too"? Are you convinced by the analogy?
3. According to Newman, why is the parallel "exact"? Does he mean that the things being compared are similar in all respects?

WRITING ASSIGNMENTS

Defend or attack Newman's distinction between the good and the useful through examples taken from another area of experience.

Newman states in a later passage that university education

> teaches him [a man] to see things as they are, to go right to the point, to disentangle a skein of thought, to detect what is sophistical, and to discard what is irrelevant.

Discuss how these aims can best be realized or fail to be realized in the required college freshman courses.

EXAMPLE

E. B. White
NEW YORK

It is a miracle that New York works at all. The whole thing is implausible. Every time the residents brush their teeth, millions of gallons of water must be drawn from the Catskills and the hills of Westchester. When a young man in Manhattan writes a letter to his girl in Brooklyn, the love message gets blown to her through a pneumatic tube—*pfft*—just like that. The subterranean system of telephone cables, power lines, steam pipes, gas mains and sewer pipes is reason enough to abandon the island to the gods and the weevils. Every time an incision is made in the pavement, the noisy surgeons expose ganglia that are tangled beyond belief. By rights New York should have destroyed itself long ago, from panic or fire or rioting or failure of some vital supply line in its circulatory system or from some deep labyrinthine short circuit. Long ago the city should have experienced an insoluble traffic snarl at some impossible bottleneck. It should have perished of hunger when food lines failed for a few days. It should have been wiped out by a plague starting in its slums or carried in by ships' rats. It should have been overwhelmed by the sea that licks at it on every side. The workers in its myriad cells should have succumbed to nerves, from the fearful pall of smoke-fog that drifts over every few days from Jersey, blotting out all light at noon and leaving the high offices suspended, men groping and depressed, and the sense of world's end. It should have been touched in the head by the August heat and gone off its rocker.

DISCUSSION: EXAMPLE

An idea may be illustrated by a series of short examples or by a long example that is needed to make it clear. The word *example* originally

NEW YORK: From pp. 24–25 in *Here Is New York* by E. B. White. Copyright, 1949 by E. B. White. By permission of Harper & Row, Publishers, Inc. Selection title by editor.

meant a sample or typical instance; but for many writers it is an out-standing instance, or even one that is essential in exposition. To say that New York is different today from the New York of fifty years ago means little unless we illustrate the difference. To persuade the person who believes it is always wrong to split the infinitive, we must provide a sentence in which the infinitive must be split. The experiments of Galileo with falling bodies are inseparably bound with our understanding of an important law of gravity. Einstein depended on "thought-experiments" involving elevators in free fall and other imagined phenomena to explain his exceedingly difficult ideas. In such experiments examples are not merely outstanding instances in exposition; they are essential.

QUESTIONS

1. White implicitly compares New York City to a human being. What are the similarities, and how does the comparison help to emphasize the "miracle" he is describing?
2. Does White depend on formal transitions to connect his examples and relate them to his topic sentence?

WRITING ASSIGNMENTS

In a well-developed paragraph state an idea about your hometown or city and develop it by a series of short examples. Make your examples vivid and lively.

Develop one of the following statements by example:
a. The insupportable labor of doing nothing.—Sir Richard Steele
b. The first blow is half the battle.—Oliver Goldsmith
c. Ask yourself whether you are happy, and you cease to be so.—John Stuart Mill

Tom Wolfe
THURSDAY MORNING IN A NEW YORK SUBWAY STATION

1. Love! Attar of libido in the air! It is 8:45 A.M. Thursday morning in the IRT subway station at 50th Street and Broadway

THURSDAY MORNING IN A NEW YORK SUBWAY STATION: Reprinted with the permission of Farrar, Straus & Giroux, Inc. from *The Kandy Kolored Tangerine Flake Streamline Baby* by Tom Wolfe, copyright © 1964 by New York Herald Tribune Inc. Selection title by editor.

EXAMPLE 77

and already two kids are hung up in a kind of herringbone weave of arms and legs, which proves, one has to admit, that love is not *confined* to Sunday in New York. Still, the odds! All the faces come popping in clots out of the Seventh Avenue local, past the King Size Ice Cream machine, and the turnstiles start whacking away as if the world were breaking up on the reefs. Four steps past the turnstiles everybody is already backed up haunch to paunch for the climb up the ramp and the stairs to the surface, a great funnel of flesh, wool, felt, leather, rubber and steaming alumicron, with the blood squeezing through everybody's old sclerotic arteries in hopped-up spurts from too much coffee and the effort of surfacing from the subway at the rush hour. Yet there on the landing are a boy and a girl, both about eighteen, in one of those utter, My Sin, backbreaking embraces.

2.   He envelops her not only with his arms but with his chest, which has the American teen-ager concave shape to it. She has her head cocked at a 90-degree angle and they both have their eyes pressed shut for all they are worth and some incredibly feverish action going with each other's mouths. All round them, ten, scores, it seems like hundreds, of faces and bodies are perspiring, trooping and bellying up the stairs with arteriosclerotic grimaces past a showcase full of such novel items as Joy Buzzers, Squirting Nickels, Finger Rats, Scary Tarantulas and spoons with realistic dead flies on them, past Fred's barbershop, which is just off the landing and has glossy photographs of young men with the kind of baroque haircuts one can get in there, and up onto 50th Street into a madhouse of traffic and shops with weird lingerie and gray hair-dyeing displays in the windows, signs for free teacup readings and a pool-playing match between the Playboy Bunnies and Downey's Showgirls, and then everybody pounds on toward the Time-Life Building, the Brill Building or NBC.

3.   The boy and the girl just keep on writhing in their embroilment. Her hand is sliding up the back of his neck, which he turns when her fingers wander into the intricate formal gardens of his Chicago Boxcar hairdo at the base of the skull. The turn causes his face to start to mash in the ciliated hull of her beehive hairdo, and so she rolls her head 180 degrees to the other side, using their mouths for the pivot. But aside from good hair grooming, they are oblivious to everything but each other. Everybody gives them a once-over. Disgusting! Amusing! How touching! A few kids pass by and say things like "Swing it,

baby." But the great majority in that heaving funnel up the stairs
seem to be as much astounded as anything else. The vision of
love at rush hour cannot strike anyone exactly as romance. It is a
feat, like a fat man crossing the English Channel in a barrel. It is
an earnest accomplishment against the tide. It is a piece of
slightly gross heroics, after the manner of those knobby, varicose
old men who come out from some place in baggy shorts every
year and run through the streets of Boston in the Marathon race.
And somehow that is the gaffe against love all week long in New
York, for everybody, not just two kids writhing under their coif-
fures in the 50th Street subway station; too hurried, too crowded,
too hard, and no time for dalliance.

QUESTIONS

1. Wolfe illustrates "the gaffe against love all week long in New York."
   What precisely is the "gaffe"? What do the details suggest about the
   Thursday morning mood of New Yorkers?
2. What does the description of the showcase and of 50th Street imply
   about the world of the lovers? Would they seem comical in any setting?

WRITING ASSIGNMENTS

Every piece of writing suggests something about the personality, interests, and ideas of the author, even when he speaks to us through a nar-
rator. Discuss the impression you receive of the author of this selection.

Describe one or two people in a situation made comical by the setting.
Allow your reader to visualize the setting as well as the situation.

Hamilton Fish Armstrong
NEW YORK AT THE TURN OF THE CENTURY

1.   When I was nine the time came for me to go to a "real"
school uptown, and unless it was pouring rain or snowing I

NEW YORK AT THE TURN OF THE CENTURY: From pp. 68–70 in *Those Days* by Hamilton Fish
Armstrong. Copyright © 1963 by Hamilton Fish Armstrong. By permission of Harper & Row,
Publishers, Inc. Selection title by editor.

EXAMPLE   **79**

went, of course, on skates. When the weather ruled this out I used the Fifth Avenue stage or the Sixth Avenue El.

2.   On the stage I rode by choice on the outside, either perched up behind the driver or, if I was lucky, alongside him. You mounted to this vantage point by the hub and two widely spaced iron footholds. Thence, as the stage rumbled heavily along, New York unrolled before you. First came the sedate brownstone houses of lower Fifth Avenue; then the Flatiron Building, to some a thing of soaring beauty, to others an architectural monstrosity, but in everyone's eyes, including those on the top of the stage, a continuing wonder (height, 307 feet); then Madison Square with the Farragut of Saint-Gaudens, one of his best, conspicuous for all the passing traffic to see (until relegated by Mr. Moses to obscurity among the trees in the middle of the park); and the Worth Monument opposite, marking the burial place of the Mexican War hero, since invaded by a marble comfort station which hopefully does not disturb the general's bones. Then came the Holland House and the Brunswick Hotel, where in spring there might be a four-in-hand coach drawn up, making ready to tool up to Claremont or Pelham or out to Tuxedo, grooms holding the horses, while on top several feather-bedecked ladies preened themselves before a group of dazzled onlookers. On you went past the Waldorf up Murray Hill and along the old reservoir resembling an Egyptian tomb, afterwards replaced by the Public Library guarded by the two lions with Horace Greeley faces.

3.   If you secured the seat beside the driver you took care not to interfere with a leather strap attached to his leg, for it performed an important function. Passing through an aperture under the seat, it led along the ceiling of the stage to the top of the rear door; and by it the driver controlled the door's opening and closing. When he stopped to take on passengers he moved his leg back, allowing the door to swing open by its own weight; then he would slide his leg forward, banging the door to, and start his horses off again. If you had to ride inside, where in winter it was stuffy and smelt of the stable, with a touch of kerosene added after dusk from the flickering lamp, the procedure was to wriggle your way forward and deposit your nickel in a box situated under the driver's seat. He could peer down through a small window and verify that your fare had been paid; if you were slow about it, he would mortify you by angrily thumping.

If you needed change, you attracted his attention by ringing a bell and passing your money up to him through a small sliding panel; and he would hand the change back to you in an envelope colored according to the amount involved. Often there was much bowing by gentlemen offering to pass along the money for ladies, and sometimes an argument, in which everyone joined, as to whether or not a certain fare had been paid. When you wanted to get off you gave notice via the driver's leg by jerking the strap on the ceiling.

4.   His various duties kept the driver busy, especially in winter when an extra horse was needed to help scale the slippery slope of Murray Hill. Gradually I became intimate with certain drivers, who let me help with handing down envelopes; and when the stage was full I would wave grandly to groups waiting on the corners to signify that we couldn't stop.

5.   My station for the Sixth Avenue El was at Eighth Street. When I reached the corner of Tenth Street and saw a train just rounding the curve from Bleecker Street I knew exactly whether or not it was worth while sprinting the two blocks and tearing up the long iron stairs to try to make it. If only the first car was in view I could catch it quite surely; if two or three cars, it would be a close shave; more than that, hopeless, and I could save my breath and leave my oatmeal and Postum untroubled in my innards. Sometimes, against all rules, the friendly ticket chopper would let me save a vital second or two by pushing my nickel into his hands rather than stopping for a ticket at the little wicket.

6.   The El stations have been described as "Renaissance-Gothic in style, like a Swiss chalet on stilts." In winter, the atmosphere in the tightly sealed waiting room was semi-solid; the pot-bellied stove, with a mushroom top to spread the heat, mingled its coal fumes with the smell of tobacco juice from the spittoons and the powerful antiseptic from the "retiring rooms." When spring came, the colored-glass windows of the stations were reluctantly opened up, and on the trains you rode breezily on the car platforms, although there you missed the latest jingles of Phoebe Snow, the pleadings of the Gold Dust twins to let them do your work, Sapolio's report on the doings of the mayor, the butcher and other happy workers in Spotless Town, and the threats of the balding-headed man, "Going!—Going!!—Gone!! Too Late for Herpicide!!!"

QUESTIONS

1. What differences in riding the stage and riding the El does the writer stress in his details? What dominant impression does he create of his experience?
2. The detailed account of the ride on the stage and the duties of the driver are essential for understanding modes of travel in New York at the turn of the century. What other features of life at that time does the account illustrate?
3. What impression does the writer create of the El stations? How does he communicate his attitude toward them?

WRITING ASSIGNMENT

Develop one of the following situations through example:
a. the hazards of rush-hour traffic
b. the nervous or inexperienced driver
c. cycling in heavy traffic
d. driving by oneself for the first time

PROCESS ANALYSIS

Florence H. Pettit
HOW TO SHARPEN YOUR KNIFE

If you have never done any whittling or wood carving before, the first skill to learn is how to sharpen your knife. You may be surprised to learn that even a brand-new knife needs sharpening. Knives are never sold honed (finely sharpened), although some gouges and chisels are. It is essential to learn the firm stroke on the stone that will keep your blades sharp. The sharpening stone must be fixed in place on the table, so that it will not move around. You can do this by placing a piece of rubber inner tube or a thin piece of foam rubber under it. Or you can tack four strips of wood, if you have a rough worktable, to frame the stone and hold it in place. Put a generous puddle of oil on the stone—this will soon disappear into the surface of a new stone, and you will need to keep adding more oil. Press the knife blade flat against the stone in the puddle of oil, using your index finger. Whichever way the cutting edge of the knife faces is the side of the blade that should get a little more pressure. Move the blade around three or four times in a narrow oval about the size of your fingernail, going *counterclockwise* when the sharp edge is facing right. Now turn the blade over in the same spot on the stone, press hard, and move it around the small oval *clockwise,* with more pressure on the cutting edge that faces left. Repeat the ovals, flipping the knife blade over six or seven times, and applying lighter pressure to the blade the last two times. Wipe the blade clean with a piece of rag or tissue and rub it flat on the piece of leather strop at least twice on each side. Stroke *away* from the cutting edge to remove the little burr of metal that may be left on the blade.

DISCUSSION: PROCESS ANALYSIS

An important method of paragraph development is that of tracing or analyzing a mechanical, natural, or historical process—that is, a series of connected stages, each stage developing from the preceding one; or a series of connected events, each event developing from the preceding one. Though the stages or events are presented chronologically, the author may interrupt his account to discuss the implications or details of a particular stage or event. In complex processes, various stages may individually contain a number of steps and each step must be carefully distinguished for the reader. Process analysis is often closely related to causal analysis and may be combined with it.

QUESTIONS

1. What steps of the mechanical process described by Florence Pettit need to be visualized to be understood? What details help the reader to visualize them?
2. Are the stages of the process presented chronologically? If not, why not?
3. What terms, in your opinion, need to be defined for the amateur? What terms are explained by the context—that is, by the description of the process?

WRITING ASSIGNMENT
Describe a mechanical process comparable to sharpening a knife—for example, sharpening the blades of a hand mower or pruning a tree or painting the exterior of a house.

Rachel Carson
THE HABITATION OF THE SHRIMP

1.   The intricate passageways, the shelter and available food they offer, have attracted many small creatures to live within the sponge. Some come and go; others never leave the sponge once they have taken up residence within it. One such permanent lodger is a small shrimp—one of the group known as snapping shrimp because of the sound made by snapping the large claw. Although the adults are imprisoned, the young shrimp, hatched from eggs adhering to the appendages of their mothers, pass out with the water currents into the sea and live for a time in the currents and tides, drifting, swimming, perhaps carried far afield. By mischance they may occasionally find their way into deep water where no sponges grow. But many of the young shrimp will in time find and approach the dark bulk of some loggerhead sponge and, entering it, will take up the strange life of their parents. Wandering through its dark halls, they scrape food from the walls of the sponge. As they creep along these cylindrical passageways, they carry their antennae and their large claws extended before them, as though to sense the approach of a larger and possibly dangerous creature, for the sponge has many lodgers of many species—other shrimps, amphipods, worms, isopods—and their numbers may reach into the thousands if the sponge is large.

2.   There, on the flats off some of the Keys, I have opened small loggerheads and heard the warning snapping of claws as the resident shrimps, small, amber-colored beings, hurried into the deeper cavities. I had heard the same sound filling the air

about me, as, on an evening low tide, I waded in to the shore. From all the exposed reef rock there were strange little knockings and hammerings, yet the sounds, to a maddening degree, were impossible to locate. Surely this nearby hammering came from this particular bit of rock; yet when I knelt to examine it closely there was silence; then from all around, from everywhere but this bit of rock at hand, all the elfin hammering was resumed. I could never find the little shrimps in the rocks, yet I knew they were related to those I had seen in the loggerhead sponges. Each has one immense hammer claw almost as long as the rest of its body. The movable finger of the claw bears a peg that fits into a socket in the rigid finger. Apparently the movable finger when raised, is held in position by suction. To lower it, extra muscular force must be applied, and when the suction is overcome, it snaps into place with audible sound, at the same time ejecting a spurt of water from its socket. Perhaps the water jet repels enemies and aids in capturing prey, which may also be stunned by a blow from the forcibly retracted claw. Whatever the value of the mechanism, the snapping shrimps are so abundant in the shallows of tropical and subtropical regions, and snap their claws so incessantly, that they are responsible for much of the extraneous noise picked up on underwater listening devices, filling the water world with a continuous sizzling, crackling sound.

QUESTIONS

1. What natural process does Rachel Carson describe in paragraph 1? What stages does she distinguish? What natural process does she describe in paragraph 2?
2. Is the account of each process chronological? If not, how do you explain the departure from chronological order?
3. This process analysis serves to develop an impression of the Florida Keys. What is that impression, and what do the details of the passage contribute to it?

WRITING ASSIGNMENT

Describe a process you have performed or observed in a science course or on a field trip. If you depart from strict chronological order, be ready to justify your departure.

Bernard DeVoto
THE HUNTING OF THE BUFFALO

1.   Stewart first saw buffalo in late May along the Platte east
of the forks, a usual time and place for fur caravans to meet them.
This was calf-time, and so the cows, at other seasons incompara-
bly the best meat, would be poor and stringy. The greenhorn had
envisoned enormous herds whose passing shook the earth and
whose bellowing made sleep impossible at night, but such herds
would not form till the mating or "running" season, well past
mid-summer. Before that season the buffalo would be encountered in small bands—from twenty or thirty up to a hundred or
so—more or less cohesive, moving toward water or feeding on
the short grama which was the most nutritious of all grasses.
There might be many bands near together, mounting up to several thousand all told; or, even in what would be considered
good buffalo country, a day's travel might reveal only two or
three. The calves would be light in color, sandy red or even
yellow; packs of wolves and coyotes would be trailing them but
the bulls would be on guard. Yearlings would be darker and
"spike bulls," the four-year-olds whose horns had smooth, clean
points, would begin to show the colors of maturity. There was
much individual variation, but a typical bull would shade from a
bright blond at the forequarters and hump to dark brown or even
black at the hindquarters and under the belly. At calf-time the
thick woolly hair would be shedding toward the near-nudity of
mid-summer and the resulting patchiness would make a full-
grown bull look even more ferocious and demoniac than a greenhorn's fantasy had painted him. Such a bull, say eight or ten
years old, would weigh just short of a ton, seventeen hundred or
eighteen hundred pounds. He would stand six feet at the shoulders. From muzzle to rump he might be ten feet long.
2.   Sighting a bunch, the hunter tightened his saddle girth
and verified the charge and priming of his weapons. He tried to
get as close as possible, approaching upwind. Grazing buffalo
could be stalked within certain bowshot—fifty to a hundred

yards—by careful Indians or whites, crawling up draws, pushing a sagebrush ahead like military snipers, or even, as in a celebrated print of Catlin's, wearing wolfskins. If a successful approach were made, such a hunter might kill half the bunch, even with firearms, before the survivors showed any curiosity about what was going on. There was no such placidity, however, if the ungainly beasts caught the man-scent or saw any rapid or unusual movement. The sportsman hoped to ride undiscovered within three hundred yards but seldom did. Usually he was half a mile away when first one and then the whole bunch broke into a run, quartering downwind to keep the scent and yet escape from it. That was what the sportsman had come for: he began the chase.

3.   Any tolerably good horse could overtake the fastest buffalo, but had to go full gallop to do so and sometimes had to gallop four or five miles, which was what broke horses down. This first wild run—most exhilarating in early morning when the thin air was electric in your lungs—was headlong over unknown ground which might have buffalo wallows or small gullies or sizable ravines in it and was certain to be pitted by innumerable burrows of gophers and prairie dogs. A fall might mean a broken leg for the horse, broken bones or concussion or death for the rider. In Frémont's report Kit Carson, as expert a hunter as ever lived, is first seen in action picking himself up from such a fall: "though considerably hurt he had the good fortune to break no bones." But long before the hunter overtook the buffalo he was, in Frémont's words, "sensible to nothing else." His heart was pounding in time with the horse's hoofs, he was straining forward in his saddle, and he was shouting at the top of his voice.

4.   The buffalo were making by instinct for country too broken for a horse to follow, deep ravines or wooded coulees. If they were overtaken, the hunter's excitement became delirium. "I could see nothing but a cloud of dust," Francis Parkman wrote. "In a moment I was in the midst of the cloud, half suffocated by the dust and stunned by the trampling of the flying herd; but I was drunk with the chase and cared for nothing but the buffalo." There were buffalo all round, enormous in the murk, butting at the horse or trying to gore it (impossible if it kept its feet, of course), sometimes charging at it. Their hoofs flung dirt and clods into the hunter's eyes; his ears roared with a confusion of noises. There was no seeing what was ahead, but he had to select a victim, and at any season but calf-time the victim had to be a

cow, a young one for preference. A trained buffalo horse, guided entirely by the pressure of the rider's thighs, side-stepped the sidelong charges and dodged the direct ones, coming up behind the right shoulder. When Indians coursed buffalo they used a lance or an arrow; one arrow was enough if properly placed and it was frequently driven clear through the beast so that it slid along the plain on the other side. The white man used his rifle and reloaded it on the dead run, pounding the butt-plate on the saddle to seat the bullet which normally had to be rammed home. If he succeeded in that doubtful operation—pouring powder haphazardly from his horn, perhaps in a double or triple charge, and spitting into the muzzle a ball he had been carrying in his mouth—he was ready for another kill. If not, he used his pistols, less effectively. No matter: by now he was a madman and had to keep galloping, yelling, firing, till his horse was spent, his powder gone, or the bunch of buffalo dispersed as stragglers. Suddenly there was silence again. Far away other half-dozens were galloping ahead of other hunters, whose rifles might spout smoke as their companion looked up. Here and there over the plain was the fallen carcass of a buffalo, here and there a wounded beast sinking to its kness. Consciousness came back. The horse was snorting for breath and bathed with foam. "I myself," Parkman says, "felt as if drenched in warm water."

QUESTIONS

1. What purpose does the description of the buffalo serve in the passage as a whole? How does the detail illuminate the difficulties the hunter faced or the opportunities he could exploit in hunting the buffalo?
2. How does De Voto distinguish the stages of the hunt? Does the passage constitute one connected series of stages, or is the description of the hunt organized in a different way?
3. Why does De Voto introduce the contrast between the Indian and the white hunter where he does? Could this contrast have appeared elsewhere?
4. How does De Voto mark the climax of the hunt and give emphasis to it?

WRITING ASSIGNMENT

Describe the process by which you learned to ride a horse or to operate a power tool or other kind of machinery. In the course of your description indicate the emotions you felt as you developed the necessary skills.

CAUSE AND EFFECT

Will Durant
THE POLITICAL CAUSES OF THE DECAY OF ROME

The political causes of decay were rooted in one fact—that increasing despotism destroyed the citizen's civic sense and dried up statesmanship at its source. Powerless to express his political will except by violence, the Roman lost interest in government and became absorbed in his business, his amusements, his legion, or his individual salvation. Patriotism and the pagan religion had been bound together, and now together decayed. The Senate, losing ever more of its power and prestige after Pertinax, relapsed into indolence, subservience, or venality; and the last barrier fell that might have saved the state from militarism and anarchy. Local governments, overrun by imperial *correctores* and *exactores*, no longer attracted first-rate men. The responsibility of municipal officials for the tax quotas of their areas, the rising expense of their unpaid honors, the fees, liturgies, benefactions, and games expected of them, the dangers incident to invasion and class war, led to a flight from office corresponding to the flight from taxes, factories, and farms. Men deliberately made themselves ineligible by debasing their social category; some fled to other towns, some became farmers, some monks. In 313 Constantine extended to the Christian clergy that exemption from municipal office, and from several taxes, which pagan priests had traditionally enjoyed; the Church was soon swamped with can-

THE POLITICAL CAUSES OF THE DECAY OF ROME: From *Caesar and Christ,* by Will Durant. Copyright, 1944, by Will Durant. Reprinted by permission of Simon and Schuster, Inc. Selection title by editor.

didates for ordination, and cities complained of losses in revenue and senators; in the end Constantine was compelled to rule that no man eligible for municipal position should be admitted to the priesthood. The imperial police pursued fugitives from political honors as it hunted evaders of taxes or conscription; it brought them back to the cities and forced them to serve; finally it decreed that a son must inherit the social status of his father, and must accept election if eligible to it by his rank. A serfdom of office rounded out the prison of economic caste.

DISCUSSION: CAUSE AND EFFECT

A paragraph may be developed by tracing causes of effects or by tracing effects from causes. Causal analysis takes several forms, depending on how *cause* is defined. The simplest and most informal distinction is that between mediate or *remote* and immediate or *proximate* causes—those standing at a distance from the event and those immediately preceding it. Where there is a causal chain of events (a student fails to study for an exam, flunks the exam, flunks the course, fails to meet the minimum grade requirement of the college, is denied a degree), the proximate cause is the immediately preceding event (failure to meet the minimum grade requirement is the proximate cause of the denial of the degree; flunking the course, the proximate cause of the failure to meet the grade requirement, and so on). Whether we are concerned with proximate or remote causes depends on the nature of our concern (the parents of the student will probably be concerned about the remote causes). The writer usually indicates which causes—proximate or remote—he wishes to emphasize.

A more complex kind of analysis distinguishes four related causes: the *material*, the *formal*, the *efficient*, and the *final*. An example will clarify their meanings. The material cause of a dictionary is the paper, ink, and other materials used in its manufacture; the formal cause is the shape of the dictionary, the arrangement of words according to a plan; the efficient cause is the dictionary maker; the final cause is the use intended for the dictionary.

The most complex kind of causal analysis—dealing chiefly with natural and historical phenomena and occurrences—distinguishes between *necessary condition* and *sufficient condition* as kinds of causes. A necessary condition is "a circumstance in whose absence the event cannot occur"; a sufficient condition is "a circumstance in whose presence the event must occur." [1] For example, given an effect, sunburn, a necessary

---

[1] Irving M. Copi, *Introduction to Logic*, 4th ed. (New York: The Macmillan Company, 1972), pp. 369–70.

condition would be the sun, whose absence would prevent the effect from occurring; a sufficient condition would be prolonged exposure, which always produces the effect. (Sun is not a sufficient condition because sunburn does not always occur in its presence.) When a writer is concerned with tracing cause to effect and effect from cause, "cause is identified with sufficient condition, and sufficient condition is regarded as the conjunction of all necessary conditions." [1] In this sense a cause is a complex interaction of conditions (sun, prolonged exposure, and so on), each of which is necessary for the effect. Such causal analysis can be highly probable but never certain in its conclusions because new conditions may remain to be discovered. Scientific investigation is continually adding to our understanding of the world about us. If it were discovered that only a certain type of skin was susceptible to sunburn, that type of skin would become one of the necessary conditions.

In dealing with human behavior a writer may not wish to think of causes as "necessary" or "sufficient," although this inference may be drawn from the discussion. He may refer to motives or traits of character without defining them exactly, and may indicate that his analysis is probable in light of our current knowledge.

QUESTIONS

1. According to Durant, what were the immediate effects on the citizens—that is, effects that became manifest in public life—of the primary cause of the fall of Rome? Does Durant discuss any mediate effects that became manifest gradually?
2. How does Durant show this primary cause to have been a necessary condition of the fall of Rome?
3. How does Durant give the primary cause emphasis—by continually indicating that it is primary, by repeating it, by developing it in detail, or by a combination of all of these means?

WRITING ASSIGNMENTS

Investigate the historical facts of one of the following events. Then distinguish the four causes—material, formal, efficient, final.
a. Versailles Treaty
b. Emancipation Proclamation
c. Geneva Accords of 1956
d. Monroe Doctrine

[1] *Ibid.*, p. 371.

Develop one of the following statements, with attention to causes and effects:
a. Students should (not) be given a voice in the approval of new courses.
b. Examinations are (not) a necessary teaching device.
c. Grades are (not) a necessary motivation in learning.

Kenneth Keniston
BIG MAN ON CAMPUS

1. With the extension of democratic rights in the first half of the nineteenth century and the ensuing decline of the Federalist establishment, a new conception of education began to emerge. Education was no longer a confirmation of a pre-existing status, but an instrument in the acquisition of higher status. For a new generation of upwardly mobile students, the goal of education was not to prepare them to live comfortably in the world into which they had been born, but to teach them new virtues and skills that would propel them into a different and better world. Education became training; and the student was no longer the gentleman-in-waiting, but the journeyman *apprentice* for upward mobility.

2. In the nineteenth century a college education began to be seen as a way to get ahead in the world. The founding of the land-grant colleges opened the doors of higher education to poor but aspiring boys from non-Anglo-Saxon, working-class, and lower-middle-class backgrounds. The myth of the poor boy who worked his way through college to success drew millions of poor boys to the new campuses. And with this shift, education became more vocational: its object was the acquisition of practical skills and useful information.

3. For the gentleman-in-waiting, virtue consisted above all in grace and style, in doing well what was appropriate to his position; education was merely a way of acquiring polish. And vice was manifested in gracelessness, awkwardness, in behaving

BIG MAN ON CAMPUS: From "Faces in the Lecture Room." Reprinted by permission of *Daedalus*, Journal of the American Academy of Arts and Sciences, Boston, Massachusetts. *The Contemporary University: U.S.A.*, edited by Robert S. Morison, 1966. Selection title by editor.

inappropriately, discourteously, or ostentatiously. For the apprentice, however, virtue was evidenced in success through hard work. The requisite qualities of character were not grace or style, but drive, determination, and a sharp eye for opportunity. While casual liberality and even prodigality characterized the gentleman, frugality, thrift, and self-control came to distinguish the new apprentice. And while the gentleman did not aspire to a higher station because his station was already high, the apprentice was continually becoming, striving, struggling upward. Failure for the apprentice meant standing still, not rising.

4.   In the early twentieth century still another type of student began to appear. As American society became more developed economically and more bureaucratized, upward mobility was no longer guaranteed by ambition, drive, and practical knowledge. In addition, those who aspired to success had to possess the ability to make friends and influence people. Mastering the human environment became more important than mastering the physical and economic environment. The function of education thus became not vocational training, but teaching the ability to be likable and persuasive and to get along with all kinds of people. College life was increasingly seen as an informal training ground for social skills; virtue was defined as popularity; and a new type, exemplified by the *Big Men on Campus,* began to emerge.

5.   Students who sought popularity and skill in dealing with people were naturally likely to emphasize the social rather than the academic or vocational aspects of higher education. Fraternities, student governments, even casual walks across the college campus, calling friends by name and saying "Hi" to strangers, were the new classrooms. Vocational skills became secondary— or, more precisely, the most important skills in *any* vocation were the capacity to make oneself respected, well liked, and a leader. The new sin was not gaucheness or standing still, but unpopularity. To the Big Man on Campus, academic and intellectual interests were irrelevant: whatever intelligence he possessed went into a rather calculated effort to please and impress others, win their respect, and dominate them without their knowing they were being dominated.

6.   The emergence of the Big Man on Campus as an ideal type among American students coincided with the appearance of a distinctively nonacademic youth culture. The gentleman and

the apprentice were both oriented primarily to the adult world: their most relevant models were adults—either the parental generation of gentlemen or the older generation of upwardly mobile and successful entrepreneurs. For the Big Man on Campus, however, the adult world was less immediately important. He looked mainly to his peers, for only by establishing his popularity in their eyes could he demonstrate his merit. Thus student cultures became more and more insulated both from academic culture and from adult society, developing their own rites, rituals, and traditions. The world of students became a separate world, not merely a reflection of or a preparation for adulthood. And as many observers have noted, the outlooks of this world were clearly distinguishable from the outlooks of adulthood—the student youth culture emphasized immediacy, enjoyment of the moment, popularity, attractiveness, sports, daring, and intellectual indifference. Walls, barricades, and fences of apathy, deafness, and blindness were built between students and the more academic, intellectual values of their teachers. The power of these fortifications is suggested by the monotonous finding of research done before World War II that so many students were so little affected by the values their colleges sought to promote.

7.   Since that time, yet another type of student has begun to emerge. Today "superior academic performance" is a prerequisite for admission to any desirable college, let alone graduate school. Grace, ambition, and popularity have fallen into secondary position, for, without good grades and the ability to do well on IQ tests, the gentlemanly, ambitious, or popular student is not even considered by the admissions office. From an early age students are therefore exposed and overexposed to academic demands: they are taught from kindergarten onward that prestige and rewards are impossible without intellectual competence, cognitive efficiency, intellectual skill, and a high degree of specialization.

QUESTIONS

1. By what principle does Keniston divide students in the course of his analysis? Does he intend the division to be exhaustive?
2. Keniston uses this division of students to trace an historical process. What points is he making about American education through this analysis?

3. Keniston is arguing that attitudes toward education are shaped by the cultural situation. How does he establish this cause and effect relationship?
4. How does the emergence of the Big Man on Campus illustrate the impact of social and cultural change?
5. What conditions were necessary to the emergence of the "youth culture" discussed in paragraph 6?

WRITING ASSIGNMENTS

Discuss the extent to which students in your high school conformed to one or more of the types Keniston distinguishes.

Discuss the extent to which students in your college differ from students you knew in high school. State what you consider the probable causes of these differences.

Oscar Handlin
THE AMERICAN IMMIGRANT

1.   How could this man, so recently removed from an altogether different life, explain to himself the productive system in which he was enmeshed? Now he was a part of something altogether unnatural. It was that, rather than the length or laboriousness of his work, that was harshest. Indeed the factory was not at all like the field, the field over which he had once bent in piety, the field over which he had once cast forth the sacred seeds that would bring forth God's fruit on a morrow. At best, there was this cardinal fault in the new work, that it was separated from the soil; and, at least, it required this adjustment of the peasant, that he reconcile himself to a life away from the earth, that he cut himself off from the process of birth and death, from the cycle of growth, aging, and regeneration that had once given meaning to his being. Now he was to act within a realm of inanimate things. Senseless iron shapes will everlastingly be about him, and stone will hem him in—on city street, in mill or

THE IMMIGRANT: From *The Uprooted* by Oscar Handlin. Copyright 1951, © 1973 by Oscar Handlin. By permission of Little, Brown and Co. in association with The Atlantic Monthly Press. Selection title by editor.

mine. In his own estimation he would be that much the less a man.

2.   In all matters, the New World made the peasant less a man. Often he toiled at intangibles, labored to produce objects he never would see. In the laborer's perspective, the factory turned out only parts of things: not a shoe, a coat, a plow, a cart—but a sole, a sleeve, a blade, a wheel. Bound to the monotony of a minute task, endlessly repeated, the worker sometimes could not envisage the whole of which his bit would be a part. He through whose hands all of production had then passed, from the dropped seed to the eaten bread, often now could not tell what manner of thing his labor made—its shape, its quality, its function. Such labor was labor for its own sake and meaningless.

3.   Actions no longer related to the rhythms of the soil now seemed related to nothing at all. In the new context, all sorts of old judgments became irrelevant. Formerly the peasant's life had been guided by standards he accepted as fixed and immutable. Now his life made a mockery of those very standards. Could he here, as at home, expect the relationships of reciprocal goodness between master and men, between just employer and true employee? Could he count on neighborly loans, on the mutual help of men working together? Those who thought it were quickly disabused.

4.   As in the crossing, there was a reversal of roles. The loyal dutiful man, faithful to tradition, the man who was the son and grandson of substantial peasants, was reduced to the indignity of hired labor, while shrewd, selfish, unscrupulous upstarts thrived. Clearly the attributes the immigrants held in high esteem were not those that brought success in America. The idea of success was itself strange; to thrust oneself above one's station in life called for harsh competitive qualities the peasant had always despised. Of course there was a satisfaction in the knowledge that even the well-to-do worked here and a man's cap was not worn out from lifting it to the gentry. But the satisfaction was mixed with a sense of impropriety. And to the extent that the immigrant lacked fixity of place, he felt again the less a man for it.

5.   He was not a man at all. Whether he worked or was idle, whether he prospered or starved, was quite unrelated to his qualities as a human being, to his virtues as an individual. The line would move forward by the hiring boss, and then suddenly stop. The rest would be turned away, not through any deficiency

of their own, not through lack of skill or will, but because the system operated impersonally. Where the line stopped was unpredictable. Those figures on the line who got in or did not felt part of an entity vast beyond their comprehension, certainly beyond their control. Driven in a helpless alternation of fortunes by the power of remote forces, these were no longer men, not any more men than the cogs spinning in their great machines.

6.   If the system was also wasteful, that only added to the irony of the situation for those entangled in it. The American economy operated in the mass; it was prodigal of resources of human energies and of raw materials; yet it never yielded enough. In the midst of plenty was always want; in the midst of shortages, much that seemed usable continued to be discarded. This the peasant could not grasp, that serviceable articles should not have a market, that other men should throw away what he needed. Buildings razed within the decade of their erection, the immense accumulations of junkyards and dumps, made no sense to him. What he could not understand was not that some were rich while he was poor, but that so much was wasted' that he could use.

QUESTIONS

1. In paragraph 1 Handlin says that the peasant's bewilderment is the result of his separation from the soil. Such a separation is a necessary condition of this bewilderment: all human beings have certain needs. How does Handlin seek to persuade us that these needs exist?

2. How do paragraphs 2–5 develop the main point of paragraph 1? To what extent does Handlin depend on examples, analogy, comparison and contrast, or process analysis?

3. Paragraph 6 returns to a consideration of paragraph 1: "How could this man, so recently removed from an altogether different life, explain to himself the productive system in which he was enmeshed?" How is this transition made?

4. Does Handlin state what he considers to be an ideal productive system, or must we infer his ideal from his comments?

5. Do you believe that men and women are best fulfilled as human beings by work that they can conceive as a whole process? Do you believe that men and women have basic needs of work and play, or do you believe that these needs are the product of social conditioning?

WRITING ASSIGNMENT

Respond to Handlin's view of men and women by stating and defending your ideal of work. Support your statements from your own experience—perhaps by commenting on schoolwork.

VARIETY OF
PARAGRAPH DEVELOPMENT

Dwight MacDonald
FUNCTIONAL CURIOSITY

Henry Luce has built a journalistic empire on this national weakness for being "well informed." *Time* attributes its present two-million circulation to a steady increase, since it first appeared in 1925, in what it calls "functional curiosity." Unlike the old-fashioned idle variety, this is "a kind of searching, hungry interest in what is happening everywhere—born not of an idle desire to be entertained or amused, but of a solid conviction that the news intimately and vitally affects the lives of everyone now. Functional curiosity grows as the number of educated people grows." The curiosity exists, but it is not functional since it doesn't help the individual function. A very small part of the mass of miscellaneous Facts offered in each week's issue of *Time* (or, for that matter, in the depressing quantity of newspapers and magazines visible on any large newsstand) is useful to the reader; they don't help him make more money, take some political or other action to advance his interests, or become a better person. About the only functional gain (though the *New York Times*, in a recent advertising campaign, proclaimed that reading

FUNCTIONAL CURIOSITY: From *Against the American Grain*, by Dwight MacDonald. Copyright © 1962 by Dwight MacDonald. Reprinted by permission of Random House, Inc. Selection title by editor.

it would help one to "be more interesting") the reader gets out of them is practice in reading. And even this is a doubtful advantage. *Times's* educated people read too many irrelevant words—irrelevant, that is, to any thoughtful idea of their personal interests, either narrow (practical) or broad (cultural). Imagine a similar person of, say the sixteenth century confronted with a copy of *Time* or the *New York Times*. He would take a whole day to master it, perhaps two, because he would be accustomed to take the time to think and even to feel about what he read; and he could take the time because there *was* time, there being comparatively little to read in that golden age. (The very name of Luce's magazine is significant: *Time,* just because we don't have it.) Feeling a duty—or perhaps simply a compulsion—at least to glance over the printed matter that inundates us daily, we have developed of necessity a rapid, purely rational, classifying habit of mind, something like the operations of a Mark IV calculating machine, making a great many small decisions every minute: read or not read? If read, then take in this, skim over that, and let the rest go by. This we do with the surface of our minds, since we "just don't have time" to bring the slow, cumbersome depths into play, to ruminate, speculate, reflect, wonder, *experience* what the eye flits over. This gives a greatly extended coverage to our minds, but also makes them, compared to the kind of minds similar people had in past centuries, coarse, shallow, passive, and unoriginal. Such reading habits have produced a similar kind of reading matter, since, except for a few stubborn old-fashioned types—the handcraftsmen who produce whatever is written today of quality, whether in poetry, fiction, scholarship or journalism—our writers produce work that is to be read quickly and then buried under the next day's spate of "news" or the next month's best seller; hastily slapped-together stuff which it would be foolish to waste much time or effort on either writing or reading. For those who, as readers or as writers, would get a little under the surface, the real problem of our day is how to *escape* being "well informed," how to resist the temptation to acquire too much information (never more seductive than when it appears in the chaste garb of duty), and how in general to elude the voracious demands on one's attention enough to think a little. The problem is as acute in the groves of Academe as in the profane world of journalism—one has only to consider the appalling mass of words available in any large college library on any topic of scholarly interest (that is, now that the "social sciences" have so proliferated, on any topic). The amount of verbal pomposity, elaboration of the obvious, repetition, trivia, low-grade statistics, tedious factification, drudging recapitulations of the half comprehended, and generally inane and laborious junk that one encounters suggests that the thinkers of earlier ages had one decisive advantage over those of today: they could draw on very little research.

DISCUSSION: VARIETY OF PARAGRAPH DEVELOPMENT

We have seen that paragraphs are often developed by more than one method: comparison and definition may be used to analyze the causes of an event, definition and analogy to explain a difficult idea. Earlier we considered the problem of unifying diverse ideas in a single paragraph so that the reader is able to give attention to one idea at a time. Obviously the greater number of ways we develop a paragraph, the more difficult it is to maintain unity; the greatest care must be given to the arrangement of ideas and transitions between them so that the reader does not lose his way. We noted that parallel phrasing and formal transitions help to clarify the relationship of ideas; another useful way is to subordinate several methods of development to the one method most necessary to the analysis.

QUESTIONS

1. Does MacDonald accept the *Time* distinction between idle and functional curiosity? Is he denying that there is such a thing as functional curiosity?
2. How does MacDonald account for the difference in attitude between sixteenth-century man and modern man? What causes does he cite for the attitude of modern man?
3. What are the effects of modern man's reading habits?
4. Is "the appalling mass of words" that have proliferated in Academe a result of functional curiosity?
5. What is the topic sentence of the paragraph? Is it stated explicitly? How are division, causal analysis, example, and contrast used to develop it?
6. How is the paragraph organized to deal with one idea at a time?

WRITING ASSIGNMENTS

Analyze a news story in *Time* or *Newsweek* to determine what interests it appeals to in its audience. What does the magazine seek to inform its audience about, and how does it do it?

Analyze your daily consumption of news (either from written material, television, or radio) to determine the extent to which your curiosity is idle, functional, or neither.

THE
SENTENCE

EMPHASIS

Mark Twain
THE MESMERIZER

[1] Every night for three nights I sat in the row of candidates on the platform and held the magic disk in the palm of my hand and gazed at it and tried to get sleepy, but it was a failure; I remained wide awake and had to retire defeated, like the majority. [2] Also, I had to sit there and be gnawed with envy of Hicks, our journeyman; I had to sit there and see him scamper and jump when Simmons the enchanter exclaimed, "See the snake! See the snake!" and hear him say, "My, how beautiful!" in response to the suggestion that he was observing a splendid sunset; and so on—the whole insane business. [3] I couldn't laugh, I couldn't applaud; it filled me with bitterness to have others do it and to have people make a hero of Hicks and crowd around him when the show was over and ask him for more and more particulars of the wonders he had seen in his visions and manifest in many ways that they were proud to be acquainted with him. [4] Hicks—the idea! [5] I couldn't stand it; I was getting boiled to death in my own bile.

[6] On the fourth night temptation came and I was not strong enough to resist. [7] When I had gazed at the disk a while I pretended to be sleepy and began to nod. [8] Straightway came the professor and made passes over my head and down my body and legs and arms, finishing each pass with a snap of his fingers in the air to discharge the surplus electricity; then he began to "draw" me with the disk, holding it in his fingers and telling me I could not take my eyes off it, try as I might; so I rose slowly, bent and gazing, and followed that disk all over the place, just as I had seen the others do. [9] Then I was put through the other paces. [10] Upon suggestion I fled from snakes, passed buckets at a fire, became excited over hot steamboat-races, made love to

THE MESMERIZER: From pp. 51–52 in *The Autobiography of Mark Twain*, edited by Charles Neider. Copyright © 1959 by The Mark Twain Company. Copyright © 1959 by Charles Neider. By permission of Harper & Row, Publishers, Inc. Selection title by editor.

imaginary girls and kissed them, fished from the platform and landed mud cats that out-weighed me—and so on, all the customary marvels. [11] But not in the customary way. [12] I was cautious at first and watchful, being afraid the professor would discover that I was an imposter and drive me from the platform in disgrace; but as soon as I realized that I was not in danger, I set myself the task of terminating Hicks's usefulness as a subject and of usurping his place.

[13] It was a sufficiently easy task. [14] Hicks was born honest, I without that incumbrance—so some people said. [15] Hicks saw what he saw and reported accordingly, I saw more than was visible and added to it such details as could help. [16] Hicks had no imagination; I had a double supply. [17] He was born calm, I was born excited. [18] No vision could start a rapture in him and he was constipated as to language, anyway; but if I saw a vision I emptied the dictionary onto it and lost the remnant of my mind into the bargain.

DISCUSSION: EMPHASIS

In our everyday speech we vary our sentences with little if any conscious effort to give certain words emphasis. The speaker of the following sentence, a witness before a congressional committee, becomes grammatically incoherent in trying to give emphasis to certain ideas:

My experience is that we hold people sometimes in jail, young people in jail, for days at a time with a complete lack of concern of the parents, if they do live in homes where parents live together, a complete lack of concern in many instances on the part of the community or other agencies as to where these young people are or what they are doing.

Spoken sentences like this may be clear to the listener because the speaker depends on vocal inflection to stress key words and phrases. If written, the sentence would have to be more tightly constructed to be clear: the number of modifiers that expand the core sentence would have to be reduced. The writer cannot depend directly on vocal inflection for clarity and emphasis; he can and will suggest these inflections by shaping the sentence in accord with familiar patterns of speech. Good sentences remain close to these patterns, though they are more consciously put together.

In a large number of English sentences the familiar subject-verb-complement pattern (*He read the book, His emotions made him feel strange*) provides the core. How much a writer is able to expand the core depends on his ability to keep the main clause from disappearing into its modifiers:

> *His emotions made him feel strange* in the presence of men who talked excitedly of a prospective battle as of a drama they were about to witness, with nothing but eagerness and curiosity in their faces.—Stephen Crane, *The Red Badge of Courage*

Any variation from the familiar subject-verb-complement pattern will give more than usual emphasis to certain words. In the following sentences the subject and predicate are given emphasis through their separation:

> When another night came *the columns,* changed to purple streaks, *filed across* two pontoon *bridges.* A glaring fire wine-tinted the waters of the river. *Its rays,* shining upon the moving masses of troops, *brought forth* here and there sudden *gleams* of silver or gold. Upon the other shore a dark and mysterious *range of hills was curved* against the sky.—*The Red Badge of Courage*

These variations conform to familiar patterns of speech; the speaker or writer need not have planned them. To achieve even greater emphasis he may vary the sentence even more, perhaps by making special use of the end of the sentence—the position that in English tends to be the most emphatic:

> The cold passed reluctantly from the earth, and the retiring fogs revealed an army stretched out on the hills, *resting.*—*The Red Badge of Courage*

Or he may break up the sentence so that individual ideas or experiences receive separate emphasis:

> The youth stopped. He was transfixed by this terrific medley of all noises. It was as if worlds were being rended. There was the ripping sound of musketry and the breaking crash of the artillery.—*The Red Badge of Courage*

These sentences may also be coordinated, either by *and, but, for, yet, nor,* or by a semicolon—with a corresponding distribution of emphasis.

The relationship of subordinate clauses to other elements in a sentence is controlled largely by the requirements of English word order. The position of subordinate clauses that serve as nouns and adjectives (noun and adjective clauses) is rather fixed; the position of subordinate clauses that serve as adverbs (adverb clauses) is not. The position of the adverb clause depends chiefly on its importance as an idea in the sentence and on its length:

> I majored in zoology *because I enjoy working with animals.*
> *Because I enjoy working with animals* I majored in zoology.

The position of the subordinate clause determines what information is stressed: in the first sentence the subordinate clause seems to express the more important idea because it follows the main clause; in the second sentence, the main clause receives the emphasis by virtue of its position. Subordinate clauses may in fact contain ideas as important as, if not more important than, those of the main clauses:

The writer *I admire most* is Mark Twain.

The adjective clause—(*that*) *I admire most*—contains the important information. It should be noted that the end of the sentence will not take the thrust of meaning if ideas appearing toward the beginning are given special emphasis, possibly through repetition. Main clauses placed at the end will usually seem emphatic.

Any variation from normal colloquial patterns—whether extremely short, disconnected sentences or a large number of coordinated clauses, with relatively few modifiers—will contribute greater than usual emphasis. The kind and amount of sentence variation is determined by the occasion and the audience, the impression we want to give of ourselves, the mood we want to create, and the degree of formality suited to the subject.

Our informal spoken sentences show the least variation and depend heavily on coordination. The so-called "run-on" sentence in writing—a series of ideas strung together with *and* and other conjunctions—is a heavily coordinated sentence without the customary vocal markers. The sentence "fragment" usually derives from the clipped sentences and phrases that we depend on in speech.

QUESTIONS

1. Compare the following sentences:
   a. Every night for three nights I sat in the row of candidates on the platform and held the magic disk in the palm of my hand and gazed at it and tried to get sleepy, but it was a failure.
   b. Every night for three nights, as I sat in the row of candidates on the platform, I held the magic disk in the palm of my hand, gazed at it, and tried to get sleepy, but it was a failure.

   How does Twain connect his verbs in *a* (the original sentence) to achieve special emphasis? In *b*, how does the omission of *and* before *held* and before *gazed* affect the degree of emphasis given these verbs in *a*?
2. Repetition of words and phrases provides additional emphasis. What words or phrases are repeated in sentences 2 and 3? What is the effect of this repetition on the mood of the first paragraph?
3. Rewrite sentence 5, subordinating one of the clauses. How does the revision affect the emphasis of ideas in the original sentence?

4. Does sentence 8 describe one connected experience, or could the sentence be divided into two without affecting the meaning? Would the meaning of sentences 12 and 18 be altered if they were similarly divided?

5. What personal emotions does Twain want to convey—rage, exultation, sober pride—and how does the sentence construction help to convey them and create a mood?

WRITING ASSIGNMENTS

Twain shows that deception requires abundant imagination. Write a short essay developing this idea from personal experience. Be as specific as Twain is in describing the deception.

Twain says earlier in his autobiography: "The truth is, a person's memory has no more sense than his conscience and no appreciation whatever of values and proportions." Develop this idea from your experience.

Carl Sandburg
THE FUNERAL OF GENERAL GRANT

¹ The Galesburg Marine Band marched past, men walking and their mouths blowing into their horns as they walked. ² One man had a big horn that seemed to be wrapped around him and I was puzzled how he got into it. ³ They had on blue coats and pants and the stripe down the sides of the pants was either red or yellow and looked pretty. ⁴ Their music was slow and sad. ⁵ General Grant was dead and this was part of his funeral and the music should be sad. ⁶ It was only twenty years since the war ended and General Grant was the greatest general in the war and they wanted to show they were sad because he was dead. ⁷ That was the feeling I had and I could see there were many others had this same feeling. ⁸ Marching past came men wearing dark-blue coats and big black hats tied round with a little cord of what looked like gold with a knot and a little tassel. ⁹ They were the G.A.R., the Grand Army of the Republic, and I heard that some

THE FUNERAL OF GENERAL GRANT: From *Always the Young Strangers* by Carl Sandburg. Reprinted by permission of Harcourt Brace Jovanovich, Inc. Selection title by editor.

of these men had seen General Grant and had been in the war with him and could tell how he looked on a horse and what made him a great general. [10] Eight or ten of these G.A.R. men walked along the sides of a long black box on some kind of a black car pulled by eight black horses. [11] The body of General Grant wasn't in the box, but somewhere far away General Grant was being buried in a box like this one. [12] I could see everybody around was more quiet when this part of the parade passed.

QUESTIONS

1. Sandburg depends on the repetition of certain words, particularly in sentences 4–6, to convey a dominant mood. What is that mood, and what words are most repeated?
2. Sentences 2, 5, 6, and 7 are heavily coordinated and seem monotonous. Is that effect appropriate to the mood generated by details in these sentences?
3. How would changing *black horses* to *ebony horses* and changing the second *box* to *coffin* in sentences 10 and 11 alter the mood?
4. How would the substitution of the following revisions for sentences 5 and 6 affect the paragraph?
   a. Because General Grant was dead and this was part of his funeral, the music should be sad.
   b. Because it was only twenty years since the war ended and General Grant was the greatest general in the war, they wanted to show that his death saddened them.

WRITING ASSIGNMENT

Describe a parade or celebration and construct your sentences so that they convey the mood of the event.

Ferdinand (Jelly Roll) Morton
THE PARADES OF NEW ORLEANS

[1] Those parades were really tremendous things. [2] The drums would start off, the trumpets and trombones rolling into some-

thing like *Stars and Stripes* or *The National Anthem* and everybody would strut off down the street, the bass-drum player twirling his beater in the air, the snare drummer throwing his sticks up and bouncing them off the ground, the kids jumping and hollering, the grand marshal and his aides in their expensive uniforms moving along dignified, women on top of women strutting along back of the aides, and out in front of everybody—the second line, armed with sticks and bottles and baseball bats and all forms of ammunition ready to fight the foe when they reached the dividing line.

QUESTIONS

1. How is sentence 2 constructed to contrast the various lines of the parade and give special emphasis to the second line, which served to protect the paraders as they passed through certain districts of the city?
2. How does this passage differ in effect from the Sandburg passage, and how does the sentence construction contribute to this effect? What change, if any, would occur if the second sentence were broken into a series of short sentences—comparable to those in Sandburg's passage?

WRITING ASSIGNMENT

Contrast the passage with Sandburg's to show how sentence construction is used to convey mood.

Norman Mailer
THE DEATH OF BENNY PARET

¹ Paret was a Cuban, a proud club fighter who had become welterweight champion because of his unusual ability to take a punch. ² His style of fighting was to take three punches to the head in order to give back two. ³ At the end of ten rounds, he

THE DEATH OF BENNY PARET: Reprinted by permission of G. P. Putnam's Sons from *The Presidential Papers* by Norman Mailer. Copyright © 1960, 1961, 1962, 1963 by Norman Mailer. Selection title by editor.

would still be bouncing, his opponent would have a headache. ⁴ But in the last two years, over the fifteen-round fights, he had started to take some bad maulings.

⁵ This fight had its turns. ⁶ Griffith won most of the early rounds, but Paret knocked Griffith down in the sixth. ⁷ Griffith had trouble getting up, but made it, came alive and was dominating Paret again before the round was over. ⁸ Then Paret began to wilt. ⁹ In the middle of the eighth round, after a clubbing punch had turned his back to Griffith, Paret walked three disgusted steps away, showing his hindquarters. ¹⁰ For a champion, he took much too long to turn back around. ¹¹ It was the first hint of weakness Paret had ever shown, and it must have inspired a particular shame, because he fought the rest of the fight as if he were seeking to demonstrate that he could take more punishment than any man alive. ¹² In the twelfth, Griffith caught him. ¹³ Paret got trapped in a corner. ¹⁴ Trying to duck away, his left arm and his head became tangled on the wrong side of the top rope. ¹⁵ Griffith was in like a cat ready to rip the life out of a huge boxed rat. ¹⁶ He hit him eighteen right hands in a row, an act which took perhaps three or four seconds, Griffith making a pent-up whimpering sound all the while he attacked, the right hand whipping like a piston rod which has broken through the crankcase, or like a baseball bat demolishing a pumpkin. ¹⁷ I was sitting in the second row of that corner—they were not ten feet away from me, and like everybody else, I was hypnotized. ¹⁸ I had never seen one man hit another so hard and so many times. ¹⁹ Over the referee's face came a look of woe as if some spasm had passed its way through him, and then he leaped on Griffith to pull him away. ²⁰ It was the act of a brave man. ²¹ Griffith was uncontrollable. ²² His trainer leaped into the ring, his manager, his cut man, there were four people holding Griffith, but he was off on an orgy, he had left the Garden, he was back on a hoodlum's street. ²³ If he had been able to break loose from his handlers and the referee, he would have jumped Paret to the floor and whaled on him there.

²⁴ And Paret? ²⁵ Paret died on his feet. ²⁶ As he took those eighteen punches something happened to everyone who was in psychic range of the event. ²⁷ Some part of his death reached out to us. ²⁸ One felt it hover in the air. ²⁹ He was still standing in the ropes, trapped as he had been before, he gave some little half-smile of regret, as if he were saying, "I didn't know I was

going to die just yet," and then, his head leaning back but still erect, his death came to breathe about him. [30] He began to pass away. [31] As he passed, so his limbs descended beneath him, and he sank slowly to the floor. [32] He went down more slowly than any fighter had ever gone down, he went down like a large ship which turns on end and slides second by second into its grave. [33] As he went down, the sound of Griffith's punches echoed in the mind like a heavy ax in the distance chopping into a wet log.

QUESTIONS

1. Each of the sentences in the second paragraph focuses on a distinct moment of the action. Could any of these sentences be combined without blurring the action?
2. Sentence 22 joins a number of actions occurring simultaneously. How does the sentence convey the jarring confusion of the moment?
3. Does sentence 29 describe a continuous action? Would the mood of the paragraph be changed if the sentence were broken up or punctuated differently?
4. How does repetition in sentence 32 reinforce the feeling Mailer is trying to communicate in the final paragraph?
5. Mailer's writing is closer to spoken patterns than the writing of others we have been studying. In how many of his sentences does Mailer depart from the subject-verb-complement pattern—and to what effect?

WRITING ASSIGNMENT

Summarize what you think are the implications of the passage, including what the passage suggests about Mailer's attitude toward Benny Paret.

LOOSE AND PERIODIC SENTENCES

John Steinbeck
THE TURTLE

¹ The sun lay on the grass and warmed it, and in the shade under the grass the insects moved, ants and ant lions to set traps for them, grasshoppers to jump into the air and flick their yellow wings for a second, sow bugs like little armadillos, plodding restlessly on many tender feet. ² And over the grass at the roadside a land turtle crawled, turning aside for nothing, dragging his high-domed shell over the grass. ³ His hard legs and yellow-nailed feet threshed slowly through the grass, not really walking, but boosting and dragging his shell along. ⁴ The barley beards slid off his shell, and the clover burrs fell on him and rolled to the ground. ⁵ His horny beak was partly open, and his fierce, humorous eyes, under brows like fingernails, stared straight ahead. ⁶ He came over the grass leaving a beaten trail behind him, and the hill, which was the highway embankment, reared up ahead of him. ⁷ For a moment he stopped, his head held high. ⁸ He blinked and looked up and down. ⁹ At last he started to climb the embankment. ¹⁰ Front clawed feet reached forward but did not touch. ¹¹ The hind feet kicked his shell along, and it scraped on the grass, and on the gravel. ¹² As the embankment grew steeper and steeper, the more frantic were the efforts of the land turtle. ¹³ Pushing hind legs strained and slipped, boosting the shell along, and the horny head protruded as far as the neck could stretch. ¹⁴ Little by little the shell slid up the embankment until at last a parapet cut straight across its line of march, the shoulder of the road, a concrete wall four inches high. ¹⁵ As though they worked independently the hind legs pushed the shell against the wall. ¹⁶ The head upraised and peered over the wall to the broad

smooth plain of cement. [17] Now the hands, braced on top of the wall, strained and lifted, and the shell came slowly up and rested its front end on the wall. [18] For a moment the turtle rested. [19] A red ant ran into the shell, into the soft skin inside the shell, and suddenly head and legs snapped in, and the armored tail clamped in sideways. [20] The red ant was crushed between body and legs. [21] And one head of wild oats was clamped into the shell by a front leg. [22] For a long moment the turtle lay still, and then the neck crept out and the old humorous frowning eyes looked about and the legs and tail came out. [23] The back legs went to work, straining like elephant legs, and the shell tipped to an angle so that the front legs could not reach the level cement plain. [24] But higher and higher the hind legs boosted it, until at last the center of balance was reached, the front tipped down, the front legs scratched at the pavement, and it was up. [25] But the head of wild oats was held by its stem around the front legs.

DISCUSSION: LOOSE AND PERIODIC SENTENCES

The mood of a passage—from plodding monotony to extreme excitement—may be promoted by loose or periodic sentence construction. In a loose sentence the basic grammatical form and meaning are completed near the beginning or the middle; qualifying phrases and clauses follow:

> *The squares were quite big, and absolutely desert,* save for the posts for clothes lines, and people passing, children playing on the hard earth.—D. H. Lawrence, "Nottingham and the Mining Countryside"

In a periodic sentence form and meaning are completed only near the end:

> To believe your own thought, to believe that what is true for you in your private heart is true for all men—that is genius.—Ralph Waldo Emerson, "Self-Reliance"

The markedly periodic sentence, like Emerson's, is usually reserved for very special effects. The distinction between these two types is especially useful in distinguishing relatively simple sentences that begin or end with an accumulation of supporting or explanatory details.

Heavily coordinated, compound sentences (a series of clauses joined by coordinating conjunctions like *and* and *but*) tend to be loose because emphasis is distributed throughout the sentence. Compound sentences also seem loose when succeeding coordinate clauses serve as afterthoughts or qualifications rather than as ideas equal in importance to the opening idea:

> I was very conscious of the crowds at first, almost despairing to have to perform in front of them, and I never got used to it.—George Plimpton, *Paper Lion*

The sequence of coordinate clauses—arranged loosely—may increase in emphasis, even with a sense of rising excitement:

> Sometimes on the blocking sleds the players would gag around, and at the hike number I would be the only one to drive forward at the sled, the others holding up on some secret signal, and without the others to help, and with Bingaman's weight, it was like jarring a shoulder into a wall.—*Paper Lion*

Explanatory phrases and clauses may also contribute to a sense of rising excitement:

> Ellie was typical of the orphan children—a thin, desiccated, anxious old maid with tiny, red-rimmed eyes, a little scrap of grey hair screwed up under her old-fashioned cap, and a tiny, tormented voice.—Frank O'Connor, *An Only Child*

> Similarly, the works of mankind often achieve great aesthetic beauty or intellectual grandeur, even though they were not planned with this end in mind—as if they were the product of an unconscious process.—Jules Dubos, *The Torch of Life*

Modern English prose uses periodic sentences sparingly, with a distribution of emphasis through the whole sentence, even though the main idea is completed only at the end:

> But not all the power and simplicity of Swift's prose, nor the imaginative effort that has been able to make not one but a whole series of impossible worlds more credible than the majority of history books—none of this would enable us to enjoy Swift if his world-view were truly wounding or shocking.—George Orwell, "Politics vs. Literature"

Sometimes two moderately periodic sentences will be coordinated, with a corresponding distribution of emphasis:

> Though reliable narration is by no means the only way of conveying to the audience the facts on which dramatic irony is based, it is a useful way, and in some works, works in which no one but the author can conceivably know what needs to be known, it may be indispensable.—Wayne C. Booth, *The Rhetoric of Fiction*

QUESTIONS

1. The essential element of sentence 2 by Steinbeck is *a land turtle crawled.* If the concluding modifiers were moved toward the beginning of the sentence, would the shift in emphasis alter the meaning?
2. How does the moderately periodic construction of sentence 12 create a sense of action?
3. Convert sentence 3 into a periodic sentence. What is gained or lost by moving the phrase *dragging his shell along* to another part of the sentence?
4. Rewrite sentence 15 as a loose sentence. What is gained or lost in effect by your revision?
5. Combine sentences 7, 8, and 9 into one sentence. Which is more effective—your sentence or the original arrangement of sentences—and why?
6. Do the sentences in the passage, considered as a whole, seem predominantly loose or periodic? How does the dominant pattern affect the mood of the passage and contribute to its meaning? In general, what kind of sentence construction conveys a greater sense of anticipation and suspense, and why?
7. The following loose and periodic sentences are characteristic of some eighteenth- and nineteenth-century British and American prose. Rewrite them as loose or periodic sentences, changing the wording where necessary. Be ready to argue which is the more effective sentence and why.

   a. Considering that natural disposition in many men to lie, and in multitudes to believe, I have been perplexed what to do with that maxim so frequent in everybody's mouth, that truth will at last prevail.—Jonathan Swift
   b. To this knowledge which all men carry about with them, and to these sympathies in which without any other discipline than that of our daily life, we are fitted to take delight, the poet principally directs his attention.—William Wordsworth
   c. Who first reduced lying into an art, and adapted it to politics, is not so clear from history, although I have made some diligent inquiries.—Swift
   d. Plants and animals, biding their time, closely followed the retiring ice, bestowing quick and joyous animation on the new-born landscape.—John Muir

WRITING ASSIGNMENT

Write an interpretation of the passage, with particular attention to how Steinbeck may be using the turtle to make a general statement about life. Analyze the detail with care.

Jonathan Bishop
THE BLACK FLIES

¹ How can something become a significant event, unless it already is one? ² One winter or rather spring morning while on my usual way to work along the shores of Beebe lake I saw a curious sight. ³ A scattering of wingless flies, I did not know what kind, were crawling across the surface of the new snow. ⁴ All were moving in the same direction, from the slope on the lake side of the path across it toward the trees. ⁵ It was an immense journey through a barren wilderness for the tiny creatures, over drifts of empty snow, down into valleys formed by footprints, up the other bank to the tree trunks which seemed to be their goal. ⁶ They struggled on, each alone, one about every two feet. ⁷ Some had failed already and lay quiet, black specks on the white expanse. ⁸ There must have been scores, perhaps hundreds altogether; I could not see, looking along the slope, where the movement ended. ⁹ These flies must have been hatched by the force of the early spring sun on the slope, which faced south. ¹⁰ Their emergence had been premature. ¹¹ Several were very feeble, and struggled on with an effort painful to see. ¹² But how could one help black flies? ¹³ It was some relief to watch one or two reach the rough junction of snow and bark and tumble into the crevices. ¹⁴ I trust these found what they wanted. ¹⁵ The March snow must have interrupted a brood which should otherwise have been able to feed immediately. ¹⁶ Nature had anticipated herself. ¹⁷ Here was Israel in the wilderness indeed.

QUESTIONS

1. Sentences 4–7 are moderately loose. Which of them can be made periodic merely by transposing sentence elements? How many other sentences in the passage are also loose?
2. Does Bishop wish to invest the incident with a sense of the extraordinary and the dramatic? Does the paragraph build to a climax?

THE BLACK FLIES: George Braziller, Inc.—from *Something Else* by Jonathan Bishop; reprinted with the permission of the publisher. Copyright © 1972 by George Braziller, Inc. Selection title by editor.

WRITING ASSIGNMENT

Contrast Steinbeck's view of the turtle with Bishop's view of the wingless flies. Comment on sentence construction as well as on the details of the descriptions.

PARALLELISM

Joseph Conrad
THE WEST WIND

¹ He is the war-lord who sends his battalions of Atlantic rollers to the assault of our seaboard. ² The compelling voice of the West Wind musters up to his service all the might of the ocean. ³ At the bidding of the West Wind there arises a great commotion in the sky above these Islands, and a great rush of waters falls upon our shores. ⁴ The sky of the Westerly Weather is full of flying clouds, of great big white clouds coming thicker and thicker till they seem to stand welded into a solid canopy, upon whose grey face the lower wrack of the gale, thin, black, and angry-looking, flies past with vertiginous speed. ⁵ Denser and denser grows this dome of vapors, descending lower and lower upon the sea, narrowing the horizon around the ship. ⁶ And the characteristic aspect of Westerly Weather, the thick, grey, smoky, and sinister tone sets in, circumscribing the view of the men, drenching their bodies, oppressing their souls, taking their breath away with booming gusts, deafening, blinding, driving, rushing them onwards in a swaying ship towards our coasts lost in mists and rain.

DISCUSSION: PARALLELISM

The italicized words in the following sentences serve the same grammatical function and are alike or parallel in structure:

THE WEST WIND: From *The Mirror of the Sea* by Joseph Conrad. Reprinted by permission of J. M. Dent and Sons, Ltd. Selection title by editor.

He *replaced the morsel of food on his plate* and *read the paragraph attentively.* Then he *drank a glass of water, pushed his plate to one side, doubled the paper down before him between his elbows* and *read the paragraph over and over again.*—James Joyce, "A Painful Case"

It is difficult to avoid making these verbs parallel. Only the very inattentive speaker or writer would say:

Then he drank a glass of water, his plate was pushed to one side, doubled the paper down before him between his elbows and read the paragraph over and over again.

We tend to finish a sentence in the way we begin it. Occasionally there may be a break in sentence parallelism to throw emphasis on a key word:

He replaced the morsel of food on his plate and the *paragraph* was read attentively.

Handbooks usually tell us to maintain strict parallelism following correlatives:

He wanted *not only* to walk down Broadway *but also* to see Wall Street.
Either we walk down Broadway *or* we see Wall Street.

In practice many writers depart from strict parallelism in these instances to avoid too formal an effect:

His evenings were spent either *before his landlady's piano* or *roaming about the outskirts of the city.*—James Joyce, "A Painful Case"

In modern English parallelism is not and need not be exact unless the sentence would be unclear or grossly awkward without it.

QUESTIONS

1. Which words and phrases in sentences 4 and 6 by Conrad are parallel? Which phrases in sentence 5?
2. The two main clauses of sentence 3 are not parallel in structure. What change in the second clause would make it parallel to the first?
3. Conrad avoids too formal an effect by varying his sentences slightly. In which sentences is a close parallel structure of words and phrases impossible to avoid?
4. How does the sentence structure help to convey the effect of the West Wind?

WRITING ASSIGNMENT

Describe a lightning storm or a heavy snowfall or another natural phenomenon. Vary the construction of your sentences to avoid too formal an impression.

Wallace Stegner
DROUGHT ON THE GREAT PLAINS

[1] There, a cabin had characteristically neither tree nor shrub nor grass. [2] Standard practice demanded that the yard be made "mud-proof" and fireproof by throwing the soapy wash- and dishwater out religiously until the whitish earth glared like an alkali flat, which it was. [3] As summer came on and the green of spring faded, Hamlin Garland says, "the sky began to scare us with its light." [4] From that sky like hot metal the sun blazed down on bare flats, bare yard, bare boards, tarpaper roof. [5] Anything metal blistered the hands, the inside of any shack was a suffocating oven, outside there was no tree or shade for miles. [6] There was no escape: east, west, north, south, July, August, September, the sun burned into the brain, the barrenness and loneliness and ugliness ate at man and woman alike but at woman most. [7] Three hundred and sixty degrees of horizon ringed them, the sky fitted the earth like a bell jar. [8] They smothered under it, watching the delusive south or east where thunderheads formed and heat lightning flared in the evenings. [9] For a while they could watch the rain-directions with hope. [10] After one ruined crop, or two, or three, their watchfulness was a kind of cursing from a circle of Hell. [11] The prairie sloughs that in the good years had grown tules and sheltered mallards and teal were dried up, the ducks gone somewhere else. [12] Windmills brought up sand. [13] Only the chinch bugs multiplied. [14] And down from the unseen mountains to the west the air currents that made their climate poured across the powder-dry plains and dust rose up ahead of them a hundred, two hundred, four hundred feet high.

DROUGHT ON THE GREAT PLAINS: From *Beyond the Hundredth Meridian.* Copyright, 1953, 1954 by Wallace E. Stegner. Reprinted by permission of Houghton Mifflin Company. Selection title by editor.

15 Grim-faced leathery women, seeing the cloud coming, slammed down windows and shut doors, and the family gathered inside with the thin, exciting smell of dust in their nostrils and wordlessly listened to the wind and watched the small gray drifts grow on window sills, below the doors.

QUESTIONS

1. Would sentence 5 gain in clarity if its three parts were parallel in structure? How is emphasis gained by departing from a strict parallel construction?
2. What elements in sentence 6 are parallel? Could these elements be varied in structure without loss of clarity?
3. The two parts of sentence 7 are grammatically parallel. Are the ideas parallel?
4. How is parallel structure used to promote clarity and avoid awkwardness in sentence 15?
5. How does the mood of the passage differ from that of Conrad's? To what extent is the greater variation in sentence structure by Stegner responsible for this difference?

WRITING ASSIGNMENT

Show how the selection of detail is used to convey the feeling of the people toward the drought. Comment on the point of view of the passage.

Ernesto Galarza
BOYHOOD IN A SACRAMENTO *BARRIO*

1.   Our family conversations always occurred on our own kitchen porch, away from the gringos. One or the other of the adults would begin: *Se han fijado?* Had we noticed—that the Americans do not ask permission to leave the room; that they had no respectful way of addressing an elderly person; that they spit brown over the railing of the porch into the yard; that when

BOYHOOD IN A SACRAMENTO *BARRIO:* Reprinted from *Barrio Boy,* by Ernesto Galarza (University of Notre Dame Press, 1971). Reprinted by permission of the publisher. Selection title by editor.

they laughed they roared; that they never brought *saludos* to everyone in your family from everyone in their family when they visited; that *General Delibree* was only a clerk; that *zopilotes* were not allowed on the streets to collect garbage; that the policemen did not carry lanterns at night; that Americans didn't keep their feet on the floor when they were sitting; that there was a special automobile for going to jail; that a rancho was not a rancho at all but a very small hacienda; that the saloons served their customers free eggs, pickles, and sandwiches; that instead of bullfighting, the gringos for sport tried to kill each other with gloves?

2.   I did not have nearly the strong feelings on these matters that Doña Henriqueta expressed. I felt a vague admiration for the way Mr. Brien could spit brown. Wayne, my classmate, laughed much better than the Mexicans, because he opened his big mouth wide and brayed like a donkey so he could be heard a block away. But it was the kind of laughter that made my mother tremble, and it was not permitted in our house.

3.   Rules were laid down to keep me, as far as possible, *un muchacho bien educado*. If I had to spit I was to do it privately, or if in public, by the curb, with my head down and my back to people. I was never to wear my cap in the house and I was to take it off even on the porch if ladies or elderly gentlemen were sitting. If I wanted to scratch, under no circumstances was I to do it right then and there, in company, like the Americans, but I was to excuse myself. If Catfish or Russell yelled to me from across the street I was not to shout back. I was never to ask for tips for my errands or other services to the tenants of 418 L, for these were *atenciones* expected of me.

4.   Above all I was never to fail in *respeto* to grownups, no matter who they were. It was an inflexible rule; I addressed myself to *Señor* Big Singh, *Señor* Big Ernie, *Señora* Dodson, *Señor* Cho-ree Lopez.

5.   My standing in the family, but especially with my mother depended on my keeping these rules. I was not punished for breaking them. She simply reminded me that it gave her acute *vergüenza* to see me act thus, and that I would never grow up to be a correct *jefe de familia* if I did not know how to be a correct boy. I knew what *vergüenza* was from feeling it time and again; and the notion of growing up to keep a tight rein over a family of my own was somehow satisfying.

6.   In our musty apartment in the basement of 418 L, ours

remained a Mexican family. I never lost the sense that we were the same, from Jalco to Sacramento. There was the polished cedar box, taken out now and then from the closet to display our heirlooms. I had lost the rifle shells of the revolution, and Tio Tonche, too, was gone. But there was the butterfly sarape, the one I had worn through the Battle of Puebla; a black lace mantilla Doña Henriqueta modeled for us; bits of embroidery and lace she had made; the tin pictures of my grandparents; my report card signed by Señorita Bustamante and Don Salvador; letters from Aunt Esther; and the card with the address of the lady who had kept the Ajax for us. When our mementos were laid out on the bed I plunged my head into the empty box and took deep breaths of the aroma of *puro cedro,* pure Jalcocotán mixed with camphor.

7.   We could have hung on the door of our apartment a sign like those we read in some store windows—*Aquí se habla español.* We not only spoke Spanish, we read it. From the *Librería Española,* two blocks up the street, Gustavo and I bought novels for my mother, like *Genoveva de Brabante,* a paperback with the poems of Amado Nervo and a handbook of the history of Mexico. The novels were never read aloud, the poems and the handbook were. Nervo was the famous poet from Tepic, close enough to Jalcocotán to make him our own. And in the history book I learned to read for myself, after many repetitions by my mother, about the deeds of the great Mexicans Don Salvador had recited so vividly to the class in Mazatlán. She refused to decide for me whether Abraham Lincoln was as great as Benito Juarez, or George Washington braver than the priest Don Miguel Hidalgo. At school there was no opportunity to settle these questions because nobody seemed to know about Juarez or Hidalgo; at least they were never mentioned and there were no pictures of them on the walls.

8.   The family talk I listened to with the greatest interest was about Jalco. Wherever the conversation began it always turned to the pueblo, our neighbors, anecdotes that were funny or sad, the folk tales and the witchcraft, and our kinfolk, who were still there. I usually lay on the floor those winter evenings, with my feet toward the kerosene heater, watching on the ceiling the flickering patterns of the light filtered through the scrollwork of the chimney. As I listened once again I chased the *zopilote* away from Coronel, or watched José take Nerón into the forest in a sack. Certain things became clear about the *rurales* and why the

young men were taken away to kill Yaqui Indians, and about the Germans, the Englishmen, the Frenchmen, the Spaniards, and the Americans who owned the haciendas, the railroads, the ships, the big stores, the breweries. They owned Mexico because President Porfirio Díaz had let them steal it, José explained as I listened. Now Don Francisco Madero had been assassinated for trying to get it back. On such threads of family talk I followed my own recollection of the years from Jalco—the attack on Mazatlán, the captain of Acaponeta, the camp at El Nanchi and the arrival at Nogales on the flatcar.

9.   Only when we ventured uptown did we feel like aliens in a foreign land. Within the *barrio* we heard Spanish on the streets and in the alleys. On the railroad tracks, in the canneries, and along the riverfront there were more Mexicans than any other nationality. And except for the foremen, the work talk was in our language. In the secondhand shops, where the *barrio* people sold and bought furniture and clothing, there were Mexican clerks who knew the Mexican ways of making a sale. Families doubled up in decaying houses, cramping themselves so they could rent an extra room to *chicano* boarders, who accented the brown quality of our Mexican *colonia.*

QUESTIONS

1. Compare paragraphs 1 and 6. How is parallel construction used to distribute emphasis and maintain sentence unity?
2. In which paragraphs are particular sentences parallel in construction? How does this construction help to underscore the topic or controlling idea?

WRITING ASSIGNMENTS

The author uses his account of his Sacramento boyhood to comment on Mexican and American folkways and on the changes that occur in an alien world. Discuss the comment he is making and what you see as his attitude toward these changes.

Discuss the increased importance that manners assume when a person finds himself in an alien world. Consider speech habits as well as ordinary behavior.

George Bird Grinnell
EDUCATION OF THE BLACKFOOT CHILDREN

1.   If a number of boys were in a lodge where older people
were sitting, very likely the young people would be talking and
laughing about their own concerns, and making so much noise
that the elders could say nothing. If this continued too long, one
of the older men would be likely to get up and go out and get a
long stick and bring it in with him. When he had seated himself,
he would hold it up, so that the children could see it and would
repeat a cautionary formula, "I will give you gum!" This was a
warning to them to make less noise, and was always heeded—for
a time. After a little, however, the boys might forget and begin to
chatter again, and presently the man, without further warning,
would reach over and rap one of them on the head with the stick,
when quiet would again be had for a time.

2.   In the same way, in winter, when the lodge was full of
old and young people, and through lack of attention the fire died
down, some older person would call out, "Look out for the
skunk!" which would be a warning to the boys to put some
sticks on the fire. If this was not done at once, the man who had
called out might throw a stick of wood across the lodge into the
group of children, hitting and hurting one or more of them. It
was taught also that, if, when young and old were in the lodge
and the fire had burned low, an older person were to lay the un-
burned ends of the sticks upon the fire, all the children in the
lodge would have the scab, or itch. So, at the call "Look out for
the scab!" some child would always jump to the fire, and lay up
the sticks.

3.   There were various ways of teaching and training the
children. Men would make long speeches to groups of boys,
playing in the camps, telling them what they ought to do to be
successful in life. They would point out to them that to accomplish anything they must be brave and untiring in war; that
long life was not desirable; that the old people always had a hard
time, were given the worst side of the lodge and generally ne-

EDUCATION OF THE BLACKFOOT CHILDREN: Reprinted by permission of Charles Scribner's
Sons from *Pawnee, Blackfoot and Cheyenne* by George Bird Grinnell. Copyright © 1961 Charles
Scribner's Sons. Selection title by editor.

glected; that when the camp was moved they suffered from cold; that their sight was dim, so that they could not see far; that their teeth were gone, so that they could not chew their food. Only discomfort and misery await the old. Much better, while the body is strong and in its prime, while the sight is clear, the teeth sound, and the hair still black and long, to die in battle fighting bravely. The example of successful warriors would be held up to them, and the boys urged to emulate their brave deeds. To such advice some boys would listen, while others would not heed it.

4.   The girls also were instructed. All Indians like to see women more or less sober and serious-minded, not giggling all the time, not silly. A Blackfoot man who had two or three girls would, as they grew large, often talk to them and give them good advice. After watching them, and taking the measure of their characters, he would one day get a buffalo's front foot and ornament it fantastically with feathers. When the time came, he would call one of his daughters to him and say to her: "Now I wish you to stand here in front of me and look me straight in the eye without laughing. No matter what I may do, do not laugh." Then he would sing a funny song, shaking the foot in the girl's face in time to the song, and looking her steadily in the eye. Very likely before he had finished, she would begin to giggle. If she did this, the father would stop singing and tell her to finish laughing; and when she was serious again, he would again warn her not to laugh, and then would repeat his song. This time perhaps she would not laugh while he was singing. He would go through with this same performance before all his daughters. To such as seemed to have the steadiest characters, he would give good advice. He would talk to each girl of the duties of a woman's life and warn her against the dangers which she might expect to meet.

5.   At the time of the Medicine Lodge, he would take her to the lodge and point out to her the Medicine Lodge woman. He would say: "There is a good woman. She has built this Medicine Lodge, and is greatly honored and respected by all the people. Once she was a girl just like you; and you, if you are good and live a pure life, may some day be as great as she is now. Remember this, and try to live a worthy life."

6.   At the time of the Medicine Lodge, the boys in the camp also gathered to see the young men count their *coups*. A man would get up, holding in one hand a bundle of small sticks,

and, taking one stick from the bundle, he would recount some brave deed, throwing away a stick as he completed the narrative of each *coup*, until the sticks were all gone, when he sat down, and another man stood up to begin his recital. As the boys saw and heard all this, and saw how respected those men were who had done the most and bravest things, they said to themselves, "That man was once a boy like us, and we, if we have strong hearts, may do as much as he has done." So even the very small boys used often to steal off from the camp, and follow war parties. Often they went without the knowledge of their parents, and poorly provided, without food or extra moccasins. They would get to the enemy's camp, watch the ways of the young men, and so learn about going to war, how to act when on the war trail so as to be successful. Also they came to know the country.

QUESTIONS

1. As certain of the long sentences in Grinnell's selection show, a sentence can be lengthened without the reader losing track of the ideas if parallelism is maintained. What short sentences in the passage might be combined through parallel construction?
2. The semicolons in the third sentence of paragraph 3 are obligatory because of the number of elements within the subordinate clauses. To what extent are these elements themselves parallel in construction?
3. Parallelism is an important means to economy in sentence construction. How does the parallelism of the second sentence of paragraph 4 reduce the number of words the author might have employed?

WRITING ASSIGNMENT

George Bird Grinnell (1849–1938), a conservationist, the editor of *Field and Stream* from 1876 to 1911, and the founder of the Audubon Society in 1886, observed Indian life first-hand and wrote about it in a number of books. Investigate the education of the children of other Indian nations in other nineteenth- and twentieth-century studies and write several paragraphs on important similarities or differences.

BALANCE

Robert Ardrey
THE HERRING GULL

[1] The herring gull is a creature of sufficient ingenuity that if he picks up a mussel with a shell too hard for his beak to break, he will carry it to a height and drop it on a hard road. [2] He is a creature of sufficient loyalty and perception to guarantee that he will never attack his own mate, and will recognize her among dozens flying into the colony at a distance to defy human binoculars. [3] He is a creature of sufficient social sophistication that, while many arrive in the spring already paired, definite areas in the colony which Tinbergen calls "clubs" will be set aside as meeting places for the unpaired. [4] He is a creature also, as we have seen, of such sensitive social adjustment that the arriving flock will make "decisions" of mood and readiness as if it were one being. [5] So dependent is the herring gull on the community of his citizenship that he would probably be unable to breed were he to return in the spring to the wrong gull town. [6] So powerful and incomprehensible is his attachment for home that, like the albatross, a pair may return year after year to nest in precisely the same spot, although the North Sea's winter storms will have effaced all landmarks to guide his eye.

DISCUSSION: BALANCE

The parallelism of long sentences and sentences in sequence may occur without our planning it. Some writers, particularly in earlier centuries, did seek a balance of parallel phrases, clauses, and even sentences to give special emphasis to ideas alike in meaning and function. The following sentences, describing the English Puritans of the early seventeenth century, develop similar ideas, are grammatically parallel, and equal in weight and proportion:

THE HERRING GULL: From *The Territorial Imperative* by Robert Ardrey. Copyright © 1966 by Robert Ardrey. Reprinted by permission of Atheneum Publishers. Selection title by editor.

If they were unacquainted with the works of philosophers and poets, they were deeply read in the oracles of God. If their names were not found in the registers of heralds, they were recorded in the Book of Life. If their steps were not accompanied by a splendid train of menials, legions of ministering angels had charge over them.— Thomas Babington Macaulay, *Milton*

Not only whole sentence but also words, phrases and clauses may be so balanced:

He had been wrested by no common deliverer from the grasp
of no common foe.
He had been ransomed by the sweat of no vulgar agony,
by the blood of no earthly sacrifice.
It was for him that the sun had been darkened,
that the rocks had been rent,
that the dead had risen,
that all nature had shuddered at the sufferings of her
expiring God.—*Milton*

The stately, formal construction of these sentences is appropriate to the impression of the Puritans Macaulay is conveying.

Sentence balance is by no means absent in modern prose, but writers avoid so studied an effect. A writer on modern prose style comments: "Many writers today, if they make two sentences elaborately parallel, are likely to qualify the effect by some means, perhaps by a contrast between the elaboration of the grammar and the colloquial tone of the vocabulary or between the high-flown expression and the humble content." [1]

QUESTIONS

1. What phrases or clauses in sentences 1–4 by Ardrey are balanced? How do the balanced constructions in these sentences give emphasis to similar ideas?
2. What parts of sentences 5 and 6 are balanced for emphasis? Is the patterning more or less exact than that of sentences 1–4?
3. Is the topic idea of the paragraph stated explicitly?

WRITING ASSIGNMENT

Analyze Ardrey's paragraph in light of Sledd's statement quoted earlier.

[1] James Sledd, *A Short Introduction to English Grammar* (Chicago: Scott, Foresman, 1959), p. 293.

John F. Kennedy
THE SPACE PROGRAM, 1962

1.   If this capsule history of our progress teaches us any-thing, it is that man, in his quest for knowledge and progress, is determined and cannot be deterred. The exploration of space will go ahead, whether we join in it or not. And it is one of the great adventures of all time, and no nation which expects to be the leader of other nations can expect to stay behind in this race for space.

2.   Those who came before us made certain that this country rode the first waves of the industrial revolution, the first waves of modern invention and the first wave of nuclear power, and this generation does not intend to founder in the backwash of the coming age of space. We mean to be a part of it. We mean to lead it, for the eyes of the world now look into space, to the moon and to the planets beyond; and we have vowed that we shall not see it governed by a hostile flag of conquest, but by a banner of freedom and peace. We have vowed that we shall not see space filled with weapons of mass destruction, but with instruments of knowledge and understanding.

3.   Yet the vows of this nation can only be fulfilled if we in this nation are first, and therefore we intend to be first. In short, our leadership in science and in industry, our hopes for peace and security, our obligations to ourselves as well as others, all require us to make this effort, to solve these mysteries, to solve them for the good of all men, and to become the world's leading space-faring nation.

4.   We set sail on this new sea because there is new knowl-edge to be gained, and new rights to be won, and they must be won and used for the progress of all people. For space science, like nuclear science and all technology, has no conscience of its own. Whether it will become a force for good or ill depends on man, and only if the United States occupies a position of pre-eminence can we help decide whether this new ocean will be a sea of peace or a new, terrifying theater of war. I do not say that we should or will go unprotected against the hostile misuse of

THE SPACE PROGRAM, 1962: From *The Burden and the Glory* by John F. Kennedy (Harper & Row, Publishers, Inc., 1964). Selection title by editor.

space any more than we go unprotected against the hostile use of land or sea, but I do say that space can be explored and mastered without feeding the fires of war, without repeating the mistakes that man has made in extending his writ around this globe of ours.

5.   There is no strife, no prejudice, no national conflict in outer space as yet. Its hazards are hostile to us all. Its conquest deserves the best of all mankind, and its opportunity for peaceful cooperation may never come again. But why, some say, the moon? Why choose this as our goal? And they may well ask, why climb the highest mountain? Why, thirty-five years ago, fly the Atlantic? Why does Rice play Texas?

6.   We choose to go to the moon. We choose to go to the moon in this decade, and do the other things, not because they are easy but because they are hard; because that goal will serve to organize and measure the best of our energies and skills; because that challenge is one that we are willing to accept, one we are unwilling to postpone, and one which we intend to win—and the others, too.

QUESTIONS

1. This 1962 statement on space exploration is typical of President Kennedy's style of public address: phrases, clauses, and sentences are balanced in the course of the statement. Find examples of each kind of balancing. To what extent is the formal balance of the examples you located varied by the length of sentences in individual paragraphs?
2. How is the formal balance qualified by "the colloquial tone of the vocabulary" or the "humble content," to quote James Sledd?
3. To what extent is the repetition of key words an element of formal balance in certain sentences?

WRITING ASSIGNMENTS

Discuss the degree to which you are persuaded by the argument of paragraphs 4 and 5. Do you believe that the reason Rice plays Texas is a sufficient explanation for the space program?

Discuss the similarities between Kennedy's reasoning on space exploration and Newman's on the nature and value of education.

Paul Goodman
THE MOON LANDING, 1969

[1] Esthetically, our great achievement is not epic. [2] (Therefore it has no pedagogic value, especially for adolescents.) [3] Objectively it is as arduous and dangerous and important for the tribe as any epic exploration, battle, or city-founding of the past. [4] But what is lacking is the dual nature that belongs to epic heroism: epic heroes are representative champions of the people, with the virtues specific to carrying out their great tasks, but at the same time they are serious and suffering persons, with a commitment and destiny and often a tragic frailty and doom that are their own. [5] So the epic feelings are admiration and pride, often mixed with pity and fear. [6] But at present, instead of being champions and persons, the agents of great deeds are becoming personnel of the collective.

[7] This has occurred rapidly in the past century. [8] Pasteur was an epic figure; Fleming and Salk have been much less so. [9] Laying the railroad and the cable and digging the Panama Canal were more epic than building the big dams and orbiting Telstar. [10] Going to the Poles was more epic than going to the Moon. [11] Even among professionals, Wright and LeCorbusier were more Architects than their successors have been, and J. J. Thomson, Einstein, and Bohr were more Scientists than their successors have been. [12] No doubt our contemporaries are persons just as forceful and interesting, but there is much less public belief in the relevance of their personalities. [13] Previously, even when deeds were essentially corporate, people personalized them; now, even when deeds are very much the work of individual genius, people regard them as corporate.

[14] There is no less hunger for personal identification. [15] But the arduous and dangerous deeds of individuals are taken as romantic or eccentric rather than as epic and important. [16] These can range from Thor Heyerdahl's efforts to prove that the Polynesians and Egyptians could cross the oceans with primitive means, to aging Mr. Chichester sailing alone around the world in

THE MOON LANDING, 1969: From *New Reformation: Notes of a Neolithic Conservative* by Paul Goodman. Copyright © 1970 by Paul Goodman. Reprinted by permission of Random House, Inc. Selection title by editor.

a ketch and proving that there will always be an England—he was properly knighted for it—to the gentleman who recently crossed Lake Michigan in a bathtub and proved that there is an America. [17] The agents of such exploits become celebrities.

[18] There *is* identification with the Moon landing, but it is not with its champions or model heroes. [19] My guess is that astronauts are celebrities for only a few days, because it is not felt that there is anything in *them*. [20] Rather, the identification is massive, a social bond, quasi-religious, expressing how we are in the world. [21] It will appear most strikingly as a style of Space toys, successor to the trains and cars, bought by those over thirty for those under ten. [22] We have added explosive fire to force and speed. [23] Rockets are guns as well as flying machines.

QUESTIONS

1. The rhythm of Goodman's sentences depends on a frequent balancing of phrases:

   So the epic feelings are admiration and pride,
           often mixed with pity and fear.

   What elements in sentence 4 are grammatically parallel as well as parallel in idea? How are these elements balanced?
2. How are key words in sentence 11 repeated for emphasis? What parts of the sentence are in balance? What parts of sentence 13 are also in balance?
3. What parts of sentence 16 are in balance? How is the balancing of the sentence loosened sufficiently to avoid too formal an effect?

WRITING ASSIGNMENTS

Discuss what Goodman means by *epic* and the kind of definition he employs.

Contrast the attitude of Goodman toward the space program with the attitude of President Kennedy. In particular, comment on the explanation offered for the impetus to the space program.

ANTITHESIS

Bernard Shaw
DON JUAN SPEAKING TO THE DEVIL

DON JUAN. Pooh! why should I be civil to them or to you? In this Palace of Lies a truth or two will not hurt you. Your friends are all the dullest dogs I know. They are not beautiful: they are only decorated. They are not clean: They are only shaved and starched. They are not dignified: they are only fashionably dressed. They are not educated: they are only college passmen. They are not religious: they are only pewrenters. They are not moral: they are only conventional. They are not virtuous: they are only cowardly. They are not even vicious: they are only "frail." They are not artistic: they are only lascivious. They are not prosperous: they are only rich. They are not loyal, they are only servile; not dutiful, only sheepish; not public spirited, only patriotic; not courageous, only quarrelsome; not determined, only obstinate; not masterful, only domineering; not self-controlled, only obtuse; not self-respecting, only vain; not kind, only senti-mental; not social, only gregarious; not considerate, only polite; not intelligent, only opinionated; not progressive, only factious; not imaginative, only superstitious; not just, only vindictive; not generous, only propitiatory; not disciplined, only cowed; and not truthful at all—liars every one of them, to the very backbone of their souls.

DISCUSSION: ANTITHESIS

When contrasting ideas are balanced in sentences and paragraphs, they are said to be in antithesis:

> But the arduous and dangerous deeds of individuals are taken *as romantic or eccentric* rather than as *epic and important.*
> But at present, instead of *being champions and persons,* the agents of great deeds are *becoming personnel of the collective.*—Paul Goodman

DON JUAN SPEAKING TO THE DEVIL: From *Man and Superman,* by Bernard Shaw. Reprinted by permission of The Society of Authors, as Agent for the Bernard Shaw Estate. Selection title by editor.

As in the first of these statements, the antithesis may be exact and epigrammatic. The second type of sentence appears more frequently, contrasting only roughly equivalent phrases. Whole sentences in antithesis are even more frequent:

> Rome did not invent education, but she developed it on a scale unknown before, gave it state support, and formed the curriculum that persisted till our harassed youth. She did not invent the arch, the vault, or the dome, but she used them with such audacity and magnificence that in some fields her architecture has remained unequaled. . . . She did not invent philosophy, but it was in Lucretius and Seneca that Epicureanism and Stoicism found their most finished form.—Will Durant, *Caesar and Christ*

The balancing of phrases within each sentence heightens the contrast of ideas in the whole passage.

QUESTIONS

1. Shaw uses antithesis strictly throughout. Does he vary the pattern in any way? What use does he make of semicolons?
2. In the passage Don Juan is replying to the Devil's query as to why he is not civil to "his friends" in Hell: they are "the dullest dogs I know," he says; and he proceeds to explain why they are. How are clarity and emphasis achieved through the use of antithesis?
3. Explain the difference between the contrasted ideas, beginning with *beautiful* and *decorated* and ending with *disciplined* and *cowed*.

WRITING ASSIGNMENT

Write an essay on one of Shaw's contrasts, basing your discussion on observation and personal experience. Make use of antithesis in some of your sentences.

Martin Luther King, Jr.
NONVIOLENT RESISTANCE

1.   Oppressed people deal with their oppression in three characteristic ways. One way is acquiescence: the oppressed re-

NONVIOLENT RESISTANCE: From pp. 211–14 in *Stride Toward Freedom*. Copyright © 1958 by Martin Luther King, Jr. By permission of Harper & Row, Publishers, Inc. Selection title by editor.

sign themselves to their doom. They tacitly adjust themselves to oppression, and thereby become conditioned to it. In every movement toward freedom some of the oppressed prefer to remain oppressed. Almost 2800 years ago Moses set out to lead the children of Israel from the slavery of Egypt to the freedom of the promised land. He soon discovered that slaves do not always welcome their deliverers. They become accustomed to being slaves. They would rather bear those ills they have, as Shakespeare pointed out, than flee to others that they know not of. They prefer the "fleshpots of Egypt" to the ordeals of emancipation.

2.   There is such a thing as the freedom of exhaustion. Some people are so worn down by the yoke of oppression that they give up. A few years ago in the slum areas of Atlanta, a Negro guitarist used to sing almost daily: "Ben down so long that down don't bother me." This is the type of negative freedom and resignation that often engulfs the life of the oppressed.

3.   But this is not the way out. To accept passively an unjust system is to coöperate with that system; thereby the oppressed become as evil as the oppressor. Noncoöperation with evil is as much a moral obligation as is coöperation with good. The oppressed must never allow the conscience of the oppressor to slumber. Religion reminds every man that he is his brother's keeper. To accept injustice or segregation passively is to say to the oppressor that his actions are morally right. It is a way of allowing his conscience to fall asleep. At this moment the oppressed fails to be his brother's keeper. So acquiescence—while often the easier way—is not the moral way. It is the way of the coward. The Negro cannot win the respect of his oppressor by acquiescing; he merely increases the oppressor's arrogance and contempt. Acquiescence is interpreted as proof of the Negro's inferiority. The Negro cannot win the respect of the white people of the South or the peoples of the world if he is willing to sell the future of his children for his personal and immediate comfort and safety.

4.   A second way that oppressed people sometimes deal with oppression is to resort to physical violence and corroding hatred. Violence often brings about momentary results. Nations have frequently won their independence in battle. But in spite of temporary victories, violence never brings permanent peace. It solves no social problem; it merely creates new and more complicated ones.

5.   Violence as a way of achieving racial justice is both impractical and immoral. It is impractical because it is a descending spiral ending in destruction for all. The old law of an eye for an eye leaves everybody blind. It is immoral because it seeks to humiliate the opponent rather than win his understanding; it seeks to annihilate rather than to convert. Violence is immoral because it thrives on hatred rather than love. It destroys community and makes brotherhood impossible. It leaves society in monologue rather than dialogue. Violence ends by defeating itself. It creates bitterness in the survivors and brutality in the destroyers. A voice echoes through time saying to every potential Peter, "Put up your sword." History is cluttered with the wreckage of nations that failed to follow this command.

6.   If the American Negro and other victims of oppression succumb to the temptation of using violence in the struggle for freedom, future generations will be the recipients of a desolate night of bitterness, and our chief legacy to them will be an endless reign of meaningless chaos. Violence is not the way.

7.   The third way open to oppressed people in their quest for freedom is the way of nonviolent resistance. Like the synthesis in Hegelian philosophy, the principle of nonviolent resistance seeks to reconcile the truths of two opposites—acquiescence and violence—while avoiding the extremes and immoralities of both. The nonviolent resister agrees with the person who acquiesces that one should not be physically aggressive toward his opponent; but he balances the equation by agreeing with the person of violence that evil must be resisted. He avoids the nonresistance of the former and the violent resistance of the latter. With nonviolent resistance, no individual or group need submit to any wrong, nor need anyone resort to violence in order to right a wrong.

8.   It seems to me that this is the method that must guide the actions of the Negro in the present crisis in race relations. Through nonviolent resistance the Negro will be able to rise to the noble height of opposing the unjust system while loving the perpetrators of the system. The Negro must work passionately and unrelentingly for full stature as a citizen, but he must not use inferior methods to gain it. He must never come to terms with falsehood, malice, hate, or destruction.

9.   Nonviolent resistance makes it possible for the Negro to remain in the South and struggle for his rights. The Negro's problem will not be solved by running away. He cannot listen to

the glib suggestion of those who would urge him to migrate en masse to other sections of the country. By grasping his great opportunity in the South he can make a lasting contribution to the moral strength of the nation and set a sublime example of courage for generations yet unborn.

10.   By nonviolent resistance, the Negro can also enlist all men of good will in his struggle for equality. The problem is not a purely racial one, with Negroes set against whites. In the end, it is not a struggle between people at all, but a tension between justice and injustice. Nonviolent resistance is not aimed against oppressors but against oppression. Under its banner consciences, not racial groups, are enlisted.

11.   If the Negro is to achieve the goal of integration, he must organize himself into a militant and nonviolent mass movement. All three elements are indispensable. The movement for equality and justice can only be a success if it has both a mass and militant character; the barriers to be overcome require both. Nonviolence is an imperative in order to bring about ultimate community.

12.   A mass movement of militant quality that is not at the same time committed to nonviolence tends to generate conflict, which in turn breeds anarchy. The support of the participants and the sympathy of the uncommitted are both inhibited by the threat that bloodshed will engulf the community. This reaction in turn encourages the opposition to threaten and resort to force. When, however, the mass movement repudiates violence while moving resolutely toward its goal, its opponents are revealed as the instigators and practitioners of violence if it occurs. Then public support is magnetically attracted to the advocates of nonviolence, while those who employ violence are literally disarmed by overwhelming sentiment against their stand.

QUESTIONS

1. A moderate balancing and antithetical arrangement of phrases with a minimum balancing and antithetical arrangement of clauses creates a formal effect and, at the same time, moderates the tension of the passage. Note the sentences that conclude paragraph 1:

> They would rather *bear those ills they have,* as Shakespeare pointed out,
>> than *flee to others that they know not of.*

> They prefer *the "fleshpots of Egypt"*
> to *the ordeals of emancipation.*

What sentences in paragraph 5 contain antithetical elements? How exact is the antithesis? How many of these sentences are balanced to emphasize similar ideas?
2. How exact is the antithesis of ideas in paragraphs 8 and 10?
3. One way to moderate the tension of a passage containing considerable balance and antithesis is to vary the length of sentences. To what extent are the sentences of paragraphs 5, 8, and 10 varied in their length?

WRITING ASSIGNMENTS

Compare King's sentence style with that of another of his writings, for example, "Letter from Birmingham Jail." Discuss how the relative exactness of sentence balance and antithesis is used to moderate or increase the tension of the writing.

Compare a letter by Saint Paul in the King James Version of the Bible with the rendering of the same letter in the Goodspeed or the Revised Standard versions.

LENGTH

Ernest Hemingway
THE SHOOTING OF THE BUFFALO

¹ The car was going a wild forty-five miles an hour across the open and as Macomber watched, the buffalo got bigger and bigger until he could see the gray, hairless, scabby look of one huge bull and how his neck was a part of his shoulders and the shiny black of his horns as he galloped a little behind the others that

THE SHOOTING OF THE BUFFALO: From "The Short Happy Life of Francis Macomber" by Ernest Hemingway. Copyright 1936 Ernest Hemingway; renewal copyright © 1964 Ernest Hemingway. Reprinted by permission of Charles Scribner's Sons from *The Short Stories of Ernest Hemingway*. Selection title by editor.

were strung out in that steady plunging gait; and then, the car swaying as though it had just jumped a road, they drew up close and he could see the plunging hugeness of the bull, and the dust in his sparsely haired hide, the wide boss of horn and his outstretched, wide-nostrilled muzzle, and he was raising his rifle when Wilson shouted, "Not from the car, you fool!" and he had no fear, only hatred of Wilson, while the brakes clamped on and the car skidded, plowing sideways to an almost stop and Wilson was out on one side and he on the other, stumbling as his feet hit the still speeding-by of the earth, and then he was shooting at the bull as he moved away, hearing the bullets whunk into him, emptying his rifle at him as he moved steadily away, finally remembering to get his shots forward into the shoulder, and as he fumbled to re-load, he saw the bull was down. [2] Down on his knees, his big head tossing, and seeing the other two still galloping he shot at the leader and hit him. [3] He shot again and missed and he heard the *carawonging* roar as Wilson shot and saw the leading bull slide forward onto his nose.

DISCUSSION: LENGTH

There is nothing intrinsically effective or ineffective, superior or inferior, about long or short sentences, just as there is nothing intrinsically effective in a single note of the scale. Effectiveness depends on the use or function of sentence length in a given context.

Ordinary exposition usually begins with the main idea and accumulates detail:

> She was a spirited-looking young woman, with dark curly hair cropped and parted on the side, a short oval face with straight eyebrows, and a large curved mouth.—Katherine Anne Porter, "Old Mortality"

How much detail a writer can provide depends on how effectively he can keep the main idea before the reader: detail becomes excessive when the main idea seems to disappear into it. In prose that describes physical action, the sentence may depict one connected action:

> Morrall would duck his head in the huddle and if it was feasible he would call a play which took the ball laterally across the field—a pitchout, perhaps, and the play would eat up ground toward the girls, the ball carrier sprinting for the sidelines, with his running guards in front of him, running low, and behind them the linemen coming too, so that twenty-two men were converging on them at a fair clip.—George Plimpton, *Paper Lion*

Sentences longer than this are rarely used, partly because of the difficulty of maintaining clarity.

By contrast, a paragraph may be constructed of very short, disconnected sentences, resulting in an effect that resembles "primer style." Hemingway uses such sentences in a short story to express the monotony felt by a veteran of the First World War on his return home:

> He sat there on the porch reading a book on the war. It was a history and he was reading about all the engagements he had been in. It was the most interesting reading he had ever done. He wished there were more maps. He looked forward with a good feeling to reading all the really good histories when they would come out with good detail maps. Now he was really learning about the war. He had been a good soldier. That made a difference.—Ernest Hemingway, "Soldier's Home"

QUESTIONS

1. Read aloud the first sentence of Hemingway's "The Shooting of the Buffalo," noting the main clauses. In light of the considerable length of the sentence, how are these clauses given emphasis? Read the sentence aloud again, this time breaking it into shorter sentences. What change in effect do you notice? Is there an *equivalence* between the original sentence, particularly in its length, and the experience described?
2. Why does Hemingway end the sentence with *he saw the bull was down* rather than continue into the next sentence?
3. Change the subordinate elements in sentence 2 into main clauses and the first two main clauses of sentence 3 into subordinate clauses. How do these changes affect the passage?
4. Use your dictionary to determine whether there are synonyms for the following words: *scabby, plunging, hugeness, speeding-by, whunk, carawonging*. Would any synonyms you found be more suitable than Hemingway's words? How do you explain the absence of some of these words in the dictionary?

WRITING ASSIGNMENT

Rewrite the entire passage by breaking it into shorter sentences. In a second paragraph discuss the ways in which the revision alters the mood.

Richard E. Byrd
ALONE IN THE ANTARCTIC

[1] May was a round boulder sinking before a tide. [2] Time sloughed off the last implication of urgency, and the days moved imperceptibly one into the other. [3] The few world news items which Dyer read to me from time to time seemed almost as meaningless and blurred as they might to a Martian. [4] My world was insulated against the shocks running through distant economies. [5] Advance Base was geared to different laws. [6] On getting up in the morning, it was enough for me to say to myself: Today is the day to change the barograph sheet, or, Today is the day to fill the stove tank. [7] The night was settling down in earnest. [8] By May 17th, one month after the sun had sunk below the horizon, the noon twilight was dwindling to a mere chink in the darkness, lit by a cold reddish glow. [9] Days when the wind brooded in the north or east, the Barrier became a vast stagnant shadow surmounted by swollen masses of clouds, one layer of darkness piled on top of the other. [10] This was the polar night, the morbid countenance of the Ice Age. [11] Nothing moved; nothing was visible. [12] This was the soul of inertness. [13] One could almost hear a distant creaking as if a great weight were settling.

QUESTIONS

1. In the winter of 1934, during his second Antarctic expedition, Admiral Byrd maintained by himself a meteorological observation station some distance from the expedition base. What is the central impression or mood that he wishes to convey—that of time moving quickly or that of inertness?
2. How does the first sentence introduce a dominant image and motif? How is this image carried into later sentences? Pay particular attention to the adjectives and verbs in sentences 7–9 and 12–13.
3. Byrd's sentences are obviously much shorter than Hemingway's in "The Shooting of the Buffalo." Do Byrd's sentences or the clauses in his compound sentences seem clipped and abrupt? In the longer sentences, are there many dependent elements, as in the first sentence by Hemingway?

ALONE IN THE ANTARCTIC: From *Alone*, by Richard E. Byrd. Copyright, 1938, by Richard E. Byrd. Reprinted by permission of G. P. Putnam's Sons. Selection title by editor.

4. Convert the last four sentences into one long, carefully constructed sentence. What is gained or lost in effect? In general, what does the sentence construction contribute to the overall mood?

WRITING ASSIGNMENT

Describe an experience that was exciting, but at the same time frightening or painful. Vary the length of your sentences to control the degree of excitement or emotion you want to convey.

Graham Billing
LIFE IN THE ANTARCTIC

[1] Even the freezing of the sea helped to regulate the animal tide, for it released cold salt-heavy water which played its motivating part in the endless circulation of the Southern Ocean so that the sea was continually and richly replenished by nutrient chemicals, with vegetable plankton forming and using the endless summer sunlight to generate almost infinite quantities of itself, like the endless generation of grasslands across North America, Europe and Asia. [2] And in the vast vegetable seas the whalefeed, the shrimp-like krill, multiplied in geometric progression. [3] And on the krill fed fish, and the penguins and flying birds fed on fish and krill, and the seals fed on fish and krill and penguins, and the giant whales tending their circumpolar pastures rolled ceaselessly among the endless west-wind driven storms and swells opening and closing their cavernous jaws to suck in the oceans thick with krill and eat their fill and breed and suckle their monstrous calves from monstrous breasts rich with the milk of the Mother of Waters.

QUESTIONS

1. In sentences as long as those of this passage, subjects and predicates should be divided as little as possible so that the reader need

LIFE IN THE ANTARCTIC: From *Forbush & the Penguins* by Graham Billing. Reprinted by permission of Holt, Rinehart and Winston, Inc. Selection title by author.

not hunt for the main idea. To what extent are the subjects and predicates divided in the several clauses of sentences 1 and 3?

2. Hemingway's sentences imitate the physical experience they describe. Do you see a relation between the content and the structure of Billing's sentences?

WRITING ASSIGNMENT

Contrast the paragraphs by Byrd and Billing to illustrate the different effects long and short sentences can achieve.

CLIMAX

William Faulkner
THE BEAR

[1] This time the bear didn't strike him down. [2] It caught the dog in both arms, almost loverlike, and they both went down. [3] He was off the mule now. [4] He drew back both hammers of the gun but he could see nothing but moiling spotted houndbodies until the bear surged up again. [5] Boon was yelling something, he could not tell what; he could see Lion still clinging to the bear's throat and he saw the bear, half erect, strike one of the hounds with one paw and hurl it five or six feet and then, rising and rising as though it would never stop, stand erect again and begin to rake at Lion's belly with its forepaws. [6] Then Boon was running. [7] The boy saw the gleam of the blade in his hand and watched him leap among the hounds, hurdling them, kicking them aside as he ran, and fling himself astride the bear as he had hurled himself onto the mule, his legs locked around the bear's belly, his left arm under the bear's throat where Lion clung, and the glint of the knife as it rose and fell.

DISCUSSION: CLIMAX

Our discussion of periodic sentences indicated one important way that climax can be achieved—by delaying the main idea or the completion of the main idea until the end of the sentence. We saw also that, even in loose sentences, modifying or qualifying phrases and clauses that follow the main idea can be arranged in the order of rising importance—as in *I came, I saw, I conquered.* A necessary condition of climax is a sense of anticipation, promoted chiefly through the ideas themselves. Obviously anticlimax will result if we make the culminating idea less significant than what has gone before. The letdown that results may be deliberately comic, as in this sentence by Thomas De Quincey:

> If once a man indulges himself in murder, very soon he comes to think little of robbery; and from robbing he next comes to drinking and Sabbath-breaking, and from that to incivility and procrastination.

QUESTIONS

1. Sentence 5 by Faulkner might have been divided into several sentences. How does the length of the sentence give weight to the details that conclude it?
2. The final clause of sentence 4 is grammatically subordinate to the earlier parts. Is it subordinate in idea as well? Could it be made grammatically coordinate without changing the meaning?
3. How are parallelism and balance used in sentence 7 to increase the tension of the scene? Note that the sentence is loose, yet builds to a climax. How is this sense of climax achieved?

WRITING ASSIGNMENT

Rewrite the passage, breaking the long sentences into shorter ones. Discuss whether your revision is less effective than Faulkner's or achieves the same effect in different ways.

John Updike
MY GRANDMOTHER

[1] When we were all still alive, the five of us in that kerosene-lit house, on Friday and Saturday nights, at an hour when in the spring and summer there was still abundant light in the air, I would set out in my father's car for town, where my friends lived. [2] I had, by moving ten miles away, at last acquired friends: an illustration of that strange law whereby, like Orpheus leading Eurydice, we achieve our desire by turning our back on it. [3] I had even gained a girl, so that the vibrations were as sexual as social that made me jangle with anticipation as I clowned in front of the mirror in our kitchen, shaving from a basin of stove-heated water, combing my hair with a dripping comb, adjusting my reflection in the mirror until I had achieved just that electric angle from which my face seemed beautiful and everlastingly, by the very volumes of air and sky and grass that lay mutely banked about our home, beloved. [4] My grandmother would hover near me, watching fearfully, as she had when I was a child, afraid that I would fall from a tree. [5] Delirious, humming, I would swoop and lift her, lift her like a child, crooking one arm under her knees and cupping the other behind her back. [6] Exultant in my height, my strength, I would lift that frail brittle body weighing perhaps a hundred pounds and twirl with it in my arms while the rest of the family watched with startled smiles of alarm. [7] Had I stumbled, or dropped her, I might have broken her back, but my joy always proved a secure cradle. [8] And whatever irony was in the impulse, whatever implicit contrast between this ancient husk, scarcely female, and the pliant, warm girl I would embrace before the evening was done, direct delight flooded away: I was carrying her who had carried me, I was giving my past a dance, I had lifted the anxious caretaker of my childhood from the floor, I was bringing her with my boldness to the edge of danger, from which she had always sought to guard me.

QUESTIONS

1. How does the ending of sentence 3 vary the normal sentence pattern to take advantage of the strong terminal position? Is the double emphasis given to *beloved* justified by the context?
2. Sentence 3 develops through an accumulation of detail. Does the sentence develop a single idea? Could it be broken up without interrupting the meaning or disturbing the effect?
3. How is climax achieved in sentences 5 and 8? Is it achieved through the same kind of sentence construction?

WRITING ASSIGNMENTS

Describe an episode or a series of incidents involving a close relative or friend. Let your details reveal your attitude toward him or her; do not state the attitude directly.

Discuss how the sense of anticipation built into Updike's paragraph is conveyed through sentence climax.

DICTION

VARIETIES OF
USAGE

Edmund Wilson
THE DREAMS AND PREMONITIONS
OF ABRAHAM LINCOLN

1.   The dreams and premonitions of Lincoln are also a part
of this drama, to which they contribute an element of imagery
and tragic foreshadowing that one finds sometimes in the lives of
poets—Dante's visions or Byron's last poem—but that one does
not expect to encounter in the career of a political figure: Lincoln's recurrent dream of a ship on its steady way to some dark
and indefinite shore, which seemed to prophesy that the war
would be going well, since it had always been followed by a victory; his ominous hallucination, after the election of 1860, when,
lying exhausted on a sofa, he saw in a mirror on the wall a double reflection of his face, with one image paler than the other,
which his wife had taken as a sign that he would be elected to a
second term but that he would not live to complete it. He repeated this story to John Hay and others the night of his second
election, and a few days before his death he had spoken of a
more recent dream, in which he had seen a crowd of people hur-
rying to the East Room of the White House and, when he followed them, found his own body laid out and heard voices saying, "Lincoln is dead." Herndon tells us that in the early days in
Springfield, Lincoln would say to him, "Billy, I fear that I shall
meet with some terrible end." But although he had been shot at
in '62 when he was riding in the streets of Washington, he would
not have a bodyguard; he explained that he wanted the people to
know that "I come among them without fear." He would take
walks in the middle of the night alone. It was only in the November of 1864 that four plain-clothesmen were posted at the

THE DREAMS AND PREMONITIONS OF ABRAHAM LINCOLN: Reprinted by permission of Farrar,
Straus, & Giroux, Inc. From *Patriotic Gore* by Edmund Wilson, published by Oxford University Press, copyright © 1962 by Edmund Wilson. Selection title by editor.

White House. On his way back to Washington from his visit to
Richmond just after the city's surrender, he read to his com-
panions on the boat the scene from *Macbeth* that contains the
lines:

> Duncan is in his grave;
> After life's fitful fever he sleeps well;
> Treason has done his worst: nor steel, nor poison,
> Malice domestic, foreign levy, nothing,
> Can touch him further.

2.   The night before Lincoln was murdered, he dreamed
again of the ship approaching its dark destination. He had foreseen and accepted his doom; he knew it was part of the drama.
He had in some sense imagined this drama himself—had even
prefigured Booth and the aspect he would wear for Booth when
the latter would leap down from the Presidential box crying,"*Sic
semper tyrannis!*" Had he not once told Herndon that Brutus was
created to murder Caesar and Caesar to be murdered by Brutus?
And in that speech made so long before to the Young Men's
Lyceum in Springfield, he had issued his equivocal warning
against the ambitious leader, describing this figure with a fire
that seemed to derive as much from admiration as from apprehension—that leader who would certainly arise among them and
"seek the gratification of [his] ruling passion," that "towering
genius" who would "burn for distinction, and, if possible . . .
have it, whether at the expense of emancipating slaves or enslaving freemen." It was as if he had not only foreseen the drama but
had even seen all around it with a kind of poetic objectivity,
aware of the various points of view that the world must take
toward its protagonist. In the poem that Lincoln lived, Booth had
been prepared for, too, and the tragic conclusion was necessary
to justify all the rest.

3.   It is not to be doubted that Lincoln, in spite of his firm
hand on policy, had found his leadership a harrowing experience. He had himself, one supposes, grown up in pain. The
handicaps imposed by his origins on his character and aspirations must have constrained him from his earliest years, and his
unhappy relations with women, the tantrums and aspirations of
his rather vulgar wife, and the death of two of his sons must
have saddened and worried and humiliated him all through his
personal life. The humorous stories and readings that his cabinet

sometimes found so incongruous only served, as he once explained, as a relief from his fits of despondency, his constant
anxiety about the war. Though not warm in his personal relationships, he was sensitive to the pain of others. He had remembered from fourteen years before that the sight of the slaves on
the steamboat had been "a continual torment," and though he
had pardoned, whenever it was possible, the soldiers who had
been sentenced to death, he had been compelled by his office to
authorize the executions of two hundred and sixty-seven men.
He must have suffered far more than he ever expressed from the
agonies and griefs of the war, and it was morally and drama-
tically inevitable that this prophet who had crushed opposition
and sent thousands of men to their deaths should finally attest
his good faith by laying down his own life with theirs.

DISCUSSION: VARIETIES OF USAGE

Our choice of words depends on the occasion of their use more than
we may recognize: the constructions and vocabulary of a graduation
speech, a letter to a prospective employer, and our breakfast-table and
locker-room conversations differ in important ways. In addition, we
belong to many groups, each with its own formal and informal language
and standards for judging what is effective and ineffective in both; and,
as individuals, we have our personal usages and standards.

We shall not be concerned here with special idioms and expressions
peculiar to certain dialects and regions, but rather with the standard English spoken and written by educated people in the United States, Canada, Great Britain, and elsewhere. Differences in vocabulary, idiom,
and even grammar in these countries and their regions are sometimes
striking, but the similarities are great enough to make the following distinctions in usage possible:

a. *Formal*   more often written than spoken, and addressed to a special, often professional, audience (and sometimes to a general audience—as in an inaugural address); usually associated with an abstract or a technical subject matter and vocabulary. Its sentences are
   sometimes long and complex, occasionally periodic, with moderate
   parallelism and balance. At its less extreme, Formal approaches
b. *General*   spoken and written by educated people in everyday situations and business affairs; the language of magazines, newspapers,
   and books with a general circulation. The subject matter and vocabulary tend to be concrete, dealing with familiar situations and ideas;
   the sentences are usually simple or compound, often loose, with
   little marked parallelism and balance. In more casual situations,
   General approaches

c. *Informal* spoken by educated people at home or among friends, and written in letters, diaries, newspaper and magazine columns, as well as in books. It differs from General primarily in its considerable use of colloquial expressions (those typical of ordinary conversation), contracted forms, and occasional slang (racy, hybrid, usually short-lived expressions).

Here are examples of these varieties of usage:

[*Formal*] It is an interesting question whether the functioning and evolution of human mentality can be accommodated within the framework of physical explanation, as presently conceived, or whether there are new principles, now unknown, that must be invoked, perhaps principles that emerge only at higher levels of organization than can now be submitted to physical investigation. —Noam Chomsky, *Language and Mind*

[*General*] Malicious gossip—which takes the place of creation in noncreative lives—of course draws heavily on the imagination. Fear and superstition have their roots in imagination. The fact is that imagination is antisocial in that it is not in any relation at all to everyday reality.—Nancy Hale, "The Two-Way Imagination"

[*Informal*] It felt as I would have expected: wonderful. The lights went out; flickering matches transformed the Garden into a giant planetarium. Dylan and The Band came back for a reprise of "Most Likely You'll Go Your Way," left, came back again, and ended with a rousing electric version of "Blowin' in the Wind." I went home as high on Dylan as I'd ever been.—Ellen Willis, *The New Yorker*, February 18, 1974 [on Bob Dylan's Madison Square Garden concert]

The ideas in these statements could be presented in any of the ways indicated. The most abstract ideas can be stated in the most informal language. But usage is a matter of convention as well as personal choice, and if we would not be surprised to find Chomsky's paragraph on language stated in a variety of ways, we probably would be surprised to find the description of the Bob Dylan concert stated in as formal a language as that of the first statement. It should be pointed out that much discourse today is mixed. We may use words of one variety of usage with those of another in a way that is startling and vigorous: we may combine colloquialisms with an abstract vocabulary in markedly formal sentences, or we may introduce into an informal discussion sentences containing striking parallelism and balance. As a rule, informal writing is closer to the patterns of ordinary speech; formal writing often seems impersonal because it departs widely from these patterns (few people would speak Chomsky's sentence). The following sentence states a complex idea informally; the pauses and qualifications suggest the way we speak:

There is a whole folklore, a whole tangle of something only a cultural anthropologist could begin to disentangle, that has grown up around the American frontier; there is—the already old-fashioned and somewhat disapproved word has to be used—a fascinating *myth* of the American frontier, the West.—Crane Brinton, *A History of Western Morals*

QUESTIONS

1. Perhaps the most formal and abstract writing is to be found in insurance policies and government pamphlets. In them we are seldom aware of someone speaking to us and revealing his interests and background; the "voice" is impersonal and neither friendly nor unfriendly. Wilson's discussion of Lincoln shows that writing can be formal without being impersonal. The formality of paragraph 1 is promoted by the careful parallelism and balance in several of the sentences. What contribution, if any, does the vocabulary make to this sense of formality? Is the formality of the sentence construction offset by a colloquial vocabulary?
2. How is repetition of key words used for emphasis in paragraph 2?
3. How much do the sentences of paragraphs 2 and 3 depart from the rather loose constructions of ordinary speech? Do you get a sense of a cultivated sentence construction?
4. Somber, tragic experiences and ideas encourage a formal language. Do you think the experiences Wilson recounts could be dealt with as effectively in informal language—for example, with contractions (can't, won't, and so on)?
5. Are the three paragraphs developed in the same way?

WRITING ASSIGNMENTS

Discuss what Wilson is saying about Lincoln as a man and a President through these statements on his dreams and premonitions.

Examine the essays and letters of Emerson or another writer and comment on his or her formal and informal treatment of similar ideas and the obvious differences in language.

George Plimpton
FOOTBALL RUNNING STYLES

[1] The running styles were as different as the physical characteristics. [2] Dick Crompton, a small Texan scatback, ran with sharp exhalations when he had the ball, *ah-ah-ah*, like piston strokes—a habit he had picked up in high school which he felt gave power to his run. [3] He could be heard across the width of a field. [4] The "Gasper" some of the players called him, and he was also nicknamed "Roadrunner"—after the quick-running desert bird of his home state. [5] Jake Greer also had a distinctive run—moving his spindly body in leaps like a high jumper moving for the crossbar, high, bouncy steps, and then he stretched out fast, and when he got to the defending back he feinted with his small high-boned head, sometimes with a tiny bit of toothpick working in it. [6] Then he'd fly on past or off at an angle, his hands splayed out wide, looking back for the ball honing in to intercept his line of flight, and then he'd *miss* it—good moves but bad hands in those early training sessions, they said—and the shouts would go up, "Squeeze that thing, baby," "Hands, man, hands." [7] Greer would circle back, stricken, staring into his big hands as if they had betrayed him as he bent down to pick up the ball. [8] His face would remain long and melancholy, and when his signal came up again, Scooter McLean would shout: "Look like you want it, Al, come *on*, baby."

QUESTIONS

1. Spoken sentences tend to be looser than periodic sentences, though a string of clauses may increase in importance—even build to a climax if the context warrants (see page 143). How loosely constructed are Plimpton's sentences? How close are they to spoken ones? Are they appropriate to the content?
2. Would the passage increase in clarity if sentences 5 and 6 were broken up?
3. Sports writing can be overly colorful if adjectives are used to excess in describing action. Effective action sentences rely on specific verbs and employ adjectives to heighten the sense of the verb. How spe-

FOOTBALL RUNNING STYLES: From p. 62 in *Paper Lion* by George Plimpton. Copyright © 1966 by George Plimpton. Reprinted by permission of Harper & Row, Publishers, Inc. Selection title by editor.

cific are the verbs in Plimpton's sentences? To what extent does he rely on adjectives to express the whole action?

4. Sports writing communicates little to a person unfamiliar with sports jargon. Some jargon is, of course, necessary in reporting a sports event or any other activity that uses a special vocabulary. Does Plimpton depend on jargon in the passage?

5. What expressions are slang? Does the context justify their use?

WRITING ASSIGNMENT

Describe the batting styles of a number of baseball players or the performing styles of a jazz, rock, or classical musician. Write in a style appropriate to the subject.

Dereck Williamson
TELL IT LIKE IT WAS

A browse through the Little League Baseball Official Rules indicates that times have changed since my sandlot baseball days. I'll tell it like it is now, and then try to tell it like it was then.

PLAYING EQUIPMENT—Each team must have at least twelve conventional baseball uniforms. The Official Little League Shoulder Patch must be affixed to the upper left sleeve of the uniform blouse. Games may not be played except in uniforms. These uniforms are the property of the League, and are to be loaned to the players for such period as the League may determine.

Playing equipment—Each guy came out to the ballfield looking like a bum. Shirts were optional. Patches went on pants because they were torn up sliding. Anybody wearing a clean or neat garment was jumped on, and rubbed around in the dirt.

Each League must provide in each dugout at least six (6) protective helmets approved by Little League Headquarters. The wearing of such approved helmets by the batter, all base run-

TELL IT LIKE IT WAS: From Martin Levin's "Phoenix Nest," *Saturday Review*, June 21, 1969. Reprinted by permission of Martin Levin.

ners, and coaches is mandatory. Shoes with metal spikes or cleats are prohibited. Catchers must wear masks during practice, pitcher warm-up, and regular games.

There were no dugouts—only the ditch that ran across the field just behind second base. In the ditch were at least sixty (60) frogs. Headgear was optional. The most popular were brimless caps and capless brims. There was only one helmet in the league—a leather aviator's helmet, with goggles, owned by Spike Snyder. Shoes with metal spikes or cleats could not be worn, because they all belonged to big brothers in high school and didn't fit. Catchers didn't wear masks. To avoid being hit in the head they stood eight feet behind the plate and let the ball bounce once.

PITCHERS—Any player on the team roster may pitch. A player shall not pitch in more than six (6) innings in a calendar week. Delivery of a single pitch shall constitute having pitched in an inning.

Pitchers—Any player who owned the ball pitched. A player could not pitch on more than seven (7) days in a calendar week, or more than one hundred (100) innings a day, because it got too dark. Delivery of a pitch straight down and the pitcher falling senseless beside the ball constituted exhaustion.

EQUIPMENT—The ball shall weigh not less than five ounces or more than five and one-quarter (5¼) ounces avoirdupois. It shall measure not less than nine (9) inches nor more than nine and one-quarter (9¼) inches in circumference. The bat shall be round and made of wood. It shall not be more than thirty-three (33) inches in length. Bats may be taped for a distance not exceeding sixteen (16) inches from the small end. The first baseman is the only fielder who may wear a mitt. All other fielders must use fielder's gloves.

Equipment—The ball could be of any weight, and anybody stupid enough to say "avoirdupois" out loud deserved what he got. Circumferences of the ball depended on the amount of tape wrapped around it. Sometimes the tape came loose when you hit the ball, and the circumference changed rapidly. Sometimes it was just tape by the time it reached the fielder, and the circumference was zero (0).

Bats were made of wood and were round unless they had been used for hitting rocks. After bats were broken they were taped for their entire length and it was hard to tell which was the small end. The first baseman was lucky if he got either a mitt or a glove. The only mitt belonged to the fat right fielder, who wore it even when he was at bat.

PROTESTS—Protests shall be considered only when based on the violation or interpretation of a playing rule or the use of an ineligible player. No protest shall be considered on a decision involving an umpire's judgment.

Protests—A protest was considered only when you were awfully sure you could lick the other guy. There was no umpire, unless some kid was on crutches and couldn't play. Nobody paid any attention to his calls, because he was just another kid.

FIELD DECORUM—The actions of players, managers, coaches, umpires, and League officials must be above reproach.

Field decorum—There were no managers, or coaches, or any of those big people. Only players who swore and spat. Anyone caught being above reproach got clobbered.

QUESTIONS

1. Williamson contrasts two kinds of baseball through two attitudes toward it—attitudes expressed not only in the details of the games but in ways of talking or writing about it. What is the chief difference between the language of Little League Baseball Official Rules and that of his account of sandlot baseball?
2. Is Williamson approving of Little League baseball, critical of it, or merely amused? Or is his feeling neutral?

WRITING ASSIGNMENTS

Rewrite the Little League Baseball Official Rules for the information of the boys who play the game. Then analyze the changes that you made in vocabulary and sentence construction and the reasons for these changes.

Write a one-paragraph letter to a former high-school teacher asking for advice about a present course or a possible future career. Write a second one-paragraph letter to a friend who has taken the course or embarked on such a career, asking the same advice. In a third paragraph discuss the adjustments in usage you made and the reasons for them.

James Baldwin
THE FUNERAL

It seemed to me, of course, that it was a very long funeral. But it was, if anything, a rather shorter funeral than most, nor, since there were no overwhelming, uncontrollable expressions of grief, could it be called—if I dare to use the word—successful. The minister who preached my father's funeral sermon was one of the few my father had still been seeing as he neared his end. He presented to us in his sermon a man whom none of us had ever seen—a man thoughtful, patient, and forbearing, a Christian inspiration to all who knew him, and a model for his children. And no doubt the children, in their disturbed and guilty state, were almost ready to believe this; he had been remote enough to be anything and, anyway, the shock of the incontrovertible, that it was really our father lying up there in that casket, prepared the mind for anything. His sister moaned and this grief-stricken moaning was taken as corroboration. The other faces held a dark, non-committal thoughtfulness. This was not the man they had known, but they had scarcely expected to be confronted with *him*; this was, in a sense deeper than questions of fact, the man they had not known, and the man they had not known may have been the real one. The real man, whoever he had been, had suffered and now he was dead: this was all that was sure and all that mattered now. Every man in the chapel hoped that when his hour came he, too, would be eulogized, which is to say forgiven, and that all of his lapses, greeds, errors, and strayings from the truth would be invested with coherence and looked upon with charity. This was perhaps the last thing human beings could give each other and it was what they demanded, after all, of the Lord. Only the Lord saw the midnight tears, only He was present when one of His children, moaning and wringing hands, paced up and

THE FUNERAL: From *Notes of a Native Son,* by James Baldwin. Copyright © 1955 by James Baldwin. Reprinted by permission of Beacon Press. Selection title by editor.

down the room. When one slapped one's child in anger the recoil in the heart reverberated through heaven and became part of the pain of the universe. And when the children were hungry and sullen and distrustful and one watched them, daily, growing wilder, and further away, and running headlong into danger, it was the Lord who knew what the charged heart endured as the strap was laid to the backside; the Lord alone who knew what one *would* have said if one had had, like the Lord, the gift of the living word. It was the Lord who knew of the impossibility every parent in that room faced: how to prepare the child for the day when the child would be despised and how to *create* in the child—by what means?—a stronger antidote to this poison than one had found for oneself. The avenues, side streets, bars, billiard halls, hospitals, police stations, and even the playgrounds of Harlem—not to mention the houses of correction, the jails, and the morgue—testified to the potency of the poison while remaining silent as to the efficacy of whatever antidote, irresistibly raising the question of whether or not such an antidote existed; raising, which was worse, the question of whether or not an antidote was desirable; perhaps poison should be fought with poison. With these several schisms in the mind and with more terrors in the heart than could be named, it was better not to judge the man who had gone down under an impossible burden. It was better to remember: *Thou knowest this man's fall; but thou knowest not his wrassling.*

QUESTIONS

1. The passage is formal in certain of its characteristics, informal in others. The author probably would not speak to members of his family as he writes here. Words like *incontrovertible* and *non-committal thoughtfulness* are chosen probably because they deepen the sense of formality. How does this sense of formality help to shape the meaning or to express an attitude toward the funeral?
2. Are there noticeable contrasts between the sentence construction and the diction?
3. How is repetition used for emphasis? What ideas or experiences are given the most emphasis and why?
4. How do the variations in diction and sentence construction suggest the different thoughts and relative maturity of the people at the funeral? How are transitions made from one person's thoughts to another person's?

Analyze three paragraphs from different articles in an issue of a newspaper or a news magazine to show how usage can vary according to the subject and the attitude and approach of individual writers. You might compare the diction of two reports of the same event (in a newspaper and a news magazine) to illustrate the possible variations.

TONE

C. Northcote Parkinson
INJELITITIS

¹ The first sign of danger is represented by the appearance in the organization's hierarchy of an individual who combines in himself a high concentration of incompetence and jealousy. ² Neither quality is significant in itself and most people have a certain proportion of each. ³ But when these two qualities reach a certain concentration —represented at present by the formula I^3J^5—there is a chemical reaction. ⁴ The two elements fuse, producing a new substance that we have termed "injelitance." ⁵ The presence of this substance can be safely inferred from the actions of any individual who, having failed to make anything of his own department, tries constantly to interfere with other departments and gain control of the central administration. ⁶ The specialist who observes this particular mixture of failure and ambition will at once shake his head and murmur, "Primary or idiopathic injelitance." ⁷ The symptoms, as we shall see, are quite unmistakable.

⁸ The next or secondary stage in the progress of the disease is reached when the infected individual gains complete or partial control of the central organization. ⁹ In many instances this stage is reached without any period of primary infection, the individ-

INJELITITIS: From *Parkinson's Law*, by C. Northcote Parkinson. Copyright © 1957 by C. Northcote Parkinson. Reprinted by permission of Houghton Mifflin Company.

ual having actually entered the organization at that level. [10] The injelitant individual is easily recognizable at this stage from the persistence with which he struggles to eject all those abler than himself, as also from his resistance to the appointment or promotion of anyone who might prove abler in course of time. [11] He dare not say, "Mr. Asterisk is too able," so he says, "Asterisk? Clever perhaps—but is he *sound*? I incline to prefer Mr. Cypher." [12] He dare not say, "Mr. Asterisk makes me feel small," so he says, "Mr. Cypher appears to me to have the better judgment." [13] Judgment is an interesting word that signifies in this context the opposite of intelligence; it means, in fact, doing what was done last time. [14] So Mr. Cypher is promoted and Mr. Asterisk goes elsewhere. [15] The central administration gradually fills up with people stupider than the chairman, director, or manager. [16] If the head of the organization is second-rate, he will see to it that his immediate staff are all third-rate; and they will, in turn, see to it that their subordinates are fourth-rate. [17] There will soon be an actual competition in stupidity, people pretending to be even more brainless than they are.

DISCUSSION: TONE

We have referred to the tone of a piece of writing, and we may define it now as the reflection of the author's attitude toward his subject or toward his reader. The author may reveal one or several attitudes: he may show himself to be mildly or strongly sarcastic, bitter, angry, mocking, whimsical, jocular, facetious, admiring, awe-struck, perhaps indifferent; and he will reveal his attitude in one or more ways, depending on what he assumes about his audience and depending on the effect he wants to produce. If he does not directly state his attitude, he may indicate it indirectly: he may exaggerate to the point of absurdity for a humorous effect; or understate in such a way that there is an obvious discrepancy between what is shown and what is said, producing an ironic effect; or merely present the facts without deliberate exaggeration or understatement, so that his attitude emerges gradually, but unmistakably, from his selection of detail. He will be aware that the tone of a statement can *qualify* meaning—in the way a sarcastic tone indicates that we intend our words to be caustic.

In short, the tone of a paragraph or an essay is to be found in the voice we hear as we read. Whether or not he intends to do so, every writer expresses himself in a voice that conveys an impression of himself—if nothing else, an impression of an unreflecting, dull person whose monotonous sentences indicate that he takes little interest in what he says or how he says it. A writer interested in his subject and his audience is less likely to be dull; his attitude toward them will emerge unmistakably. Occasionally, as the writer proceeds, he will discover something about himself or his subject, perhaps even that he has made a false start and needs to begin again. False starts in writing are often failures to discover the right voice—that is, the proper tone—to use in expressing an idea or developing an impression. And just as our ideas and attitudes will change from one piece of writing to another, the tone of an essay may change in response to shifts in attitude and emphasis. For an essay need not reveal one dominant tone: the voice of the writer may take on the nuances of meaning we hear in speech. In writing, these shifts in voice will be reflected in the modulations and rhythms of the sentences and paragraphs, which in turn reflect something of the rhythms and stresses of speech.

QUESTIONS

1. What effect does the formula I^3J^5 in sentence 3 in Parkinson's article have on the tone of the first paragraph? How may Parkinson have derived the term *injelitance?* How does his discussion of it affect the tone of the paragraph?
2. Is Parkinson being humorous about a potentially serious matter—incompetence and jealousy? Or is he making a serious point without intending to be humorous?
3. What is the tone of sentence 13—in particular, the word *interesting?* What is the tone of sentence 17?
4. What is the overall tone of the passage?

WRITING ASSIGNMENTS

Discuss *injelititis* in the classroom or on the playing field. Decide on your tone before you write and maintain it throughout the essay.

Discuss how tone qualifies meaning in Strachey's, "Queen Victoria at the End of Her Life."

Charles Dickens
A SUNDAY EVENING IN LONDON

¹ It was a Sunday evening in London, gloomy, close and stale. ² Maddening church bells of all degrees of dissonance, sharp and

A SUNDAY EVENING IN LONDON: From *Little Dorrit* by Charles Dickens.

flat, cracked and clear, fast and slow, made the brick-and-mortar echoes hideous. [3] Melancholy streets in a penitential garb of soot, steeped the souls of the people who were condemned to look at them out of windows in dire despondency. [4] In every thoroughfare, up almost every alley, and down almost every turning, some doleful bell was throbbing, jerking, tolling, as if the Plague were in the city and the dead-carts were going round. [5] Everything was bolted and barred that could by possibility furnish relief to an overworked people. [6] No pictures, no unfamiliar animals, no rare plants or flowers, no natural or artificial wonders of the ancient world—all *taboo* with that enlightened strictness, that the ugly South Sea gods in the British Museum might have supposed themselves at home again. [7] Nothing to see but streets, streets, streets. [8] Nothing to breathe but streets, streets, streets. [9] Nothing to change the brooding mind, or raise it up. [10] Nothing for the spent toiler to do, but to compare the monotony of his seventh day with the monotony of his six days, think what a weary life he led, and make the best of it—or the worst, according to the probabilities.

QUESTIONS

1. List the adjectives Dickens uses to describe the atmosphere of a Sunday evening in London. How do these adjectives help to specify the tone? How early in the paragraph is the tone evident?
2. What effect does the repetition in sentences 8–10 have on the tone?
3. How has Dickens exaggerated in order to convey the depression and monotony of a London Sunday?

WRITING ASSIGNMENT

Write an essay comparing the way the tone is achieved in Dickens with the way it is in the following passage:

> Anyone who has ever lived alone in a New York apartment knows or remembers the special quality of a Sunday. The slow, late awakening in the midst of a city suddenly and preposterously still, the coffee cups and the mountainous tons of newspapers, the sense of indolence and boredom, and the back yards, sunlit, where slit-eyed cats undulate along fences and pigeons wheel about, and a church bell lets fall its chimes upon the quiet, hopelessly and sadly. It is a time of real torpor, but a time too of a vague yet unfaltering itch and uneasiness—over what I have never been able to figure out, unless

because in this most public of cities one's privacy is momentarily en-
forced and those old questions *What am I doing? Where am I going?*
are insistent in a way they could never be on a Monday.—William
Styron [1]

John W. Aldridge
CIVILIZATION IN THE UNITED STATES

1.   That America is not yet a physically completed or settled
country is everywhere so evident that just possibly it is too evident to be noticed. Certainly, it is a fact we have had to do our
best to ignore if we were to live with it at all. But virtually everything we, rather than God, have created here—except in the old
areas of the original colonies—is stamped with the brand of the
prairie and the frontier settlement. The typical main street of
Anywhere-Nowhere, U.S.A., is still essentially that of a Montana
cowtown of the 1880's. The false fronts may be brick rather than
wooden; the signs may be neon rather than painted; the saloons
may have become cocktail lounges and the livery stables gas stations, but the effect is otherwise the same. It all has the appearance of having been thrown together in a great hurry to provide
temporary shelter and the bare essentials of life for a people who
are still in a migratory stage of development. We take it for
granted that new houses will not be spacious or well-built or
pleasant to look upon, that they will offer no luxury or ease
beyond that provided by the average motel, that we can litter the
countryside around them with all manner of industrial and commercial defecation. And we take this for granted because, even
though we know better, the assumption is somehow built into us
that the new houses will not be needed for very long, that settlements of still newer houses will be built further along the trail,
and the people on the move will stay in them for a while before
moving on again—moving always through a landscape which we

[1] From *Set This House on Fire* by William Styron. Copyright © 1960 by William Styron. Reprinted
by permission of Random House, Inc.

CIVILIZATION IN THE UNITED STATES: From pp. 18–20 in *In the Country of the Young* by John
W. Aldridge. Copyright © 1969, 1970 by John W. Aldridge. Reprinted by permission of
Harper & Row, Publishers, Inc. Selection title by editor.

secretly recognize to be expendable, which is already so far gone in ugliness that it can hardly matter if it is made still uglier. Like an eternally advancing army Americans have grown accustomed to leaving their garbage wherever they happened to drop it. They cannot take pride in an environment which looks to them like enemy territory, and it is part of their national heritage to suppose that they will never stay in one place long enough to be obliged to police the area and bury their beer cans.

2.   The experience of driving by car from coast to coast is a case in point. The very physical structure of the drive is illustrative of our sense that the environment we are passing through is not only not worth looking at, but is as alien to us as the wilderness must have seemed to the first pioneers. The whole requirement imposed by the superhighway system is that we drive as fast as we dare and for as long as we can stand the strain to get where we are going as quickly as possible. No provision is made for dawdling, sight-seeing, or exploring side roads or picturesque villages, if any were to be found. In fact, there is a distinct implication that to leave the highway is dangerous, a descent into a hostile world of aborigines and savage beasts, and that to enter it is to risk never being heard of again. Everything seems to be arranged to make very certain that one will not have an *experience* of travel of any kind, that absolutely nothing will happen except perhaps a blowout or at the very worst a collision with another car. Motels and filling stations are so located that one need never venture beyond the immediate vicinity of the highway to refuel or spend the night. The chains of roadside restaurants are obviously not intended to be places where food and drink are tasted and enjoyed but rather way stations where people are provisioned like caravans or safaris with the bare increments of nourishment required to keep them alive until they reach their destination. Destination is the lone reality in the vacuum of such travel. We always move, it seems, both physically and philosophically through a present we do not care to experience toward some future time and place at which real life will finally begin. Like Gatsby, we are all believers in the green light, the orgiastic future—not only the young and idealistic but all of us. And a principal reason we are is that the physical world we inhabit from day to day affords us so few grounds for satisfaction and such abundant grounds for believing that tomorrow cannot help but be better.

QUESTIONS

1. Aldridge expresses his opinion of American civilization directly. Is this opinion expressed with amusement or sarcasm or deep anger?
2. Consider the ending of paragraph 2 carefully. Is Aldridge wholly critical of "the green light, the orgiastic future"? Is the reference to Gatsby meant to be condemnatory? Is Aldridge saying, in general, that Americans are misdirected idealists?
3. Do you agree that a coast-to-coast drive is a good illustration of the points made in the first paragraph? Or do you reject those points and the details of the illustration?

WRITING ASSIGNMENTS

Aldridge states: "We always move, it seems, both physically and philosophically through a present we do not care to experience toward some future time and place at which real life will finally begin." Discuss whether Aldridge is stating or implying that the American environment has conditioned this attitude, that the American character shaped the environment, or that the causal relation is to be explained in another way.

Aldridge states: "That America is not yet a physically completed or settled country is everywhere so evident that just possibly it is too evident to be noticed." Discuss the extent to which this statement is descriptive of your hometown or your college town.

IMAGERY

James Joyce
MEMORIES OF CHILDHOOD

1.   The cold slime of the ditch covered his whole body; and, when the bell rang for study and the lines filed out of the

playrooms, he felt the cold air of the corridor and staircase inside his clothes. He still tried to think what was the right answer. Was it right to kiss his mother or wrong to kiss his mother? What did that mean, to kiss? You put your face up like that to say good-night and then his mother put her face down. That was to kiss. His mother put her lips on his cheek; her lips were soft and they wetted his cheek; and they made a tiny little noise: kiss. Why did people do that with their two faces?

.   .   .

2.   There was a cold night smell in the chapel. But it was a holy smell. It was not like the smell of the old peasants who knelt at the back of the chapel at Sunday mass. That was a smell of air and rain and turf and corduroy. But they were very holy peas-ants. They breathed behind him on his neck and sighed as they prayed. They lived in Clane, a fellow said: there were little cot-tages there and he had seen a woman standing at the halfdoor of a cottage with a child in her arms, as the cars had come past from Sallins. It would be lovely to sleep for one night in that cottage before the fire of smoking turf, in the dark lit by the fire, in the warm dark, breathing the smell of the peasants, air and rain and turf and corduroy. But, O, the road there between the trees was dark! You would be lost in the dark. It made him afraid to think of how it was.

DISCUSSION: IMAGERY

Images convey sensory impressions: impressions of sight, hearing, smell, taste, or touch. The following passage from a story by James Joyce illustrates most of these:

> The cold air stung us and we played till our bodies glowed. Our shouts echoed in the silent street. The career of our play brought us through the dark muddy lanes behind the houses where we ran the gauntlet of the rough tribes from the cottages, to the back doors of the dark dripping gardens where odors arose from the ashpits, to the dark odorous stables where a coachman smoothed and combed the horse or shook music from the buckled harness.—"Araby"

According to Herbert Read, "Intention is connected with the power of evoking images"; he means that we think through images constantly. Joyce could not have expressed his sense of a particular street on a par-ticular night in abstract language. The more evocative our imagery, when the situation calls for vivid impressions, the more directly will our words express experience. A passage will seem over-written if a vivid representation of experience is not needed; so-called fine writing tries to be too evocative of sense experience. In the passage quoted above, Joyce selects only those details that will give the reader an impression of the physical sensations experienced in the darkness. The imagery suggests the vitality of imagination with which the story is concerned; that vitality could not have been conveyed without it.

QUESTIONS

1. In these paragraphs from *A Portrait of the Artist as a Young Man* the images that crowd the reverie of the young Stephen Dedalus are inseparable from the emotions they evoke. At Clongowes School, Stephen is pushed into a stagnant moat; afterwards he remembers the cold slime, and his horror is intensified by the recollection that "a fellow had once seen a big rat jump plop into the scum." His reverie shifts to the corridor and staircase and then to his mother. How does the tactile imagery express this shift as well as the gradual change of mood? What do the visual and auditory images contribute to the total experience?
2. The second paragraph differs from the first in imagery and mood. Is the mood one of awe or mystery or one of passive indifference? How frightened is Stephen? What kind of imagery dominates the paragraph, and what other kinds do you find? What do the images contribute to the mood?

WRITING ASSIGNMENT

Describe a childhood experience that had its painful moments. Depend on images to convey your emotions; do not comment at length on them, if you comment at all.

Truman Capote
A CHRISTMAS MEMORY

1.   Morning. Frozen rime lusters the grass; the sun, round as an orange and orange as hot-weather moons, balances on the

horizon, burnishes the silvered winter woods. A wild turkey calls. A renegade hog grunts in the undergrowth. Soon, by the edge of knee-deep, rapid-running water, we have to abandon the buggy. Queenie wades the stream first, paddles across barking complaints at the swiftness of the current, the pneumonia-making coldness of it. We follow, holding our shoes and equipment (a hatchet, a burlap sack) above our heads. A mile more: of chastising thorns, burs and briers that catch at our clothes; of rusty pine needles brilliant with gaudy fungus and molted feathers. Here, there, a flash, a flutter, an ecstasy of shrillings remind us that not all the birds have flown south. Always, the path unwinds through lemony sun pools and pitch vine tunnels. Another creek to cross: a disturbed armada of speckled trout froths the water round us, and frogs the size of plates practice belly flops; beaver workmen are building a dam. On the farther shore, Queenie shakes herself and trembles. My friend shivers, too: not with cold but enthusiasm. One of her hat's ragged roses sheds a petal as she lifts her head and inhales the pine-heavy air. "We're almost there; can you smell it, Buddy?" she says, as though we were approaching an ocean.

2.   And, indeed, it is a kind of ocean. Scented acres of holiday trees, prickly leafed holly. Red berries shiny as Chinese bells: black crows swoop upon them screaming. Having stuffed our burlap sacks with enough greenery and crimson to garland a dozen windows, we set about choosing a tree. "It should be," muses my friend, "twice as tall as a boy. So a boy can't steal the star." The one we pick is twice as tall as me. A brave handsome brute that survives thirty hatchet strokes before it keels with a creaking rending cry. Lugging it like a kill, we commence the long trek out. Every few yards we abandon the struggle, sit down and pant. But we have the strength of triumphant huntsmen; that and the tree's virile, icy perfume revive us, goad us on. Many compliments accompany our sunset return along the red clay road to town; but my friend is sly and noncommittal when passers-by praise the treasure perched on our buggy: what a fine tree and where did it come from? "Yonderways," she murmurs vaguely. Once a car stops and the rich mill owner's lazy wife leans out and whines: "Giveya two-bits cash for that ol tree." Ordinarily my friend is afraid of saying no; but on this occasion she promptly shakes her head: "We wouldn't take a dollar." The mill owner's wife persists. "A dollar, my foot! Fifty cents. That's my last offer.

Goodness, woman, you can get another one." In answer, my friend gently reflects: "I doubt it. There's never two of anything."

QUESTIONS

1. "There's never two of anything," the woman of "sixty-something" and a distant cousin of the seven-year-old boy says, and the details of the passage show us why. What aspects of the scene does the speaker focus on? To what senses does he appeal in his description of the morning?
2. At various points the speaker refers to the distance he and his friend had to travel and to the vastness of the field where they cut the tree. How different would the experience seem if they had cut the tree in a nearby wood?
3. How has Capote transformed an ordinary event—the cutting of a Christmas tree—into an experience that seems epic to the boy?
4. How does Capote convey the importance of odor to the total experience? Notice that smells, like taste, are difficult to describe. But we can be reminded of objects we associate with vivid odors, and this reminder makes the odors alive to us.
5. What impressions do you get of the character of the friend? How does Capote convey that impression?

WRITING ASSIGNMENT

Describe a Christmas morning or another holiday that stands apart from other such mornings in your memory. Try to render the sights and smells of the morning through images that you think will convey the experience to others.

FIGURATIVE LANGUAGE

Robert Penn Warren
JEFF YORK

¹ You have seen him a thousand times. ² You have seen him standing on the street corner on Saturday afternoon, in the little county-seat towns. ³ He wears blue jean pants, or overalls washed to a pale pastel blue like the color of sky after a shower in spring, but because it is Saturday he has on a wool coat, an old one, perhaps the coat left from the suit he got married in a long time back. ⁴ His long wrist bones hang out from the sleeves of the coat, the tendons showing along the bone like the dry twist of grapevine still corded on the stove-length of a hickory sapling you would find in his wood box beside his cookstove among the split chunks of gum and red oak. ⁵ The big hands, with the knotted, cracked joints and the square, horn-thick nails, hang loose off the wrist bone like clumsy, home-made tools hung on the wall of a shed after work. ⁶ If it is summer, he wears a straw hat with a wide brim, the straw fraying loose around the edge. ⁷ If it is winter, he wears a felt hat, black once, but now weathered with streaks of dark gray and dull purple in the sunlight. ⁸ His face is long and bony, the jawbone long under the drawn-in cheeks. ⁹ The flesh along the jawbone is nicked in a couple of places where the unaccustomed razor has been drawn over the leather-coarse skin. ¹⁰ A tiny bit of blood crusts brown where the nick is. ¹¹ The color of the face is red, a dull red like the red clay mud or clay dust which clings to the bottom of his pants and to the cast-iron-looking brogans on his feet, or a red like the color of a piece of hewed cedar which has been left in the weather. ¹² The face does not look alive. ¹³ It seems to be molded from the clay or hewed from the cedar. ¹⁴ When the jaw moves, once, with its deliberate, massive motion on the quid of tobacco, you are still not convinced. ¹⁵ That motion is but the cunning triumph of a mechanism concealed within.

JEFF YORK: From "The Patented Gate and the Mean Hamburger," copyright, 1947, by Robert Penn Warren. Reprinted from his volume *The Circus in the Attic and Other Essays* by permission of Harcourt Brace Jovanovich, Inc. Selection title by editor.

DISCUSSION: FIGURATIVE LANGUAGE

A simile is an explicit comparison (using *like* or *as*) that usually develops or implies more than one simple point of resemblance:

Will Brangwen ducked his head and looked at his uncle with swift, mistrustful eyes, like a caged hawk.—D. H. Lawrence, *The Rainbow*

A metaphor is an implicit comparison in which an object is presented as if it were something else:

Some people are molded by their admirations, others by their hostilities.—Elizabeth Bowen, *The Death of the Heart*

Personification is the attribution of human qualities to abstract ideas or objects:

So some random light directing them with its pale footfall upon stair and mat, from some uncovered star, or wandering ship, or the Lighthouse even, the little airs mounted the staircase and nosed round bedroom doors.—Virginia Woolf, *To the Lighthouse*

Simile, metaphor, and personification unite in the following passage:

Then Sunday light raced over the farm as fast as the chickens were flying. Immediately the first straight shaft of heat, solid as a hickory stick, was laid on the ridge.—Eudora Welty, *Losing Battles*

One purpose of figures of speech is to evoke the qualities of experience and give shape or substance to an emotion or awareness that up to the moment of its expression may be indefinite. T. S. Eliot has described the act of language as a means of discovery, a form of knowledge:

The only way of expressing emotion in the form of art is by finding an "objective correlative"; in other words, a set of objects, a situation, a chain of events which shall be the formula of that *particular* emotion; such that when the external facts, which must terminate in sensory experience, are given, the emotion is immediately evoked.—T. S. Eliot, *Selected Essays*

In exposition a writer will depend on metaphor because of its property of expressing an attitude as well as representing an idea:

England is not the jewelled isle of Shakespeare's much-quoted passage, nor is it the inferno depicted by Dr. Goebbels. More than either it resembles a family, a rather stuffy Victorian family, with not many black sheep in it but with all its cupboards bursting with skeletons. It has rich relations who have to be kow-towed to and poor relations who are horribly sat upon, and there is a deep conspiracy of silence about the source of the family income. It is a family in which the young are generally thwarted and most of the power is in the hands of irresponsible uncles and bedridden aunts.—George Orwell, "England, Your England"

QUESTIONS

1. Sentence 3 of "Jeff York" develops through an accretion of detail and simile that specifies the blue jeans. What is made specific in sentence 4 through a similar accretion of detail?
2. How do the hanging wristbones and hands, described in sentences 4 and 5, make concrete the dominant impression that concludes the passage? How does sentence 5 extend the impression developed in sentence 4?
3. How do similes in sentences 4 and 5 help to characterize Jeff York's world? Where else is simile employed for the same purpose?
4. How is the detail in sentences 9 and 10 related to the sentences that follow them? Why does Warren mention the razor nicks?
5. According to what principle is the detail of the description of Jeff York organized?

WRITING ASSIGNMENT

Describe a friend or relative through the clothing he or she wears and the world you associate with the person.

James Agee
BUSTER KEATON

[1] No other comedian could do as much with the dead pan. [2] He used this great, sad, motionless face to suggest various related things: a one-track mind near the track's end of pure insanity; mulish imperturbability under the wildest of circumstances; how dead a human being can get and still be alive; an awe-inspiring sort of patience and power to endure, proper to granite but uncanny in flesh and blood. [3] Everything that he was and did bore out this rigid face and played laughs against it. [4] When he moved his eyes, it was like seeing them move in a

BUSTER KEATON: From *Agee on Film, I,* by James Agee. Copyright 1958 by the James Agee Trust. Reprinted by permission of Ivan Oblensky, Inc. Selection title by editor.

statue. [5] His short-legged body was all sudden, machinelike angles, governed by a daft aplomb. [6] When he swept a semaphore-like arm to point, you could almost hear the electrical impulse in the signal block. [7] When he ran from a cop his transitions from accelerating walk to easy jogtrot to brisk canter to headlong gallop to flogged-piston sprint—always floating, above this frenzy, the untroubled, untouchable face—were as distinct and as soberly in order as an automatic gearshift.

QUESTIONS

1. What do the similes and metaphors in sentences 5 and 7 of "Buster Keaton" have in common? What are the explicit or implied points of resemblance? In sentence 7 what image does *flogged-piston sprint* bring to mind? What is described as *floating,* and is the word meant literally or metaphorically?
2. How are the similes and metaphors in sentences 5 and 7 connected to the statement in sentence 2 that Keaton's face suggested "a one-track mind near the track's end of pure insanity"?
3. Analyze the similes and metaphors of sentences 3, 4, and 6. How are they connected to those of 5 and 7?
4. What is the essence of Keaton's comic style for Agee? How do the similes and metaphors focus on the key aspect of this style?

WRITING ASSIGNMENTS

Rewrite Agee's paragraph, eliminating the similes and metaphors. Then discuss the ideas you found it difficult to express without them.

Describe a contemporary comedian, using similes and metaphors to reveal his style.

Sean O'Casey
DUBLIN HOUSES

[1] There were the houses, too—a long, lurching row of discontented incurables, smirched with the age-long marks of ague,

DUBLIN HOUSES: Reprinted with permission of Macmillan Publishing Co., Inc. and Macmillan, London and Basingstoke. From *Inishfallen, Fare Thee Well* by Sean O'Casey. Copyright © 1949 by Sean O'Casey. Selection title by editor.

fevers, cancer, and consumption, the soured tears of little children, and the sighs of disappointed newly-married girls. 2 The doors were scarred with time's spit and anger's hasty knocking; the pillars by their sides were shaky, their stuccoed bloom long since peeled away, and they looked like crutches keeping the trembling doors standing on their palsied feet. 3 The gummy-eyed windows blinked dimly out, lacquered by a year's tired dust from the troubled street below. 4 Dirt and disease were the big sacraments here—outward and visible signs of an inward and spiritual disgrace. 5 The people bought the cheapest things in food they could find in order to live, to work, to worship: the cheapest spuds, the cheapest tea, the cheapest meat, the cheapest fat; and waited for unsold bread to grow stale that they might buy that cheaper, too. 6 Here they gathered up the fragments so that nothing would be lost. 7 The streets were long haggard corridors of rottenness and ruin. 8 What wonderful mind of memory could link this shrinking wretchedness with the flaunting gorgeousness of silk and satin; with bloom of rose and scent of lavender? 9 A thousand years must have passed since the last lavender lady was carried out feet first from the last surviving one of them. 10 Even the sun shudders now when she touches a roof, for she feels some evil has chilled the glow of her garment. 11 The flower that here once bloomed is dead forever. 12 No wallflower here has crept into a favoured cranny; sight and sign of the primrose were far away; no room here for a dance of daffodils; no swallow twittering under a shady eave; and it was sad to see an odd sparrow seeking a yellow grain from the mocking dust; not even a spiky-headed thistle, purple mitred, could find a corner here for a sturdy life. 13 No Wordsworth here wandered about as lonely as a cloud.

QUESTIONS

1. The description of Dublin houses is governed by a basic figure of speech, the personification of the houses as *discontented incurables*. What emotional aura does the personification evoke? What is gained by making the houses seem alive, rather than merely describing them as rickety?
2. How does sentence 3 develop the initial personification?
3. People are usually described as *haggard*, not streets. How does the word differ connotatively from *worn* and *tired*? What is gained by the use of *haggard*?

4. What other words and phrases involve personification, and what do they contribute to the general impression of Dublin houses?
5. O'Casey might have written *discolored* rather than *smirched* in the first sentence. Which word is better suited to the passage and why?

WRITING ASSIGNMENTS

Paraphrase sentences 10, 11, and 12. Then discuss what is missing in tone and meaning when figurative words are replaced by literal equivalents.

Describe an unusual room or building. Use imagery and figurative language to create an overall impression. Try to control the emotional response of your reader through a chain of images and associations, as O'Casey does.

CONCRETENESS

Claude Brown
A BUILDING IN UPPER HARLEM

¹ There is a building in upper Harlem on a shabby side street with several other buildings that resemble it in both appearance and condition. ² "This building" is in an advanced state of deterioration; only cold water runs through the water pipes, the rats here are as large as cats. ³ The saving grace of this building might very well be the erratic patterns of the varied and brilliant colors of the graffiti which adorn it internally and externally from basement to roof. ⁴ This building has no electricity in the apartments, but the electricity in the hallway lamp fixtures is still on. ⁵ Some of the apartments have garbage piled up in them five feet high and that makes opening the door a very difficult task for those whose nasal passages are sufficiently insensitive to permit entry. ⁶ In some of the apartments and on the rooftop, the garbage and

assorted debris are piled only one or two feet high, and the trash has been there so long that plant life has generated. [7] The most rapid tour possible through this building will necessitate boiling oneself in a hot tub of strong disinfectant for a couple of hours, and even then this astonishingly formidable breed of lice will continue to make its presence felt throughout a long itchy night. [8] This building is adjacent to a fully occupied tenement whose inhabitants are families, some of which include several children. [9] This building has a few steps missing from the staircase above the second floor and there are no lightbulbs in the hallway; it's a very unsafe place for trespassers, even during the day. [10] This building's last family of tenants was emancipated several weeks ago; they hit the numbers and moved to the Bronx, shouting, "Free at last, free at last; thank God for the number man." [11] Prior to their liberation, the "last family" had lived a most un- usual existence. [12] Somebody had to be at home at all times to protect the family's second-hand-hot television from becoming a third-hand-hot television; there were too many junkies in and out who used the vacant apartments to stash their loot until they could "down" it and who also used some of the apartments for sleeping and as "shooting galleries." [13] For protection, the last family had a large, vicious German shepherd. [14] This dog was needed for the rats as well as the junkies. [15] A cat would be no help at all. [16] The sight of the rats in this building would give any cat smaller than a mountain lion instant heart failure. [17] The last family considered itself fortunate, despite the many unpleas- ant, unhealthy and unsafe aspects of its residence. [18] "We ain't paid no rent in two years. [19] I guess the city just forgot that we was here or they was just too embarrassed to ask for it," said the head of the last family. [20] This building has holes in the walls large enough for a man to walk through two adjacent apartments. [21] This building has holes in the ceilings on the fourth and fifth floors, and when it rains, the rain settles on the floor of a fourth- story apartment. [22] This building is not unique, there are many others like it in the ghettos of New York City; and like many others . . . this building is owned by the City of New York.

DISCUSSION: CONCRETENESS

Writing concretely means giving substance to an abstract idea, an awareness, or an insight—making the idea perceptible to the senses and giving it immediacy. In some instances making an idea or awareness concrete may simply mean giving the details of an overall impression; but writers may also use imagery and figurative language to heighten the impression. Again, the context will determine the kind of development suited to the subject. It should be remembered that excessive detail will blur the focus and perhaps make the writing incoherent. Voltaire said, "The secret of being a bore is to tell everything." A boring film may show everything in a seemingly endless stream of detail; a boring paragraph or essay does the same thing. Effective detail is *selected* to develop an idea or impression. Good writing, as we suggested in our discussion of figurative language, always reveals an economy of style.

QUESTIONS

1. Compared to O'Casey's description of Dublin houses, Brown's description of a Harlem slum building depends little on simile, metaphor, and personification and much on an accretion of detail. From what physical angle of vision is the building described in sentences 1–9? Are we given an overall view from a single point of observation?
2. What is gained by reserving the information about the adjacent building to the middle of the paragraph—following the description of the deserted building? What is gained in the whole paragraph by saving the information about the owner of the building for the end? What is the principle of order in the whole paragraph?
3. The final sentence indicates that the author is making the building representative or symbolic of an *attitude,* reflected in a particular environment. What is that attitude and how does the selection of detail help us to understand it?

WRITING ASSIGNMENT

Discuss the implications of the details of the paragraph: what the building reveals about the city that owns it and what it suggests about the lives of its inhabitants.

Lawrence Durrell
A FISHING SCENE IN EGYPT

1.   The circle of boats had narrowed now to encompass the
pans and in the hot dusk matches began to spark, while soon the
carbide lamps attached to the prows blossomed into trembling
yellow flowers, wobbling up into definition, enabling those who
were out of line to correct their trim. Narouz bent over his guest
with an apology and groped at the prow. Mountolive smelt the
sweat of his strong body as he bent down to test the rubber tube
and shake the old bakelite box of the lamp, full of rock-carbide.
Then he turned a key, struck a match, and for a moment the
dense fumes engulfed them both where they sat, breath held,
only to clear swiftly while beneath them also flowered, like some
immense coloured crystal, a semicircle of lake water, candent and
faithful as a magic lantern to the startled images of fish scattering
and reforming with movements of surprise, curiosity, perhaps
even pleasure. Narouz expelled his breath sharply and retired to
his place. "Look down" he urged, and added "But keep your
head well down." And as Mountolive, who did not understand
this last piece of advice, turned to question him, he said "Put a
coat around your head. The kingfishers go mad with the fish and
they are not night-sighted. Last time I had my cheek cut open;
and Sobhi lost an eye. Face forwards and down."
2.   Mountolive did as he was bidden and lay there floating
over the nervous pool of lamplight whose floor was now peerless
crystal not mud and alive with water-tortoises and frogs and sliding fish—a whole population disturbed by this intrusion from
the overworld. The punt lurched again and moved while the cold
bilge came up around his toes. Out of the corner of his eye he
could see that now the great half-circle of light, the chain of blos-
soms, was closing more rapidly; and as if to give the boats orientation and measure, there arose a drumming and singing, subdued and melancholy, yet authoritative. He felt the tug of the
turning boat echoed again in his backbone. His sensations recalled nothing he had ever known, were completely original.
3.   The water had become dense now, and thick; like an oat-

meal soup that is slowly stirred into thickness over a slow fire. But when he looked more closely he saw that the illusion was caused not by the water but by the multiplication of the fish themselves. They had begun to swarm, darting in schools, excited by the very consciousness of their own numbers, yet all sliding and skirmishing one way. The cordon too had tightened like a noose and only twenty feet now separated them from the next boat, the next pool of waxen light. The boatmen had begun to utter hoarse cries and pound the waters around them, themselves excited by the premonition of those fishy swarms which crowded the soft lake bottom, growing more and more excited as the shallows began and they recognized themselves trapped in the shining circle. There was something like delirium in their swarming and circling now. Vague shadows of men began to unwind hand-nets in the boats and the shouting thickened. Mountolive felt his blood beating faster with excitement. "In a moment" cried Narouz. "Lie still."

4.   The waters thickened to glue and silver bodies began to leap into the darkness only to fall back, glittering like coinage, into the shallows. The circles of light touched, overlapped, and the whole ceinture was complete, and from all around it there came the smash and crash of dark bodies leaping into the shallows, furling out the long hand-nets which were joined end to end and whose dark loops were already bulging like Christmas stockings with the squirming bodies of fish. The leapers had taken fright too and their panic-stricken leaps ripped up the whole surface of the pan, flashing back cold water upon the stuttering lamps, falling into the boats, a shuddering harvest of cold scales and drumming tails. Their exciting death-struggles were as contagious as the drumming had been. Laughter shook the air as the nets closed. Mountolive could see Arabs with their long white robes tucked up to the waist pressing forwards with steadying hands held to the dark prows beside them, pushing their linked nets slowly forward. The light gleamed upon their dark thighs. The darkness was full of their barbaric blitheness.

5.   And now came another unexpected phenomenon—for the sky itself began to thicken above them as the water had below. The darkness was suddenly swollen with unidentifiable shapes for the jumpers had alerted the sleepers from the shores of the lakes, and with shrill incoherent cries the new visitants from the sedge-lined outer estuary joined in the hunt—hundreds of

pelican, flamingo, crane and kingfisher—coming in on irregular
trajectories to career and swoop and snap at the jumping fish.
The waters and the air alike seethed with life as the fishermen
aligned their nets and began to scoop the swarming catch into
the boats, or turned out their nets to let the rippling cascades of
silver pour over the gunwales until the helmsmen were sitting
ankle-deep in the squirming bodies. There would be enough and
to spare for men and birds, and while the larger waders of the
lake folded and unfolded awkward wings like old-fashioned
painted parasols, or hovered in ungainly parcels above the
snapping, leaping water, the kingfishers and herring-gulls came
in from every direction at the speed of thunderbolts, half mad
with greed and excitement, flying on suicidal courses, some to
break their necks outright upon the decks of the boats, some to
flash beak forward into the dark body of a fisherman to split
open a cheek or a thigh in their terrifying cupidity. The splash of
water, the hoarse cries, the snapping of beaks and wings, and
the mad tattoo of the finger-drums gave the whole scene an unforgettable splendour, vaguely recalling to the mind of Mountolive forgotten Pharaonic frescoes of light and darkness.

6.   Here and there too the men began to fight off the birds,
striking at the dark air around them with sticks until amid the
swarming scrolls of captured fish one could see surprisingly rainbow feathers of magical hue and broken beaks from which blood
trickled upon the silver scales of the fish. For three-quarters of an
hour the scene continued thus until the dark boats were brimming. Now Nessim was alongside, shouting to them in the darkness. "We must go back." He pointed to a lantern waving across
the water, creating a warm cave of light in which they glimpsed
the smooth turning flanks of a horse and the serrated edge of
palm-leaves. "My mother is waiting for us" cried Nessim. His
flawless head bent down to take the edge of a light-pool as he
smiled. His was a Byzantine face such as one might find among
the frescoes of Ravenna—almond-shaped, dark-eyed, clear-fea-
tured. But Mountolive was looking, so to speak, through the face
of Nessim and into that of Leila who was so like him, his mother.
"Narouz," he called hoarsely, for the younger brother had
jumped into the water to fasten a net. "Narouz!" One could
hardly make oneself heard in the commotion. "We must go
back."

QUESTIONS

1. The unity of the long sentences of paragraph 1 is maintained; one thing is described fully before the focus shifts to another. To what extent are the details presented chronologically in the third and fourth sentences?
2. What details in paragraphs 1 and 2 generate a mood of anticipation?
3. The images of paragraphs 3 and 4 join opposites: the dense water, "thickened to glue"; the fish leaping, squirming. What other images fall into this pattern? Does the human world reveal this tension?
4. Against what landscape are the swooping birds projected? To what extent do they exhibit contrasts of image and mood already established? What other such contrasts and patterns do you notice?
5. Durrell introduces details of the landscape gradually, as elements of a mood and impression of nature. How do these details fit into patterns noted above?

WRITING ASSIGNMENT

Durrell describes a struggle among fish, birds, men. Describe a similar struggle, introducing details of landscape as part of the general mood and impression.

FAULTY DICTION

George Orwell
POLITICS AND THE ENGLISH LANGUAGE

1.   Most people who bother with the matter at all would admit that the English language is in a bad way, but it is generally assumed that we cannot by conscious action do anything about it. Our civilization is decadent and our language—so the

POLITICS AND THE ENGLISH LANGUAGE: From *Shooting an Elephant and Other Essays* by George Orwell, copyright, 1945, 1946, 1949, 1950, by Sonia Brownell Orwell. Reprinted by permission of Harcourt Brace Jovanovich, Inc. Also by permission of A. M. Heath & Company, Ltd. for Mrs. Sonia Brownell Orwell and Secker & Warburg.

argument runs—must inevitably share in the general collapse. It follows that any struggle against the abuse of language is a sentimental archaism, like preferring candles to electric light or hansom cabs to aeroplanes. Underneath this lies the half-conscious belief that language is a natural growth and not an instrument which we shape for our own purposes.

2.   Now, it is clear that the decline of a language must ultimately have political and economic causes: it is not due simply to the bad influence of this or that individual writer. But an effect can become a cause, reinforcing the original cause and producing the same effect in an intensified form, and so on indefinitely. A man may take to drink because he feels himself to be a failure, and then fail all the more completely because he drinks. It is rather the same thing that is happening to the English language. It becomes ugly and inaccurate because our thoughts are foolish, but the slovenliness of our language makes it easier for us to have foolish thoughts. The point is that the process is reversible. Modern English, especially written English, is full of bad habits which spread by imitation and which can be avoided if one is willing to take the necessary trouble. If one gets rid of these habits one can think more clearly, and to think clearly is a necessary first step toward political regeneration: so that the fight against bad English is not frivolous and is not the exclusive concern of professional writers. I will come back to this presently, and I hope that by that time the meaning of what I have said here will have become clearer. Meanwhile, here are five specimens of the English language as it is now habitually written.

3.   These five passages have not been picked out because they are especially bad—I could have quoted far worse if I had chosen—but because they illustrate various of the mental vices from which we now suffer. They are a little below the average, but are fairly representative samples. I number them so that I can refer back to them when necessary:

> (1) I am not, indeed, sure whether it is not true to say that the Milton who once seemed not unlike a seventeenth-century Shelley had not become, out of an experience ever more bitter in each year, more alien [sic] to the founder of that Jesuit sect which nothing could induce him to tolerate.
>
> Professor Harold Laski (Essay in *Freedom of Expression*)

> (2) Above all, we cannot play ducks and drakes with a native battery of idioms which prescribes such egregious colloca-

tions of vocables as the Basic *put up with* for *tolerate* or *put at a loss* for *bewilder*.

Professor Lancelot Hogben (*Interglossa*)

(3) On the one side we have the free personality: by definition it is not neurotic, for it has neither conflict nor dream. Its desires, such as they are, are transparent, for they are just what institutional approval keeps in the forefront of consciousness; another institutional pattern would alter their number and intensity; there is little in them that is natural, irreducible, or culturally dangerous. But *on the other side,* the social bond itself is nothing but the mutual reflection of these self-secure integrities. Recall the definition of love. Is not this the very picture of a small academic? Where is there a place in this hall of mirrors for either personality or fraternity?

Essay on psychology in *Politics* (New York)

(4) All the "best people" from the gentlemen's clubs, and all the frantic fascist captains, united in common hatred of Socialism and bestial horror of the rising tide of the mass revolutionary movement, have turned to acts of provocation, to foul incendiarism, to medieval legends of poisoned wells, to legalize their own destruction of proletarian organizations, and rouse the agitated petty-bourgeoisie to chauvinistic fervor on behalf of the fight against the revolutionary way out of the crisis.

Communist pamphlet

(5) If a new spirit *is* to be infused into this old country, there is one thorny and contentious reform which must be tackled, and that is the humanization and galvanization of the B.B.C. Timidity here will bespeak canker and atrophy of the soul. The heart of Britain may be sound and of strong beat, for instance, but the British lion's roar at present is like that of Bottom in Shakespeare's *Midsummer Night's Dream*—as gentle as any sucking dove. A virile new Britain cannot continue indefinitely to be traduced in the eyes or rather ears, of the world by the effete languors of Langham Place, brazenly masquerading as "standard English." When the Voice of Britain is heard at nine o'clock, better far and infinitely less ludicrous to hear aitches honestly dropped than the present priggish, inflated, inhibited, school-ma'amish arch braying of blameless bashful mewing maidens!

Letter in *Tribune*

4.   Each of these passages has faults of its own, but, quite apart from avoidable ugliness, two qualities are common to all of them. The first is staleness of imagery; the other is lack of precision. The writer either has a meaning and cannot express it, or he inadvertently says something else, or he is almost indifferent as to whether his words mean anything or not. This mixture of vagueness and sheer incompetence is the most marked characteristic of modern English prose, and especially of any kind of political writing. As soon as certain topics are raised, the concrete melts into the abstract and no one seems able to think of turns of speech that are not hackneyed: prose consists less and less of *words* chosen for the sake of their meaning, and more and more of *phrases* tacked together like the sections of a prefabricated henhouse. I list below, with notes and examples, various of the tricks by means of which the work of prose-construction is habitually dodged:

5.   *Dying metaphors.* A newly invented metaphor assists thought by evoking a visual image, while on the other hand a metaphor which is technically "dead" (e.g. *iron resolution*) has in effect reverted to being an ordinary word and can generally be used without loss of vividness. But in between these two classes there is a huge dump of worn-out metaphors which have lost all evocative power and are merely used because they save people the trouble of inventing phrases for themselves. Examples are: *Ring the changes on, take up the cudgels for, toe the line, ride roughshod over, stand shoulder to shoulder with, play into the hands of, no axe to grind, grist to the mill, fishing in troubled waters, on the order of the day, Achilles' heel, swan song, hotbed.* Many of these are used without knowledge of their meaning (what is a "rift," for instance?), and incompatible metaphors are frequently mixed, a sure sign that the writer is not interested in what he is saying. Some metaphors now current have been twisted out of their original meaning without those who use them even being aware of the fact. For example, *toe the line* is sometimes written *tow the line.* Another example is *the hammer and the anvil,* now always used with the implication that the anvil gets the worst of it. In real life it is always the anvil that breaks the hammer, never the other way about: a writer who stopped to think what he was saying would be aware of this, and would avoid perverting the original phrase.

6.   *Operators* or *verbal false limbs.* These save the trouble of

picking out appropriate verbs and nouns, and at the same time pad each sentence with extra syllables which give it an appearance of symmetry. Characteristic phrases are *render inoperative, militate against, make contact with, be subjected to, give rise to, give grounds for, have the effect of, play a leading part (role) in, make itself felt, take effect, exhibit a tendency to, serve the purpose of, etc., etc.* The keynote is the elimination of simple verbs. Instead of being a single word, such as *break, stop, spoil, mend, kill,* a verb becomes a *phrase,* made up of a noun or adjective tacked on to some general-purpose verb such as *prove, serve, form, play, render.* In addition, the passive voice is wherever possible used in preference to the active, and noun constructions are used instead of gerunds (*by examination of* instead of *by examining*). The range of verbs is further cut down by means of the *-ize* and *de-* formations, and the banal statements are given an appearance of profundity by means of the *not un-* formation. Simple conjunctions and prepositions are replaced by such phrases as *with respect to, having regard to, the fact that, by dint of, in view of, in the interests of, on the hypothesis that;* and the ends of sentences are saved from anticlimax by such resounding commonplaces as *greatly to be desired, cannot be left out of account, a development to be expected in the near future, deserving of serious consideration, brought to a satisfactory conclusion,* and so on and so forth.

7.   *Pretentious diction.* Words like *phenomenon, element, individual* (as noun), *objective, categorical, effective, virtual, basic, primary, promote, constitute, exhibit, exploit, utilize, eliminate, liquidate,* are used to dress up simple statement and give an air of scientific impartiality to biased judgments. Adjectives like *epochmaking, epic, historic, unforgettable, triumphant, age-old, inevitable, inexorable, veritable,* are used to dignify the sordid processes of international politics, while writing that aims at glorifying war usually takes on an archaic color, its characteristic words being: *realm, throne, chariot, mailed fist, trident, sword, shield, buckler, banner, jackboot, clarion.* Foreign words and expressions such as *cul de sac, ancien régime, deus ex machina, mutatis mutandis, status quo, gleichschaltung, weltanschauung,* are used to give an air of culture and elegance. Except for the useful abbreviations *i.e., e.g.,* and *etc.,* there is no real need for any of the hundreds of foreign phrases now current in English. Bad writers, and especially scientific, political, and sociological writers, are nearly always haunted by the notion that Latin or Greek words are

grander than Saxon ones, and unnecessary words like *expedite, ameliorate, predict, extraneous, deracinated, clandestine, subaqueous,* and hundreds of others constantly gain ground from their Anglo-Saxon opposite numbers.* The jargon peculiar to Marxist writing (*hyena, hangman, cannibal, petty bourgeois, these gentry, lackey, flunkey, mad dog, White Guard,* etc.) consists largely of words and phrases translated from Russian, German, or French; but the normal way of coining a new word is to use a Latin or Greek root with the appropriate affix and, where necessary, the size formation. It is often easier to make up words of this kind (*deregionalize, impermissible, extramarital, nonfragmentary* and so forth) than to think up the English words that will cover one's meaning. The result, in general, is an increase in slovenliness and vagueness.

8.   *Meaningless words.* In certain kinds of writing, particularly in art criticism and literary criticism, it is normal to come across long passages which are almost completely lacking in meaning.† Words like *romantic, plastic, values, human, dead, sentimental, natural, vitality,* as used in art criticism, are strictly meaningless, in the sense that they not only do not point to any discoverable object, but are hardly ever expected to do so by the reader. When one critic writes, "The outstanding feature of Mr. X's work is its living quality," while another writes, "The immediately striking thing about Mr. X's work is its peculiar deadness," the reader accepts this as a simple difference of opinion. If words like *black* and *white* were involved, instead of the jargon words *dead* and *living,* he would see at once that language was being used in an improper way. Many political words are similarly abused. The word *Fascism* has now no meaning except in so far as it signifies "something not desirable." The words *democracy, socialism, freedom, patriotic, realistic, justice,* have each of them several different meanings which cannot be reconciled with one another. In the case of a word like *democracy,* not only is

---

* An interesting illustration of this is the way in which the English flower names which were in use till very recently are being ousted by Greek ones, *snapdragon* becoming *antirrhinum, forget-me-not* becoming *myosotis,* etc. It is hard to see any practical reason for this change of fashion: it is probably due to an instinctive turning away from the more homely word and a vague feeling that the Greek word is scientific.

† Example: "Comfort's catholicity of perception and image, strangely Whitmanesque in range, almost the exact opposite in aesthetic compulsion, continues to evoke that trembling atmospheric accumulative hinting at a cruel, an inexorably serene timelessness. . . . Wrey Gardiner scores by aiming at simple bull's-eyes with precision. Only they are not so simple, and through this contented sadness runs more than the surface bittersweet of resignation." (*Poetry Quarterly.*)

there no agreed definition, but the attempt to make one is resisted from all sides. It is almost universally felt that when we call a country democratic we are praising it: consequently the defenders of every kind of régime claim that it is a democracy, and fear that they might have to stop using the word if it were tied down to any one meaning. Words of this kind are often used in a consciously dishonest way. That is, the person who uses them has his own private definition, but allows his hearer to think he means something quite different. Statements like *Marshal Pétain was a true patriot, The Soviet press is the freest in the world, The Catholic Church is opposed to persecution,* are almost always made with intent to deceive. Other words used in variable meanings, in most cases more or less dishonestly, are: *class, totalitarian, science, progressive, reactionary, bourgeois, equality.*

9.   Now that I have made this catalogue of swindles and perversions, let me give another example of the kind of writing that they lead to. This time it must of its nature be an imaginary one. I am going to translate a passage of good English into modern English of the worst sort. Here is a well-known verse from *Ecclesiastes:*

> I returned and saw under the sun, that the race is not to the swift, nor the battle to the strong, neither yet bread to the wise, nor yet riches to men of understanding, nor yet favour to men of skill; but time and chance happeneth to them all.

Here it is in modern English:

> Objective consideration of contemporary phenomena compels the conclusion that success or failure in competitive activities exhibits no tendency to be commensurate with innate capacity, but that a considerable element of the unpredictable must invariably be taken into account.

10.   This is a parody, but not a very gross one. Exhibit (3), above, for instance, contains several patches of the same kind of English. It will be seen that I have not made a full translation. The beginning and ending of the sentence follow the original meaning fairly closely, but in the middle the concrete illustrations—race, battle, bread—dissolve into the vague phrase "success or failure in competitive activities." This had to be so, because no modern writer of the kind I am discussing—no one capable of using phrases like "objective consideration of contem-

porary phenomena"—would ever tabulate his thoughts in that precise and detailed way. The whole tendency of modern prose is away from concreteness. Now analyze these two sentences a little more closely. The first contains forty-nine words but only sixty syllables, and all its words are those of everyday life. The second contains thirty-eight words of ninety syllables: eighteen of its words are from Latin roots, and one from Greek. The first sentence contains six vivid images, and only one phrase ("time and chance") that could be called vague. The second contains not a single fresh, arresting phrase, and in spite of its ninety syllables it gives only a shortened version of the meaning contained in the first. Yet without a doubt it is the second kind of sentence that is gaining ground in modern English. I do not want to exaggerate. This kind of writing is not yet universal, and outcrops of simplicity will occur here and there in the worst-written page. Still, if you or I were told to write a few lines on the uncertainty of human fortunes, we should probably come much nearer to my imaginary sentence than to the one from *Ecclesiastes*.

11.   As I have tried to show, modern writing at its worst does not consist in picking out words for the sake of their meaning and inventing images in order to make the meaning clearer. It consists in gumming together long strips of words which have already been set in order by someone else, and making the results presentable by sheer humbug. The attraction of this way of writing is that it is easy. It is easier—even quicker, once you have the habit—to say *In my opinion it is not an unjustifiable assumption that* than to say *I think*. If you use ready-made phrases, you not only don't have to hunt about for words; you also don't have to bother with the rhythms of your sentences, since these phrases are generally so arranged as to be more or less euphonious. When you are composing in a hurry—when you are dictating to a stenographer, for instance, or making a public speech—it is natural to fall into a pretentious, Latinized style. Tags like *a consideration which we should do well to bear in mind* or *a conclusion to which all of us would readily assent* will save many a sentence from coming down with a bump. By using stale metaphors, similes, and idioms, you save much mental effort, at the cost of leaving your meaning vague, not only for your reader but for yourself. This is the significance of mixed metaphors. The sole aim of a metaphor is to call up a visual image. When these images clash—as in *The Fascist octopus has sung its swan song, the jackboot*

is thrown into the melting pot—it can be taken as certain that the
writer is not seeing a mental image of the objects he is naming;
in other words he is not really thinking. Look again at the examples I gave at the beginning of this essay. Professor Laski (1)
uses five negatives in fifty-three words. One of these is superfluous, making nonsense of the whole passage, and in addition
there is the slip—*alien* for akin—making further nonsense, and
several avoidable pieces of clumsiness which increase the general
vagueness. Professor Hogben (2) plays ducks and drakes with a
battery which is able to write prescriptions, and, while disap-
proving of the everyday phrase *put up with*, is unwilling to look
egregious up in the dictionary and see what it means; (3), if one
takes an uncharitable attitude towards it, is simply meaningless:
probably one could work out its intended meaning by reading
the whole of the article in which it occurs. In (4), the writer
knows more or less what he wants to say, but an accumulation of
stale phrases chokes him like tea leaves blocking a sink. In (5),
words and meaning have almost parted company. People who
write in this manner usually have a general emotional meaning—
they dislike one thing and want to express solidarity with another—but they are not interested in the detail of what they are
saying. A scrupulous writer, in every sentence that he writes,
will ask himself at least four questions, thus: What am I trying to
say? What words will express it? What image or idiom will make
it clearer? Is this image fresh enough to have an effect? And he
will probably ask himself two more: Could I put it more shortly?
Have I said anything that is avoidably ugly? But you are not
obliged to go to all this trouble. You can shirk it by simply
throwing your mind open and letting the ready-made phrases
come crowding in. They will construct your sentences for you—
even think your thoughts for you, to a certain extent—and at
need they will perform the important service of partially concealing your meaning even from yourself. It is at this point that
the special connection between politics and the debasement of
language becomes clear.

12.   In our time it is broadly true that political writing is
bad writing. Where it is not true, it will generally be found that
the writer is some kind of rebel, expressing his private opinions
and not a "party line." Orthodoxy, of whatever color, seems to
demand a lifeless, imitative style. The political dialects to be
found in pamphlets, leading articles, manifestoes, White Papers

and the speeches of undersecretaries do, of course, vary from
party to party, but they are all alike in that one almost never
finds in them a fresh, vivid, homemade turn of speech. When
one watches some tired hack on the platform mechanically repeating the familiar phrases—*bestial atrocities, iron heel, blood-
stained tyranny, free peoples of the world, stand shoulder to
shoulder*—one often has a curious feeling that one is not watching
a live human being but some kind of dummy: a feeling which
suddenly becomes stronger at moments when the light catches
the speaker's spectacles and turns them into blank discs which
seem to have no eyes behind them. And this is not altogether
fanciful. A speaker who uses that kind of phraseology has gone
some distance toward turning himself into a machine. The appropriate noises are coming out of his larynx, but his brain is not
involved as it would be if he were choosing his words for himself. If the speech he is making is one that he is accustomed to
make over and over again, he may be almost unconscious of
what he is saying, as one is when one utters the responses in
church. And this reduced state of consciousness, if not indispensable, is at any rate favorable to political conformity.

13.   In our time, political speech and writing are largely the
defense of the indefensible. Things like the continuance of British rule in India, the Russian purges and deportations, the
dropping of the atom bombs on Japan, can indeed be defended,
but only by arguments which are too brutal for most people to
face, and which do not square with the professed aims of political parties. Thus political language has to consist largely of euphemism, question-begging and sheer cloudy vagueness.
Defenseless villages are bombarded from the air, the inhabitants
driven out into the countryside, the cattle machine-gunned, the
huts set on fire with incendiary bullets: this is called *pacification.*
Millions of peasants are robbed of their farms and sent trudging
along the roads with no. more than they can carry: this is called
transfer of population or *rectification of frontiers.* People are imprisoned for years without trial, or shot in the back of the neck or
sent to die of scurvy in Arctic lumber camps: this is called *elimination of unreliable elements.* Such phraseology is needed if one
wants to name things without calling up mental pictures of them.
Consider for instance some comfortable English professor defending Russian totalitarianism. He cannot say outright, "I believe in killing off your opponents when you can get good results

by doing so." Probably, therefore, he will say something like this:

"While freely conceding that the Soviet régime exhibits certain features which the humanitarian may be inclined to deplore, we must, I think, agree that a certain curtailment of the right to political opposition is an unavoidable concomitant of transitional periods, and that the rigors which the Russian people have been called upon to undergo have been amply justified in the sphere of concrete achievement."

14.   The inflated style is itself a kind of euphemism. A mass of Latin words falls upon the facts like soft snow, blurring the outlines and covering up all the details. The great enemy of clear language is insincerity. When there is a gap between one's real and one's declared aims, one turns as it were instinctively to long words and exhausted idioms, like a cuttlefish squirting out ink. In our age there is no such thing as "keeping out of politics." All issues are political issues, and politics itself is a mass of lies, evasions, folly, hatred, and schizophrenia. When the general atmosphere is bad, language must suffer. I should expect to find— this is a guess which I have not sufficient knowledge to verify— that the German, Russian and Italian languages have all deteriorated in the last ten or fifteen years, as a result of dictatorship.

15.   But if thought corrupts language, language can also corrupt thought. A bad usage can spread by tradition and imitation, even among people who should and do know better. The debased language that I have been discussing is in some ways very convenient. Phrases like *a not unjustifiable assumption, leaves much to be desired, would serve no good purpose, a consideration which we should do well to bear in mind,* are a continuous temptation, a packet of aspirins always at one's elbow. Look back through this essay, and for certain you will find that I have again and again committed the very faults I am protesting against. By this morning's post I have received a pamphlet dealing with conditions in Germany. The author tells me that he "felt impelled" to write it. I open it at random, and here is almost the first sentence that I see: "[The Allies] have an opportunity not only of achieving a radical transformation of Germany's social and political structure in such a way as to avoid a nationalistic reaction in Germany itself, but at the same time of laying the foundations of a co-operative and unified Europe." You see, he "feels impelled" to write—feels, presumably, that he has something new to say—and yet his

words, like cavalry horses answering the bugle, group themselves automatically into the familiar dreary pattern. This invasion of one's mind by ready-made phrases (*lay the foundations,
achieve a radical transformation*) can only be prevented if one is
constantly on guard against them, and every such phrase anaes-
thetizes a portion of one's brain.

16.   I said earlier that the decadence of our language is
probably curable. Those who deny this would argue, if they produced an argument at all, that language merely reflects existing
social conditions, and that we cannot influence its development
by any direct tinkering with words and constructions. So far as
the general tone or spirit of a language goes, this may be true,
but it is not true in detail. Silly words and expressions have often
disappeared, not through any evolutionary process but owing to
the conscious action of a minority. Two recent examples were
explore every avenue and *leave no stone unturned*, which were
killed by the jeers of a few journalists. There is a long list of
flyblown metaphors which could similarly be got rid of if enough
people would interest themselves in the job; and it should also
be possible to laugh the *not un-* formation out of existence,* to
reduce the amount of Latin and Greek in the average sentence, to
drive out foreign phrases and strayed scientific words, and, in
general, to make pretentiousness unfashionable. But all these are
minor points. The defense of the English language implies more
than this, and perhaps it is best to start by saying what it does
not imply.

17.   To begin with it has nothing to do with archaism, with
the salvaging of obsolete words and turns of speech, or with the
setting up of a "standard English" which must never be departed
from. On the contrary, it is especially concerned with the scrap-
ping of every word or idiom which has outworn its usefulness. It
has nothing to do with correct grammar and syntax, which are of
no importance so long as one makes one's meaning clear, or with
the avoidance of Americanisms, or with having what is called a
"good prose style." On the other hand it is not concerned with
fake simplicity and the attempt to make written English colloquial. Nor does it even imply in every case preferring the Saxon
word to the Latin one, though it does imply using the fewest and
shortest words that will cover one's meaning. What is above all

---

* One can cure oneself of the *not un-* formation by memorizing this sentence: *A not unblack
dog was chasing a not unsmall rabbit across a not ungreen field.*

needed is to let the meaning choose the word, and not the other way about. In prose, the worst thing one can do with words is to surrender to them. When you think of a concrete object, you think wordlessly, and then, if you want to describe the thing you have been visualizing you probably hunt about till you find the exact words that seem to fit it. When you think of something abstract you are more inclined to use words from the start, and unless you make a conscious effort to prevent it, the existing dialect will come rushing in and do the job for you, at the expense of blurring or even changing your meaning. Probably it is better to put off using words as long as possible and get one's meaning as clear as one can through pictures or sensations. Afterward one can choose—not simply *accept*—the phrases that will best cover the meaning, and then switch round and decide what impression one's words are likely to make on another person. This last effort of the mind cuts out all stale or mixed images, all prefabricated phrases, needless repetitions, and humbug and vagueness generally. But one can often be in doubt about the effect of a word or a phrase, and one needs rules that one can rely on when instinct fails. I think the following rules will cover most cases:

(i) Never use a metaphor, simile, or other figure of speech which you are used to seeing in print.
(ii) Never use a long word where a short one will do.
(iii) If it is possible to cut a word out, always cut it out.
(iv) Never use the passive where you can use the active.
(v) Never use a foreign phrase, a scientific word, or a jargon word if you can think of an everyday English equivalent.
(vi) Break any of these rules sooner than say anything outright barbarous.

These rules sound elementary, and so they are, but they demand a deep change of attitude in anyone who has grown used to writing in the style now fashionable. One could keep all of them and still write bad English, but one could not write the kind of stuff that I quoted in those five specimens at the beginning of this article.
18.   I have not here been considering the literary use of language, but merely language as an instrument for expressing and not for concealing or preventing thought. Stuart Chase and others have come near to claiming that all abstract words are

meaningless, and have used this as a pretext for advocating a kind of political quietism. Since you don't know what Fascism is, how can you struggle against Fascism? One need not swallow such absurdities as this, but one ought to recognize that the present political chaos is connected with the decay of language, and that one can probably bring about some improvement by starting at the verbal end. If you simplify your English, you are freed from the worst follies of orthodoxy. You cannot speak any of the necessary dialects, and when you make a stupid remark its stupidity will be obvious, even to yourself. Political language—and with variations this is true of all political parties, from Conservatives to Anarchists—is designed to make lies sound truthful and murder respectable, and to give an appearance of solidity to pure wind. One cannot change this all in a moment, but one can at least change one's own habits, and from time to time one can even, if one jeers loudly enough, send some worn-out and useless phrase—some *jackboot, Achilles' heel, hotbed, melting pot, acid test, veritable inferno,* or other lump of verbal refuse—into the dustbin where it belongs.

DISCUSSION: FAULTY DICTION

Diction can be faulty for the same reasons sentences are: imprecision, inflation, inappropriateness. These faults sometimes arise, as Orwell points out, because the writer wishes to disguise his thoughts and intentions. They also arise when, in seeking to avoid the looseness that can be found in speech, we depart too far from the usual speech patterns. The following suggestions may help you avoid awkward, monotonous, or overloaded sentences:

1. Needless repetition of a word can be awkward and monotonous; it may also be confusing if the word is used to express a different meaning each time it occurs:

   We entertained a motion to provide entertainment and food for the guests.

2. Trying to avoid repeating a word in the same sentence can lead to confusion or misunderstanding:

   The person who entered the room was not the individual we were expecting.

   Individual is a common synonym for *person,* but there is no reason to avoid using *person* a second time. Since *individual* has other meanings, the reader may think we intend one of these. H. W. Fowler calls needless substitution of this kind "elegant variation."

3. The following sentence contains deadwood—needless repetition and words and phrases for which there are simple, precise equivalents:

> There are necessary skills a writer needs to make his ideas easy to grasp and comprehensible to each and every reader.

4. Euphemism is a mild substitute for a possibly shocking or offensive or blunt expression. Readers of Victorian novels routinely decipher such euphemisms as *ruined* and *betrayed* as descriptions of certain women; these readers, in turn, employ euphemisms that people fifty years from now will have to decipher. (We still use *limbs* to refer to women's legs without realizing that the word was originally a euphemism; some know they are employing euphemism when asking for *white meat* when chicken is on the table). We may employ euphemism to avoid giving offense. In a recent film offended children complain, "Momma! You went out with a *garbage man?*" This useful, but often despised, occupation may seem a little more desirable if any of the standard, and sometimes absurd, euphemisms are substituted for garbage man: *janitor, custodian, sanitary engineer.* The last of these can be confused with other occupations. And confusion and pain result when unspecified qualities are made to seem sinister or contemptible by being left unnamed, as in the widely-used term *exceptional* to describe certain kinds of children. But are the words *slow* and *retarded* kinder to the less intelligent child or to the mentally deficient? What words should be used in speaking to them or about them? There is no easy advice to give: the writer must be as honest, and at the same time as considerate of feelings, as he can.

5. Euphemisms and other substitutions are sometimes called *genteelisms:*

> By *genteelism* is here to be understood the substituting for the ordinary natural word that first suggests itself to the mind, of a synonym that is thought to be less soiled by the lips of the common herd, less familiar, less plebian, less vulgar, less improper, less apt to come unhandsomely betwixt the wind and our nobility.—H. W. Fowler, *Modern English Usage*

Fowler cites the following: *peruse* for *read, hither* for *here, inquire* for *ask.* Usage determines what is pretentious, and usage has made some genteelisms cited by Fowler routine today: *assist* for *help, stomach* for *belly, proceed* for *go, place* for *put.*

6. Clichés and bromides rob prose of conviction and vigor. A cliché is a phrase or saying that once may have been original and startling but has become trite through overuse: *honey of a girl, sweet as sugar, conspicuous by his absence, more sinned against than sin-*

ning. A bromide is a dull platitude thought to be comforting: *It's the effort that counts, not the winning.*

7. Mixed metaphors can make sentences unintentionally comic:

> Blows to one's pride stick in the craw.

8. Foreign expressions like *distingué* (for *distinguished* or *well-bred*) can be pretentious when standard English words would serve as well.

9. Overlapping words will obscure the meaning of a sentence. Fowler cites this example:

> The *effect* of the tax is not likely to be *productive* of much real damage.

The italicized words mean the same thing.

10. Awkwardness may result when we needlessly avoid splitting infinitives, ending sentences with prepositions, or opening them with *but* and *and;* Fowler refers to these "rules" as superstitions and fetishes. Formal and informal English sentences have ended with prepositions and will contine to do so—and opened with *and* and *but.* The following sentence comes about because the writer wishes not to break a rule:

> That's the ladder up which I climbed.

No one would speak such a sentence, but sentences like it are written. Similarly, we must sometimes split the infinitive. Note the effect of avoiding the split in the following sentence—ambiguity:

> Our object is further to cement trade relations. [cited by Fowler]

The ear must be the guide in most instances; a sensible practice is not to split the infinitive with long modifiers.

QUESTIONS

1. How do the passages cited by Orwell in paragraph 3 help to explain the statement in paragraph 4 that "the concrete melts into the abstract"?

2. What visual image did *iron resolution* in paragraph 5 originally convey? What other dead metaphors can you cite, and what was their original significance? What current meanings of *rift* seem to have originated in metaphor?

3. Among the characteristic phrases cited in paragraph 6, Orwell might have included *in terms of.* Compare the following:

> He explained his failure in terms of his attitude toward school.

Einstein was a creative thinker in physics because he thought in terms of mathematics instead of mystical concepts.

In which sentence is the phrase used less awkwardly, and why?

4. Use several of the words cited in the second to last sentence of paragraph 7 in two or three sentences of your own. Then rewrite the sentences, substituting "English words that will cover one's meaning."

5. Why is the passage cited in the footnote to paragraph 8 "almost completely lacking in meaning"? Given Orwell's criticisms in paragraph 8, what would be the proper use of language in art criticism?

6. Do you agree with Orwell's statement in paragraph 8 that the use of words for which there is "no agreed definition" usually indicates dishonesty?

7. Compare the passage from *Ecclesiastes* quoted in paragraph 9 (King James Version) with modern renderings of it. Do you think these modern renderings are superior to Orwell's parody or to the King James version? Why?

8. "If you or I were told to write a few lines on the uncertainty of human fortunes," why would the writing come nearer to Orwell's parody than to the sentence from *Ecclesiastes?*

9. Why should dictation promote the Latinized style Orwell criticizes in paragraph 11? What examples of such a style do you find in the letter column of your daily newspaper?

10. Given the assumptions Orwell makes in the whole essay, why are all issues "political issues"?

11. Orwell states in paragraph 15: "Look back through this essay, and for certain you will find that I have again and again committed the very faults I am protesting against." Has he?

12. Orwell says in paragraph 17 that his concern has not been to promote a "standard English" or "to make written English colloquial." Explain what he means here. Has he not recommended the use of plain English words? What exceptions would he allow?

13. Rewrite the following sentences to eliminate the faults in diction:
    a. Once you have heard him speak in his highly unorthodox manner, his grating rasping voice and his often repeated phrases that are hackneyed, you will never forget him.
    b. His version of the story was not the rendering we had heard a week before.
    c. He has more regard for his honor than he has respect for money.
    d. There is a not uncommon way of expressing that idea.
    e. He had unfortunate luck in dealing with the man who owned the premises where he lived and to whom he paid rent.
    f. There is no candy in the jar there.

g. He is the man with whom she came with.
h. A free economy is the linchpin on which a progressive tariff policy must be built.
i. The result of the conference is certain to effect a change in the present tariff policy.

WRITING ASSIGNMENTS

Analyze a paragraph from the catalog of your college or university to discover its tone and judge the writing according to the criteria Orwell proposes.

Analyze a letter to the editor of a newspaper or magazine and indicate the impression the writer wishes to create of himself, the qualities of the prose, and the virtues or defects of the letter.

Analyze three paragraphs from a current textbook in one of your courses to determine how much needless jargon is employed and how well the writing meets the standard of good writing Orwell proposes.

Analyze a published speech of a major political figure (see *The New York Times* or *Vital Speeches* or *Congressional Record*). How honest is the use of language? Compare this speech with another by the same person. How consistent is he in his use of language?

the
whole
essay

THE
ORDERING
OF
IDEAS

THESIS

Peggy and Pierre Streit
A WELL IN INDIA

1.   The hot dry season in India. . . . A corrosive wind drives rivulets of sand across the land; torpid animals stand at the edge of dried-up water holes. The earth is cracked and in the rivers the sluggish, falling waters have exposed the sludge of the mud flats. Throughout the land the thoughts of men turn to water. And in the village of Rampura these thoughts are focused on the village well.

2.   It is a simple concrete affair, built upon the hard earth worn by the feet of five hundred villagers. It is surmounted by a wooden structure over which ropes, tied to buckets, are lowered to the black, placid depths twenty feet below. Fanning out from the well are the huts of the villagers—their walls white from sun, their thatched roofs thick with dust blown in from the fields.

3.   At the edge of the well is a semi-circle of earthen pots and, crouched at some distance behind them, a woman. She is an untouchable—a sweeper in Indian parlance—a scavenger of the village. She cleans latrines, disposes of dead animals and washes drains. She also delivers village babies, for this—like all her work—is considered unclean by most of village India.

4.   Her work—indeed, her very presence—is considered polluting, and since there is no well for untouchables in Rampura, her water jars must be filled by upper-caste villagers.

5.   There are dark shadows under her eyes and the flesh has fallen away from her neck, for she, like her fellow outcastes, is at the end of a bitter struggle. And if, in her narrow world, shackled by tradition and hemmed in by poverty, she had been unaware of the power of the water of the well at whose edge she waits—she knows it now.

6.   Shanti, 30 years old, has been deserted by her husband, and supports her three children. Like her ancestors almost as far

back as history records, she has cleaned the refuse from village huts and lanes. Hers is a life of inherited duties as well as inherited rights. She serves, and her work calls for payment of one chapatty—a thin wafer of unleavened bread—a day from each of the thirty families she cares for.

7.   But this is the hiatus between harvests; the oppressive lull before the burst of monsoon rains; the season of flies and dust, heat and disease, querulous voices and frayed tempers— and the season of want. There is little food in Rampura for anyone, and though Shanti's chores have continued as before, she has received only six chapatties a day for her family—starvation wages.

8.   Ten days ago she revolted. Driven by desperation, she defied an elemental law of village India. She refused to make her sweeper's rounds—refused to do the work tradition and religion had assigned her. Shocked at her audacity, but united in desperation, the village's six other sweeper families joined in her protest.

9.   Word of her action spread quickly across the invisible line that separates the untouchables' huts from the rest of the village. As the day wore on and the men returned from the fields, they gathered at the well—the heart of the village—and their voices rose, shrill with outrage: a *sweeper* defying them all! Shanti, a sweeper *and* a woman challenging a system that had prevailed unquestioned for centuries! Their indignation spilled over. It was true, perhaps, that the sweepers had not had their due. But that was no fault of the upper caste. No fault of theirs that sun and earth and water had failed to produce the food by which they could fulfill their obligations. So, to bring the insurgents to heel, they employed their ultimate weapon; the earthern water jars of the village untouchables would remain empty until they returned to work. For the sweepers of Rampura the well had run dry.

10.   No water: thirst, in the heat, went unslaked. The embers of the hearth were dead, for there was no water for cooking. The crumbling walls of outcaste huts went untended, for there was no water for repairs. There was no fuel, for the fires of the village were fed with dung mixed with water and dried. The dust and the sweat and the filth of their lives congealed on their skins and there it stayed, while life in the rest of the village— within sight of the sweepers—flowed on.

11.   The day began and ended at the well. The men, their dhotis wrapped about their loins, congregated at the water's edge in the hushed post-dawn, their small brass water jugs in hand, their voices mingling in quiet conversation as they rinsed their bodies and brushed their teeth. The buffaloes were watered, their soft muzzles lingering in the buckets before they were driven off to the fields. Then came the women, their brass pots atop their heads, to begin the ritual of water drawing: the careful lowering of the bucket in the well, lest it come loose from the rope; the gratifying splash as it touched the water; the maneuvering to make it sink; the squeal of rope against wooden pulley as it ascended. The sun rose higher. Clothes were beaten clean on the rocks surrounding the well as the women gossiped. A traveler from a near-by road quenched his thirst from a villager's urn. Two little boys, hot and bored, dropped pebbles into the water and waited for their hollow splash, far below.

12.   As the afternoon wore on and the sun turned orange through the dust, the men came back from the fields. They doused the parched, cracked hides of their water buffaloes and murmured contentedly, themselves, as the water coursed over their own shoulders and arms. And finally, as twilight closed in, came the evening procession of women, stately, graceful, their bare feet moving smoothly over the earth, their full skirts swinging about their ankles, the heavy brass pots once again balanced on their heads.

13.   The day was ended and life was as it always was—almost. Only the fetid odor of accumulated refuse and the assertive buzz of flies attested to strife in the village. For, while tradition and religion decreed that sweepers must clean, it also ordained that the socially blessed must not. Refuse lay where it fell and rotted.

14.   The strain of the water boycott was beginning to tell on the untouchables. For two days they had held their own. But on the third their thin reserve of flesh had fallen away. Movements were slower; voices softer; minds dull. More and more the desultory conversation turned to the ordinary; the delicious memory of sliding from the back of a wallowing buffalo into a pond; the feel of bare feet in wet mud; the touch of fresh water on parched lips; the anticipation of monsoon rains.

15.   One by one the few tools they owned were sold for food. A week passed, and on the ninth day two sweeper children

were down with fever. On the tenth day Shanti crossed the path that separated outcaste from from upper caste and walked through familiar, winding alleyways to one of the huts she served.

16.   "Your time is near," she told the young, expectant mother. "Tell your man to leave his sickle home when he goes to the fields. I've had to sell mine." (It is the field sickle that cuts the cord of newborn babies in much of village India.) Shanti, the instigator of the insurrection, had resumed her ancestral duties; the strike was broken. Next morning, as ever, she waited at the well. Silently, the procession of upper-caste women approached. They filled their jars to the brim and without a word they filled hers.

17.   She lifted the urns to her head, steadied them, and started back to her quarters—back to a life ruled by the powers that still rule most of the world: not the power of atoms or electricity, nor the power of alliances or power blocs, but the elemental powers of hunger, of disease, of tradition—and of water.

DISCUSSION: THESIS

The thesis of an essay is its central or controlling idea, the proposition or chief argument—the point of the discussion. The topic sentence of a paragraph may be a full or partial statement of the controlling idea or an indication of the subject: the thesis is always a full statement. Where the thesis appears in the essay depends on what the writer assumes about the audience. If he knows the audience well and believes no introduction to the thesis is required, he may start the essay with a statement of it. The Federalist papers of Hamilton, Jay, and Madison often start in this way:

> A firm Union will be of the utmost moment to the peace and liberty of the States, as a barrier against domestic faction and insurrection.—Alexander Hamilton, *The Federalist* No. 9

> Among the numerous advantages promised by a well-constructed Union, none deserves to be more accurately developed than its tendency to break and control the violence of faction.—James Madison, *The Federalist* No. 10

If the subject is an unfamiliar one or the thesis would be difficult to understand without background and careful discussion, the writer may build to a preliminary or full statement of it—or perhaps reserve a full statement of it to the end of the essay. The following opening sentences state the subject of the essay only, the topics to be explored:

> Saints should always be judged guilty until they are proved in-
> nocent, but the tests that have to be applied to them are not, of
> course, the same in all cases. In Gandhi's case the questions one
> feels inclined to ask are: to what extent was Gandhi moved by
> vanity—by the consciousness of himself as a humble, naked old
> man, sitting on a praying mat and shaking empires by sheer spiritual
> power—and to what extent did he compromise his own principles
> by entering politics, which of their nature are inseparable from coer-
> cion and fraud?—George Orwell, "Reflections on Gandhi"

Important terms need to be defined, attitudes clarified, and a climate of
opinion and the world of the essay's subject portrayed before the thesis
can be stated fully.

In some essays the writer leads the reader to draw conclusions from
the details provided and their presentation. In these instances the
thesis is said to be *implicit*.

Rhetorical considerations—that is, considerations of audience and
the most effective ways of making ideas understandable and convincing—have much to do with the placing of the thesis, as well as with
the ways main ideas are distinguished from subordinate ones. Such
considerations also influence the uses made of the beginning and the
ending of the essay, its tone and transitions, its order of ideas, and its
unity and style. The rhetoric of the paragraph thus is relevant to the
essay.

QUESTIONS

1. The authors build to a statement of the thesis at the end of paragraph 5. Why is it necessary to portray the world of the untouchable
   before stating the thesis?
2. Where in the essay is the thesis restated? Is the restatement more in-
   formative or detailed than the original statement of it?
3. What is the attitude of the authors toward the world they portray and
   the fate of Shanti? Do they seem to be taking sides?
4. Is it important to the thesis that Shanti is a woman? Are the authors
   concerned with her as a woman, in addition to their concern for her
   as an untouchable?
5. Is the concern of the essay equally with the power of water and the
   power of tradition? Or are these considerations subordinate to the
   portrayal of the untouchable and the courage shown?
6. Are we given a motive directly for what Shanti does—or is the motive
   implied?
7. How are transitions made through the seventeen short paragraphs?

WRITING ASSIGNMENT

Develop an idea relating to the power of tradition and illustrate it from personal observation. Provide enough background so that your reader understands why the tradition is important to the people who observe it.

George Orwell
SHOOTING AN ELEPHANT

1.   In Moulmein, in lower Burma, I was hated by large numbers of people—the only time in my life that I have been important enough for this to happen to me. I was sub-divisional police officer of the town, and in an aimless, petty kind of way anti-European feeling was very bitter. No one had the guts to raise a riot, but if a European woman went through the bazaars alone somebody would probably spit betel juice over her dress. As a police officer I was an obvious target and was baited whenever it seemed safe to do so. When a nimble Burman tripped me up on the football field and the referee (another Burman) looked the other way, the crowd yelled with hideous laughter. This happened more than once. In the end the sneering yellow faces of young men that met me everywhere, the insults hooted after me when I was at a safe distance, got badly on my nerves. The young Buddhist priests were the worst of all. There were several thousands of them in the town and none of them seemed to have anything to do except stand on street corners and jeer at Europeans.

2.   All this was perplexing and upsetting. For at that time I had already made up my mind that imperialism was an evil thing and the sooner I chucked up my job and got out of it the better. Theoretically—and secretly, of course—I was all for the Burmese and all against their oppressors, the British. As for the job I was doing, I hated it more bitterly than I can perhaps make clear. In a job like that you see the dirty work of Empire at close quarters.

The wretched prisoners huddling in the stinking cages of the lock-ups, the gray, cowed faces of the long-term convicts, the scarred buttocks of the men who had been flogged with bamboos—all these oppressed me with an intolerable sense of guilt. But I could get nothing into perspective. I was young and ill educated and I had had to think out my problems in the utter silence that is imposed on every Englishman in the East. I did not even know that the British Empire is dying, still less did I know that it is a great deal better than the younger empires that are going to supplant it. All I knew was that I was stuck between my hatred of the empire I served and my rage against the evil-spirited little beasts who tried to make my job impossible. With one part of my mind I thought of the British Raj as an unbreakable tyranny, as something clamped down, in *saecula saeculorum,* upon the will of prostrate peoples; with another part I thought that the greatest joy in the world would be to drive a bayonet into a Buddhist priest's guts. Feelings like these are the normal by-products of imperialism; ask any Anglo-Indian official, if you can catch him off duty.

3.   One day something happened which in a roundabout way was enlightening. It was a tiny incident in itself, but it gave me a better glimpse than I had had before of the real nature of imperialism—the real motives for which despotic governments act. Early one morning the sub-inspector at a police station the other end of the town rang me up on the 'phone and said that an elephant was ravaging the bazaar. Would I please come and do something about it? I did not know what I could do, but I wanted to see what was happening and I got on to a pony and started out. I took my rifle, an old .44 Winchester and much too small to kill an elephant, but I thought the noise might be useful *in terrorem.* Various Burmans stopped me on the way and told me about the elephant's doings. It was not, of course, a wild elephant, but a tame one which had gone "must." It had been chained up, as tame elephants always are when their attack of "must" is due, but on the previous night it had broken its chain and escaped. Its mahout, the only person who could manage it when it was in that state, had set out in pursuit, but had taken the wrong direction and was now twelve hours' journey away, and in the morning the elephant had suddenly reappeared in the town. The Burmese population had no weapons and were quite helpless against it. It had already destroyed somebody's bamboo

hut, killed a cow and raided some fruit-stalls and devoured the stock; also it had met the muncipal rubbish van and, when the driver jumped out and took to his heels, had turned the van over and inflicted violences upon it.

4.　　The Burmese sub-inspector and some Indian constables were waiting for me in the quarter where the elephant had been seen. It was a very poor quarter, a labyrinth of squalid bamboo huts, thatched with palm-leaf, winding all over a steep hillside. I remember that it was a cloudy, stuffy morning at the beginning of the rains. We began questioning the people as to where the elephant had gone and, as usual, failed to get any definite information. That is invariably the case in the East; a story always sounds clear enough at a distance, but the nearer you get to the scene of events the vaguer it becomes. Some of the people said that the elephant had gone in one direction, some said that he had gone in another, some professed not even to have heard of any elephant. I had almost made up my mind that the whole story was a pack of lies, when we heard yells a little distance away. There was a loud, scandalized cry of "Go away, child! Go away this instant!" and an old woman with a switch in her hand came round the corner of a hut, violently shooing away a crowd of naked children. Some more women followed, clicking their tongues and exclaiming; evidently there was something that the children ought not to have seen. I rounded the hut and saw a man's dead body sprawling in the mud. He was an Indian, a black Dravidian coolie, almost naked, and he could not have been dead many minutes. The people said that the elephant had come suddenly upon him round the corner of the hut, caught him with its trunk, put its foot on his back and ground him into the earth. This was the rainy season and the ground was soft, and his face had scored a trench a foot deep and a couple of yards long. He was lying on his belly with arms crucified and head sharply twisted to one side. His face was coated with mud, the eyes wide open, the teeth bared and grinning with an expression of unendurable agony. (Never tell me, by the way, that the dead look peaceful. Most of the corpses I have seen looked devilish.) The friction of the great beast's foot had stripped the skin from his back as neatly as one skins a rabbit. As soon as I saw the dead man I sent an orderly to a friend's house nearby to borrow an elephant rifle. I had already sent back the pony, not wanting it to go mad with fright and throw me if it smelt the elephant.

5.   The orderly came back in a few minutes with a rifle and five cartridges, and meanwhile some Burmans had arrived and told us that the elephant was in the paddy fields below, only a few hundred yards away. As I started forward practically the whole population of the quarter flocked out of the houses and followed me. They had seen the rifle and were all shouting excitedly that I was going to shoot the elephant. They had not shown much interest in the elephant when he was merely ravaging their homes, but it was different now that he was going to be shot. It was a bit of fun to them, as it would be to an English crowd; besides they wanted the meat. It made me vaguely uneasy. I had no intention of shooting the elephant—I had merely sent for the rifle to defend myself if necessary—and it is always unnerving to have a crowd following you. I marched down the hill, looking and feeling a fool, with the rifle over my shoulder and an ever-growing army of people jostling at my heels. At the bottom, when you got away from the huts, there was a metalled road and beyond that a miry waste of paddy fields a thousand yards across, not yet ploughed but soggy from the first rains and dotted with coarse grass. The elephant was standing eight yards from the road, his left side toward us. He took not the slightest notice of the crowd's approach. He was tearing up bunches of grass, beating them against his knees to clean them, and stuffing them into his mouth.

6.   I had halted on the road. As soon as I saw the elephant I knew with perfect certainty that I ought not to shoot him. It is a serious matter to shoot a working elephant—it is comparable to destroying a huge and costly piece of machinery—and obviously one ought not to do it if it can possibly be avoided. And at that distance, peacefully eating, the elephant looked no more dangerous than a cow. I thought then and I think now that his attack of "must" was already passing off; in which case he would merely wander harmlessly about until the mahout came back and caught him. Moreover, I did not in the least want to shoot him. I decided that I would watch him for a little while to make sure that he did not turn savage again, and then go home.

7.   But at that moment I glanced round at the crowd that had followed me. It was an immense crowd, two thousand at the least and growing every minute. It blocked the road for a long distance on either side. I looked at the sea of yellow faces above the garish clothes—faces all happy and excited over this bit of fun, all cer-

tain that the elephant was going to be shot. They were watching me as they would watch a conjurer about to perform a trick. They did not like me, but with the magical rifle in my hands I was momentarily worth watching. And suddenly I realized that I should have to shoot the elephant after all. The people expected it of me and I had got to do it; I could feel their two thousand wills pressing me forward, irresistibly. And it was at this moment, as I stood there with the rifle in my hands, that I first grasped the hollowness, the futility of the white man's dominion in the East. Here was I, the white man with his gun, standing in front of the unarmed native crowd—seemingly the leading actor of the piece; but in reality I was only an absurd puppet pushed to and fro by the will of those yellow faces behind. I perceived in this moment that when the white man turns tyrant it is his own freedom that he destroys. He becomes a sort of hollow, posing dummy, the conventionalized figure of a sahib. For it is the condition of his rule that he shall spend his life in trying to impress the "natives," and so in every crisis he has got to do what the "natives" expect of him. He wears a mask, and his face grows to fit it. I had got to shoot the elephant. I had committed myself to doing it when I sent for the rifle. A sahib has got to act like a sahib; he has got to appear resolute, to know his own mind and do definite things. To come all that way, rifle in hand, with two thousand people marching at my heels, and then to trail feebly away, having done nothing—no, that was impossible. The crowd would laugh at me. And my whole life, every white man's life in the East, was one long struggle not to be laughed at.

8.   But I did not want to shoot the elephant. I watched him beating his bunch of grass against his knees with that preoccupied grandmotherly air that elephants have. It seemed to me that it would be murder to shoot him. At that age I was not squeamish about killing animals, but I had never shot an elephant and never wanted to. (Somehow it always seems worse to kill a *large* animal.) Besides, there was the beast's owner to be considered. Alive, the elephant was worth at least a hundred pounds; dead, he would only be worth the value of his tusks, five pounds, possibly. But I had got to act quickly. I turned to some experienced-looking Burmans who had been there when we arrived, and asked them how the elephant had been behaving. They all said the same thing: he took no notice of you if you left him alone, but he might charge if you went too close to him.

9.   It was perfectly clear to me what I ought to do. I ought to walk up to within, say, twenty-five yards of the elephant and test his behavior. If he charged, I could shoot; if he took no notice of me, it would be safe to leave him until the mahout came back. But also I knew that I was going to do no such thing. I was a poor shot with a rifle and the ground was soft mud into which one would sink at every step. If the elephant charged and I missed him, I should have about as much chance as a toad under a steam-roller. But even then I was not thinking particularly of my own skin, only of the watchful yellow faces behind. For at that moment, with the crowd watching me, I was not afraid in the ordinary sense, as I would have been if I had been alone. A white man mustn't be frightened in front of "natives"; and so, in general, he isn't frightened. The sole thought in my mind was that if anything went wrong those two thousand Burmans would see me pursued, caught, trampled on, and reduced to a grinning corpse like that Indian up the hill. And if that happened it was quite probable that some of them would laugh. That would never do. There was only one alternative. I shoved the cartridges into the magazine and lay down on the road to get a better aim.

10.   The crowd grew very still, and a deep, low, happy sigh, as of people who see the theater curtain go up at last, breathed from innumerable throats. They were going to have their bit of fun after all. The rifle was a beautiful German thing with cross-hair sights. I did not then know that in shooting an elephant one would shoot to cut an imaginary bar running from ear-hole to ear-hole. I ought, therefore, as the elephant was sideways on, to have aimed straight at his ear-hole; actually I aimed several inches in front of this, thinking the brain would be further forward.

11.   When I pulled the trigger I did not hear the bang or feel the kick—one never does when a shot goes home—but I heard the devilish roar of glee that went up from the crowd. In that instant, in too short a time, one would have thought, even for the bullet to get there, a mysterious, terrible change had come over the elephant. He neither stirred nor fell, but every line of his body had altered. He looked suddenly stricken, shrunken, immensely old, as though the frightful impact of the bullet had paralyzed him without knocking him down. At last, after what seemed a long time—it might have been five seconds, I dare say—he sagged flabbily to his knees. His mouth slobbered. An

enormous senility seemed to have settled upon him. One could have imagined him thousands of years old. I fired again into the same spot. At the second shot he did not collapse but climbed with desperate slowness to his feet and stood weakly upright, with legs sagging and head drooping. I fired a third time. That was the shot that did for him. You could see the agony of it jolt his whole body and knock the last remnant of strength from his legs. But in falling he seemed for a moment to rise, for as his hind legs collapsed beneath him he seemed to tower upward like a huge rock toppling, his trunk reaching skyward like a tree. He trumpeted, for the first and only time. And then down he came, his belly toward me, with a crash that seemed to shake the ground even where I lay.

12.   I got up. The Burmans were already racing past me across the mud. It was obvious that the elephant would never rise again, but he was not dead. He was breathing very rhythmically with long rattling gasps, his great mound of a side painfully rising and falling. His mouth was wide open—I could see far down into caverns of pale pink throat. I waited a long time for him to die, but his breathing did not weaken. Finally I fired my two remaining shots into the spot where I thought his heart must be. The thick blood welled out of him like red velvet, but still he did not die. His body did not even jerk when the shots hit him, the tortured breathing continued without a pause. He was dying, very slowly and in great agony, but in some world remote from me where not even a bullet could damage him further. I felt that I had got to put an end to that dreadful noise. It seemed dreadful to see the great beast lying there, powerless to move and yet powerless to die, and not even to be able to finish him. I sent back for my small rifle and poured shot after shot into his heart and down his throat. They seemed to make no impression. The tortured gasps continued as steadily as the ticking of a clock.

13.   In the end I could not stand it any longer and went away. I heard later that it took him half an hour to die. Burmans were bringing dahs and baskets even before I left, and I was told they had stripped his body almost to the bones by the afternoon.

14.   Afterward, of course, there were endless discussions about the shooting of the elephant. The owner was furious, but he was only an Indian and could do nothing. Besides, legally I had done the right thing, for a mad elephant has to be killed, like a mad dog, if its owner fails to control it. Among the Europeans

opinion was divided. The older men said I was right, the younger men said it was a damn shame to shoot an elephant for killing a coolie, because an elephant was worth more than any damn Coringhee coolie. And afterward I was very glad that the coolie had been killed; it put me legally in the right and it gave me a sufficient pretext for shooting the elephant. I often wondered whether any of the others grasped that I had done it solely to avoid looking a fool.

QUESTIONS

1. Orwell states in paragraph 3: "One day something happened which in a roundabout way was enlightening. It was a tiny incident in itself, but it gave me a better glimpse than I had had before of the real nature of imperialism—the real motives for which despotic governments act." The incident, in all its particularity, reveals the psychology of the imperialist ruler. What effect do the atmosphere (the stuffy, cloudy weather) and the behavior of the Burmans and their attitude toward the elephant have on this psychology? Why is the dead coolie described in detail in paragraph 4? Why is the shooting of the elephant described in detail in paragraph 11? In general, how does the incident reveal the motives Orwell mentions?
2. The incident reveals more than just the motives of the imperialist ruler: it reveals much about mob and crisis psychology and the man in the middle. What does it reveal specifically?
3. Where in the essay is the thesis stated, and how do you account for its placement?
4. The exactness of the diction contributes greatly to the development of the thesis, for Orwell does not merely *tell* us, he makes us *see*. In paragraph 11, for example, he states: ". . . I heard the devilish roar of *glee* that went up from the crowd." He might have chosen *laughter, hilarity,* or *mirth* to describe the behavior of the crowd, but *glee* is the exact word because it connotes something that the other three words do not—malice. And the elephant "*sagged* flabbily to his knees," not *dropped* or *sank,* because *sagged* connotes weight and, in the context of the passage, age. What does Orwell mean in the same paragraph by "His mouth slobbered" and "An enormous senility seemed to have settled upon him"? In paragraph 12 why "*caverns* of pale pink throat" rather than *depths*? In paragraph 4 why is the corpse *grinning* rather than *smiling*? (Consult the synonym listings in your dictionary.)

WRITING ASSIGNMENT

Illustrate the last sentence of the essay from your own experience. Be careful to build to your climax—the moment when you acted to avoid looking like a fool. Make your reader see and feel what you saw and felt.

Eric Sevareid
VELVA, NORTH DAKOTA

1.   My home town has changed in these thirty years of the American story. It is changing now, will go on changing as America changes. Its biography, I suspect, would read much the same as that of all other home towns. Depression and war and prosperity have all left their marks; modern science, modern tastes, manners, philosophies, fears and ambitions have touched my town as indelibly as they have touched New York or Panama City.

2.   Sights have changed: there is a new precision about street and home, a clearing away of chicken yards, cow barns, pigeon-crested cupolas, weed lots and coulees, the dim and secret adult-free rendezvous of boys. An intricate metal "jungle gym" is a common backyard sight, the sack swing uncommon. There are wide expanses of clear windows designed to let in the parlor light, fewer ornamental windows of colored glass designed to keep it out. Attic and screen porch are slowly vanishing and lovely shades of pastel are painted upon new houses, tints that once would have embarrassed farmer and merchant alike.

3.   Sounds have changed; I heard not once the clopping of a horse's hoof, nor the mourn of a coyote. I heard instead the shriek of brakes, the heavy throbbing of the once-a-day Braniff airliner into Minot, the shattering sirens born of war, the honk of a diesel locomotive which surely cannot call to faraway places the heart of a wakeful boy like the old steam whistle in the night. You can walk down the streets of my town now and hear from

VELVA, NORTH DAKOTA: From *This Is Eric Sevareid* by Eric Sevareid. Copyright © 1964 by Eric Sevareid. Reprinted by permission of The Harold Matson Company Inc. Selection title by editor.

open windows the intimate voices of the Washington commentators in casual converse on the great affairs of state; but you cannot hear on Sunday morning the singing in Norwegian of the Lu-
theran hymns; the old country seems now part of a world left
long behind and the old-country accents grow fainter in the
speech of my Velva neighbors.

4.   The people have not changed, but the *kinds* of people
have changed: there is no longer an official, certified town drunk,
no longer a "Crazy John," spitting his worst epithet, "rotten
chicken legs," as you hurriedly passed him by. People so sick are
now sent to places of proper care. No longer is there an official
town joker, like the druggist MacKnight, who would spot a customer in the front of the store, have him called to the phone, then
slip to the phone behind the prescription case, and imitate the
man's wife to perfection with orders to bring home more bread
and sausage and Cream of Wheat. No longer anyone like the
early attorney, J. L. Lee, who sent fabulous dispatches to that
fabulous tabloid, the *Chicago Blade,* such as his story of the wild
man captured on the prairie and chained to the wall in the drugstore basement. (This, surely, was Velva's first notoriety; inquiries came from anthropologists all over the world.)

5.   No, the "characters" are vanishing in Velva, just as they
are vanishing in our cities, in business, in politics. The "well-
rounded, socially integrated" personality that the progressive
schoolteachers are so obsessed with is increasing rapidly, and I
am not at all sure that this is good. Maybe we need more personalities with knobs and handles and rugged lumps of individuality. They may not make life more smooth; more interesting
they surely make it.

6.   They eat differently in Velva now; there are frozen fruits
and sea food and exotic delicacies we only read about in novels
in those meat-and-potato days. They dress differently. The hard
white collars of the businessmen are gone with the shiny alpaca
coats. There are comfortable tweeds now, and casual blazers with
a touch in their colors of California, which seems so close in time
and distance.

7.   It is distance and time that have changed the most and
worked the deepest changes in Velva's life. The telephone, the
car, the smooth highway, radio and television are consolidating
the entities of our country. The county seat of Towner now seems
no closer than the state capital of Bismarck; the voices and con-

cerns of Presidents, French premiers and Moroccan pashas are no
farther away than the portable radio on Aunt Jessey's kitchen
table. The national news magazines are stacked each week in
Harold Anderson's drugstore beside the new soda fountain, and
the excellent *Minot Daily News* smells hot from the press each afternoon.

8.   Consolidation. The nearby hamlets of Sawyer and Logan
and Voltaire had their own separate banks and papers and
schools in my days of dusty buggies and Model Ts marooned in
the snowdrifts. Now these hamlets are dying. A bright yellow
bus takes the Voltaire kids to Velva each day for high school.
Velva has grown—from 800 to 1,300—because the miners from
the Truax coal mine can commute to their labors each morning
and the nearby farmers can live in town if they choose. Minot
has tripled in size to 30,000. Once the "Magic City" was a distant
and splendid Baghdad, visited on special occasions long prepared for. Now it is a twenty-five minute commuter's jump
away. So P. W. Miller and Jay Louis Monicken run their businesses in Minot but live on in their old family homes in Velva.
So Ray Michelson's two girls on his farm to the west drive up
each morning to their jobs as maids in Minot homes. Aunt Jessey
said, "Why, Saturday night I counted sixty-five cars just between
here and Sawyer, all going up to the show in Minot."

9.   The hills are prison battlements no longer; the prairies
no heart-sinking barrier, but a passageway free as the swelling
ocean, inviting you to sail home and away at your whim and
your leisure. (John and Helen made an easy little jaunt of 700
miles that weekend to see their eldest daughter in Wyoming.)

10.   Consolidation. Art Kumm's bank serves a big region
now; its assets are $2,000,000 to $3,000,000 instead of the $200,000
or $300,000 in my father's day. Eighteen farms near Velva are
under three ownerships now. They calculate in sections; "acres"
is an almost forgotten term. Aunt Jessey owns a couple of farms,
and she knows they are much better run. "It's no longer all take
out and no put in," she said. "Folks strip farm now; they know
all about fertilizers. They care for it and they'll hand on the land
in good shape." The farmers gripe about their cash income, and
not without reason at the moment, but they will admit that life is
good compared with those days of drought and foreclosure, ma-
nure banked against the house for warmth, the hand pump frozen at 30 below and the fitful kerosene lamp on the kitchen table.

Electrification has done much of this, eased back-breaking chores that made their wives old as parchment at forty, brought life and music and the sound of human voices into their parlors at night.

11.   And light upon the prairie. "From the hilltop," said Aunt Jessey, "the farms look like stars at night."

12.   Many politicians deplore the passing of the old family-size farm, but I am not so sure. I saw around Velva a release from what was like slavery to the tyrannical soil, release from the ignorance that darkens the soul and from the loneliness that corrodes it. In this generation my Velva friends have rejoined the general American society that their pioneering fathers left behind when they first made the barren trek in the days of the wheat rush. As I sit here in Washington writing this, I can feel their nearness. I never felt it before save in my dreams.

13.   But now I must ask myself: Are they nearer to one another? And the answer is no; yet I am certain that this is good. The shrinking of time and distance has made contrast and relief available to their daily lives. They do not know one another quite so well because they are not so much obliged to. I know that democracy rests upon social discipline, which in turn rests upon personal discipline; passions checked, hard words withheld, civic tasks accepted, work well done, accountings honestly rendered. The old-fashioned small town was this discipline in its starkest, most primitive form; without this discipline the small town would have blown itself apart.

14.   For personal and social neuroses festered under this hard scab of conformity. There was no place to go, no place to let off steam; few dared to voice unorthodox ideas, read strange books, admire esoteric art or publicly write or speak of their dreams and their soul's longings. The world was not "too much with us," the world was too little with us and we were too much with one another.

15.   The door to the world stands open now, inviting them to leave anytime they wish. It is the simple fact of the open door that makes all the difference; with its opening the stale air rushed out. So, of course, the people themselves do not have to leave, because, as the stale air went out, the fresh air came in.

16.   Human nature is everywhere the same. He who is not forced to help his neighbor for his own existence will not only give him help, but his true good will as well. Minot and its hospital are now close at hand, but the people of Velva put their

purses together, built their own clinic and homes for the two young doctors they persuaded to come and live among them. Velva has no organized charity, but when a farmer falls ill, his neighbors get in his crop; if a townsman has a financial catastrophe his personal friends raise a fund to help him out. When Bill's wife, Ethel, lay dying so long in the Minot hospital and nurses were not available, Helen and others took their turns driving up there just to sit with her so she would know in her gathering dark that friends were at hand.

17.   It is personal freedom that makes us better persons, and they are freer in Velva now. There is no real freedom without privacy, and a resident of my home town can be a private person much more than he could before. People are able to draw at least a little apart from one another. In drawing apart, they gave their best human instincts room for expansion.

QUESTIONS

1. Where does Sevareid indicate his attitude toward his home town? What is his thesis?
2. How does the selection of detail in the whole essay support the dominating impression Sevareid creates of the town in his opening paragraph? Is any of this detail unrelated to this dominant impression?
3. What is the tone of the comment on the story of the wild man, and how is it related to the thesis?
4. How does Sevareid emphasize the causes of the change in life in Velva? Does he indicate a main cause?
5. What does Sevareid mean by the statement that concludes paragraph 13, "without this discipline the small town would have blown itself apart"?
6. Sevareid points up a series of paradoxes toward the end. What are these, and what do they contribute to the tone of the conclusion?

WRITING ASSIGNMENTS

Analyze the shifts in tone and relate these to Sevareid's thesis. Analyze also how Sevareid introduces his thesis and keeps it before the reader.

Describe the changes that have occurred in the neighborhood in which you grew up and discuss the reasons for these changes.

James Thurber
THE TIGER WHO WOULD BE KING

One morning the tiger woke up in the jungle and told his mate that he was king of beasts.

"Leo, the lion, is king of beasts," she said.

"We need a change," said the tiger. "The creatures are crying for a change."

The tigress listened but she could hear no crying, except that of her cubs.

"I'll be king of beasts by the time the moon rises," said the tiger. "It will be a yellow moon with black stripes, in my honor."

"Oh, sure," said the tigress as she went to look after her young, one of whom, a male, very like his father, had got an imaginary thorn in his paw.

The tiger prowled through the jungle till he came to the lion's den. "Come out," he roared, "and greet the king of beasts! The king is dead, long live the king!"

Inside the den, the lioness woke her mate. "The king is here to see you," she said.

"What king?" he inquired, sleepily.

"The king of beasts," she said.

"I am the king of beasts," roared Leo, and he charged out of the den to defend his crown against the pretender.

It was a terrible fight, and it lasted until the setting of the sun. All the animals of the jungle joined in, some taking the side of the tiger and others the side of the lion. Every creature from the aardvark to the zebra took part in the struggle to overthrow the lion or to repulse the tiger, and some did not know which they were fighting for, and some fought for both, and some fought whoever was nearest, and some fought for the sake of fighting.

"What are we fighting for?" someone asked the aardvark.

"The old order," said the aardvark.

"What are we dying for?" someone asked the zebra.

"The new order," said the zebra.

When the moon rose, fevered and gibbous, it shone upon a jungle in which nothing stirred except a macaw and a cockatoo, screaming in horror. All the beasts were dead except the tiger, and his days were numbered and his time was ticking away. He was monarch of all he surveyed, but it didn't seem to mean anything.

MORAL: *You can't very well be king of beasts if there aren't any.*

James Thurber
THE WEAVER AND THE WORM

A weaver watched in wide-eyed wonder a silkworm spinning its cocoon in a white mulberry tree.

"Where do you get that stuff?" asked the admiring weaver.

"Do you want to make something out of it?" inquired the silkworm, eagerly.

Then the weaver and the silkworm went their separate ways, for each thought the other had insulted him. We live, man and worm, in a time when almost everything can mean almost anything, for this is the age of gobbledygook, doubletalk, and gudda.

MORAL: *A word to the wise is not sufficient if it doesn't make any sense.*

QUESTIONS

1. How does Thurber establish a voice in the two fables through his selection of detail and his diction? What other qualities help to suggest a voice?
2. The morals of these fables are a kind of thesis. What is the relation of the moral to the second fable? Is a particular word at issue? Why should the silkworm think he has been insulted?
3. To what extent does the humor of each fable depend on incongruity and exaggeration?

WRITING ASSIGNMENT

Analyze the sources of Thurber's humor in these fables. Give particular attention to his treatment of animals.

White

JT MYSELF

1.   I am a man of medium height. I keep my records in a Weis Folder Re-order Number 8003. The unpaid balance of my estimated tax for the year 1945 is item 3 less the sum of items 4 and 5. My eyes are gray. My Selective Service order number is 10789. The serial number is T1654. I am in Class IV-A, and have been variously in Class 3-A, Class I-A(H), and Class 4-H. My social security number is 067-01-9841. I am married to U.S. Woman Number 067-01-9807. Her eyes are gray. This is not a joint declaration, nor is it made by an agent; therefore it need be signed only by me—and, as I said, I am a man of medium height.

2.   I am the holder of a quit-claim deed recorded in Book 682, Page 501, in the county where I live. I hold Fire Insurance Policy Number 424747, continuing until the 23 day of October in the year nineteen hundred forty-five, at noon, and it is important that the written portions of all policies covering the same property read exactly alike. My cervical spine shows relatively good alignment with evidence of proliferative changes about the bodies consistent with early arthritis. (Essential clinical data: pain in neck radiating to mastoids and occipito-temporal region, not constant, moderately severe; patient in good general health and working.) My operator's licence is Number 16200. It expired December 31, 1943, more than a year ago, but I am still carrying it and it appears to be serving the purpose. I shall renew it when I get time. I have made, published, and declared my last will and testament, and it thereby revokes all other wills and codicils at any time heretofore made by me. I hold Basic A Mileage Ration 108950, O.P.A. Form R-525-C. The number of my car is 18-388. Tickets A-14 are valid through March 21st.

3.   I was born in District Number 5903, New York State. My birth is registered in Volume 3/58 of the Department of Health. My father was a man of medium height. His telephone number was 484. My mother was a housewife. Her eyes were blue. Neither parent had a social security number and neither was secure socially. They drove to the depot behind an unnumbered horse.

4.   I hold Individual Certificate Number 4320-209 with the Equitable Life Assurance Society, in which a corporation hereinafter called the employer has contracted to insure my life for the sum of two thousand dollars. My left front tire is Number 48KE8846, my right front tire is Number 63T6895. My rear tires are, from left to right, Number 6N4M5384 and Number A26E5806D. I brush my hair with Whiting-Adams Brush Number 010 and comb my hair with Pro-Phy-Lac-Tic Comb Number 1201. My shaving brush is sterilized. I take Pill Number 43934 after each meal and I can get more of them by calling ELdorado 5-6770. I spray my nose with De Vilbiss Atomizer Number 14. Sometimes I stop the pain with Squibb Pill, Control Number 3K49979 (aspirin). My wife (Number 067-01-9807) takes Pill Number 49345.

5.   I hold War Ration Book 40289EW, from which have been torn Airplane Stamps Numbers 1, 2, and 3. I also hold Book 159378CD, from which have been torn Spare Number 2, Spare Number 37, and certain other coupons. My wife holds Book 40288EW and Book 159374CD. In accepting them, she recognized that they remained the property of the United States Government.

6.   I have a black dog with cheeks of tan. Her number is 11032. It is an old number. I shall renew it when I get time. The analysis of her prepared food is guaranteed and is Case Number 1312. The ingredients are: Cereal Flaked feeds (from Corn, Rice, Bran, and Wheat), Meat Meal, Fish Liver and Glandular Meal, Soybean Oil Meal, Wheat Bran, Corn Germ Meal, 5% Kel-Centrate [containing Dried Skim Milk, Dehydrated Cheese, Vitamin B_1 (Thiamin), Flavin Concentrate, Carotene, Yeast, Vitamin A and D Feeding Oil (containing 3,000 U.S.P. units Vitamin A and 400 U.S.P. units Vitamin D per gram), Diastase (Enzyme), Wheat Germ Meal, Rice Polish Extract], 1½% Calcium Carbonate, .00037% Potassium Iodide, and ¼% Salt. She prefers offal.

7.   When I finish what I am now writing it will be late in the day. It will be about half past five. I will then take up Purchase Order Number 245-9077-B-Final, which I received this morning from the Office of War Information and which covers the use of certain material they want to translate into a foreign language. Attached to the order are Standard Form Number 1034 (white) and three copies of Standard Form Number 1034a (yellow), also "Instructions for Preparation of Voucher by Vendor and Example of Prepared Voucher." The Appropriation Symbol of the Purchase Order is 1153700.001-501. The requisition number is B-827.

The allotment is X5-207.1-R2-11. Voucher shall be prepared in ink, indelible pencil, or typewriter. For a while I will be vendor preparing voucher. Later on, when my head gets bad and the pain radiates, I will be voucher preparing vendor. I see that there is a list of twenty-one instructions which I will be following. Number One on the list is: "Name of payor agency as shown in the block 'appropriation symbol and title' in the upper left-hand corner of the Purchase Order." Number Five on the list is: "Vendor's personal account or invoice number," but whether that means Order Number 245-9077-B-Final, or Requisition B-827, or Allotment X5-207.1-R2-11, or Appropriation Symbol 1153700.001-501, I do not know, nor will I know later on in the evening after several hours of meditation, nor will I be able to find out by consulting Woman 067-01-9807, who is no better at filling out forms than I am, nor after taking Pill Number 43934, which tends merely to make me drowsy.

8.   I owe a letter to Corporal 32413654, Hq and Hq Sq., VII AAF S.C., APO 953, c/o PM San Francisco, Calif., thanking him for the necktie he sent me at Christmas. In 1918 I was a private in the Army. My number was 4,345,016. I was a boy of medium height. I had light hair. I had no absences from duty under G.O. 31, 1912, or G.O. 45, 1914. The number of that war was Number One.

QUESTIONS

1. E. B. White develops his thesis *implicitly*. Before we try to state the thesis, we shall have to consider the details and the nature of the presentation. Let us begin with paragraph 2. Why does White state "My cervical spine shows relatively good alignment with evidence of proliferative changes about the bodies consistent with early arthritis" instead of "I have the symptoms of arthritis"? Why does he provide the number of his fire insurance policy and paraphrase its language? Why in paragraph 3 does he say that neither of his parents was "secure socially" instead of "had much money"? And why does he tell us the number of the district in which he was born? On what aspect of his life does this detail focus?

2. How does the detail of paragraphs 2 and 3 resemble that of paragraph 1? What do the numbers and classifications, even the reorder number of his Weis folder, tell us about him? What do they *not* tell us? In short, what impression of him do they create?

3. Up to paragraph 6 White has been talking about himself. In para-

graph 6, however, he lists the ingredients of dogfood. Why does he? What is the implication of "She prefers offal"?

4. In the last paragraph why does White give the full address of the corporal and then indicate that he is writing to thank him for the necktie?

5. Why in the concluding paragraph does he repeat the fact that he "was a boy of medium height"? Why does he conclude the essay as he does? How serious is the tone of the last sentence? Is the tone of the essay as a whole serious? Is it humorous in any way?

6. State the thesis explicitly and be ready to discuss how the precise, exhaustive detail develops it.

7. White does not state his thesis directly. What is the value of being indirect, given his thesis?

8. How else might White have presented his thesis? To what kind of audience is he writing? To state the question in another way, what can you tell about the audience from how he approaches it?

WRITING ASSIGNMENT

Write a paragraph developing an impression of yourself through details about your life. Organize it to reveal a series of characteristics or one dominant characteristic. Do not comment on these details. In a second paragraph develop the same impression by stating the characteristic(s) and illustrating them. The thesis of your first paragraph will be implicit in the details; it will be explicit in the second paragraph.

W. S. Merwin
UNCHOPPING A TREE

1.   Start with the leaves, the small twigs, and the nests that have been shaken, ripped, or broken off by the fall; these must be gathered and attached once again to their respective places. It is not arduous work, unless major limbs have been smashed or mutilated. If the fall was carefully and correctly planned, the chances of anything of the kind happening will have been reduced. Again, much depends upon the size, age, shape, and species of the tree. Still, you will be lucky if you can get through

UNCHOPPING A TREE: From *The Miner's Pale Child* by W. S. Merwin. Copyright © 1969, 1970 by W. S. Merwin. Reprinted by permission of Atheneum Publishers.

this stage without having to use machinery. Even in the best of circumstances it is a labor that will make you wish often that you had won the favor of the universe of ants, the empire of mice, or at least a local tribe of squirrels, and could enlist their labors and their talents. But no, they leave you to it. They have learned, with time. This is men's work. It goes without saying that if the tree was hollow in whole or in part, and contained old nests of bird or mammal or insect, or hoards of nuts or such structures as wasps or bees build for their survival, the contents will have to be repaired where necessary, and reassembled, insofar as possible, in their original order, including the shells of nuts already opened. With spiders' webs you must simply do the best you can. We do not have the spider's weaving equipment, nor any substitute for the leaf's living bond with its point of attachment and nourishment. It is even harder to simulate the latter when the leaves have once become dry—as they are bound to do, for this is not the labor of a moment. Also it hardly needs saying that this is the time for repairing any neighboring trees or bushes or other growth that may have been damaged by the fall. The same rules apply. Where neighboring trees were of the same species it is difficult not to waste time conveying a detached leaf back to the wrong tree. Practice, practice. Put your hope in that.

2.   Now the tackle must be put into place or the scaffolding, depending on the surroundings and the dimensions of the tree. It is ticklish work. Almost always it involves, in itself, further damage to the area, which will have to be corrected later. But as you've heard, it can't be helped. And care now is likely to save you considerable trouble later. Be careful to grind nothing into the ground.

3.   At last the time comes for the erecting of the trunk. By now it will scarcely be necessary to remind you of the delicacy of this huge skeleton. Every motion of the tackle, every slight upward heave of the trunk, the branches, their elaborately reassembled panoply of leaves (now dead) will draw from you an involuntary gasp. You will watch for a leaf or a twig to be snapped off yet again. You will listen for the nuts to shift in the hollow limb and you will hear whether they are indeed falling into place or are spilling in disorder—in which case, or in the event of anything else of the kind—operations will have to cease, of course, while you correct the matter. The raising itself is no small enterprise, from the moment when the chains tighten

around the old bandages until the bole hangs vertical above the stump, splinter above splinter. Now the final straightening of the splinters themselves can take place (the preliminary work is best done while the wood is still green and soft, but at times when the splinters are not badly twisted most of the straightening is left until now, when the torn ends are face to face with each other). When the splinters are perfectly complementary the appropriate fixative is applied. Again we have no duplicate of the original substance. Ours is extremely strong, but it is rigid. It is limited to surfaces, and there is no play in it. However the core is not the part of the trunk that conducted life from the roots up into the branches and back again. It was relatively inert. The fixative for this part is not the same as the one for the outer layers and the bark, and if either of these is involved in the splintered section they must receive applications of the appropriate adhesives. Apart from being incorrect and probably ineffective, the core fixative would leave a scar on the bark.

4.   When all is ready the splintered trunk is lowered onto the splinters of the stump. This, one might say, is only the skeleton of the resurrection. Now the chips must be gathered, and the sawdust, and returned to their former positions. The fixative for the wood layers will be applied to chips and sawdust consisting only of wood. Chips and sawdust consisting of several substances will receive applications of the correct adhesives. It is as well, where possible, to shelter the materials from the elements while working. Weathering makes it harder to identify the smaller fragments. Bark sawdust in particular the earth lays claim to very quickly. You must find your own ways of coping with this problem. There is a certain beauty, you will notice at moments, in the pattern of the chips as they are fitted back into place. You will wonder to what extent it should be described as natural, to what extent man-made. It will lead you on to speculations about the parentage of beauty itself, to which you will return.

5.   The adhesive for the chips is translucent, and not so rigid as that for the splinters. That for the bark and its subcutaneous layers is transparent and runs into the fibers on either side, partially dissolving them into each other. It does not set the sap flowing again but it does pay a kind of tribute to the preoccupations of the ancient thoroughfares. You could not roll an egg over the joints but some of the mine-shafts would still be pass-

able, no doubt. For the first exploring insect who raises its head in the tight echoless passages. The day comes when it is all restored, even to the moss (now dead) over the wound. You will sleep badly, thinking of the removal of the scaffolding that must begin the next morning. How you will hope for sun and a still day!

6.   The removal of the scaffolding or tackle is not so dangerous, perhaps, to the surroundings, as its installation, but it presents problems. It should be taken from the spot piece by piece as it is detached, and stored at a distance. You have come to accept it there, around the tree. The sky begins to look naked as the chains and struts one by one vacate their positions. Finally the moment arrives when the last sustaining piece is removed and the tree stands again on its own. It is as though its weight for a moment stood on your heart. You listen for a thud of settlement, a warning creak deep in the intricate joinery. You cannot believe it will hold. How like something dreamed it is, standing there all by itself. How long will it stand there now? The first breeze that touches its dead leaves all seems to flow into your mouth. You are afraid the motion of the clouds will be enough to push it over. What more can you do? What more can you do?

7.   But there is nothing more you can do.

8.   Others are waiting.

9.   Everything is going to have to be put back.

QUESTIONS

1. What are the chief indications of the writer's purpose in this essay? Does he state that purpose directly?

2. Examine the following statement from paragraph 4 carefully: "You will wonder to what extent it should be described as natural, to what extent man-made. It will lead you on to speculations about the parentage of beauty itself, to which you will return." What is the tone of the statement—that is, what seems to be the writer's attitude toward his reader as well as toward the act of unchopping a tree? Is an attitude *implied* in the whole essay that no single statement expresses? Could you accept such an implication as embodying the thesis?

3. The writer has chosen a strategy to deal with his idea—that is, he approaches his reader in a particular way to achieve a particular effect. What does he want his reader to think and feel at the end of the essay, and what is his strategy in realizing these aims?

4. The essay ends with three single-sentence paragraphs. To what effect?

WRITING ASSIGNMENT

Write an essay on a similar topic, for example, undoing an insult. Be consistent in conveying a tone and building to your conclusion. Be ready to defend the strategy you adopt in the essay.

Dee Brown
WOUNDED KNEE

There was no hope on earth, and God seemed to have forgotten us. Some said they saw the Son of God; others did not see Him. If He had come, He would do some great things as He had done before. We doubted it because we had seen neither Him nor His works.

The people did not know; they did not care. They snatched at the hope. They screamed like crazy men to Him for mercy. They caught at the promise they heard He had made.

The white men were frightened and called for soldiers. We had begged for life, and the white men thought we wanted theirs. We heard that soldiers were coming. We did not fear. We hoped that we could tell them our troubles and get help. A white man said the soldiers meant to kill us. We did not believe it, but some were frightened and ran away to the Badlands.

—RED CLOUD

Had it not been for the sustaining force of the Ghost Dance religion, the Sioux in their grief and anger over the assassination of Sitting Bull might have risen up against the guns of the soldiers. So prevalent was their belief that the white men would soon disappear and that with the next greening of the grass their dead relatives and friends would return, they made no retaliations. By the hundreds, however, the leaderless Hunkpapas fled from Standing Rock, seeking refuge in one of the Ghost Dance camps or with the last of the great chiefs, Red Cloud, at Pine Ridge. In the Moon When the Deer Shed Their Horns (December 17) about a hundred of these fleeing Hunkpapas reached Big Foot's Minneconjou camp near Cherry Creek. That same day the War Department issued orders for the arrest and imprisonment of Big Foot. He was on the list of "fomenters of disturbances."

As soon as Big Foot learned that Sitting Bull had been killed, he started his people toward Pine Ridge, hoping that Red Cloud could protect them from the soldiers. En route, he fell ill of pneumonia, and when hemorrhaging began, he had to travel in a wagon. On December 28, as they neared Porcupine Creek, the Minneconjous sighted four troops of cavalry approaching. Big Foot immediately ordered a white flag run up over his wagon. About two o'clock in the afternoon he raised up from his blankets to greet Major Samuel Whitside, Seventh U.S. Cavalry. Big Foot's blankets were stained with blood from his lungs, and as he talked in a hoarse whisper with Whitside, red drops fell from his nose and froze in the bitter cold.

Whitside told Big Foot that he had orders to take him to a cavalry camp on Wounded Knee Creek. The Minneconjou chief replied that he was going in that direction; he was taking his people to Pine Ridge for safety.

Turning to his half-breed scout, John Shangreau, Major Whitside ordered him to begin disarming Big Foot's band.

"Look here, Major," Shangreau replied, "if you do that, there is liable to be a fight here; and if there is, you will kill all those women and children and the men will get away from you."

Whitside insisted that his orders were to capture Big Foot's Indians and disarm and dismount them.

"We better take them to camp and then take their horses from them and their guns," Shangreau declared.

"All right," Whitside agreed. "You tell Big Foot to move down to camp at Wounded Knee." *

The major glanced at the ailing chief, and then gave an order for his Army ambulance to be brought forward. The ambulance would be warmer and would give Big Foot an easier ride than the jolting springless wagon. After the chief was transferred to the ambulance, Whitside formed a column for the march to Wounded Knee Creek. Two troops of cavalry took the lead, the

* Utley, Robert M. *The Last Days of the Sioux Nation.* New Haven, Yale University Press, 1963, p. 195.

ambulance and wagons following, the Indians herded into a compact group behind them, with the other two cavalry troops and a battery of two Hotchkiss guns bringing up the rear.

Twilight was falling when the column crawled over the last rise in the land and began descending the slope toward Chankpe Opi Wakpala, the creek called Wounded Knee. The wintry dusk and the tiny crystals of ice dancing in the dying light added a supernatural quality to the somber landscape. Somewhere along this frozen stream the heart of Crazy Horse lay in a secret place, and the Ghost Dancers believed that his disembodied spirit was waiting impatiently for the new earth that would surely come with the first green grass of spring.

At the cavalry tent camp on Wounded Knee Creek, the Indians were halted and carefully counted. There were 120 men and 230 women and children. Because of the gathering darkness, Major Whitside decided to wait until morning before disarming his prisoners. He assigned them a camping area immediately to the south of the military camp, issued them rations, and as there was a shortage of tepee covers, he furnished them several tents. Whitside ordered a stove placed in Big Foot's tent and sent a regimental surgeon to administer to the sick chief. To make certain that none of his prisoners escaped, the major stationed two troops of cavalry as sentinels around the Sioux tepees, and then posted his two Hotchkiss guns on top of a rise overlooking the camp. The barrels of these rifled guns, which could hurl explosive charges for more than two miles, were positioned to rake the length of the Indian lodges.

Later in the darkness of that December night the remainder of the Seventh Regiment marched in from the east and quietly bivouacked north of Major Whitside's troops. Colonel James W. Forsyth, commanding Custer's former regiment, now took charge of operations. He informed Whitside that he had received orders to take Big Foot's band to the Union Pacific Railroad for shipment to a military prison in Omaha.

After placing two more Hotchkiss guns on the slope beside the others, Forsyth and his officers settled down for the evening with a keg of whiskey to celebrate the capture of Big Foot.

The chief lay in his tent, too ill to sleep, barely able to breathe. Even with their protective Ghost Shirts and their belief in the prophecies of the new Messiah, his people were fearful of the pony soldiers camped all around them. Fourteen years before, on the Little Bighorn, some of these warriors had helped defeat some of these soldier chiefs—Moylan, Varnum, Wallace, Godfrey, Edgerly—and the Indians wondered if revenge could still be in their hearts.

"The following morning there was a bugle call," said Wasu-maza, one of Big Foot's warriors who years afterward was to change his name to Dewey Beard. "Then I saw the soldiers mounting their horses and surrounding us. It was announced that all men should come to the center for a talk and that after the talk they were to move on to Pine Ridge agency. Big Foot was brought out of his tepee and sat in front of his tent and the older men were gathered around him and sitting right near him in the center."

After issuing hardtack for breakfast rations, Colonel Forsyth informed the Indians that they were now to be disarmed. "They called for guns and arms," White Lance said, "so all of us gave the guns and they were stacked up in the center." The soldier chiefs were not satisfied with the number of weapons surren-dered, and so they sent details of troopers to search the tepees. "They would go right into the tents and come out with bundles and tear them open." Dog Chief said. "They brought our axes, knives, and tent stakes and piled them near the guns." *

Still not satisfied, the soldier chiefs ordered the warriors to remove their blankets and submit to searches for weapons. The Indians' faces showed their anger, but only the medicine man, Yellow Bird, made any overt protest. He danced a few Ghost Dance steps, and chanted one of the holy songs, assuring the warriors that the soldiers' bullets could not penetrate their sacred garments. "The bullets will not go toward you," he chanted in Sioux. "The prairie is large and the bullets will not go toward you." †

The troopers found only two rifles, one of them a new Win-chester belonging to a young Minneconjou named Black Coyote. Black Coyote raised the Winchester above his head, shouting that he paid much money for the rifle and that it belonged to him. Some years afterward Dewey Beard recalled that Black Coyote was deaf. "If they had left him alone he was going to put his gun down where he should. They grabbed him and spinned him in

* McGregor, James H. *The Wounded Knee Massacre from the Viewpoint of the Survivors.* Bal-timore, Maryland, Wirth Brothers, 1940, pp. 105, 118, 134.

† Utley, p. 210.

the east direction. He was still unconcerned even then. He hadn't his gun pointed at anyone. His intention was to put that gun down. They came on and grabbed the gun that he was going to put down. Right after they spun him around there was the report of a gun, was quite loud. I couldn't say that anybody was shot, but following that was a crash."

"It sounded much like the sound of tearing canvas, that was the crash," Rough Feather said. Afraid-of-the-Enemy described it as a "lightning crash." *

Turning Hawk said that Black Coyote "was a crazy man, a young man of very bad influence and in fact a nobody." He said that Black Coyote fired his gun and that "immediately the soldiers returned fire and indiscriminate killing followed." †

In the first seconds of violence, the firing of carbines was deafening, filling the air with powder smoke. Among the dying who lay sprawled on the frozen ground was Big Foot. Then there was a brief lull in the rattle of arms, with small groups of Indians and soldiers grappling at close quarters, using knives, clubs, and pistols. As few of the Indians had arms, they soon had to flee, and then the big Hotchkiss guns on the hill opened up on them, firing almost a shell a second, raking the Indian camp, shredding the tepees with flying shrapnel, killing men, women, and children.

"We tried to run," Louise Weasel Bear said, "but they shot us like we were a buffalo. I know there are some good white people, but the soldiers must be mean to shoot children and women. Indian soldiers would not do that to white children."

"I was running away from the place and followed those who were running away," said Hakiktawin, another of the young women. "My grandfather and grandmother and brother were killed as we crossed the ravine, and then I was shot on the right hip clear through and on my right wrist where I did not go any further as I was not able to walk, and after the soldier picked me up where a little girl came to me and crawled into the blanket." ‡

When the madness ended, Big Foot and more than half of his people were dead or seriously wounded; 153 were known dead, but many of the wounded crawled away to die afterward. One

* McGregor, pp. 106, 109, 126.

† U.S. Bureau of Ethnology. Report. 14th, 1892–93, Part 2, p. 885.

‡ McGregor, pp. 111, 140.

estimate placed the final total of dead at very nearly three hundred of the original 350 men, women, and children. The soldiers lost twenty-five dead and thirty-nine wounded, most of them struck by their own bullets or shrapnel.

After the wounded cavalrymen were started for the agency at Pine Ridge, a detail of soldiers went over the Wounded Knee battlefield, gathering up Indians who were still alive and loading them into wagons. As it was apparent by the end of the day that a blizzard was approaching, the dead Indians were left lying where they had fallen. (After the blizzard, when a burial party returned to Wounded Knee, they found the bodies, including Big Foot's, frozen into grotesque shapes.)

The wagonloads of wounded Sioux (four men and forty-seven women and children) reached Pine Ridge after dark. Because all available barracks were filled with soldiers, they were left lying in the open wagons in the bitter cold while an inept Army officer searched for shelter. Finally the Episcopal mission was opened, the benches taken out, and hay scattered over the rough flooring.

It was the fourth day after Christmas in the Year of Our Lord 1890. When the first torn and bleeding bodies were carried into the candlelit church, those who were conscious could see Christmas greenery hanging from the open rafters. Across the chancel front above the pulpit was strung a crudely lettered banner: PEACE ON EARTH, GOOD WILL TO MEN.

QUESTIONS

1. Following the battle of Little Bighorn in 1876 and the gradual disappearance of the buffalo from the plains, the chief of the Hunkpapa Teton Sioux, Sitting Bull, in 1877 took his dwindling tribe into Canada; he surrendered to American officials in 1881. From 1883 he lived at Standing Rock Agency in South Dakota, where he staved off hunger and tried to prevent the sale of Indian land. In 1889 a resurgence of the Ghost Dance religion caused unrest among Sioux Indians; this North American Indian cult fostered the hope that a messiah of Indian origin would bring deliverance from the white man. Seeking to control the unrest, the government tried to arrest Sitting Bull; he was seized on the Grand River and shot in the struggle on December 15, 1890. In the statement that opens the account of events at Wounded Knee, the Sioux chief Red Cloud refers to the hopes raised by the Ghost Dance religion; the sentences that conclude the account refer to the Christmas season. How do these sentences help to

indicate the point of view of the author, in particular his attitude toward the events he describes?
2. Is the author chiefly concerned with the motives of the American soldiers or with the injustice done to the Sioux—or with neither of these? How do you account for the selection of detail, in particular the attention to the character and physical condition of Black Coyote?
3. Does the author suggest that no single motive can be cited for the behavior of the American soldiers and that the massacre was the fault of no one? Does he stress the role of accident in these events? Are the statements of various eyewitnesses intended to express the author's own view of the situation?

WRITING ASSIGNMENT

Accounts of the treatment of the Sioux prior to the massacre at Wounded Knee differ. Examine some of the sources cited in the notes, in addition to various other accounts and histories of the Sioux, to determine how widely interpretations of the event differ and why they do.

MAIN AND SUBORDINATE IDEAS

Irwin Edman
SINCERITY AS A FINE ART

1.   I remember often during my early adolescence listening to older people making conversation. I vowed I would never willingly be a conspirator at such transparent hypocrisies. When *I* went out to dinner, I found myself saying, I should speak only when I felt like it, and I should say only what was on my mind. I used to listen while my elders pretended to have a fascinated in-

SINCERITY AS A FINE ART: From *Under Whatever Sky* by Irwin Edman. Copyright 1951 by Irwin Edman. Reprinted by permission of The Viking Press, Inc.

terest in visitors with whom I knew they had only the most
remote concern, and hear them discuss with affected animation
matters that I knew bored them to pain. I remember having had
it explained to me that this was the least that good manners
demanded. It was at this moment that I came to the conclusion
that good manners and dubious morals had much in common.

2.   In these matters, I have become subdued to the general
color of civilized society. It has long ago been brought home to
me that a guest has obligations in addition to that of eating the
food provided by his host. It is fair enough that one should, if
not sing, at least converse for one's supper. I have even come to
believe that my elders of long ago were more interested in their
visitors than I had supposed. I have lighted upon the fact that
questions asked out of politeness may elicit answers that are fascinating on their own. An enchanting story may be the unearned
increment of a conventional inquiry.

3.   And yet I have not ceased to be troubled at the momentum with which on a social occasion one is embarked on a brief
career of insincerity. I have found myself expressing opinions on
Russia or on psychiatry that I had not known I possessed. I have
sometimes, out of sheer inability to get out of it, maintained a
position on old-age security, or on old age itself, that, save for
some impulsive remark I had let fall, I should not have considered it a point of honor to defend as my considered philosophy
on the subject. On shamefully numerous occasions, I have repeated an anecdote by which I was myself bored to death. I have
talked with dowagers about literature, art, and education, at moments when all three of these lofty themes seemed to me insuf-
ferably tedious and stuffy.

4.   I have come to admire those sturdy individualists who
say—as I once planned to say—only whatever comes into their
minds, and speak only when they are spoken to, and perhaps not
even then. But I must admit I find them difficult socially, these
high-minded boors who can be pricked into only the most mini-
mal of replies, these dedicated roughnecks who find a savage
pleasure in telling you without compromise what they think of
everything, including your loyalties and your enthusiasms—and
possibly yourself.

5.   There must be some way of acting both agreeably and
sincerely. It is a fine art, practiced, one is told, by a few witty
eighteenth-century courtiers. But wits today are rather celebrated

for their malignity. It is a difficult alternative, that between truth and charm, and I confess that I am tempted to seek the easier and more genial path. If one plumped for sincerity, one would get to be known simply as a bear, a bear who would soon be walking alone, a boorish bear who at any rate would seldom be invited out to dinner. As Santayana remarks somewhere, "For a man of sluggish mind and bad manners, there is decidedly no place like home."

DISCUSSION: MAIN AND SUBORDINATE IDEAS

One way to distinguish the main idea of the essay from subordinate ones that develop it or introduce related considerations is to repeat or restate it at key points, or indicate through transitions (*A less important consideration, But more importantly*) the relative weight of ideas. Essays in which all ideas seem equal in importance are difficult to read.

The writer, of course, must know what he wants to stress—he must have his thesis clearly in mind—and one good way to think out the relationship of ideas is to plan the organization in a sentence or topic outline. A sentence outline consists of complete sentences that briefly summarize the ideas and are arranged in the order of importance. The advantage of outlining an essay is that it lets the writer *see* the relationship of his ideas and so test their coherence before the actual writing. A sentence outline is particularly useful in writing long essays in which the proper proportioning and arrangement of ideas requires careful planning. Here is a sentence outline of Edman's essay up to the second sentence of paragraph 4:

I. In my youth I was disturbed by the hypocrisy of adults.
   A. I vowed that I would be different when I grew up.
      1. I would speak only when I wanted to.
      2. I would speak only the truth.
   B. I observed my parents among their guests.
      1. They pretended to be interested in boring conversation.
      2. They explained that good manners required a show of interest.
   C. I concluded that good manners and doubtful morals have much in common.
II. As an adult I see the matter somewhat differently.
   A. I misunderstood several things.
      1. A guest has an obligation to his host.
      2. My parents were interested in their guests.
      3. Polite questions may bring fascinating answers.

    B. I am still troubled by being forced into insincerity.
        1. I have expressed unformed opinions impulsively.
        2. I have repeated boring anecdotes.
        3. I have talked at length about tedious subjects.
    C. My attitude toward truthful, blunt individualists has changed.
        1. I admire them for speaking their minds and speaking only when they want to. . . .

Notice that the first heading (I) is a generalization extracted from what is judged to be the first part of the essay: A, B, and C under it are its breakdown—that is, its detail.

A topic outline consists of short, parallel phrases, not sentences: it indicates what is to be discussed and arranges these, again, according to their relative importance. The sentence "In my youth I was disturbed by the hypocrisy of adults" becomes in a topic outline "My youthful dislike of adult hypocrisy."

A difficulty with outlining is that it can make the writing of the essay mechanical. Used properly, the outline should be considered a preliminary plan; the writer can and should revise it as new ideas and methods of development occur to him in the writing.

QUESTIONS

1. Is the heading of the sentence outline—"In my youth I was disturbed by the hypocrisy of adults"—derived from a single sentence of Edman's essay or summarized from a number of sentences?
2. How is A under I derived? Is it explicitly or implicitly stated in paragraph 1? How is B derived?
3. I and II; A, B, and C; and 1, 2, 3, and so on are coordinate ideas—that is, ideas of equal importance. In paragraph 4, is sentence 2 a coordinate of 1 under IIC or of IIC itself?
4. Finish the outline. Notice that the first division corresponds to the first paragraph. The second division, however, may include more than just the second paragraph—it may cover the rest of the essay. There is, in other words, no necessary correspondence between the number of paragraphs in the essay and the number of divisions in the outline.
5. To what extent does Edman depend on transitions to show which ideas are main and subordinate? What is his chief means of indicating the difference?

WRITING ASSIGNMENT

Write a sentence or topic outline for one of the following. Then write an essay from the outline.

a. the art of friendly criticism
b. the art of not giving wanted advice
c. the art of persuading children without threatening

Margaret Mead and Rhoda Metraux
THE GIFT OF AUTONOMY

December, 1966

1.   Every gift we give carries with it our idea of what a present is. Perhaps it expresses our personality; perhaps, on the contrary, it is what we believe the recipient really wants, a choice based on careful listening for the slightest hint of what he longs for or needs or should have, even though he may not realize it.

2.   Gifts from parents to children always carry the most meaningful messages. The way parents think about presents goes one step beyond the objects themselves—the ties, dolls, sleds, record players, kerchiefs, bicycles and model airplanes that wait by the Christmas tree. The gifts are, in effect, one way of telling boys and girls, "We love you even though you have been a bad boy all month" or, "We love having a daughter" or, "We treat all our children alike" or, "It is all right for girls to have some toys made for boys" or, "This alarm clock will help you get started in the morning all by yourself." Throughout all the centuries since the invention of a Santa Claus figure who represented a special recognition of children's behavior, good and bad, presents have given parents a way of telling children about their love and hopes and expectations for them.

3.   When I was a child, my parents used to give me a pair of books each Christmas. One was "light," easy reading; the other was "heavy," a book I had to think about if I was to enjoy it. This combination carried with it the message that there are different kinds of pleasure to be gained through reading and that I should discover each kind for myself.

4.   If we think about all the presents we have given our children over the years, we will see how they fit into the hopes we have for each child. I do not mean this in the simple sense

that we delight in a little girl's femininity, and so give her dolls, or that we implement a boy's masculinity by giving him model planes and boxing gloves. We do, of course, speak to our children in this simplest form of symbolism. And we do, of course, personalize what we say when we give our outdoors son a fishing rod and his experiment-minded brother a microscope.

5.   However, our giving also carries more subtle and complex messages. For example, we can ask ourselves: "What am I saying to my children about growing up to be independent, autonomous people?" An abstract question of this kind can be posed in relation to a whole range of presents for children of both sexes and of different ages. Where the choice to be made is between a simple toy engine that the child himself can wind up and a more complicated one that I shall have to wind up for him, which one do I give him? Choosing a doll for a little girl, do I buy her a perishable costume doll with one beautiful dress, a washable doll with a wardrobe or a doll for which she will make dresses out of the materials I also give her? The costume doll can perhaps be dressed and undressed, but that is all. A bath would be ruinous. A sturdy doll with a ready-made wardrobe places choice in the child's own hands. She herself can dress and undress it, bathe it safely and decide whether her "little girl" will wear pink or blue, plaid or plain. Giving my child materials out of which to fashion doll dresses is a lovely idea, and may perhaps encourage her to learn how to sew. But choice and autonomy both are reduced because now I must help her at every step.

6.   We can ask questions of this kind also about the presents of money that are given our children by grandparents and godparents, aunts and uncles and family friends. What do we tell our children about the bright silver dollar tucked into the toe of a Christmas stocking or the grown-up-looking check that is made out in the child's own name? Is the money meant to be used now for some specific purpose—for the charm bracelet a little girl has admired or the radio a boy wants for his own room? Or is it an inducement, perhaps, to begin saving for the car a teen-ager must wait five years to own? Is the child told, directly or indirectly: "This is your money to do with as you like"? Or is the child asked: "Would you rather spend it or put it in the bank?"

7.   By defining the alternatives so sharply, we are, in effect, robbing the child of choice. In fact, when you tell him that the money is his and then give directions, hint at alternatives or reproach him for spending it in one way instead of another, the

gift carries a very definite message: "I don't really trust your choices. I don't really want you to choose." If, on the other hand, the message is simple and direct ("This is your money, yours, to dispose of as you like"), then the child may even solicit your advice. But there is no real turning back once you have said, "This is your money."

8.   Over the years, there are always new ways of reinforcing or detracting from our children's growing sense of independence. For example, if you give a boy a box of stationery imprinted with his name and a supply of postage stamps, you are showing him that you expect him to write, address and mail his own letters. This means, of course, that you may never see the letters he writes, or you may become a consultant on appropriate terms of address or the correct abbreviations of names of states. At this point you can give him an almanac in which he himself can look up the answers to his questions—or you can keep the almanac on your own desk and become the mediator between his questions and the information he needs.

9.   Giving a girl a diary with a key is a way in which a mother can tell her daughter (boys, on the whole, do not keep diaries) that she respects her child's growing sense of identity and independence. Giving a boy a desk is one way of fostering his sense of personal privacy; but if we continually tidy it up or complain about its untidiness, as we see it, the original message miscarries.

10.   In many families the climax, and in some the crisis, of their individual pattern of giving comes as the children approach college, when their parents prepare to give them the most expensive "gift" of all—a college education. Of course, parents are not, as a rule, literally "giving" their children an education. What they are giving them is the opportunity to become educated.

11.   Many parents today meet the responsibility of supporting their children through the college years, wholly or in part, by taking out insurance policies for this special purpose. Usually such policies, whatever their specific form, are payable to the parents. Then the choice of a college and the course of study remains firmly in the parents' hands. Americans believe very strongly that he who pays the piper calls the tune.

12.   This is the *customary* way of doing things. It carries with it the message that our children, although approaching adulthood, are still children in our eyes. But this need not be. The money instead can be set up as a fund available to the boy or

girl. Its purpose can be specified: This is not money for just anything. It is money for higher education, intended to give you
freedom and choice within this area of your life.

13.   For children who have grown up with an ever-enlarg-
ing sense of their own autonomy and independence, intelligent
handling of the opportunity for further education will come naturally and easily. They are free, if they like, to postpone going to
college for a year. Or they can drop out for a semester or a year
without fearing that the tuition money will have vanished when
they want to go back. A girl can marry before she goes to college,
or while she is still a student, knowing that the choice of when
and where she will continue her education remains open to her.
Next year or ten years from now the money will be there, waiting, ready for her when she wants and needs it.

14.   Like the small presents of early childhood that carry the
message "You need my help," the educational insurance policy
in the parents' name places responsibility in the parents' hands.
In many cases parents are not even required to spend the money
on the education of the child in whose interest the policy was
acquired. But when money is placed in the child's own name, a
trust for a special purpose, the parents are saying: "This is what I
hope to give you—the right of choice. I respect your right to
choose. My gift is intended to underwrite your freedom to be a
person. Long ago I gave you stamps so you could mail your own
letters. I gave you an allowance so you could move more freely in
your own world. Now, as then, I want you to be an autonomous,
self-starting person, someone who enjoys interdependence with
other people because instead of fighting for your independence,
you have grown into it."

15.   All our giving carries with it messages about ourselves, our feelings about those to whom we give, how we see
them as people and how we phrase the ties of relationship.
Christmas giving, in which love and hope and trust play such an
intrinsic part, can be an annual way of telling our children that
we think of each of them as a person, as we also hope they will
come to think of us.

QUESTIONS

1. The statement in paragraph 11—"Americans believe very strongly
   that he who pays the piper calls the tune"—might have served as the

thesis of the essay. If it were the thesis, how might the essay be reorganized to develop it, without omitting any of the present statements? Rewrite the opening two paragraphs to show how you would make this revision.

2. The authors use their first paragraph to build to the statement of the thesis. How? Where is the thesis restated and for what purpose?
3. The authors discuss various problems involved in giving presents. In what order are these problems discussed in paragraphs 4–10?
4. The authors devote a considerable portion of the essay to the educational insurance policy. Why?
5. Is the purpose of the essay to analyze the practice of gift giving or to give advice to parents? Do the authors address their audience as colleagues, as clients, or merely as general readers?

WRITING ASSIGNMENTS

Analyze the gifts you gave to members of your family last Christmas or another occasion and the reasons for your choice. Give particular attention to your expectations in choosing the gift for the particular person.

Discuss ways in which English teachers can and do encourage their students to think independently and to depend on their own intellectual and imaginative resources in writing essays. Focus on what you would and would not do if you were an English teacher.

BEGINNING AND ENDING

Edmund Wilson
DETROIT MOTORS

1.   On the dreary yellow Michigan waste with its gray stains of frozen water, the old cars wait like horses at the pound. Since the spring before last, Henry Ford has been buying them up at twenty dollars apiece, and people drive them in every day. Old, battered, muddy roadsters, sedans, limousines, touring cars and trucks—in strings of two or three they are dragged off to the disassembly building, following foolishly and gruesomely like corpses shaken up into life, hoods rickety and wheels turning backwards. Once inside, they are systematically and energetically dismantled: the flat road-ruined tires are stripped away; the rush-flare of an acetylene torch attacks the stems of the steering wheels; the motors are cleaned out like a bull's tripes and sent to make scrap iron for the blast furnace; the glass is taken out and kept to replace broken factory panes; the leather from the hoods and seats goes for aprons and handpads for the workers; the hair stuffing of the seats is sold again; even the bronze and babbitt metal are scraped out of the connecting rods and melted up to line new connecting rods. Then the picked and gutted carcass of the old car is shoved into a final death chamber—crushed flat by a five-ton press, which makes it scrunch like a stepped-on beetle.

2.   The home of the open-hearth furnaces is a vast loud abode of giants: groans, a continual ringing, the falling of remote loads. The old automobiles sent in on little cars are like disemboweled horses at the bull-ring whose legs are buckling under them. A fiend in blue glasses who sits in a high throne on an enormous blue chariot or float causes it to move horizontally back and forth before the white-glowing mouths of the furnaces, feeding them the flattened cars like so many metallic soft-shell crabs—ramming each one in with a sudden charge, dropping it

quickly with a twist. There are not many mouths big enough yet to accommodate a whole car at one gape, and, pending the completion of ten hundred-ton furnaces specially designed for the consumption of old cars—fifty thousand of which have been melted up since the April before last—they are being chopped up for the small-mouthed furnaces by a thousand-ton electric shear, which reduces chassis, springs, wheels, fenders and all to a junk-fodder of iron spines and bent tin shells, like horseshoe crabs cut up for pigs. When you put on blue glasses and gaze through the blinding hole in the furnace door, where the old cars are being digested with such condiments as limestone and pig iron, you see only a livid lake which vibrates with pale thickish bubbles. (The draft from the furnace heats a boiler—the boiler produces steam—the steam runs a turbine—the turbine turns the fan that makes the draft.)

3.   Twice a day the old liquefied cars are poured out through the backside of the furnace into receptacles like huge iron buckets: a hot stink, a thunderous hissing, the voiding of a molten feces of gold burned beyond gold to a white ethereal yellow, a supreme incandescence, while a spray of snow-crystal sparks explodes like tiny rockets. In the arena below the gallery, during the pouring no human beings go. Giant cranes move along the ceiling and, picking up the caldrons of golden soup, lift them across the great barn and tip them into other vats, whence the liquid runs down through holes into cylindrical ingot molds. Eleven hundred tons of steel a day.

4.   In the blooming mill's spacious gloom, ruby lights are sharp tiny watch gems under the clockwork of thin naked steel beams and the writhing of vermiform silver pipes. Hot breaths; a prolonged dull hooting; the acridity of pickling baths. A crane like a gigantic blue airplane comes sliding along the ceiling and from an elaborate suspended cab, which slides at right angles to the movement of the crane, it lifts, with great beetle-tweezers, the dark cooling ingots out of their molds, carries them across and lowers them into ovens—the soaking pits—where they soak in heat till, white-hot, they glow.

5.   Silver pipes—a deafening clack-a-clack-clack—the spilling of metallic avalanches—the groaning barks of Cerbera in labor. Transmitters like the shells of red monstrous snails, fattened behind glass in white and spotless stalls, furnish underground power for the rollers. You look down from a narrow

gallery at a runway of turning cylinders: the ingot, now cooling red-hot, lurches along it like a length of column roughly blunt-snouted and grooved. As it enters a mechanical grotto, the rollers above and below it crunch off the outer crust and a shear crops the bottom end, in which the impurities have settled, and drops it into a waiting receptacle from which it will be routed back to be melted up again.

6.   Now the pigs have been bloomed into billets and are heated to be rolled in the rolling mill. Long strips of red-hot metal timber traveling along the rollers of the slides—squeezed out thinner and thinner, as they pass through the rollers of the stands, into longer and longer red worms, which a row of men, snapping the handles of black boxes in an upper gallery, cause to coast backwards and forwards or send spinning as they leave the wringers. Squared and cut in even lengths, they make at last a hangarful of piled steel stock.

7.   Drop forges: a shattering whack-whack-whack, which, when, formerly, it whacked out crankshafts, could break down the mudflat land and shake down the very building. But the crankshafts are now made at Highland Park. Here at Dearborn the big blacksmiths with bunged-up eyes, are stamping out connecting rods. By the steady steam-blown outflare of furnaces, with deliberate implacable bangs, the impacts of the dropping black trap, on anvil-die they bring hammer-die down, and out of red-hot lengths of tongs-held stock they cut cupcake-pans that still glow red-hot.

8.   Machining: a finished connecting rod is the product of twenty-eight different processes. The rake-forks of the chain-conveyor wind zigzag in and out among benches and carry the connecting rods from one machine to the next. Each one of them must be toughened by a print heat-treat and softened by a draw heat-treat; rolled in a revolving tumbler, which rubs the scale away and turns the metal from dull to shining; straightened in swedge presses; drilled on revolving turrets; rough-turned, finish-turned, chamfered and threaded; bored with holes for the crankshaft and wristpin; the holes lined with white babbitt metal and bronze, the babbitt and bronze burnished smooth as satin; cleaned, oxidized, trimmed, washed, oil-holes drilled and oil-pocket cut (a solid man in a brown suit and round glasses has just invented a new machine for drilling all the holes at once, and he is supervising its installation); oil-groove cut, oil-pocket broached; balanced on a scale and corrected—the ones that weigh

too much or too little scrapped in thick-lipped iron buckets; holes in the babbitt and bronze bored with a diamond drill; inspected in constant-temperature greenhouses, lit blank violet by mercury tubes, and gauged to a millionth of an inch by a gauge with a diamond point.

9.   The part—the connecting rod—is now done with the production conveyor, and starts on another journey, along the subassembly conveyor, in the course of which other parts are added. The wristpins are now stuck in; the crankshaft and the piston are fitted. The rod is important, it must be a sound part: it has to withstand the wear and tear of a hundred revolutions a minute. At last it is fixed in the motor-block. The motor-block goes on its way and, piece by piece, becomes fully equipped; it acquires a queer little muzzle and two protruding eyes—takes on an animal aspect; and it finally crawls up the conveyor track on its way to the assembly room like an obedient tropical beetle.

10.   In this assembly room, to the point blank banging of hammers, the motor-block is seized and dropped down into an empty still wheelless frame which, on a double-track conveyor, is passing beneath to receive it; and now there takes shape on this track a kind of ichthyosaurus-shape that moves slowly with sprawling paws and a single long knobbed snail-eye which one recognizes soon as a gear-shaft. This shape, as it moves along, picks up wheels, shiny fenders, shiny runningboards. From above, the familiar body is dropped down on the goggle-eyed frame: the thing is a motor car now, glossy and fit to go, but still passive, still moved by another agency as if it had not yet emerged from the womb. Now it gets its last tests and touches: horns are made to speak, windshield cleaners wiped around their arc, accidental scratches painted over. Black coupés; blue town sedans; maroon tudors; buff roadsters; green trucks—they leave the conveyor for good; are pushed out, self-possessed and gleaming, with their glass goggle eyes just opened, into their first electric-lighted showroom. They stand waiting to be driven away or to be taken to the dealers on trailers, over the long dreary Michigan waste.

DISCUSSION: BEGINNING AND ENDING

Unless he has no interest in his reader, but only in himself, a writer will want to capture the reader's attention and hold it. He will lose his reader if he describes in too much detail how he intends to proceed.

Usually he will indicate a point of view and perhaps also the ways the subject is to be developed. There may be excellent reasons for beginning the essay with a statement of the thesis, as Hamilton and Madison do in certain of the Federalist papers, but in most instances the thesis requires an introduction: the writer will build to his thesis by showing why the subject is worth discussing and the thesis worth the reader's attention. The following opening paragraphs effectively accomplish this purpose:

> The administration of criminal justice and the extent of individual moral responsibility are among the crucial problems of a civilized society. They are indissolubly linked, and together they involve our deepest personal emotions. We often find it hard to forgive ourselves for our own moral failures. All of us, at some time or other, have faced the painful dilemma of when to punish and when to forgive those we love—our children, our friends. How much harder it is, then, to deal with the stranger who transgresses.—David L. Bazelon, "The Awesome Decision"

> The aim of this book is to delineate two types of clever schoolboy: the converger and the diverger. The earlier chapters offer a fairly detailed description of the intellectual abilities, attitudes and personalities of a few hundred such boys. In the later chapters, this description is then used as the basis for a more speculative discussion—of the nature of intelligence and originality and of the ways in which intellectual and personal qualities interact. Although the first half of the book rests heavily on the results of psychological tests, and the last two chapters involve psychoanalytic theory, I have done my best to be intelligible, and, wherever possible, interesting to everyone interested in clever schoolboys: parents, schoolteachers, dons, psychologists, administrators, clever schoolboys.—Liam Hudson, *Contrary Imaginations*

In the first of these opening paragraphs, the reader is eased into the subject: his interest is aroused by the personal consideration—his attitude toward himself, his children, his friends. The author assumes that this interest needs to be aroused. In the second opening paragraph, interest is challenged: no easing into the subject here, for the opening sentence announces both the subject of the book and a key distinction. The bonus is the wit of the author—and the promise of more.

An effective ending will not let the discussion drop; the reader should not have a sense of loose ends, of lines of thought left uncompleted. In the formal essay, the ending may be used for a restatement of the thesis or perhaps a full statement of it—if the writer has chosen to build to it. One of the most effective conclusions is the reference back to ideas that opened the essay.

QUESTIONS

1. Compare the opening and concluding paragraphs. What is gained by beginning and ending with the same descriptive phrase? Is the phrase merely descriptive of the scene, or is Wilson saying that the car factory has created a wasteland?
2. Is Wilson attaching significance to the fact that the factory salvages old cars by turning them into new ones? Is he seeking to make a point about this process?
3. To what extent does Wilson depend on the comparison of old cars to "horses at the pound" in the whole essay? How much does he depend on personification and on other figures of speech?
4. What adjectives and adverbs in paragraph 5 are metaphors? Notice that we need not be aware of them as metaphors. Are we made aware of them as such? How does the pattern of detail in this and other paragraphs shape our response to these words?
5. How does the sentence construction and word length in paragraph 7 convey the experience of drop forges?
6. What is the principle of order in the whole essay?

WRITING ASSIGNMENT

Write a short essay on one of the following epigrams. In your concluding paragraph return to the ideas or images that you use in your opening paragraph.

a. You can tell the ideals of a nation by its advertisements.—Norman Douglas
b. Injustice is relatively easy to bear; what stings is justice.—H. L. Mencken
c. We have all enough strength to bear the misfortunes of others.—La Rochefoucauld
d. Answer a fool according to his folly.—*Proverbs*

ORDER OF IDEAS

Arthur Koestler
THE BOREDOM OF FANTASY

1.   Once upon a time, more precisely on the 17th June, A.D. 4784, Captain Kayle Clark stepped into a public telescreen box to call up his fiancée, secret agent Lucy Rall. He was told that Lucy was not available as she had got married a week before. "To whom?" cried the exasperated Captain. "To me," said the man to whom he was talking. Taking a closer look at the telescreen, the Captain discovered with a mild surprise that the man he was talking to was himself.

2.   The startling mystery was solved by Mr. Robert Headrock, the first immortal man on earth. Headrock, using his electronic superbrain computer, discovered that Captain Clark had taken a trip in a time-machine; that he had made a loop into the past, and married Lucy Rall without his unlooped present self knowing about it. Through this little frolic, he also became the richest man on earth as he knew the movements of the Stock Exchange in advance. When the point in time was reached where Clark had looped off in the time-machine, the past Clark and the present Clark became again one, and lived happily ever after. Meanwhile, Robert Headrock, the immortal man, sent a journalist called MacAllister several million trillion years back into the past and made him cause a cosmic explosion, which gave rise to our planetary system as we know it.

3.   The book from which I was quoting is called *The Weapon Shops of Isher* by A. E. van Vogt. Mr. van Vogt is probably the most popular of contemporary American science-fiction writers. The book was recently published in England in a science-fiction series which signals, together with the founding of the British Science-Fiction Club, that the new craze, a kind of cosmic jitterbug, has crossed the Atlantic.

THE BOREDOM OF FANTASY: From *The Trail of the Dinosaur*, by Arthur Koestler. Published by The Macmillan Company and William Collins Sons & Co. Ltd. Reprinted by permission of A. D. Peters & Co.

4.   I had better confess at this point that while I lived in the United States I was a science-fiction addict myself and am still liable to occasional relapses. Reading about space travel, time travel, Martian maidens, robot civilizations and extra-galactic supermen is habit-forming like opium, murder thrillers and yoghourt diets. Few people in this country realize the extent and virulence of this addiction in the United States. According to a recent survey, the average sale of a detective story or a Western thriller in America is four thousand copies; the average sale of a science-fiction novel is six thousand copies, or fifty per cent higher. Every month, six new novels of this type are published in the U.S.A. and three large publishing firms specialize exclusively in science-fiction. There is a flood of science-fiction magazines, science-fiction clubs, science-fiction films, television programs and so on. The addicts are called "fen," which is the plural of fan. Fen gather in clubhouses called slanshacks, "slan" meaning a biologically mutated superman, and hold conferences, called fenferences. The characters in science-fiction speak a kind of cosmic R.A.F. slang (it ought to be called, evidently, "cosmilingo"). Young space cadets, for instance, dislike meeting Bems—for bug-eyed Monsters—in alien galaxies unless armed with paraguns—paralysis-causing ray-guns. They swear "By space," "By the seven rings of Saturn," or "By the gas-pits of Venus."

5.   If grown-ups betray these strange symptoms, one can imagine how the kiddies react. Your friends' children no longer plug you with six-shooters; they atomize you with nuclear blasters. They wear plastic bubbles around their heads which look like divers' helmets and enable them to breathe while floating in gravity-free interstellar space. These are sold by the thousand in department stores together with other cosmic paraphernalia, and are steadily replacing cowboy equipment, just as on the television screen Tom Corbett, Space Cadet, is in the process of replacing Hopalong Cassidy as the children's national hero. Even the housewife, listening in to the radio while on her domestic chores, is becoming cosmic-minded. The soap opera has branched out into the space opera. Imagine the opposite number of Mrs. Dale in Texas or Minnesota: "I am so worried about Richard not being back from his luncheon date on Jupiter. Maybe he's got space-happy and gone on to Venus. Or one of those nasty meteors may have deflected him from his orbit."

6.   So much for the grotesque side of science-fiction. But a craze of such vast dimensions is never entirely crazy. It always expresses, in a distorted way, some unconscious need of the time. Science-fiction is a typical product of the atomic age. The discoveries of that age weigh like an undigested lump on the stomach of mankind. Electronic brains which predict election results, lie-detectors which make you confess the truth, new drugs which make you testify to lies, radiations which produce biological monsters—all these developments of the last fifty years have created new vistas and new nightmares, which art and literature have not yet assimilated. In a crude and fumbling fashion, science-fiction is trying to fill this gap. But there is perhaps another and more hidden reason for this sudden hunger for other ages and other worlds. Perhaps, when they read about the latest hydrogen bomb tests, people are more aware than they admit to themselves, of the possibility that human civilization may be approaching its end. And together with this may go a dim, inarticulate suspicion that the cause lies deeper than Communism or Fascism, that it may lie in the nature of *homo sapiens;* in other words, that the human race may be a biological misfit doomed to extinction like the giant reptiles of an earlier age. I believe that some apocalyptic intuition of this kind may be one of the reasons for the sudden interest in life on other stars.

7.   As a branch of literature, science-fiction is, of course, not new. As early as the second century Lucian, a Greek writer, wrote a story of a journey to the moon. Swift wrote science-fiction; so did Samuel Butler, Jules Verne, H. G. Wells, Aldous Huxley, George Orwell. But while in the past such exercises were isolated literary extravaganzas, they are now mass-produced for a mass audience. Moreover, modern science-fiction takes itself very seriously. There are certain rules of the game which every practitioner must observe, otherwise he will be torn to shreds by the critics. The basic rule is that the author may only operate with future inventions, gadgets and machines which are extrapolations (that is, logical extensions) of present discoveries, and do not go against the laws of nature. A number of physicists, doctors and biologists are employed by the film and television industries to make sure that, even in the children's science-fiction show, every detail is correct. Some of the best-known science-fiction authors in America are actually scientists, several of international repute, who write under pen-names. The most recent and distinguished recruit to their ranks is Lord Russell. All

this is a guarantee of scientific accuracy, but unfortunately not of artistic quality.

8.   Mr. Gerald Heard has recently expressed the opinion that science-fiction is "the mark of the dawn of a new vision, and the rise of a new art," and simply *the* future form of the novel. Other well-known critics overseas also believe, in all seriousness, that science-fiction, now in its infancy, will grow up and one day become the literature of the future.

9.   I do not share their opinion. I believe that science-fiction is good entertainment, and that it will never become good art. It is reasonably certain that within the next hundred years we shall have space-travel, but at that stage the description of a trip to the moon will no longer be science-fiction but simple reportage. It will be fact, not fantasy, and the science-fiction of that time will have to go even further to startle the reader. What Mr. Heard's claim really amounts to is the replacement of the artist's disciplined imagination by the schoolboy's unbridled fantasy. But daydreaming is not poetry, and fantasy is not art.

10.   At first sight one would of course expect that imaginative descriptions of non-human societies on alien planets would open new vistas for the somewhat stagnant novel of our time. But most disappointingly this is not the case, and for a simple reason. Our imagination is limited; we cannot project ourselves into the distant future any more than into the distant past. This is the reason why the historical novel is practically dead today. The life of an Egyptian civil servant under the Eighteenth Dynasty, or even of a soldier in Cromwell's army, is only imaginable to us in dim outline; we are unable to identify ourselves with the strange figure moving through such a strange world. Few Englishmen can really understand the feelings and habits of Frenchmen, much less of Russians, much less of Martians. And without this act of identification, of intimate understanding, there is no art, only a thrill of curiosity which soon yields to boredom. The Martian heroes of science-fiction may have four eyes, a green skin and an accent stranger than mine—we just couldn't care less. We are tickled by them for a few pages; but because they are too strange to be true, we soon get bored.

11.   For every culture is an island. It communicates with other islands but it is only familiar with itself. And art means seeing the familiar in a new light, seeing tragedy in the trivial event; it means in the last resort broadening and deepening our understanding of ourselves. Swift's *Gulliver*, Huxley's *Brave New*

World, Orwell's *Nineteen-Eighty-Four,* are great works of literature because in them the gadgets of the future and the oddities of alien worlds serve merely as a background or pretext for a social message. In other words, they are literature precisely to the extent to which they are not science-fiction, to which they are works of disciplined imagination and not of unlimited fantasy. A similar rule holds for the detective story. Georges Simenon is probably the greatest master in that field, yet his novels become works of art precisely at the point where character and atmosphere become more important than the plot, where imagination triumphs over invention.

12.   Thus the paradoxical lesson of science-fiction is to teach us modesty. When we reach out for the stars, our limitations become grotesquely apparent. The heroes of science-fiction have unlimited power and fantastic possibilities, but their feelings and thoughts are limited within the narrow human range. Tom Corbett, Space Cadet, behaves on the third planet of Orion exactly in the same way as he does in a drugstore in Minnesota, and one is tempted to ask him: "Was your journey really necessary?" The Milky Way has become simply an extension of Main Street.

13.   Travel is no cure for melancholia; space-ships and time-machines are no escape from the human condition. Let Othello subject Desdemona to a lie-detector test; his jealousy will still blind him to the evidence. Let Oedipus triumph over gravity; he won't triumph over his fate.

14.   Some twenty years ago the German writer, Alfred Döblin, wrote a novel in which humanity discovers the secret of biological self-transformation: by a click of their fingers people can change themselves into giants, tigers, demons, or fish— much like Flook in the *Daily Mail* cartoon. At the end of the book the last specimens of this happy race sit, each on a solitary rock, in the shape of black ravens, in eternal silence. They have tried, experienced, seen and said everything under the sun, and all that is left for them to do is to die of boredom—the boredom of fantasy.

DISCUSSION: ORDER OF IDEAS

We said earlier that the order of ideas in the whole essay may be determined by assumptions the writer makes about his audience. We said that the writer may state his thesis in the first paragraph, if he is sure his audience will understand it without explanation, or he may build to it, if he believes the thesis requires explanation or will be more convincing if reserved to the end. As a result of these considerations there may be a difference between the natural or logical order of ideas (the sequence in which we think out ideas) and their rhetorical order (the order in which they finally appear). The conclusion, or thesis, is the result of a process of thought, a series of premises or evidences. If the writer believes that his conclusion is less controversial than his premises, he may choose to begin with it and build to a defense of the premises; or he may proceed in the reverse order.

Certain patterns of organization have become traditional because they reflect the natural processes of thought and argument. One pattern that influenced the formal essay is that of the classical oration. We may summarize its parts as follows:

> *exordium,* or *introduction,* which shapes the mood of the audience; appeals to its interest and good will; states the subject or thesis or point-at-issue
> *division of proofs,* which summarizes the proofs or kinds of evidence and argument to be presented
> *narration,* which states the relevant facts and background
> *confirmation,* or *proof,* which argues the thesis
> *refutation,* which attacks the arguments of opponents
> *peroration,* or *conclusion,* which reinforces the original appeal to the audience, makes new appeals, and summarizes the main argument and proofs if necessary

The advantage of following this procedure is that it helps the writer unify his argument in accord with certain traditional approaches to the audience—that is, he can if he wishes take advantage of a familiar ordering of ideas. The formal essay may omit one or several of the parts indicated above; and the "proof" may consist of mere exposition. The parts may also be arranged in a different way, the refutation possibly being combined with the narration.

The ideas of the informal essay may be as carefully organized as those of the formal essay, but the division of parts will usually be less definite or rigorous. The ideas may also be shaped to express a particular mood or attitude. For example, Orwell's "Shooting an Elephant" makes important comments on the relationship between the imperialist ruler and those ruled through an episode that defines that relationship; these comments could be made in a formal discussion of the problem, without illustrating or dramatizing it.

QUESTIONS

1. Instead of presenting his thesis in the early paragraphs, Koestler builds to it. He states it in preliminary form in paragraph 9—science-

fiction "will never become good art"—and proceeds to develop it; he distinguishes in the same paragraph between "the artist's disciplined imagination" and "the schoolboy's unbridled fantasy." What is the essential difference, and why does fantasy lead to boredom? Where in the rest of the essay does Koestler restate his thesis?

2. Paragraph 6 discusses the reason for the science-fiction cult. How does the paragraph clarify the thesis?

3. How do paragraphs 9 and 10 help to explain what Koestler means by "good art"? What does paragraph 11 add to our understanding of the phrase?

4. Paragraphs 1 and 2 constitute the main narrative of the essay, but Koestler provides additional important background in later paragraphs. What is the purpose of this later information? If Koestler were writing for science-fiction fans only, the example would be superfluous. What does he assume about his audience, and how do you know? How much does he assume his audience knows about art criticism or needs to be told?

5. The main part of the essay serves as the confirmation of the argument. Has Koestler introduced a refutation?

6. What is the function of the last paragraph? Does it introduce a new idea or summarize the argument?

WRITING ASSIGNMENT

Develop a thesis relating to the popular arts—for example, why some comic strips are uninteresting. Remember that how much you describe or explain and the order in which you introduce your ideas will depend on how much you assume your audience knows about the subject.

Loren Eiseley
SCIENCE AND THE UNEXPECTED UNIVERSE

Imagine God, as the Poet saith, *Ludere in Humanis,* to play but a game at Chesse with this world; to sport Himself with mak-

SCIENCE AND THE UNEXPECTED UNIVERSE: © 1966 by Loren C. Eiseley. Reprinted from his volume *The Unexpected Universe* by permission of Harcourt Brace Jovanovich, Inc.

ing little things great, and great things nothing; Imagine God
to be at play with us, but a gamester. . . .

—JOHN DONNE

1.   A British essayist of distinction, H. J. Massingham, once
remarked perceptively that woods nowadays are haunted not by
ghosts, but by a silence and man-made desolation that might
well take terrifying material forms. There is nothing like a stalled
train in a marsh to promote such reflections—particularly if one
has been transported just beyond the environs of a great city and
set down in some nether world that seems to partake both of nature before man came and of the residue of what will exist after
him. It was night when my train halted, but a kind of flame-
wreathed landscape attended by shadowy figures could be
glimpsed from the window.
2.   After a time, with a companion, I descended and strolled
forward to explore this curious region. It turned out to be a perpetually burning city dump, contributing its miasmas and choking vapors to the murky sky above the city. Amidst the tended
flames of this inferno I approached one of the grimy attendants
who was forking over the rubbish. In the background, other
shadows, official and unofficial, were similarly engaged. For a
moment I had the insubstantial feeling that must exist on the
borders of hell, where everything, wavering among heat waves,
is transported to another dimension. One could imagine ragged
and distorted souls grubbed over by scavengers for what might
usefully survive.
3.   I stood in silence watching this great burning. Sodden
papers were being forked into the flames, and after a while it
crossed my mind that this was perhaps the place where last
year's lace valentines had gone, along with old Christmas trees,
and the beds I had slept on in childhood.
4.   "I suppose you get everything here," I ventured to the
grimy attendant.
5.   He nodded indifferently and drew a heavy glove across
his face. His eyes were red-rimmed from the fire. Perhaps they
were red anyhow.
6.   "Know what?" He swept a hand outward toward the
flames. "No," I confessed.
7.   "Babies," he growled in my ear. "Even dead babies sometimes turn up. From there." He gestured contemptuously toward

the city and hoisted an indistinguishable mass upon his fork. I stepped back from the flare of light but it was only part of an old radio cabinet. Out of it had once come voices and music and laughter, perhaps from the twenties. And where were the voices traveling now? I looked at the dangling fragments of wire. They reminded me of something, but the engine bell sounded before I could remember.

8.   I made a parting gesture. Around me in the gloom dark shapes worked ceaselessly at the dampened fires. My eyes were growing accustomed to their light.

9.   "We get it all," the dump philosopher repeated. "Just give it time to travel, we get it all."

10.   "Be seeing you," I said irrelevantly. "Good luck."

11.   Back in my train seat, I remembered unwillingly the flames and the dangling wire. It had something to do with an air crash years ago and the identification of the dead. Anthropologists get strange assignments. I put the matter out of my mind, as I always do, but I dozed and it came back: the box with the dangling wires. I had once fitted a seared and broken skull-cap over a dead man's brains, and I had thought, peering into the scorched and mangled skull vault, it is like a beautiful, irreparably broken machine, like something consciously made to be used, and now where are the voices and the music?

12.   "We get it all," a dark figure said in my dreams. I sighed, and the figure in the murk faded into the clicking of the wheels.

13.   One can think just so much, but the archaeologist is awake to memories of the dead cultures sleeping around us, to our destiny, and to the nature of the universe we profess to inhabit. I would speak of these things not as a wise man, with scientific certitude, but from a place outside, in the role, shall we say, of a city-dump philosopher. Nor is this a strained figure of speech. The archaeologist is the last grubber among things mortal. He puts not men, but civilizations, to bed, and passes upon them final judgments. He finds, if imprinted upon clay, both our grocery bills and the hymns to our gods. Or he uncovers, as I once did in a mountain cavern, the skeleton of a cradled child, supplied, in the pathos of our mortality, with the carefully "killed" tools whose shadowy counterparts were intended to serve a tiny infant through the vicissitudes it would encounter beyond the dark curtain of death. Infinite care had been lavished upon objects that did not equate with the child's ability to use

them in this life. Was his spirit expected to grow to manhood, or had this final projection of bereaved parental care thrust into the night, in desperate anxiety, all that an impoverished and simple culture could provide where human affection could not follow?

14.   In a comparable but more abstract way, the modern mind, the scientific mind, concerned as it is with the imponderable mysteries of existence, has sought to equip oncoming generations with certain mental weapons against the terrors of ignorance. Protectively, as in the case of the dead child bundled in a cave, science has proclaimed a universe whose laws are open to discovery and, above all, it has sought, in the words of one of its greatest exponents, Francis Bacon, "not to imagine or suppose, but to *discover* what nature does or may be made to do."

15.   To discover what nature does, however, two primary restrictions are laid upon a finite creature: he must extrapolate his laws from what exists in his or his society's moment of time and, in addition, he is limited by what his senses can tell him of the surrounding world. Later, technology may provide the extension of those senses, as in the case of the microscope and telescope. Nevertheless the same eye or ear with which we are naturally endowed must, in the end, interpret the data derived from such extensions of sight or hearing. Moreover, science since the thirteenth century has clung to the dictum of William of Ockham that hypotheses must not be multiplied excessively; that the world, in essence, is always simple, not complicated, and its secrets accessible to men of astute and sufficiently penetrating intellect. Ironically, in the time of our greatest intellectual and technological triumphs one is forced to say that Ockham's long-honored precepts, however well they have served man, are, from another view, merely a more sophisticated projection of man's desire for order—and for the ability to control, understand and manipulate his world.

16.   All of these intentions are commendable enough, but perhaps we would approach them more humbly and within a greater frame of reference if we were to recognize what Massingham sensed as lying latent in his wood, or what John Donne implied more than three centuries ago when he wrote:

> I am rebegot
> of absence, darknesse, death:
> Things which are not.

17.   Donne had recognized that behind visible nature lurks an invisible and procreant void from whose incomprehensible magnitude we can only recoil. That void has haunted me ever since I handled the shattered calvarium that a few hours before had contained, in microcosmic dimensions, a similar lurking potency.

18.   Some years previously I had written a little book of essays in which I had narrated how time had become natural in our thinking, and I had gone on to speak likewise of life and man. In the end, however, I had been forced to ask How Natural is Natural?—a subject that raised the hackles of some of my scientifically inclined colleagues, who confused the achievements of their disciplines with certitude on a cosmic scale. My very question thus implied an ill-concealed heresy. That heresy it is my intent to pursue further. It will involve us, not in the denigration of science, but, rather, in a farther stretch of the imagination as we approach those distant and wooded boundaries of thought where, in the words of the old fairy tale, the fox and the hare say goodnight to each other. It is here that predictability ceases and the unimaginable begins—or, as a final heretical suspicion, we might ask ourselves whether our own little planetary fragment of the cosmos has all along concealed a mocking refusal to comply totally with human conceptions of order and secure prediction.

19.   The world contains, for all its seeming regularity, a series of surprises resembling those that in childhood terrorized us by erupting on springs from closed boxes. The world of primitive man is not dissimilar. Lightning leaps from clouds, something invisible rumbles in the air, the living body, spilling its mysterious red fluid, lies down in a sleep from which it cannot waken. There are night cries in the forest, talking waters, guiding omens, or portents in the fall of a leaf. No longer, as with the animal, can the world be accepted as given. It has to be perceived and consciously thought about, abstracted, and considered. The moment one does so, one is outside of the natural; objects are each one surrounded with an aura radiating meaning to man alone. To a universe already suspected of being woven together by unseen forces, man brings the organizing power of primitive magic. The manikin that is believed to control the macrocosm by some sympathetic connection is already obscurely present in the poppet thrust full of needles by the witch. Crude and imperfect, magic is still man's first conscious abstraction from nature, his

first attempt to link disparate objects by some unseen attraction between them.

20.   If we now descend into the early years of modern science, we find the world of the late eighteenth and early nineteenth centuries basking comfortably in the conception of the balanced world machine. Newton had established what appeared to be the reign of universal order in the heavens. The planets—indeed the whole cosmic engine—were self-regulatory. This passion for order controlled by a divinity too vast to be concerned with petty miracle was slowly extended to earth. James Hutton glimpsed, in the long erosion and renewal of the continents by subterranean uplift, a similar "beautiful machine" so arranged that recourse to the "preternatural," or "destructive accident," such as the Mosaic Deluge, was unnecessary to account for the physical features of the planet.

21.   Time had lengthened and through those eons, law, not chaos, reigned. The imprint of fossil raindrops similar to those of today had been discovered upon ancient shores. The marks of fossil ripples were also observable in uncovered strata, and buried trees had absorbed the sunlight of far millennia. The remote past was one with the present and, over all, a lawful similarity decreed by a Christian Deity prevailed.

22.   In the animal world, a similar web of organization was believed to exist, save by a few hesitant thinkers. The balanced Newtonian clockwork of the heavens had been transferred to earth and, for a few decades, was destined to prevail in the world of life. Plants and animals would be frozen into their existing shapes; they would compete but not change, for change in this system was basically a denial of law. Hutton's world renewed itself in cycles, just as the oscillations observable in the heavens were similarly self-regulatory.

23.   Time was thus law-abiding. It contained no novelty and was self-correcting. It was, as we have indicated, a manifestation of divine law. That law was a comfort to man. The restive world of life fell under the same dominion as the equally restive particles of earth. Organisms oscillated within severely fixed limits. The smallest animalcule in a hay infusion carried a message for man; the joints of an insect assured him of divine attention. "In every nature and every portion of nature which we can descry," wrote William Paley in a book characteristic of the period, "we find attention bestowed upon even the minutest parts. The

hinges in the wing of an earwig . . . are as highly wrought as if the creator had nothing else to finish. We see no signs of diminution of care by multiplicity of objects, or distraction of thought by variety. We have no reason to fear, therefore, our being forgotten, or overlooked, or neglected." Written into these lines in scientific guise is the same humanly protective gesture that long ago had heaped skin blankets, bone needles and a carved stick for killing rabbits into the burial chamber of a child.

24.   This undeviating balance in which life was locked was called "natural government" by the great anatomist John Hunter. It was, in a sense, like the cyclic but undeviating life of the planet earth itself. That vast elemental creature felt the fall of raindrops on its ragged flanks, was troubled by the drift of autumn leaves or the erosive work of wind throughout eternity. Nevertheless, the accounts of nature were strictly kept. If a continent was depressed at one point, its equivalent arose elsewhere. Whether the item in the scale was the weight of a raindrop or a dislodged boulder on a mountainside, a dynamic balance kept the great beast young and flourishing upon its course.

25.   And as it was with earth, so with its inhabitants. "There is an equilibrium kept up among the animals by themselves," Hunter went on to contend. They kept their own numbers pruned and in proportion. Expansion was always kept within bounds. The struggle for existence was recognized before Darwin, but only as the indefinite sway of a returning pendulum. Life was selected, but it was selected for but one purpose: vigor and consistency in appearance. The mutative variant was struck down. What had been was; what would be already existed. As in the case of that great animal the earth, of the living flora and fauna it could be said that there was to be found "no vestige of a beginning,—no prospect of an end." An elemental order lay across granite, sea and shore. Each individual animal peered from age to age out of the same unyielding sockets of bone. Out of no other casements could he stare; the dweller within would see leaf and bird eternally the same. This was the scientific doctrine known as uniformitarianism. It had abolished magic as it had abolished the many changes and shape shiftings of witch doctors and medieval necromancers. At last the world was genuinely sane under a beneficent Deity. Then came Darwin.

26.   At first he was hailed as another Newton who had dis-

covered the laws of life. It was true that what had once been deemed independent creations—the shells in the collector's cabinet, the flowers pressed into memory books—were now, as in the abandoned magic of the ancient past, once more joined by invisible threads of sympathy and netted together by a common ancestry. The world seemed even more understandable, more natural than natural. The fortuitous had become fashionable, and the other face of "natural government" turned out to be creation. Life's pendulum of balance was an illusion.

27.   Behind the staid face of that nature we had worshiped for so long we were unseen shapeshifters. Viewed in the long light of limitless time, we were optical illusions whose very identity was difficult to fix. Still, there was much talk of progress and perfection. Only later did we begin to realize that what Charles Darwin had introduced into nature was not Newtonian predictability but absolute random novelty. Life was bent, in the phrase of Alfred Russel Wallace, upon "indefinite departure." No living thing, not even man, understood upon what journey he had embarked. Time was no longer cyclic or monotonously repetitious.* It was historic, novel, and unreturning. Since that momentous discovery, man has, whether or not he realizes or accepts his fate, been moving in a world of contingent forms.

28.   Even in the supposedly stable universe of matter, as it was viewed by nineteenth-century scientists, new problems constantly appear. The discovery by physicists of antimatter particles having electric charges opposite to those that compose our world and unable to exist in concert with known matter raises the question of whether, after all, our corner of the universe is representative of the entire potentialities that may exist elsewhere. The existence of antimatter is unaccounted for in present theories of the universe, and such peculiarities as the primordial atom and the recently reported flash of the explosion at the birth of the universe, as recorded in the radio spectrum, lead on into unknown paths.

29.   If it were not for the fact that familiarity leads to assumed knowledge, we would have to admit that the earth's atmosphere of oxygen appears to be the product of a biological invention, photosynthesis, another random event that took place in Archeozoic times. That single "invention," for such it was, determined

* For purposes of space I have chosen to ignore the short-lived geological doctrine of the early nineteenth century known as catastrophism, since I have treated it at length elsewhere.

the entire nature of life on this planet, and there is no possibility at present of calling it preordained. Similarly, the stepped-up manipulation of chance, in the shape of both mutation and recombination of genetic factors, which is one result of the sexual mechanism, would have been unprophesiable.

30.   The brain of man, that strange gray iceberg of conscious and unconscious life, was similarly unpredictable until its appearance. A comparatively short lapse of geological time has evolved a humanity that, beginning in considerable physical diversity, has increasingly converged toward a universal biological similarity marked only by a lingering and insignificant racial differentiation. With the rise of *Homo sapiens* and the final perfection of the human brain as a manipulator of symbolic thought, the spectrum of man's possible social behavior has widened enormously. What is essentially the same brain biologically can continue to exist in the simple ecological balance of the Stone Age, or, on the other hand, may produce those enormous inflorescences known as civilizations. These growths seemingly operate under their own laws and take distinct and irreversible pathways. In an analogous way, organisms mutate and diverge through adaptive radiation from one or a few original forms.

31.   In the domain of culture, man's augmented ability to manipulate abstract ideas and to draw in this fashion enormous latent stores of energy from his brain has led to an intriguing situation: the range of his *possible* behavior is greater and more contradictory than that which can be contained within the compass of a single society, whether tribal or advanced. Thus, as man's penetration into the metaphysical and abstract has succeeded, so has his capacity to follow, in the same physical body, a series of tangential roads into the future. Likeness in body has, paradoxically, led to diversity in thought. Thought, in turn, involves such vast institutional involutions as the rise of modern science, with its intensified hold upon modern society.

32.   All past civilizations of men have been localized and have had, therefore, the divergent mutative quality to which we have referred. They have offered choices to men. Ideas have been exchanged, along with technological innovations, but never on so vast, overwhelming and single-directed a scale as in the present. Increasingly, there is but one way into the future: the technological way. The frightening aspect of this situation lies in the constriction of human choice. Western technology has re-

leased irrevocable forces, and the "one world" that has been talked about so glibly is frequently a distraught conformity produced by the centripetal forces of Western society. So great is its power over men that any other solution, any other philosophy, is silenced. Men, unknowingly, and whether for good or ill, appear to be making their last decisions about human destiny. To pursue the biological analogy, it is as though, instead of many adaptive organisms, a single gigantic animal embodied the only organic future of the world.

33.   Archaeology is the science of man's evening, not of his midday triumphs. I have spoken of my visit to a flame-wreathed marsh at nightfall. All in it had been substance, matter, trailing wires and old sandwich wrappings, broken toys and iron bedsteads. Yet there was nothing present that science could not reduce into its elements, nothing that was not the product of the urban world whose far-off towers had risen gleaming in the dusk beyond the marsh. There on the city dump had lain the shabby debris of life: the waxen fragment of an old record that had stolen a human heart, wilted flowers among smashed beer cans, the castaway knife of a murderer, along with a broken tablespoon. It was all a maze of invisible, floating connections, and would be until the last man perished. These forlorn materials had all been subjected to the dissolving power of the human mind. They had been wrenched from deep veins of rock, boiled in great crucibles, and carried miles from their origins. They had assumed shapes that, though material enough, had existed first as blueprints in the profound darkness of a living brain. They had been defined before their existence, named and given shape in the puff of air that we call a word. That word had been evoked in a skull box which, with all its contained powers and lurking paradoxes, has arisen in ways we can only dimly retrace.

34.   Einstein is reputed to have once remarked that he refused to believe that God plays at dice with the universe. But as we survey the long backward course of history, it would appear that in the phenomenal world the open-endedness of time is unexpectedly an essential element of His creation. Whenever an infant is born, the dice, in the shape of genes and enzymes and the intangibles of chance environment, are being rolled again, as when that smoky figure from the fire hissed in my ear the tragedy of the cast-off infants of the city. Each one of us is a statistical impossibility around which hover a million other lives that

were never destined to be born—but who, nevertheless, are being unmanifest, a lurking potential in the dark storehouse of the void.

35.   Today in spite of that web of law, that network of forces which the past century sought to string to the ends of the universe, a strange unexpectedness lingers about our world. This change in viewpoint, which has frequently escaped our attention, can be illustrated in the remark of Heinrich Hertz, the nineteenth-century experimenter in the electromagnetic field. "The most important problem which our conscious knowledge of nature should enable us to solve," Hertz stated, "is the anticipation of future events, so that we may arrange our present affairs in accordance with such anticipation."

36.   There is an attraction about this philosophy that causes it to linger in the lay mind and, as a short-term prospect, in the minds of many scientists and technologists. It implies a tidiness which is infinitely attractive to man, increasingly a homeless orphan lost in the vast abysses of space and time. Hertz's remark seems to offer surcease from uncertainty, power contained, the universe understood, the future apprehended before its emergence. The previous Elizabethan age, by contrast, had often attached to its legal documents a humble obeisance to life's uncertainties expressed in the phrase "by the mutability of fortune and favor." The men of Shakespeare's century may have known less of science, but they knew only too well what unexpected overthrow was implied in the frown of a monarch or a breath of the plague.

37.   The twentieth century, on the other hand, surveys a totally new universe. That our cosmological conceptions bear a relationship to the past is obvious, that some of the power of which Hertz dreamed lies in our hands is all too evident, but never before in human history has the mind soared higher and seen less to cheer its complacency. We have heard much of science as the endless frontier, but we whose immediate ancestors were seekers of gold among great mountains and gloomy forests are easily susceptible to a simplistic conception of the word *frontier* as something conquerable in its totality. We assume that, with enough time and expenditure of energy, the ore will be extracted and the forests computed in board feet of lumber. A tamed wilderness will subject itself to man.

38.   Not so the wilderness beyond the stars or concealed in the

infinitesimal world beneath the atom. Wise reflection will lead us to recognize that we have come upon a different and less conquerable region. Forays across its border already suggest that man's dream of mastering all aspects of nature takes no account of his limitations in time or space or of his own senses, augmented though they may be by his technological devices. Even the thought that he can bring to bear upon that frontier is limited in quantity by the number of trained minds that can sustain such an adventure. Ever more expensive grow the tools with which research can be sustained, ever more diverse the social problems which that research, in its technological phase, promotes. To take one single example: who would have dreamed that a tube connecting two lenses of glass would pierce into the swarming depths of our being, force upon us incredible feats of sanitary engineering, master the plague, and create that giant upsurge out of unloosened nature which we call the population explosion?

39.   The Roman Empire is a past event in history, yet by analogy it presents us with a small scale model comparable to the endless frontier of science. A great political and military machine had expanded outward to the limits of the known world. Its lines of communication grew ever more tenuous, taxes rose fantastically, the disaffected and alienated within its borders steadily increased. By the time of the barbarian invasions the vast structure was already dying of inanition. Yet that empire lasted far longer than the world of science has yet endured.

40.   But what of the empire of science? Does not its word leap fast as light, is it not a creator of incalculable wealth, is not space its plaything? Its weapons are monstrous; its eye is capable of peering beyond millions of light-years. There is one dubious answer to this buoyant optimism: science is human; it is of human devising and manufacture. It has not prevented war; it has perfected it. It has not abolished cruelty or corruption; it has enabled these abominations to be practiced on a scale unknown before in human history.

41.   Science is a solver of problems, but it is dealing with the limitless, just as, in a cruder way, were the Romans. Solutions to problems create problems; their solutions, in turn, multiply into additional problems that escape out of scientific hands like noxious insects into the interstices of the social fabric. The rate of growth is geometric, and the vibrations set up can even now be detected in our institutions. This is what the Scottish

biologist D'Arcy Thompson called the evolution of contingency. It is no longer represented by the long, slow turn of world time as the geologist has known it. Contingency has escaped into human hands and flickers unseen behind every whirl of our machines, every pronouncement of political policy.

42.   Each one of us before his death looks back upon a childhood whose ways now seem as remote as those of Rome. "Daddy," the small daughter of a friend of mine recently asked, "tell me how it was in olden days." As my kindly friend groped amidst his classical history, he suddenly realized with a slight shock that his daughter wanted nothing more than an account of his own childhood. It was forty years away and it was already "olden days." "There was a time," he said slowly to the enchanted child, "called the years of the Great Depression. In that time there was a very great deal to eat, but men could not buy it. Little girls were scarcer than now. You see," he said painfully, "their fathers could not afford them, and they were not born." He made a half-apologetic gesture to the empty room, as if to a gathering of small reproachful ghosts. "There was a monster we never understood called Overproduction. There were," and his voice trailed hopelessly into silence, "so many dragons in that time you could not believe it. And there was a very civilized nation where little girls were taken from their parents. . . ." He could not go on. The eyes from Auschwitz, he told me later, would not permit him.

43.   Recently I passed a cemetery in a particularly bleak countryside. Adjoining the multitude of stark upthrust grey stones was an incongruous row of six transparent telephone booths erected in that spot for reasons best known to the communications industry. Were they placed there for the midnight convenience of the dead, or for the midday visitors who might attempt speech with the silent people beyond the fence? It was difficult to determine, but I thought the episode suggestive of our dilemma.

44.   An instrument for communication, erected by a powerful unseen intelligence, was at my command, but I suspect—although I was oddly averse to trying to find out—that the wires did not run in the proper direction, and that there was something disconnected or disjointed about the whole endeavor. It was, I fear, symbolic of an unexpected aspect of our universe, a universe that, however strung with connecting threads, is en-

dowed with an open-ended and perverse quality we shall never completely master. Nature contains that which does not concern us, and has no intention of taking us into its confidence. It may provide us with receiving boxes of white bone as cunning in their way as the wired booths in the cemetery, but, like these, they appear to lack some essential ingredient of genuine connection. As we consider what appears to be the chance emergence of photosynthesis, which turns the light of a far star into green leaves, or the creation of the phenomenon of sex that causes the cards at the gaming table of life to be shuffled with increasing frequency and into ever more diverse combinations, it should be plain that nature contains the roiling unrest of a tornado. It is not the self-contained stately palace of the eighteenth-century philosophers, a palace whose doorstep was always in precisely the same position.

45.   From the oscillating universe beating like a gigantic heart, to the puzzling existence of antimatter, order, in a human sense, is at least partially an illusion. Ours, in reality, is the order of a time, and of an insignificant fraction of the cosmos, seen by the limited senses of a finite creature. Behind the appearances, as even one group of primitive philosophers, the Hopi, have grasped, lurks being unmanifest, whose range and number exceeds the real. This is why the unexpected will always confront us; this is why the endless frontier is really endless. This is why the half-formed chaos of the marsh moved me as profoundly as though a new prophetic shape induced by us had risen monstrously from dangling wire and crumpled cardboard.

46.   We are more dangerous than we seem and more potent in our ability to materialize the unexpected that is drawn from our own minds. "Force maketh Nature more violent in the Returne," Francis Bacon had once written. In the end this is her primary quality. Her creature man partakes of that essence, and it is well that he consider it in contemplation and not always in action. To the unexpected nature of the universe man owes his being. More than any other living creature he contains, unknowingly, the shapes and forms of an uncreated future to be drawn from his own substance. The history of this unhappy century should prove a drastic warning of his powers of dissolution, even when directed upon himself. Waste, uncertain marshes, lie close to reality in our heads. Shapes as yet unevoked had best be left lying amidst those spectral bog lights, lest the drifting smoke of

dreams merge imperceptibly, as once it did, with the choking real fumes from the ovens of Belsen and Buchenwald.

47.   "It is very unhappy, but too late to be helped," Emerson had noted in his journal, "the discovery we have made that we exist. That discovery is called the Fall of Man. Ever afterwards we suspect our instruments. We have learned that we do not see directly." Wisdom interfused with compassion should be the consequence of that discovery, for at the same moment one aspect of the unexpected universe will have been genuinely revealed. It lies deep-hidden in the human heart, and not at the peripheries of space. Both the light we seek and the shadows that we fear are projected from within. It is through ourselves that the organic procession pauses, hesitates, or renews its journey. "We have learned to ask terrible questions," exclaimed that same thinker in the dawn of Victorian science. Perhaps it is just for this that the Unseen Player in the void has rolled his equally terrible dice. Out of the self-knowledge gained by putting dreadful questions man achieves his final dignity.

QUESTIONS

1. Eiseley builds up to a preliminary statement of his thesis by describing his experience on the marsh. What "terrifying material forms" did he discover? What is the significance of the attendant's comment that "Even dead babies sometimes turn up"? How is this comment related to Eiseley's discovery of the "dead child cradled in a cave"?

2. Eiseley states his thesis at the end of paragraph 18 and restates it several times later in the essay. How has the thesis been introduced?

3. What has Eiseley told the reader about the modern world in the process of introducing his thesis?

4. What is the purpose of the contrast between our present world and that of primitive man (paragraph 19)? What does the history of uniformitarianism in paragraphs 20–25 show? How are the two considerations related?

5. What have been the consequences of thinking that nature is entirely predictable? Is the "constriction of human choice," discussed in paragraph 32, one consequence?

6. What conclusion does Eiseley derive from the fact that man is a "statistical impossibility" (paragraph 34)? If nature is less predictable than man had assumed, is man more free than he thought?

7. What does Eiseley show to be the limitations of science? What is the meaning of Emerson's statement, "We have learned that we do not

see directly" (paragraph 47)? How did Emerson interpret the Fall of
Man?

8. What is the implication of the statement that "It is through ourselves that the organic procession pauses, hesitates, or renews its
   journey" (paragraph 47)?
9. Is Eiseley suggesting that the unexpectedness of the universe reveals a higher purpose? Would it be possible to determine the nature of his religious beliefs from this essay?
10. What is the purpose of the reference to the ovens of Belsen and
    Buchenwald in the concluding paragraphs? How is this reference
    related to the introduction of the essay?
11. Where is the thesis most fully stated?
12. What does Eiseley appear to assume about the knowledge and
    background of his audience? Is he writing for the general reader or
    for a strictly scientific audience?

WRITING ASSIGNMENT

Discuss the implication of one of the following statements in relation to
the essay as a whole:

a. "Western technology has released irrevocable forces, and the 'one
   world' that has been talked about so glibly is frequently a distraught conformity produced by the centripetal forces of Western
   society" (paragraph 32).
b. "Einstein is reputed to have once remarked that he refused
   to believe that God plays at dice with the universe" (paragraph
   34).
c. "Science is a solver of problems, but it is dealing with the limitless,
   just as, in a cruder way, were the Romans" (paragraph 41).
d. "We are more dangerous than we seem and more potent in our ability to materialize the unexpected that is drawn from our own
   minds" (paragraph 46).

Ralph Ellison
LIVING WITH MUSIC

1.   In those days it was either live with music or die with
noise, and we chose rather desperately to live. In the process our

LIVING WITH MUSIC: From *High Fidelity*, December, 1955. Reprinted by permission of *High Fidelity*.

apartment—what with its booby-trappings of audio equipment, wires, discs and tapes—came to resemble the Collier mansion, but that was later. First there was the neighborhood, assorted drunks and a singer.

2.   We were living at the time in a tiny ground-floor-rear apartment in which I was also trying to write. I say "trying" advisedly. To our right, separated by a thin wall, was a small restaurant with a juke box the size of the Roxy. To our left, a night-employed swing enthusiast who took his lullaby music so loud that every morning promptly at nine Basie's brasses started blasting my typewriter off its stand. Our living room looked out across a small back yard to a rough stone wall to an apartment building which, towering above, caught every passing thorough-fare sound and rifled it straight down to me. There were also howling cats and barking dogs, none capable of music worth living with, so we'll pass them by.

3.   But the court behind the wall, which on the far side came knee-high to a short Iroquois, was a forum for various singing and/or preaching drunks who wandered back from the corner bar. From these you sometimes heard a fair barbershop style "Bill Bailey," free-wheeling versions of "The Bastard King of England," the saga of Uncle Bud, or a deeply felt rendition of Leroy Carr's "How Long Blues." The preaching drunks took on any topic that came to mind: current events, the fate of the long-sunk *Titanic* or the relative merits of the Giants and the Dodgers. Naturally there was great argument and occasional fighting—none of it fatal but all of it loud.

4.   I shouldn't complain, however, for these were rather entertaining drunks, who like the birds appeared in the spring and left with the first fall cold. A more dedicated fellow was there all the time, day and night, come rain, come shine. Up on the corner lived a drunk of legend, a true phenomenon, who could surely have qualified as the king of all the world's winos—not excluding the French. He was neither poetic like the others nor ambitious like the singer (to whom we'll presently come) but his drinking bouts were truly awe-inspiring and he was not without his sensitivity. In the throes of his passion he would shout to the whole wide world one concise command, "Shut up!" Which was disconcerting enough to all who heard (except, perhaps, the singer), but such were the labyrinthine acoustics of courtyards and areaways that he seemed to direct his command at me. The writer's

block which this produced is indescribable. On one heroic occasion he yelled his obsessive command without one interruption longer than necessary to take another drink (and with no appreciable loss of volume, penetration or authority) for three long summer days and nights, and shortly afterwards he died. Just how many lines of agitated prose he cost me I'll never know, but in all that chaos of sound I sympathized with his obsession, for I, too, hungered and thirsted for quiet. Nor did he inspire me to a painful identification, and for that I was thankful. Identification, after all, involves feelings of guilt and responsibility, and since I could hardly hear my own typewriter keys I felt in no way accountable for his condition. We were simply fellow victims of the madding crowd. May he rest in peace.

5.   No, these more involved feelings were aroused by a more intimate source of noise, one that got beneath the skin and worked into the very structure of one's consciousness—like the "fate" motif in Beethoven's Fifth or the knocking-at-the-gates scene in *Macbeth*. For at the top of our pyramid of noise there was a singer who lived directly above us; you might say we had a singer on our ceiling.

6.   Now, I had learned from the jazz musicians I had known as a boy in Oklahoma City something of the discipline and devotion to his art required of the artist. Hence I knew something of what the singer faced. These jazzmen, many of them now world-famous, lived for and with music intensely. Their driving motivation was neither money nor fame, but the will to achieve the most eloquent expression of idea-emotions through the technical mastery of their instruments (which, incidentally, some of them wore as a priest wears the cross) and the give and take, the subtle rhythmical shaping and blending of idea, tone and imagination demanded of group improvisation. The delicate balance struck between strong individual personality and the group during those early jam sessions was a marvel of social organization. I had learned too that the end of all this discipline and technical mastery was the desire to express an affirmative way of life through its musical tradition and that this tradition insisted that each artist achieve his creativity within its frame. He must learn the best of the past, and add to it his personal vision. Life could be harsh, loud and wrong if it wished, but they lived it fully, and when they expressed their attitude toward the world it was with a fluid style that reduced the chaos of living to form.

7.   The objectives of these jazzmen were not at all those of the singer on our ceiling, but though a purist committed to the mastery of the *bel canto* style, German *lieder*, modern French art songs and a few American slave songs sung as if *bel canto*, she was intensely devoted to her art. From morning to night she vocalized, regardless of the condition of her voice, the weather or my screaming nerves. There were times when her notes, sifting through her floor and my ceiling, bouncing down the walls and ricocheting off the building in the rear, whistled like tenpenny nails, buzzed like a saw, wheezed like the asthma of a Hercules, trumpeted like an enraged African elephant—and the squeaky pedal of her piano rested plumb center above my typing chair. After a year of non-co-operation from the neighbor on my left I became desperate enough to cool down the hot blast of his phonograph by calling the cops, but the singer presented a serious ethical problem: Could I, an aspiring artist, complain against the hard work and devotion to craft of another aspiring artist?

8.   Then there was my sense of guilt. Each time I prepared to shatter the ceiling in protest I was restrained by the knowledge that I, too, during my boyhood, had tried to master a musical instrument and to the great distress of my neighbors—perhaps even greater than that which I now suffered. For while our singer was concerned basically with a single tradition and style, I had been caught actively between two: that of the Negro folk music, both sacred and profane, slave song and jazz, and that of Western classical music. It was most confusing; the folk tradition demanded that I play what I heard and felt around me, while those who were seeking to teach the classical tradition in the schools insisted that I play strictly according to the book and express that which I was *supposed* to feel. This sometimes led to heated clashes of wills. Once during a third-grade music appreciation class a friend of mine insisted that it was a large green snake he saw swimming down a quiet brook instead of the snowy bird the teacher felt that Saint-Saëns' *Carnival of the Animals* should evoke. The rest of us sat there and lied like little black, brown and yellow Trojans about that swan, but our stalwart classmate held firm to his snake. In the end he got himself spanked and reduced the teacher to tears, but truth, reality and our environment were redeemed. For we were all familiar with snakes, while a swan was simply something the Ugly Duckling of the story grew up to be. Fortunately some of us grew up with a genuine

appreciation of classical music *despite* such teaching methods. But as an inspiring trumpeter I was to wallow in sin for years before being awakened to guilt by our singer.

9.   Caught mid-range between my two traditions, where one attitude often clashed with the other and one technique of playing was by the other opposed, I caused whole blocks of people to suffer.

10.   Indeed, I terrorized a good part of an entire city section. During summer vacation I blew sustained tones out of the window for hours, usually starting—especially on Sunday mornings—before breakfast. I sputtered whole days through M. Arban's (he's the great authority on the instrument) double- and triple-tonguing exercises—with an effect like that of a jackass hiccupping off a big meal of briars. During school-term mornings I practiced a truly exhibitionist "Reveille" before leaving for school, and in the evening I generously gave the ever-listening world a long, slow version of "Taps," ineptly played but throbbing with what I in my adolescent vagueness felt was a romantic sadness. For it was farewell to day and a love song to life and a peace-be-with-you to all the dead and dying.

11.   On hot summer afternoons I tormented the ears of all not blessedly deaf with imitations of the latest hot solos of Hot Lips Paige (then a local hero), the leaping right hand of Earl "Fatha" Hines, or the rowdy poetic flights of Louis Armstrong. Naturally I rehearsed also such school-band standbys as the *Light Cavalry* Overture, Sousa's "Stars and Strips Forever," the *William Tell* Overture, and "Tiger Rag." (Not even an after-school job as office boy to a dentist could stop my efforts. Frequently, by way of encouraging my development in the proper cultural direction, the dentist asked me proudly to render Schubert's *Serenade* for some poor devil with his jaw propped open in the dental chair. When the drill got going, or the forceps bit deep, I blew real strong.)

12.   Sometimes, inspired by the even then considerable virtuosity of the late Charlie Christian (who during our school days played marvelous riffs on a cigar box banjo), I'd give whole summer afternoons and the evening hours after heavy suppers of black-eyed peas and turnip greens, cracklin' bread and buttermilk, lemonade and sweet potato cobbler, to practicing hard-driving blues. Such food oversupplied me with bursting energy, and from listening to Ma Rainey, Ida Cox and Clara Smith, who

made regular appearances in our town, I knew exactly how I wanted my horn to sound. But in the effort to make it do so (I was no embryo Joe Smith or Tricky Sam Nanton) I sustained the curses of both Christian and infidel—along with the encouragement of those more sympathetic citizens who understood the profound satisfaction to be found in expressing oneself in the blues.

13.   Despite those who complained and cried to heaven for Gabriel to blow a chorus so heavenly sweet and so hellishly hot that I'd forever put down my horn, there were more tolerant ones who were willing to pay in present pain for future pride.

14.   For who knew what skinny kid with his chops wrapped around a trumpet mouthpiece and a faraway look in his eyes might become the next Armstrong? Yes, and send you, at some big dance a few years hence, into an ecstasy of rhythm and memory and brassy affirmation of the goodness of being alive and part of the community? Someone had to; for it was part of the group tradition—though that was not how they said it.

15.   "Let that boy blow," they'd say to the protesting ones. "He's got to talk baby talk on that thing before he can preach on it. Next thing you know he's liable to be up there with Duke Ellington. Sure, plenty Oklahoma boys are up there with the big bands. Son, let's hear you try those "Trouble in Mind Blues." Now try and make it sound like old Ida Cox sings it."

16.   And I'd draw in my breath and do Miss Cox great violence.

17.   Thus the crimes and aspirations of my youth. It had been years since I had played the trumpet or irritated a single ear with other than the spoken or written word, but as far as my singing neighbor was concerned I had to hold my peace. I was forced to listen, and in listening I soon became involved to the point of identification. If she sang badly I'd hear my own futility in the windy sound; if well, I'd stare at my typewriter and despair that I should ever make my prose so sing. She left me neither night nor day, this singer on our ceiling, and as my writing languished I became more and more upset. Thus one desperate morning I decided that since I seemed doomed to live within a shrieking chaos I might as well contribute my share; perhaps if I fought noise with noise I'd attain some small peace. Then a miracle: I turned on my radio (an old Philco AM set connected to a small Pilot FM tuner) and I heard the words

Art thou troubled?
Music will calm thee . . .

I stopped as though struck by the voice of an angel. It was Kathleen Ferrier, that loveliest of singers, giving voice to the aria from Handel's *Rodelinda*. The voice was so completely expressive of words and music that I accepted it without question—what lover of the vocal art could resist her?

18.   Yet it was ironic, for after giving up my trumpet for the typewriter I had avoided too close a contact with the very art which she recommended as balm. For I had started music early and lived with it daily, and when I broke I tried to break clean. Now in this magical moment all the old love, the old fascination with music superbly rendered, flooded back. When she finished I realized that with such music in my own apartment, the chaotic sounds from without and above had sunk, if not into silence, then well below the level where they mattered. Here was a way out. If I was to live and write in that apartment, it would be only through the grace of music. I had tuned in a Ferrier recital, and when it ended I rushed out for several of her records, certain that now deliverance was mine.

19.   But not yet. Between the hi-fi record and the ear, I learned, there was a new electronic world. In that realization our apartment was well on its way toward becoming an audio booby trap. It was 1949 and I rushed to the Audio Fair. I have, I confess, as much gadget-resistance as the next American of my age, weight and slight income; but little did I dream of the test to which it would be put. I had hardly entered the fair before I heard David Sarser's and Mel Sprinkle's Musician's Amplifier, took a look at its schematic and, recalling a boyhood acquaintance with such matters, decided that I could build one. I did, several times before it measured within specifications. And still our system was lacking. Fortunately my wife shared my passion for music, so we went on to buy, piece by piece, a fine speaker system, a first-rate AM-FM tuner, a transcription turntable and a speaker cabinet. I built half a dozen or more preamplifiers and record compensators before finding a commercial one that satisfied my ear, and, finally, we acquired an arm, a magnetic cartridge and—glory of the house—a tape recorder. All this plunge into electronics, mind you, had as its simple end the enjoyment of recorded music as it was intended to be heard. I was obsessed

with the idea of reproducing sound with such fidelity that even when using music as a defense behind which I could write, it would reach the unconscious levels of the mind with the least distortion. And it didn't come easily. There were wires and pieces of equipment all over the tiny apartment (I became a compulsive experimenter) and it was worth your life to move about without first taking careful bearings. Once we were almost crushed in our sleep by the tape machine, for which there was space only on a shelf at the head of our bed. But it was worth it.

20.   For now when we played a recording on our system even the drunks on the wall could recognize its quality. I'm ashamed to admit, however, that I did not always restrict its use to the demands of pleasure or defense. Indeed, with such marvels of science at my control I lost my humility. My ethical consideration for the singer up above shriveled like a plant in too much sunlight. For instead of soothing, music seemed to release the beast in me. Now when jarred from my writer's reveries by some especially enthusiastic flourish of our singer, I'd rush to my music system with blood in my eyes and burst a few decibels in her direction. If she defied me with a few more pounds of pressure against her diaphragm, then a war of decibels was declared.

21.   If, let us say, she were singing *"Depuis le Jour"* from *Louise,* I'd put on a tape of Bidu Sayão performing the same aria, and let the rafters ring. If it was some song by Mahler, I'd match her spitefully with Marian Anderson or Kathleen Ferrier; if she offended with something from *Der Rosenkavalier,* I'd attack her flank with Lotte Lehmann. If she brought me up from my desk with art songs by Ravel or Rachmaninoff, I'd defend myself with Maggie Teyte or Jennie Tourel. If she polished a spiritual to a meaningless artiness I'd play Bessie Smith to remind her of the earth out of which we came. Once in a while I'd forget completely that I was supposed to be a gentleman and blast her with Strauss' *Zarathustra,* Bartók's *Concerto for Orchestra,* Ellington's "Flaming Sword," the famous crescendo from *The Pines of Rome,* or Satchmo scatting, "I'll be Glad When You're Dead" (you rascal you!). Oh, I was living with music with a sweet vengeance.

22.   One might think that all this would have made me her most hated enemy, but not at all. When I met her on the stoop a few weeks after my rebellion, expecting her fully to slap my face, she astonished me by complimenting our music system. She even questioned me concerning the artists I had used against

her. After that, on days when the acoustics were right, she'd stop singing until the piece was finished and then applaud—not always, I guessed, without a justifiable touch of sarcasm. And although I was not getting on with my writing, the unfairness of this business bore in upon me. Aware that I could not have withstood a similar comparison with literary artists of like caliber, I grew remorseful. I also came to admire the singer's courage and control, for she was neither intimidated into silence nor goaded into undisciplined screaming; she persevered, she marked the phrasing of the great singers I sent her way, she improved her style.

23.   Better still, she vocalized more softly, and I, in turn, used music less and less as a weapon and more for its magic with mood and memory. After a while a simple twirl of the volume control up a few decibels and down again would bring a live-and-let-live reduction of her volume. We have long since moved from that apartment and that most interesting neighborhood and now the floors and walls of our present apartment are adequately thick and there is even a closet large enough to house the audio system; the only wire visible is that leading from the closet to the corner speaker system. Still we are indebted to the singer and the old environment for forcing us to discover one of the most deeply satisfying aspects of our living. Perhaps the enjoyment of music is always suffused with past experience; for me, at least, this is true.

24.   It seems a long way and a long time from the glorious days of Oklahoma jazz dances, the jam sessions at Halley Richardson's place on Deep Second, from the phonographs shouting the blues in the back alleys I knew as a delivery boy, and from the days when watermelon men with voices like mellow bugles shouted their wares in time with the rhythm of their horses' hoofs and farther still from the washerwomen singing slave songs as they stirred sooty tubs in sunny yards; and a long time, too, from those intense, conflicting days when the school music program of Oklahoma City was tuning our earthy young ears to classical accents—with music appreciation classes and free musical instruments and basic instruction for any child who cared to learn and uniforms for all who made the band. There was a mistaken notion on the part of some of the teachers that classical music had nothing to do with the rhythms, relaxed or hectic, of daily living, and that one should crook the little finger

when listening to such refined strains. And the blues and the spirituals—jazz—? they would have destroyed them and scattered the pieces. Nevertheless, we learned some of it all, for in the United States when traditions are juxtaposed they tend, regardless of what we do to prevent it, irresistibly to merge. Thus musically at least each child in our town was an heir of all the ages. One learns by moving from the familiar to the unfamiliar, and while it might sound incongruous at first, the step from the spirituality of the spirituals to that of the Beethoven of the symphonies or the Bach of the chorales is not as vast as it seems. Nor is the romanticism of a Brahms or Chopin completely unrelated to that of Louis Armstrong. Those who know their native culture and love it unchauvinistically are never lost when encountering the unfamiliar.

25.   Living with music today we find Mozart and Ellington, Kirsten Flagstad and Chippie Hill, William L. Dawson and Carl Orff all forming part of our regular fare. For all exalt life in rhythm and melody; all add to its significance. Perhaps in the swift change of American society in which the meanings of one's origin are so quickly lost, one of the chief values of living with music lies in its power to give us an orientation in time. In doing so, it gives significance to all those indefinable aspects of experience which nevertheless help to make us what we are. In the swift whirl of time music is a constant, reminding us of what we were and of that toward which we aspired. Art thou troubled? Music will not only calm, it will ennoble thee.

QUESTIONS

1. How do the opening four paragraphs establish a tone and suggest a theme or line of thought to be pursued in the whole essay? How do these paragraphs prepare the reader for the more serious consideration of "a more intimate source of noise" in paragraph 5 and the paragraphs that follow, in particular the reference to "the chaos of living" at the end of paragraph 6?
2. What do the details of the opening seven paragraphs reveal about the background and character of the writer? Notice that they constitute a narrative similar to Koestler's. How do these narratives differ in presentation and purpose?
3. Ellison states an important idea in paragraph 8: "For while our singer was concerned basically with a single tradition and style, I had been caught actively between two: that of the Negro folk music, both

sacred and profane, slave song and jazz, and that of Western classical music." Have paragraphs 1–7 anticipated this theme in any way?
Is the conflict they deal with of the same kind?
4. How do the two kinds of music represent two cultural ideals and
worlds in the whole essay? How does Ellison use his personal experience to keep the focus of the essay on these differences?
5. Ellison builds to a series of statements about music and about life in
the United States. Could one of these be considered the thesis of
the essay—a statement that explains the organization and accounts
for the various details and considerations? Or are paragraphs 24 and
25 afterthoughts or reflections? Might the essay have ended with
paragraph 23 without seeming incomplete?

WRITING ASSIGNMENTS

Characterize the author of the essay on the basis of the details he provides about himself and his interests. Build your characterization to a
statement of the quality you believe stands out most in the essay.

First describe your musical preferences, distinguishing them carefully.
Then account for them and indicate the extent to which they have
produced a conflict in your life comparable to the conflict Ellison por-
trays in paragraph 8.

STYLE

Marianne Moore
ABRAHAM LINCOLN AND
THE ART OF THE WORD

1.   "I dislike an oath which requires a man to swear he *has*
not done wrong. It rejects the Christian principle of forgiveness
on terms of repentance. I think it is enough if the man does no

ABRAHAM LINCOLN AND THE ART OF THE WORD: From *A Marianne Moore Reader*, published
by The Viking Press, Inc. Copyright © 1960, Broadcast Music, © 1961 by Marianne Moore.
Reprinted by permission of Broadcast Music.

wrong hereafter." It was Abraham Lincoln who said this—his controlled impetuosity exemplifying excellences both of the technician and of the poet.

2.   The malcontent attacks greatness by disparaging it—by libels on efficiency, interpreting needful silence as lack of initiative, by distortion, by ridicule. "As a general rule," Lincoln said, "I abstain from reading attacks upon myself, wishing not to be provoked by that to which I cannot properly offer an answer." Expert in rebuttal, however, as in strategy, he often won juries and disinterested observers alike, by anecdote or humorous implication that made argument unnecessary. His use of words became a perfected instrument, acquired by an education largely self-attained—" 'picked up,' " he said, "under pressure of necessity." That the books read became part of him is apparent in phrases influenced by the Bible, Shakespeare, *The Pilgrim's Progress, Robinson Crusoe,* Burns, Blackstone's *Commentaries;* and not least, by some books of Euclid—read and "nearly mastered," as he says, after he had become a member of Congress. The largeness of the life entered into the writing, as with a passion he strove to persuade his hearers of what he believed, his adroit, ingenious mentality framing an art which, if it is not to be designated poetry, we may call a "grasp of eternal grace"—in both senses, figurative and literal. Nor was he unaware of having effected what mattered, as we realize by his determined effort, when a first attempt failed, to obtain from the *Chicago Press and Tribune* "a set of the late debates (if they may be so called)" he wrote, "between Douglas and myself . . . two copies of each number . . . in order to lay one away in the raw and to put the other in a scrapbook." One notes that he did not neglect to say, "if any debate is on *both* sides of one sheet, it will take two sets to make one scrapbook."

3.   Of persuasive expedients, those most constant with Lincoln are antithesis, reiteration, satire, metaphor; above all *the meaning,* clear and unadorned. A determination "to express his ideas in simple terms became his ruling passion," his every word natural, impelled by ardor. In his address at the Wisconsin Agricultural Fair, he said—regarding competitive awards about to be made—"exultations and mortifications . . . are but temporary; the victor shall soon be vanquished, if he relax in his exertion; and . . . the vanquished this year may be the victor next, in spite of all competition." At the Baltimore Sanitary Fair of 1864,

in an address conspicuously combining antithesis with reiteration, he said, "The world has never had a good definition of liberty. . . . We all declare for liberty; but in using the same *word* we do not all mean the same *thing*. With some the word may mean for each man to do as he pleases with himself, and the product of his labor; while with others the same word may mean for some men to do as they please with other men, and the product of other men's labor. Here are two, not only different, but incompatible things, called by the same name—liberty. . . . The shepherd drives the wolf from the sheep's throat, for which the sheep thanks the shepherd as a *liberator*, while the wolf denounces him for the same act as the destroyer of liberty, especially as the sheep was a black one." In Lincoln's use of italics, one perceives that he is not substituting emphasis for precision but is impersonating speech. In declining an invitation to the Jefferson birthday dinner of 1859, he wrote, "The principles of Jefferson are the axioms of a free society. One dashingly calls them 'glittering generalities'; another bluntly calls them 'self-evident lies.' " And in combating repeal of the Missouri Compromise (which would have extended slavery), he said, "Repeal the Missouri Compromise—repeal all compromises—repeal the Declaration of Independence—repeal all history—you cannot repeal human nature."

4.   Crystalline logic indeed was to be his passion. He wrote to James Conkling, "You desire peace; and you blame me that we do not have it. But how can we attain it? There are but three conceivable ways. First, force of arms. . . . Are you for it? . . . A second way is to give up the Union. Are you for it? If you are, you should say so plainly. If not for force, not yet for dissolution, Compromise. I am against that. I do not believe any compromise is now possible." And to General Schurz he said, "You think I could do better; therefore you blame me. I think I could not do better, therefore I blame you for blaming me."

5.   Unsurpassed in satire, Lincoln said that Judge Douglas, in his interpretation of the Declaration of Independence, offered "the arguments that kings have made for enslaving the people in all ages of the world. They always bestrode the necks of the people, not that they wanted to do it, but that the people were better off for being ridden." Of slavery as an institution he said, "Slavery is strikingly peculiar in this, that it is the only good thing which no man seeks the good of for *himself.*"

6.   Metaphor is a force, indeed magnet, among Lincoln's arts of the word. Urgent that the new government of Louisiana be affirmed, he said, "If we reject it, we in effect say, 'You are worthless. We will neither help nor be helped by you.' To the blacks we say, 'This cup of liberty which these, your old masters, hold to your lips, we will dash from you, . . . discouraging and paralyzing both white and black. . . . If on the contrary, we recognize and sustain the new government, we are supporting its efforts to this end, to make it, to us, in your language, a Union of hearts and hands as well as of states.' " Passionate that the Union be saved, he uses a metaphor yet stronger than the cup of liberty. He says, "By general law, life *and* limb must be protected; yet often a limb must be amputated to save a life; but a life is never wisely given to save a limb. . . . I could not feel that, . . . to save slavery, . . . I should permit the wreck of government, country, and constitution altogether."

7.   Diligence underlay these verbal expedients—one can scarcely call them devices—so rapt Lincoln was in what he cared about. He had a genius for words but it was through diligence that he became a master of them—affording hope to the most awkward of us. To Isham Reavis he wrote, "If you are resolutely determined to make a lawyer of yourself, the thing is half done already. It is a small matter whether you read *with* anybody or not. . . . It is of no consequence to be in a large town. . . . I read at New Salem, which never had three hundred people living in it. The *books* and your *capacity* for understanding them, are just the same in all places."

8.   Diligence was basic. Upon hearing that George Latham, his son Robert's classmate at the Phillips Exeter Academy, had failed entrance examinations to Harvard, Lincoln wrote, "having made the attempt you *must* succeed in it. *'Must'* is the word . . . you *can* not fail if you resolutely determine that you *will* not." This intensity we see heightened in Lincoln's torment of anxiety, during the war, that the struggle be ended. "The subject is on my mind day and night," he said. During August, 1862, in a letter to Colonel Haupt on the 29th, he begged, "What news from the direction of Manassas?" On that same day to General McClellan he wrote, "What news from the direction of Manassas Junction?" On August 30th, to General Banks, "Please tell me what news?" and again "What news?" on August 30th to Colonel Haupt. The result was a man wearing down under continuous desperation

when General Meade, unable to conclude the war at Gettysburg, allowed the Confederate forces to retreat south.

9.   In speeches and in letters, Lincoln made articulate an indomitable ideal—that what the framers of the Constitution embodied in it be preserved—"and that something is the principle of 'Liberty for all,' that clears the *path* for all—gives *hope* to all—and by consequence *enterprise* and *industry* to all." Inflexible when sure he was right—as in his reply to Isaac Schermerhorn, who was dissatisfied with the management of the war, he said, "This is not a question of sentiment or taste but one of physical force which may be measured and estimated as horse-power and Steam-power are measured and estimated. . . . Throw it away and the Union goes with it."

10.   There is much to learn from Lincoln's respect for words taken separately, as when he said, "It seems to me very important that the statute laws should be made as plain and intelligible as possible, and be reduced to as small compass as may consist with the fullness and precision of the will of the legislature and the perspicuity of its language." He was "determined to be so clear," he said, "that no honest man can misunderstand me, and no dishonest one can successfully misrepresent me." Exasperated to have been misquoted, he protested "a specious and fantastic arrangement of words, by which a man can prove a horse-chestnut to be a chestnut horse." Consulted regarding a more perfect edition of his Cooper Institute speech, he said, "Of course I would not object, but would be pleased rather . . . but I do not wish the sense changed or modified, to a hair's breadth. Striking out 'upon' leaves the sense too general and incomplete. . . . The words 'quite,' 'as,' and 'or,' on the same page, I wish retained." Of Stephen Douglas he said, "Cannot the Judge perceive the difference between a purpose and an expectation? I have often expressed an expectation to die but I have never expressed a *wish* to die." The Declaration of Independence he made stronger by saying, "I think the authors of that notable instrument intended to include *all* men but they did not intend to declare all men were equal *in all respects*." And to quibblers, after the surrender of the South, he replied, "whether the seceded states, so-called, are in the Union or out of it, the question is bad . . . a pernicious abstraction!" Indelible even upon a feeble memory—we recall the phrase, "With malice toward none and charity for all," and in the second inaugural address, "Let us strive on to finish the work we

are in." We are *in*. Lincoln understood in the use of emphasis that one must be *natural*. Instead of using the word "confidential" in a letter to A. H. Stephens, he wrote in italics at the head of the page, *"For your eye only."* The result of this intensified particularity was such that in his so-called Lost Speech of 1856, which unified the Republican party, "newspaper men forgot paper and pad . . . to sit enraptured," and instead of taking down his eulogy of Henry Clay, "dropped their pens and sat as under enchantment from near the beginning, to quite the end."

11.   Lincoln attained not force only, but cadence, the melodic propriety of poetry in fact, as in the Farewell Address from Springfield he refers to "the weight of responsibility on George Washington"; then says of "that Divine being without which I cannot succeed, with that assistance, I cannot fail." Consider also the stateliness of the three cannots in the Gettysburg Address: "We cannot dedicate—we cannot consecrate—we cannot hallow—this ground. The brave men, living and dead, who struggled here, have consecrated it far above our poor power to add or detract. The world will little note nor long remember what we may say here, but it can never forget what they did here." Editors attempting to improve Lincoln's punctuation by replacing dashes with commas, should refrain—the dash, as well known, signifying prudence.

12.   With consummate reverence for God, with insight that illumined his every procedure as a lawyer, that was alive in his every decision as a President with civilian command of an army at bay, Lincoln was notable in his manner of proffering consolation; studiously avoiding insult when relieving an officer of his command; instantaneous with praise. To General Grant—made commander of the Union army after his brilliant flanking maneuver at Vicksburg—he said, "As the country trusts you, so, under God, it will sustain you." To Grant "alone" he ascribed credit for terminating the war. Constrained almost to ferocity by the sense of fairness, he begs recognition for "black men who can remember that with silent tongues, and clenched teeth, and steady eye and well-poised bayonet, they have helped mankind to this consummation" (preserving the Union). He managed to take time to retrieve the property of a barber, a Negro, who had not recorded the deed to land he owned. Emphasizing by vivid addendum his request for promotion of a "brave drummer-boy" who "had accompanied his division under heavy fire," Lincoln

said, "he should have his chance." For "a poor widow whose son was serving a long sentence without pay"—recommending the son for re-enlistment with pay—he wrote, "she says she cannot get it acted on. Please do it." In constant disfavor with officers in charge of penalties, he said, "Must I shoot a simple soldier boy who deserts while I must not touch a hair of the wily agitator who induces him to desert? To silence the agitator and save the boy is not only constitutional but withal a great mercy." Of Captain McKnabb, dismissed on the charge of being a disunionist, Lincoln wrote, "He wishes to show that the charge is false. Fair play is a jewel. Give him a chance if you can." Afflicted by self-obsessed factions in Missouri, where private grievances should have been settled locally, he summarized the matter: "I have exhausted my wits and nearly my patience in efforts to convince both [sides] that the evils they charged on the others are inherent. I am well satisfied that the preventing of the remedial raid into Missouri was the only safe way to avoid an indiscriminate massacre, including probably more innocent than guilty. Instead of condemning, I therefore approve what I understand General Schofield did in that respect. . . . Few things have been so grateful to my anxious feeling as when . . . the local force in Missouri aided General Schofield to so promptly send a large force to the relief of General Grant then investing Vicksburg and menaced by General Johnston. . . . My feeling obliges nobody to follow me and I trust obliges me to follow nobody."

13. With regard to presidential appointments, it was in 1849, during Zachary Taylor's administration, that Lincoln said, "I take the responsibility. In that phrase were the 'Samson's locks' of General Jackson, and we dare not disregard the lessons of experience"—lessons underlying the principle which he put into practice when appointing Governor Chase Secretary of the Treasury. Pressed, in fact persecuted, to appoint General Cameron, he said, "It seems to me not only highly proper but a *necessity* that Governor Chase shall take that place. His ability, firmness, and purity of character produce the propriety." Purity of character—the phrase is an epitome of Lincoln. To a young man considering law as a career, he said, "There is a vague popular belief that lawyers are necessarily dishonest. If you cannot be an honest lawyer, resolve to be honest without being a lawyer." Deploring bombast, yet tactful, he opposed investigating the Bank of Illinois: "No, Sir, it is the *politician* who is first to

sound the alarm (which, by the way, is a false one). It is he, who, by these unholy means, is endeavoring to blow up a storm that he may ride upon and direct it. . . . I say this with the greater freedom, because, being a politician, none can regard it as personal." Firm in resisting pressure, he was equally strong in exerting it, as when he wrote to "Secretary Seward & Secretary Chase" jointly, "You have respectively tendered me your resignations . . . but, after most anxious consideration, my deliberate judgment is, that the public interest does not admit of it. I therefore have to request that you will resume the duties of your departments respectively. Your Obt. Servt."

14.   In faithfulness to a trust, in saving our constituted freedom and opportunity for all, declaring that "no grievance is a fit object of redress by mob violence," made disconsolate by what he termed "a conspiracy" to "nationalize slavery," Lincoln—dogged by chronic fatigue—was a monumental contradiction of that conspiracy. An architect of justice, determined and destined to win his "case," he did not cease until he had demonstrated the mightiness of his "proposition." It is a Euclid of the heart.

DISCUSSION: STYLE

We are used to thinking of style as something habitual; the football-running styles Plimpton distinguishes vary little in the performances of the players. In discussions of writing, however, we sometimes think of style as the sum of choices we make—choices in diction as well as sentence construction and organization. If choice is essential to style in writing, it might be assumed that only writing reflects style, since so much of our speech is unplanned. But we clearly do make choices in speaking—if only in the variety of usage we deliberately or undeliberately adopt. In writing, choices may be more deliberate—and usually are when we have a particular audience in mind. It is difficult, though, to make a sharp distinction between choice and habit. For choices can be a matter of habit. The sentences we write depend for their shape and rhythm on the sentences we speak: we speak before we write. In the course of growing up, the influence of conventional usage and ways of thinking increases, and we develop habitual ways of expressing ideas. Gradually we learn to adapt these ways to various situations. Most of the time we rely on familiar phrases, and we seldom depart from familiar sentence patterns. In formal situations our choices are increasingly selective; we are far more sensitive to the appropriateness of our language, and we vary the usual sentence patterns and diction depending on the occasion. Ultimately, personal style is shaped not only by our acquired habits of thought and feeling but by our personality. Thought and expression in the literate person are inseparable processes.

QUESTIONS

1. What evidence does Marianne Moore provide to indicate that Lincoln's "art of the word" was a matter of choice? What were the origins of his writing style, and why are these origins revealing?
2. In paragraph 3, how do the examples show how Lincoln realized his aim, *"the meaning,* clear and unadorned"?
3. What does the author mean by the statement that in his use of italics Lincoln is "not substituting emphasis for precision but is impersonating speech"? Under what circumstances would a writer substitute emphasis for precision?
4. What does the author mean in paragraph 7 by the statement "Diligence underlay these verbal expedients"? Why can these expedients not be called *devices*?
5. How is this diligence in the use of words shown to reflect Lincoln's character? What in his "art of the word" reflects other aspects of his character?
6. What does paragraph 9 show? How is it related to the whole discussion?
7. What do the examples in paragraph 10 show?
8. What do paragraphs 12–14 show? Why does the author emphasize these considerations?
9. What is the meaning of the concluding phrase, "a Euclid of the heart"?

WRITING ASSIGNMENT

Analyze the style of a twentieth-century political figure by analyzing representative passages from his (or her) writings and speeches. Choose a variety of examples that exhibit different aspects of style, and discuss how these reflect the mind and character of the person.

LOGICAL
ANALYSIS

DEFINITION, DIVISION, CLASSIFICATION

John Ciardi
IS EVERYBODY HAPPY?

1.   The right to pursue happiness is issued to Americans with their birth certificates, but no one seems quite sure which way it ran. It may be we are issued a hunting license but offered no game. Jonathan Swift seemed to think so when he attacked the idea of happiness as "the possession of being well-deceived," the felicity of being "a fool among knaves." For Swift saw society as Vanity Fair, the land of false goals.

2.   It is, of course, un-American to think in terms of fools and knaves. We do, however, seem to be dedicated to the idea of buying our way to happiness. We shall all have made it to Heaven when we possess enough.

3.   And at the same time the forces of American commercialism are hugely dedicated to making us deliberately unhappy. Advertising is one of our major industries, and advertising exists not to satisfy desires but to create them—and to create them faster than any man's budget can satisfy them. For that matter, our whole economy is based on a dedicated insatiability. We are taught that to possess is to be happy, and then we are made to want. We are even told it is our duty to want. It was only a few years ago, to cite a single example, that car dealers across the country were flying banners that read "You Auto Buy Now." They were calling upon Americans, as an act approaching patriotism, to buy at once, with money they did not have, automobiles they did not really need, and which they would be required to grow tired of by the time the next year's models were released.

4.   Or look at any of the women's magazines. There, as Bernard DeVoto once pointed out, advertising begins as poetry in the front pages and ends as pharmacopoeia and therapy in the

IS EVERYBODY HAPPY?: From *Manner of Speaking* (Rutgers University Press, 1972). Reprinted by permission of the author.

back pages. The poetry of the front matter is the dream of perfect beauty. This is the baby skin that must be hers. These, the flawless teeth. This, the perfumed breath she must exhale. This, the sixteen-year-old figure she must display at forty, at fifty, at sixty, and forever.

5.   Once past the vaguely uplifting fiction and feature articles, the reader finds the other face of the dream in the back matter. This is the harness into which Mother must strap herself in order to display that perfect figure. These, the chin straps she must sleep in. This is the salve that restores all, this is her laxative, these are the tablets that melt away fat, these are the hormones of perpetual youth, these are the stockings that hide varicose veins.

6.   Obviously no half-sane person can be completely persuaded either by such poetry or by such pharmacopoeia and orthopedics. Yet someone is obviously trying to buy the dream as offered and spending billions every year in the attempt. Clearly the happiness market is not running out of customers, but what are we trying to buy?

7.   The idea "happiness," to be sure, will not sit still for easy definition: the best one can do is to try to set some extremes to the idea and then work in toward the middle. To think of happiness as acquisitive and competitive will do to set the materialistic extreme. To think of it as the idea one senses in, say, a holy man of India will do to set the spiritual extreme. That holy man's ideal of happiness is in needing nothing from outside himself. In wanting nothing, he lacks nothing. He sits immobile, rapt in contemplation, free even of his own body. Or nearly free of it. If devout admirers bring him food he eats it; if not, he starves indifferently. Why be concerned? What is physical is an illusion to him. Contemplation is his joy and he achieves it through a fantastically demanding discipline, the accomplishment of which is itself a joy within him.

8.   Is he a happy man? Perhaps his happiness is only another sort of illusion. But who can take it from him? And who will dare say it is more illusory than happiness on the installment plan?

9.   But, perhaps because I am Western, I doubt such catatonic happiness, as I doubt the dreams of the happiness market. What is certain is that his way of happiness would be torture to almost any Western man. Yet these extremes will still serve to

frame the area within which all of us must find some sort of balance. Thoreau—a creature of both Eastern and Western thought—had his own firm sense of that balance. His aim was to save on the low levels in order to spend on the high.

10. Possession for its own sake or in competition with the rest of the neighborhood would have been Thoreau's idea of the low levels. The active discipline of heightening one's perception of what is enduring in nature would have been his idea of the high. What he saved from the low was time and effort he could spend on the high. Thoreau certainly disapproved of starvation, but he would put into feeding himself only as much effort as would keep him functioning for more important efforts.

11. Effort is the gist of it. There is no happiness except as we take on life-engaging difficulties. Short of the impossible, as Yeats put it, the satisfactions we get from a lifetime depend on how high we choose our difficulties. Robert Frost was thinking in something like the same terms when he spoke of "the pleasure of taking pains." The mortal flaw in the advertised version of happiness is in the fact that it purports to be effortless.

12. We demand difficulty even in our games. We demand it because without difficulty there can be no game. A game is a way of making something hard for the fun of it. The rules of the game are an arbitrary imposition of difficulty. When the spoilsport ruins the fun, he always does so by refusing to play by the rules. It is easier to win at chess if you are free, at your pleasure, to change the wholly arbitrary rules, but the fun is in winning within the rules. No difficulty, no fun.

13. The buyers and sellers at the happiness market seem too often to have lost their sense of the pleasure of difficulty. Heaven knows what they are playing, but it seems a dull game. The Indian holy man seems dull to us, I suppose, because he seems to be refusing to play anything at all. The Western weakness may be in the illusion that happiness can be bought. Perhaps the Eastern weakness is in the idea that there is such a thing as perfect (and therefore static) happiness.

14. Happiness is never more than partial. There are no pure states of mankind. Whatever else happiness may be, it is neither in having nor in being, but in becoming. What the Founding Fathers declared for us as an inherent right, we should do well to remember, was not happiness but the *pursuit* of happiness. What they might have underlined, could they have foreseen the happi-

ness market, is the cardinal fact that happiness is in the pursuit itself, in the meaningful pursuit of what is life-engaging and life-revealing, which is to say, in the idea of *becoming*. A nation is not measured by what it possesses or wants to possess, but by what it wants to become.

15.   By all means let the happiness market sell us minor satisfactions and even minor follies so long as we keep them in scale and buy them out of spiritual change. I am no customer for either puritanism or asceticism. But drop any real spiritual capital at those bazaars, and what you come home to will be your own poorhouse.

DISCUSSION: DEFINITION, DIVISION, CLASSIFICATION

The methods of analysis we studied in paragraph development are also used to analyze the essay. In trying to convince the reader to accept unfamiliar ideas or a new way of looking at experience, the writer may wish to define his terms—perhaps theoretically or stipulatively (see pages 44-45)—to divide or classify his subject, to compare and contrast ideas, or to draw analogies. Any of these methods may be used as the chief principle of organization, even when the essay is argumentative. Thus it may be organized as an extended definition of a familiar idea that the writer believes should be considered in a new light—or of an unfamiliar idea that needs to be compared with a familiar idea if we are to understand it fully, or at all.

QUESTIONS

1. Ciardi organizes his discussion of happiness as an extended definition. What kind of definition of happiness does he employ—denotative, connotative, stipulative, or theoretical?
2. Ciardi builds to his full definition of happiness through a consideration of advertising and the Eastern holy man. Given his opening comments on Swift and the American way of thinking, why does he delay his definition until late in the essay? How do his comments on advertising and the Eastern holy man help to establish his definition?
3. Where, finally, does he state his definition?
4. What would be gained or lost if Ciardi had begun with his comments on Thoreau, Yeats, and Frost (in paragraphs 9–11)? Does the answer to this question depend on your knowing the audience Ciardi has in mind? Would the order of examples be effective with any audience?
5. The "pursuit of happiness" is so familiar a phrase that we are likely not to examine its full implications. Is Ciardi defining this phrase ac-

cording to what he believes the Founding Fathers meant by it, or is
he proposing his own definition?

WRITING ASSIGNMENTS

Ciardi deals with an abstract idea through everyday experiences. Select
another phrase in common use and define it as Ciardi does. Examine its
implications fully.

Discuss the statement "We demand difficulty even in our games"
through two different games that you enjoy playing. Indicate the extent
of your agreement with Ciardi.

Develop the following statement through your personal observations:
"Whatever else happiness may be, it is neither in having nor in being,
but in becoming."

Ciardi analyzes women's magazines in light of the idea of happiness
they purvey. Analyze a man's magazine in the same way, giving attention to the articles and the advertisements.

William O. Douglas
THE RIGHT TO DEFY AN
UNCONSTITUTIONAL STATUTE

1.   There are circumstances where the otherwise absolute
obligation of the law is tempered by exceptions for individual
conscience. As in the case of the conscientious objector to military service, the exception may be recognized by statute or, as in
the case of the flag salute for school children, it may be required
by the First Amendment. But in countless other situations the
fact that conscience counsels violation of the law can be no defense. Those are the situations in which the citizen is placed in
the dilemma of being forced to choose between violating the dictates of his conscience or violating the command of positive law.
2.   The problem is age-old. In Sophocles' play, Antigone
had this choice to make. She chose to follow the dictates of her
conscience, attempting to bury the body of her brother, Polyni-

ces, rather than conform to the edict of the tyrant, Creon, that the corpse remain unburied. Socrates, convicted of corrupting the youth of Athens, refused to "hold his tongue," preferring to face death. Even Hobbes, who wrote that civil obedience is the highest duty of a citizen, recognized that a point could be reached where conscience would demand that the command of the leviathan state must be disobeyed. But for Hobbes, civil disobedience was not justified unless to obey would be to lose the right to eternal salvation after death.

3.	The moral right to defy an unjust law was certainly not unknown in the American colonies. The Puritans fled England after they had defied the English sovereigns by adhering to their forms of worship. John Locke, an intellectual father of the American Revolution, wrote that, if the sovereign should require anything which appears unlawful to the private person, he is not obliged to obey that law against his conscience. Locke's philosophy found expression in the Declaration of Independence.

4.	Emerson wrote that "no greater American existed than Thoreau." Thoreau's insistence on his right to lead his own life and to resist the encroachment of government was typically American. In 1846, he refused to pay the town tax because he disapproved of the purposes for which the money was to be spent. For this, he spent a night in jail. He was released only after a friend had "interfered" and paid the tax. His short imprisonment resulted in Thoreau's dramatic essay on civil disobedience, where he insisted that he had the right to disobey an unjust law. "Under a government which imprisons any unjustly," he wrote, "the true place for a just man is also a prison."

5.	Thoreau's writings had a great impact on Gandhi. Gandhi's concept of *satyagraba* was one which championed the moral right to disregard an unjust law and undergo the penalty for its breach. He wrote:

> "The law-breaker breaks the law surreptitiously and tries to avoid the penalty; not so the civil resister. He ever obeys the laws of the state to which he belongs, not out of fear of the sanctions, but because he considers them to be good for the welfare of society. But there come occasions, generally rare, when he considers certain laws to be so unjust as to render obedience to them a dishonour. He then openly and civilly breaks them and quietly suffers the penalty of their breach.

And in order to register his protest against the action of the
law-givers, it is open to him to withdraw his co-operation
from the state by disobeying such other laws whose breach
does not involve moral turpitude."

6.   Unless the law applies with equal force to those who dissent from it, there can be no ordered society. The choice given
the individual is not to obey the law or to violate it with impunity, but to obey the law or incur the punishment for disobedience. Socrates recognized the obligation of the law which had
unjustly sentenced him to die, when he explained to Crito that
he would not flee from his punishment. He recognized that his
choice was to incur the punishment of the law rather than conform to it, but did not contend that he was above the law. Locke,
too, observed that the "private judgement of any person concerning a law enacted in public matters, for the public good, does not
take away the obligation of that law, nor deserve a dispensa-
tion." Rousseau, who had defended the right to resist unjust law,
still observed that no individual in a democracy should have the
right to be above the law. Both Thoreau and Gandhi recognized
that disobedience of the law may be punished.
7.   These two values, the right of the individual to follow
his own conscience and the right of society to promulgate rules
for the orderly conduct of its affairs, are sometimes antagonistic.
American democracy is not the leviathan state which Hobbes
pictured. Our society is built upon the premise that it exists only
to aid the fullest individual achievement of which each of its
members is capable. Our starting point has always been the individual, not the state. Nevertheless, democracy is built upon the
rule of the majority, and a civilized society requires orderly rules,
applicable to all alike. If a statute is otherwise valid, the law does
not consider the moral values which led to its disobedience.
8.   But the Puritan tradition of the citizen's right to shake
his fist at the legislature has found its place in American law in
the right to defy an unconstitutional statute. An unconstitutional
statute is a lawless act by the legislature. The humblest citizen,
confronted by all the forces of the state which insist that he must
obey the law, may take matters into his own hands, defy an unconstitutional statute, and risk the outcome on the ultimate decision of the courts. He may forsake the orderly processes of society and proceed as if the statute does not exist. That was

Jefferson's attitude toward the Alien and Sedition Laws. On July 22, 1804, he wrote:

". . . I discharged every person under punishment or prosecution under the sedition law, because I considered, and now consider, that law to be a nullity, as absolute and as palpable as if Congress had ordered us to fall down and worship a golden image; and that it was as much my duty to arrest its execution at every stage, as it would have been to have rescued from the fiery furnace those who should have been cast into it for refusing to worship the image. It was accordingly done in every instance, without asking what the offenders had done, or against whom they had offended, but whether the pains they were suffering were inflicted under the pretended sedition law."

9.   The clearest example of an individual's right to ignore an unconstitutional ordinance is in the area of prior restraint upon First Amendment freedoms, which I have discussed in the first lecture. *Thomas* v. *Collins,* 323 U.S. 516, involved a statute which required a labor organizer to obtain a license before he could address an assembly of laborers. He ignored that statute and spoke. His conviction for speaking without a license was overturned because the statute constituted an infringement of his right to speak. He was not required to submit to the invalid ordinance, apply for the license, and be refused the right to speak, before he was allowed to challenge the validity of the statute. Under the principle of *Thomas* v. *Collins,* a minister who is required to get a license to address his flock could not be convicted for preaching without a license.

10.   Of course, if an individual violates a statute under the mistaken view that it is unconstitutional, he may be punished. As Chief Justice Stone once said, "There is no freedom to conspire to violate a statute with impunity merely because its constitutionality is doubted. The prohibition of the statute is infringed by the intended act in any case, and the law imposes its sanctions unless the doubt proves to be well founded." *Keegan* v. *United States,* 325 U.S. 478, 505. The citizen who defies the statute takes the risk that he is mistaken. But if his views of the Constitution are accepted, he goes free.

11.   A striking analogy may be found in the Articles of the Uniform Code of Military Justice. In the Armed Forces, discipline

and obedience to orders are of primary importance. Under military discipline, respect for authority is the prime virtue. But, under Articles 90 through 92 of the Uniform Code, an American serviceman has the absolute right to disobey any unlawful order of a superior officer, for he is punished only for disobedience of a *lawful* order. A recent decision of the United States Court of Military Appeals demonstrates that this right has real value. An airman stationed in Japan, suspected of using narcotics, had been ordered by his squadron commander to furnish a urine specimen for chemical analysis. Although the airman was warned of the possibility of court-martial for failure to comply, he refused to do so. He was court-martialed for willful disobedience of the command of a superior officer. The United States Court of Military Appeals set aside the conviction, holding that the order was unlawful because it compelled the airman to furnish evidence against himself. *United States* v. *Jordan,* 7 U.S.C.M.A. 452. This was an order from a superior officer, with all the force of military discipline behind it; yet, under the Uniform Code of Military Justice, it could be disobeyed with impunity because the order itself was not legal.

12.   There will be specific instances where most people will agree that the individual's right to defy even an unconstitutional statute may be denied because of the interest of society in the continued conduct of the processes of government. For example, a taxpayer can be required to pay an unconstitutional tax and sue for its return. If he prevails, he has only been temporarily deprived of the use of his money. For this he can be compensated. On the other hand, if every taxpayer refused to pay his taxes, the business of government would grind to a halt.

13.   There has developed, however, in recent years a tendency to require the citizen to obey an extreme ordinance or statute, even though it is unconstitutional. The rights of the individual are then sacrificed to the interests of orderly conduct of the processes of government. The Court has gone far in requiring that sacrifice. The most striking example is *Poulos* v. *New Hampshire,* 345 U.S. 395. Jehovah's Witnesses had been arbitrarily denied a license to speak in a public park. The Court, in affirming their convictions for holding a religious meeting without the required license, held that their remedy for violation of their right to speak was to proceed as required by state law to compel issuance of the license.

14. The *Poulos* decision is a significant departure from prior decisions which have allowed the individual the right to resist the unconstitutional demands of government. The right to speak, guaranteed by the First Amendment, was sacrificed to the delays, the expense, and the necessities of pursuing the processes of an "orderly society." *Id.,* p. 409.

15. The risk—the great and agonizing danger—in situations of this kind is that the citizen will be caught in the treadmill of an elusive administrative remedy. While he pursues it, his constitutional rights are denied. And it may take so much time to go through the intricate administrative system with all of its hearings and appeals that any relief will come too late and the great occasion, when the right to speak, to worship, or to assemble might have been enjoyed, will be lost.

16. The right to defy an unconstitutional statute has its roots in our traditions of individualism and in our mistrust of the uncontrolled power of the state. That mistrust was written into numerous limitations on governmental power contained in the Constitution. The right to ignore a statute that is unconstitutional is a reflection of those limitations. Like them, it says—so far government may go and no farther.

17. I have said enough to indicate that the right to be let alone, though greatly impaired in recent years, still clamors for recognition. It is a sturdy part of our heritage, more American than European, more Western than Eastern. It cannot be easily stamped out on this continent, for it is a part of all of us. It can be eroded and depreciated. But it will always be one of our great rallying points.

QUESTIONS

1. Douglas begins his discussion of civil disobedience with a division of laws according to attitudes toward them. What are these attitudes, and is the division exhaustive?
2. Does Douglas believe that it is possible for a law to be "just" and at the same time in conflict with the conscience of the individual? Does he imply that the needs of the individual and the needs of society are sometimes irreconcilable?
3. In paragraphs 9 and 10 Douglas distinguishes kinds of dissent. What is the principle of his division?
4. Douglas distinguishes the illegitimate "interest of society in the continued conduct of the processes of government" from the legitimate

(paragraphs 12–15). What criterion differentiates the legitimate interest from the illegitimate?

5. Douglas defines civil disobedience through division chiefly. What
other methods of analysis does he employ?

WRITING ASSIGNMENTS

Analyze the essay to show how Douglas employs narrative, confirmation, and refutation in arguing that "the right to be let alone . . . still
clamors for recognition."

Discuss the extent to which Martin Luther King, Jr., in his analysis of
nonviolent resistance, is in agreement with the premises stated in this
essay.

Carl Cohen
WHAT CIVIL DISOBEDIENCE IS NOT

I. NOT EVERY PUBLIC DEMONSTRATION IS CIVIL DISOBEDIENCE

1.   It will be clear from what has gone before that most protest, however vehement or unusual, is not civil disobedience and
would be improperly classified as such. Because civil disobedience necessarily involves some deliberate infraction of the law,
all parades, assemblies, marches, picket lines, and other public
demonstrations that abide by the law are *not* civil disobedience.
Such lawful protests also need to be evaluated; they also may be
foolish, wrongheaded, or (even if well motivated) tactically ill-ad-
vised. But public demonstrations of protest, as such, are not disobedient and are not our present subject.

II CONSCIENTIOUS OBJECTION IS NOT CIVIL DISOBEDIENCE

2.   Civil disobedience must be conscientiously performed;
that is, it must flow from the principled and deeply held convictions of the protester. But "conscientious objection" is a special
expression, generally reserved to identify a special device of the
body politic. This device usually takes the form of a clause in cer-

WHAT CIVIL DISOBEDIENCE IS NOT: From *Civil Disobedience* by Carl Cohen. (New York: Co-
lumbia University Press, 1971). Reprinted by permission of the publisher and the author.

tain legislation that makes it possible for those who find the acts that law requires morally intolerable to comply with the law in some alternative (and to them morally unobjectionable) way. Its most common, but not exclusive, use is in conscription legislation, under which religious pacifists or other categories of conscientious objectors may apply for permission to render an equivalent period of social service to the state in some welfare organization of a noncombatant, and usually nonmilitary character. The conscientious objector—whether or not he is right in his repugnance for all military activity—acts entirely within the provisions of the law. He follows procedures specified by statute and is protected by the law once his status as conscientious objector is administratively established. He must not be viewed as a violator of the law; his conduct certainly is not civil disobedience.

3.   It is also true that some persons deliberately violate the selective service laws out of sincere respect for moral principles. Their acts *are* instances of civil disobedience. Although truly motivated by conscience, such persons are not properly classed as "conscientious objectors" as that expression is most generally used. Conscientious objection, in the normal sense, may be considered a form of protest, but it is never disobedient.

III. CIVIL DISOBEDIENCE IS NOT REVOLUTION

4.   Revolution seeks the overthrow of constituted governmental authority, or at least repudiates that authority in some sphere; civil disobedience does neither. This distinction is of the most fundamental importance in understanding civil disobedience and in appraising it.

5.   In certain circumstances, of course, even revolution may prove justifiable. Of the countless revolutions that have transpired in human history, many are the culmination of a process in which an exploited mass throws off what they believe to be their oppressive yoke; some are the work of a dedicated minority acting on behalf of the masses. We Americans think our colonial forefathers were justified in rebelling against the British Crown, and so likewise the loyal citizens of many nations believe their nationhood owed to the courage and wisdom of their revolutionary founders. In France, in Mexico, in China, and Ireland, and Cuba, and in a hundred other lands, "the Revolution" is regarded as the event of greatest national honor, and the revolu-

tionaries are gloried and revered. Of course, revolutionaries are traitors. Their treason is against an authority they believe illegitimate or cruel; nevertheless it is high crime, and when the rebel is caught he is likely to be executed. But if the act accuse, the result will excuse—provided, as Machiavelli carefully points out—that the rebel is successful. If he is, he may become the Father of his Country. Revolution is the classic case in which—at least so far as the official history of the nation will record—military success assures moral justification. Might does not make right; but in some circumstances it produces a very persuasive synthetic.

6.   Viewed objectively, of course, some revolutions have been justified and some have not. Oppressive cruelty has not been rare in human history, and the appeal to arms to end it may sometimes have been the only recourse left. Which cases are truly of that sort? The Algerian? The Bolivian? The Indonesian? The American? Reliable answers require the most careful historical study of particular cases, and even then are never beyond doubt. Some revolutions, on the other hand, seek the overthrow of a reasonably stable and generally decent government and advance chiefly the private interests of the revolutionaries. "Governments long established should not be changed," as the American revolutionaries who signed the *Declaration of Independence* wisely agreed, "for light and transient causes." Revolutions are too serious to be undertaken lightly. Almost invariably they spill human blood; sometimes, as in the American and Spanish civil wars, revolutions bequeath a legacy of misery and bitterness that cannot be forgotten for decades, or even a century. He who revolts against the constituted authority, whatever his reasons, necessarily unsettles the life of the entire community, shakes the security and peace of mind of all its members, brings on great loss of property, and renders probable the injury and death of many human beings. Revolution tears up the fabric of a nation's life; justified or not it is an awful thing.

7.   Civil disobedience is another matter entirely. It does not result in death or misery and rarely entails significant loss of property. It does not seek to unseat an existing government and does not destroy the order or stability of national or community life. It *is* a serious matter, in being a deliberate violation of the law, but it is a shallow (although common) mistake to confuse it with revolution or to view the civil disobedient as a revolutionary.

8.   The essential difference between the two lies in this: the civil disobedient does, while the revolutionary does not, accept the general legitimacy of the established authorities. While the civil disobedient may vigorously condemn some law or policy those authorities institute, and may even refuse to comply with it, he does not by any means intend to reject the larger system of laws of which that one is a very small part. In accepting that system he accepts even the technical legitimacy of the law he breaks; he recognizes that in one very important sense that law does claim obedience from him, and he knows that his defiance of that claim—while he accepts the general legitimacy of the system—requires some special justification. In short, the civil disobedient acts deliberately within the framework of established political authority; the revolutionary seeks to demolish that framework, or to capture it. The difference is monumental.

9.   Two great men, both alleged practitioners of civil disobedience, may be more fully understood in the light of this distinction. The first, Henry David Thoreau, wrote the most famous of all essays on the subject: "On the Duty of Civil Disobedience" (1849). He also refused to pay taxes lawfully imposed. The object of his attack was twofold: the American prosecution of an unjust war with Mexico and, more especially, the American retention of a system of human slavery. His conduct—deliberate violation of the law and submission to arrest without resistance—is typical of civil disobedients. His essay makes it very clear, however, that what he intended was not merely protest but the complete repudiation of governmental authority. He wished the government to "treat him as a neighbor," to recognize him as a "higher and independent power." He said:

> How does it become a man to behave toward this American government today? I answer that he cannot without disgrace be associated with it. I cannot for an instant recognize that political organization as *my* government which is the *slaves'* government also. . . . I quietly declare war with the State, after my fashion, though I will still make what use and get what advantage of her I can, as is usual in such cases. . . . I think that it is not too soon for honest men to rebel and revolutionize.

Thoreau's act may have been a noble one, but in placing himself above the law and denying its jurisdiction over him, he became a rebel. Although his essay probably introduced the expression into common speech, Thoreau himself did not, in the strict sense, defend civil disobedience.

10.   The second, Mahatma Gandhi, was one of history's most effective leaders, and the greatest exponent of the technique of "passive resistance," *satyagraha*. Gandhi's movement was exceedingly subtle and complex, but one aspect of it needs clarification for our purposes. He sought to develop and strengthen moral resistance to the British rule of India, and to do so wholly without force of arms. His strictly nonviolent methods often incorporated disobedience of some British law or decree, but it was the spiritual resistance, not the disobedience as such, that was the leading character of his acts; prolonged hunger strikes that served as symbolic defiance of British authority were more typical of him than deliberate legal infractions. Most important, the entire movement aimed at, and accomplished, the destruction of British authority in the land. Although the transfer of authority did come, at last, in a peaceful way, that transfer was the culmination of a genuinely revolutionary movement, of which Gandhi was the known and self-conscious leader. Gandhi was a rebel; had tactical considerations permitted, he would surely have been permanently banished or executed. That he was not was due to the special reverence with which he was regarded by the Indian masses, and his consequent political power. It is therefore quite misleading to treat Gandhi as a civil disobedient exclusively. To do so is to err on both sides, missing first the fundamental nature of his aims and achievements, and supposing second that civil disobedience typically seeks the overthrow of established authority.

11.   Still, the history of Gandhi's movement is evidence that although revolution and civil disobedience are conceptually distinct, it is in some cases difficult to draw a sharp line of distinction between them. He who seeks the destruction of one system of government and its replacement by another is a revolutionary; but in the slow process of building that revolution he may practice and encourage civil disobedience directed against specific acts of oppression. In this, as in every case of moral significance, what a man is *doing* depends importantly not only upon his external deeds but also upon his internal intentions. These intentions are difficult to determine in some cases—as criminal lawyers know well—but in many cases they are reasonably clear. There was never much doubt that Gandhi's intent was revolu-

tionary; he said so quite straightforwardly. In a similar but not so obvious way, some of those who practice civil disobedience in America or Great Britain may have long-range revolutionary hopes. But their hopes are one thing and their concrete acts are another. A just government must be always meticulous in prosecuting at law only established infractions of the law, not fantasy or deluded political ambition.

12.   The great majority of civil disobedients, in any event, leave no doubt about their real intentions. They abjure revolution, and, although sometimes angry at their government, they make it very clear that their act is one committed *under* the law, even if against it. In one sense revolution is the furthest thing from their minds. Their object—pursued with self-sacrificial vigor—is not to replace the system but to improve it.

IV. CIVIL RIOTS ARE NOT CIVIL DISOBEDIENCE

13.   Riots have become a serious threat in large American cities. Periodic onsets of civil chaos have recently become much more frequent and much more destructive than ever before, creating a widely felt sense of national insecurity and disorder. The causes of these social paroxysms lie very deep—in history, in the selves of their participants, and in the structure of the society that gives birth to them. Linking these fundamental causes with the riots themselves are a set of intermediate disorders that are both ugly and humiliating: rotten housing, bad schools, broken families, general filth, and a widespread feeling of powerlessness and alienation. These are running sores on the body politic. Leaders of all parties talk much about the need to heal them, but in fact very little is being accomplished toward that end; the fundamental causes are little understood and rarely dealt with. Minor patches of improvement emerge here and there, with fairer employment practices and more public housing, but the infection still spreads in the Nation, showing new and ever more virulent symptoms.

14.   The riot is one way—violent, destructive, and irrational, but for many concrete and satisfying—of reacting against a set of social injustices for which we seem to have no foreseeable effective remedy and no rational problem-solving system that promises remedy. It is important to differentiate these unhappy outbreaks of disorder from civil disobedience.

15.   In the first place, civil disobedience, unlike riots, is not

violent or destructive, and even the slightest use of physical force
directly against persons or property will be avoided wherever
possible. Nonviolence is usually a principle of importance to the
civil disobedient; rampant violence is anathema to him and is inconsistent with both the strategy and the objective of his protest.
16.   In the second place, civil disobedience, unlike riots, is
(whether or not it proves ultimately justified) a rational tactic, intellectually chosen and pursued. It is undertaken thoughtfully
and deliberately, with careful limits self-imposed. The civil disobedient breaks the law, but he does not disregard it; his acts are
coolly and calmly performed and are never, as civil riots are,
sheer bursts of passion or blind ventings of fury. In its tranquil-
ity, forethoughtfulness, and ultimate respect for authority, civil
disobedience is as much unlike civil rioting as anything can be.
17.   There are, it is true, some features in common. Both violate the law. Both are, in some rough sense, protests, and the
object of attack is sometimes the same general sort of injustice—
racial discrimination, felt oppression. But the differences are
more important than the likenesses. Riots, in the final analysis,
are revolutionary in intent. Their participants do not—at least for
that time in that place—accept the legitimacy of the authorities or
their laws. They have no real plan for the replacement of these
authorities by another, and probably no serious intention of
forming such a plan. To that degree their revolt is partial and
chaotic, and doomed to accomplish little but destruction. A revolt
it is, nevertheless. The law is blatantly defied. Looting, arson,
mad rampaging, and even beatings and deadly assaults, follow
one another without reason, not in a spirit of civic dedication but
in that of fiery anger, and with exultation that the chains of "the
system" are, at least for a few wild hours or days, defiantly cast
aside, without apparent danger of arrest or punishment.
18.   Rioting is a kind of civic madness. Of course the
sickness is no more to be cured with tanks and guns than is the
sickness of insanity cured by the use of a strait-jacket. In both
cases the patient may be quieted until he regains his senses; but
in both cases the repeated and severe application of physical restraint is likely to increase hostility and alienation, providing yet
more fuel for the next fire. In neither case does sheer force even
approach the roots of the malady.
19.   The riots that have beset American cities, and promise
to continue to do so, are, in a word, uprisings. The descriptive

term used by the participants themselves, and their leaders, is *rebellion*. That is on the whole an accurate description, and it clearly marks off these disorders from all varieties of civil disobedience.

QUESTIONS

1. To what class are parades, assemblies, marches, and picket lines fitted in paragraph 1?
2. In paragraphs 2 and 3 Cohen shows that conscientious objection and civil disobedience do not belong to the same classification. Why not?
3. Riots and civil disobedience are classified in Part IV. To what purpose? On what basis are they distinguished in paragraph 17?
4. How are revolutions divided in paragraph 6, and how is revolution distinguished from civil disobedience? Is the statement in paragraph 7 that civil disobedience "does not result in death or misery and rarely entails significant loss of property" basic to the distinction?
5. Cohen argues that Thoreau was not performing an act of civil disobedience. Was he a rebel, by Cohen's definition?
6. Division and classification are used in this extended definition of civil disobedience. Given his organization of ideas and his method of definition and examples, for how specialized an audience is Cohen writing? If that audience consisted of jurists solely, do you think he might have proceeded in another way and included or excluded information of any kind? Would you characterize the writing as expository rather than persuasive—that is, is Cohen seeking merely to inform his readers about civil disobedience, or is he seeking or encouraging action of some kind?

WRITING ASSIGNMENT

Analyze Thoreau's reasoning in his essay "Civil Disobedience" to determine whether he advocates or implicitly is recommending rebellion as Cohen defines it.

DEDUCTIVE REASONING

H. L. Mencken
REFLECTIONS ON WAR

1.   The thing constantly overlooked by those hopefuls who
talk of abolishing war is that it is by no means an evidence of
decay but rather a proof of health and vigor. To fight seems to be
as natural to man as to eat. Civilization limits and wars upon the
impulse but it can never quite eliminate it. Whenever the effort
seems to be most successful—that is, whenever man seems to be
submitting most willingly to discipline, the spark is nearest to
the powder barrel. Here repression achieves its inevitable work.
The most warlike people under civilization are precisely those
who submit most docilely to the rigid inhibitions of peace. Once
they break through the bounds of their repressed but steadily ac-
cumulating pugnacity, their destructiveness runs to great
lengths. Throwing off the chains of order, they leap into the air
and kick their legs. Of all the nations engaged in the two World
Wars the Germans, who were the most rigidly girded by conceptions of renunciation and duty, showed the most gusto for war
for its own sake.
2.   The powerful emotional stimulus of war, its evocation of
motives and ideals which, whatever their error, are at least more
stimulating than those which impel a man to get and keep a safe
job—this is too obvious to need laboring. The effect on the individual soldier of its very horror, filling him with a sense of the
heroic, increases enormously his self-respect. This increase in
self-respect reacts upon the nation, and tends to save it from the
deteriorating effects of industrial discipline. In the main, soldiers
are men of humble position and talents—laborers, petty mechan-
ics, young fellows without definite occupation. Yet no one can
deny that the veteran shows a certain superiority in dignity to
the average man of his age and experience. He has played his

part in significant events; he has been a citizen in a far more profound sense than any mere workman can ever be. The effects of all this are plainly seen in his bearing and his whole attitude of mind. War may make a fool of man, but it by no means degrades him; on the contrary, it tends to exalt him, and its net effects are much like those of motherhood on women.

3.　　That war is a natural revolt against the necessary but extremely irksome discipline of civilization is shown by the difficulty with which men on returning from it re-adapt themselves to a round of petty duties and responsibilities. This was notably apparent after the Civil War. It took three or four years for the young men engaged in that conflict to steel themselves to the depressing routine of everyday endeavor. Many of them, in fact, found it quite impossible. They could not go back to shovelling coal or tending a machine without intolerable pain. Such men flocked to the West, where adventure still awaited them and discipline was still slack. In the same way, after the Franco-Prussian War, thousands of young German veterans came to the United States, which seemed to them one vast Wild West. True enough, they soon found that discipline was necessary here as well as at home, but it was a slacker discipline and they themselves exaggerated its slackness in their imagination. At all events, it had the charm of the unaccustomed.

4.　　We commonly look upon the discipline of war as vastly more rigid than any discipline necessary in time of peace, but this is an error. The strictest military discipline imaginable is still looser than that prevailing in the average assembly-line. The soldier, at worst, is still able to exercise the highest conceivable functions of freedom—that is, he is permitted to steal and to kill. No discipline prevailing in peace gives him anything even remotely resembling this. He is, in war, in the position of a free adult; in peace he is almost always in the position of a child. In war all things are excused by success, even violations of discipline. In peace, speaking generally, success is inconceivable except as a function of discipline.

.　　.　　.

5.　　The hope of abolishing war is largely based upon the fact that men have long since abandoned the appeal to arms in their private disputes and submitted themselves to the jurisdiction of courts. Starting from this fact, it is contended that disputes between nations should be settled in the same manner, and that the

adoption of the reform would greatly promote the happiness of
the world.

6.   Unluckily, there are three flaws in the argument. The
first, which is obvious, lies in the circumstance that a system of
legal remedies is of no value if it is not backed by sufficient force
to impose its decisions upon even the most powerful litigants—a
sheer impossibility in international affairs, for even if one powerful litigant might be coerced, it would be plainly impossible to
coerce a combination, and it is precisely a combination of the
powerful that is most to be feared. The second lies in the fact that
any legal system, to be worthy of credit, must be administered
by judges who have no personal interest in the litigation before
them—another impossibility, for all the judges in the international court, in the case of disputes between first-class powers,
would either be appointees of those powers, or appointees of inferior powers that were under their direct influence, or obliged to
consider the effects of their enmity. The third objection lies in
the fact, frequently forgotten, that the courts of justice which
now exist do not actually dispense justice, but only law, and that
this law is frequently in direct conflict, not only with what one
litigant honestly believes to be his rights, but also with what he
believes to be his honor. Practically every litigation, in truth,
ends with either one litigant or the other nursing what appears to
him as an outrage upon him. For both litigants to go away satisfied that justice has been done is almost unheard of.

7.   In disputes between man and man this dissatisfaction is
not of serious consequence. The aggrieved party has no feasible
remedy; if he doesn't like it, he must lump it. In particular, he
has no feasible remedy against a judge or a juryman who, in his
view, has treated him ill; if he essayed vengeance, the whole
strength of the unbiased masses of men would be exerted to destroy him, and that strength is so enormous, compared to his
own puny might, that it would swiftly and certainly overwhelm
him. But in the case of first-class nations there would be no such
overwhelming force in restraint. In a few cases the general opinion of the world might be so largely against them that it would
force them to acquiesce in the judgment rendered, but in perhaps
a majority of important cases there would be sharply divided
sympathies, and it would constantly encourage resistance.
Against that resistance there would be nothing save the counter-
resistance of the opposition—*i.e.,* the judge against the aggrieved
litigant, the twelve jurymen against the aggrieved litigant's

friends, with no vast and impersonal force of neutral public opinion behind the former.

DISCUSSION: DEDUCTIVE REASONING

When the United Nations was formed in 1945, many people hoped that war could be abolished. But opinions differed. Hanson W. Baldwin wrote that mankind should not despair over war even if it took centuries to abolish it:

> The guiding star still shines; it cannot be attained in a century or two. But it is nevertheless worth struggling forward, pushing on; it would be worth the effort even if we knew the star was a mirage. *Death is an accepted part of life. Yet death is no cause for despair. The whole philosophy of man is keyed to the conception of the ultimate triumph of life over death.* Why, then, despair because war recurs?—*The New York Times,* May 21, 1945 [italics added—Ed.]

Notice the reasoning here. The italicized statements are presented as certain and well-established truths that provide decisive evidence for the conclusion: they are stated as if they were self-evident. One writer, Barrows Dunham, disagreed with Baldwin:

> Why despair? Because in war one's friends get killed, one's children get killed, and one gets killed oneself. Because everything one has built may be destroyed. Because it is idiocy to fight one war for the sake of fighting another later on. If human nature really does inevitably produce war, let us accept the fact without surrounding it with this comfortless nonsense.—*Man Against Myth*

Notice the difference in reasoning. Dunham moves from particular experiences to a generalization about them: the consequences of war are serious enough to make people despair. Dunham does not, however, assert that *all* men despair over war. His generalization is a probability only, not a certainty. Baldwin's reasoning is typical of deductive arguments; Dunham's, of inductive arguments.

Deductive reasoning concerning matters of fact begins with truths held to be certain—assumptions, beliefs, and suppositions about men and women and the world:

> We hold these truths to be self-evident; that all men are created equal; that they are endowed by their creator with certain unalienable rights; that among these are life, liberty, and the pursuit of happiness. . . .

Where do such "self-evident" truths come from? Some philosophers believe they are inborn in the human mind; others believe that they come from observation and experience. However derived, these assumptions or beliefs can be stated as propositions—statements that can be affirmed or denied, that can be asserted as true or false—and serve as the premises of deductive arguments, providing decisive evidence for the certitude of the conclusion. In inductive arguments, by contrast, premises are taken to provide only probable evidence; the conclusion is not taken to be certain.

Like the axioms of geometry, the premises of deductive arguments may be established by definition. The proposition that all squares have four sides is a premise of this kind: a body observed to contain five sides would not be *called* a square. Or a generalization based on a series of instances or experiences (the process that we call induction) may be regarded as so well established that it can serve as a premise: the statement that all men are mortal is such a generalization or induction. Or thinkers in a particular age may agree to consider a group of propositions as given and draw inferences from them: the propositions in the Declaration of Independence are of this kind.

The foremost characteristic of deductive arguments is that they may be considered valid or invalid. Validity is a function of the form or the arrangement of the terms in the premises that are stated in support of the conclusion. Validity is not concerned with the contents, or the subject matter, of the premises or the conclusion. If all the items mentioned in the conclusion are mentioned in the premises, and, if the terms are properly arranged, then, whether or not the premises are true in fact, the argument is a valid argument.

A simple but rigorous form of deductive argument that lends itself readily to a fairly easy decision about validity or invalidity is called a syllogism:

Major Premise	All men are mortal.
Minor Premise	John is a man.
Conclusion	John is mortal.

Premises are classified according to the subject and predicate terms of the conclusion: *John is mortal.* The major premise contains the predicate term (*mortal*), the minor premise the subject term (*John*). If the major and minor premises are accepted as true, the conclusion necessarily follows from them when they are related to each other in the manner indicated. A deductive argument is *valid* if the form of the argument is correct; the argument is *sound* if the premises and conclusion are true. It should be noted that a deductive argument may be valid, yet unsound, because it is correct in form but false in one or both of its premises:

All books contain one hundred pages.
War and Peace is a book.
War and Peace contains one hundred pages.

One of the premises and the conclusion of this syllogism are false, yet the argument is valid. What we seek, of course, is an argument valid in its form and sound in its premises.

Syllogisms may be defective for a number of reasons. We shall consider a few of these reasons. First, the *middle term* of the syllogism may be undistributed. The middle term is the term that appears in the premises but not in the conclusion. The following syllogism is valid:

All *property owners* are taxpayers.
My neighbors are *property owners*.
My neighbors are taxpayers.

The middle term is *property owners*. It is "distributed" if it refers to *all* of the members of the class; it is "undistributed" if it refers only to *some* of the members of the class. In the above syllogism a characteristic of all property owners is that they are taxpayers; this characteristic or fact is distributed among all members of the class; it is true of all property owners, and therefore is true of all my neighbors. But if the syllogism is written

All property owners are *taxpayers*.
My neighbors are *taxpayers*.
My neighbors are property owners.

the middle term is *taxpayers* and is undistributed in relation to the conclusion. Not all taxpayers are property owners, only *some* are; therefore only *some* of my neighbors are property owners. Yet the conclusion states all of my neighbors are. The syllogism is invalid.

A syllogism is defective if the middle term is ambiguous. In the syllogism

Whoever thrusts a knife into a person is a murderer.
A surgeon is *someone who thrusts a knife into a person*.
A surgeon is a murderer.

the middle term is incompletely defined and therefore ambiguous.

Finally, both premises must be affirmative if the conclusion is to be affirmative; if one of the premises is negative, the conclusion must be negative. The following syllogism is valid:

No dogs are allowed in the grocery store.
Rover is a dog.
Rover is not allowed in the grocery store.

The following syllogism is invalid:

No dogs are allowed in the store.
Rover is not a dog.
Rover is allowed in the store.

If the two premises are negative, no conclusion may be drawn. The argument is invalid.

The tests of logical validity are complex and cannot be reviewed in this brief discussion. But we should return to our discussion of the premises themselves and point out that arguments considered sound in one age may be rejected as unsound at a later time. Physicists before the twentieth century made deductions from the premise that space contains an "ether" that alters the speed of light in the vicinity of large bodies. This premise had to be discarded when Einstein's theory that the speed of light is unaltered by the motion of the earth or of any other body in the universe seemed confirmed. Einstein revised other fundamental assumptions about the nature of space and time. His theories have proved remarkably durable, but, like Newton's theory of gravitation, they may ultimately be revised or qualified by new observations.

Thus it is erroneous to think that disagreement over deductive reasoning arises mainly over conclusions. Disagreement is more likely to arise over premises, for there is general agreement on what constitutes a valid deductive argument. How premises are established is therefore of major importance, and writers may devote considerable discussion to explaining premises that are self-evident to them, but perhaps not to all of their readers.

Deductive arguments therefore can be developed in more than one way. The premises may be stated without discussion, or perhaps they may be illustrated by showing how they were originally established through induction. In this instance deduction and induction will be joined: the main argument may be deductive; the illustrations will demonstrate the process of inductive reasoning.

QUESTIONS

1. In paragraphs 1–4, Mencken argues that war will not be easily abolished, and he states his major assumption explicitly: "To fight seems to be as natural to man as to eat." How does the wording of this statement and the wording of others in these paragraphs show that Mencken regards these assumptions as certain and decisive evidence for his conclusions? What conclusions does he reach, based on these assumptions?

2. Though he regards these assumptions as certain, Mencken nevertheless defends them, knowing that not everyone will accept them as true. What evidence does he present? Does he discuss one civilization, or does he instead generalize about "warlike people" on the basis of observations made over a period of time?

3. Not all of Mencken's assumptions are explicitly stated. Does he as-

sume, for example, that human nature is a constant (Human nature never changes) or a variable (Man is a product of heredity and environment)? What other assumptions about the world or about people are implied?

4. In testing the logic of an essay, it is sometimes necessary to restate the premises to conform to the standard syllogism described above. Paragraph 1 contains several syllogisms; in the first of these, the major premise may be stated in these words: The expression of a natural instinct is evidence of health and vigor. What are the minor premise and the conclusion?

5. In paragraph 1 Mencken argues that repression of a natural instinct leads to increased destructiveness. What are the minor premise and the conclusion?

6. L. A. White, in *Science of Culture,* argues that the need for military conscription refutes the assumption that people are naturally warlike. Given his assumptions and evidence, how might Mencken answer this objection? What do paragraphs 5–7 suggest?

7. In paragraphs 5–7 Mencken challenges "the hope of abolishing war," a hope based on the assumption that men have long since "submitted themselves to the jurisdiction of courts." What flaws does Mencken find in the argument, and what kind of evidence does he present in refutation? Does he deal with particular instances or, instead, generalize from observations made over a period of time—observations he regards as obvious enough not to require substantiation?

8. In paragraph 6, are the three flaws discussed in the order of their importance, interest, or probability—or according to some other principle?

9. Evaluate the following arguments. It may be necessary to reword the premises.
   a. Since all voters are citizens and I am a voter, I am a citizen.
   b. Since all voters are citizens and I am a citizen, I am a voter.
   c. Since beneficent acts are virtuous and losing at poker benefits others, losing at poker is virtuous.
   d. Since the Irish are vegetarians and G. B. Shaw was Irish, Shaw was a vegetarian.
   e. I am permitted to enroll in Abnormal Psychology because freshmen are not permitted to enroll in the course, and I am a sophomore.
   f. This car has seat belts because all cars manufactured in this state have them, and this car was manufactured here.
   g. People who take things that are not theirs are thieves. Trash collectors take things that are not theirs. Trash collectors are thieves.
   h. Those who made 93 or better on the exam will receive an A in

the course. Seven of us received an A in the course and must have made 93 or better on the exam.

10. An *enthymeme* is a condensed syllogism in which one of the premises is implied: Because I am a man, I am mortal; I pay taxes because I own property. Reconstruct the original syllogism by supplying the missing premise, and evaluate the argument. The premises and conclusions may need rewording.

    a. Lord Haw Haw was a traitor to England because he resided in Germany during the Second World War.

    b. Lord Haw Haw committed treason by broadcasting anti-British propaganda for Germany during the war.

    c. Columbus did not discover America because the Vikings explored the North American continent before his time.

    d. I am a successful businessman because I had a paper route as a boy.

    e. I am an Independent, just as my father and grandfather were.

WRITING ASSIGNMENTS

Many thinkers have considered the problem of war: William James, in his essay "The Moral Equivalent of War"; Ruth Benedict, in *Patterns of Culture;* L. A. White, in *Science of Culture;* Sigmund Freud and Albert Einstein, in their correspondence entitled . . . *Why War?* Compare the assumptions of two of these writers (or any others) with those of Mencken and discuss how each writer seems to have arrived at them.

Mencken states that "of all the nations engaged in the two World Wars the Germans, who were the most rigidly girded by conceptions of renunciation and duty, showed the most gusto for war for its own sake." Examine W. L. Shirer's *The Rise and Fall of the Third Reich* and *Berlin Diary,* Howard K. Smith's *Last Train from Berlin,* A. J. P. Taylor's *Origins of the Second World War,* Hannah Arendt's *The Origins of Totalitarianism* and *Eichmann in Jerusalem,* and other books dealing with Germany in the 1930s to discover evidence that would support or refute Mencken's contention. Discuss and document your findings.

Lewis Mumford
MASS-SPORT AND THE CULT OF DEATH

1.   The romantic movements were important as a corrective to the machine because they called attention to essential elements in life that were left out of the mechanical world-picture: they themselves prepared some of the materials for a richer synthesis. But there is within modern civilization a whole series of compensatory functions that, so far from making better integration possible, only serve to stabilize the existing state—and finally they themselves become part of the very regimentation they exist to combat. The chief of these institutions is perhaps mass-sports. One may define these sports as those forms of organized play in which the spectator is more important than the player, and in which a good part of the meaning is lost when the game is played for itself. Mass-sport is primarily a spectacle.

2.   Unlike play, mass-sport usually requires an element of mortal chance or hazard as one of its main ingredients: but instead of the chance's occurring spontaneously, as in mountain climbing, it must take place in accordance with the rules of the game and must be increased when the spectacle begins to bore the spectators. Play in one form or another is found in every human society and among a great many animal species: but sport in the sense of a mass-spectacle, with death to add to the underlying excitement, comes into existence when a population has been drilled and regimented and depressed to such an extent that it needs at least a vicarious participation in difficult feats of strength or skill or heroism in order to sustain its waning life-sense. The demand for circuses, and when the milder spectacles are still insufficiently life-arousing, the demand for sadistic exploits and finally for blood is characteristic of civilizations that are losing their grip: Rome under the Caesars, Mexico at the time of Montezuma, Germany under the Nazis. These forms of surrogate manliness and bravado are the surest signs of a collective impotence and a pervasive death wish. The dangerous symptoms of that ultimate decay one finds everywhere today in machine civilization under the guise of mass-sport.

3.   The invention of new forms of sport and the conversion
of play into sport were two of the distinctive marks of the last
century: baseball is an example of the first, and the transformation of tennis and golf into tournament spectacles, within our
own day, is an example of the second. Unlike play, sport has an
existence in our mechanical civilization even in its most abstract
possible manifestation: the crowd that does not witness the ball
game will huddle around the scoreboard in the metropolis to
watch the change of counters. If it does not see the aviator finish
a record flight around the world, it will listen over the radio to
the report of his landing and hear the frantic shouts of the mob
on the field; should the hero attempt to avoid a public reception
and parade, he would be regarded as cheating. At times, as in
horse-racing, the elements may be reduced to names and betting
odds: participation need go no further than the newspaper and
the betting booth, provided that the element of chance be there.
Since the principal aim of our mechanical routine in industry is
to reduce the domain of chance, it is in the glorification of chance
and the unexpected, which sport provides, that the element ex-
truded by the machine returns, with an accumulated emotional
charge, to life in general. In the latest forms of mass-sport, like
air races and motor races, the thrill of the spectacle is intensified
by the promise of immediate death or fatal injury. The cry of horror that escapes from the crowd when the motor car overturns or
the airplane crashes is not one of surprise but of fulfilled expectation: is it not fundamentally for the sake of exciting just such
bloodlust that the competition itself is held and widely attended?
By means of the talking picture that spectacle and that thrill are
repeated in a thousand theatres throughout the world as a mere
incident in the presentation of the week's news: so that a steady
habituation to bloodletting and exhibitionistic murder and sui-
cide accompanies the spread of the machine and, becoming stale
by repetition in its milder forms, encourages the demand for
more massive and desperate exhibitions of brutality.
4.   Sport presents three main elements: the spectacle, the
competition, and the personalities of the gladiators. The spectacle
itself introduces the esthetic element, so often lacking in the pa-
leotechnic industrial environment itself. The race is run or the
game is played within a frame of spectators, tightly massed: the
movements of this mass, their cries, their songs, their cheers, are
a constant accompaniment of the spectacle: they play, in effect,

the part of the Greek chorus in the new machine-drama, announcing what is about to occur and underlining the events of the contest. Through his place in the chorus, the spectator finds his special release: usually cut off from close physical associations by his impersonal routine, he is now at one with a primitive undifferentiated group. His muscles contract or relax with the progress of the game, his breath comes quick or slow, his shouts heighten the excitement of the moment and increase his internal sense of the drama: in moments of frenzy he pounds his neighbor's back or embraces him. The spectator feels himself contributing by his presence to the victory of his side, and sometimes, more by hostility to the enemy than encouragement to the friend, he does perhaps exercise a visible effect on the contest. It is a relief from the passive rôle of taking orders and automatically filling them, of conforming by means of a reduced "I" to a magnified "It," for in the sports arena the spectator has the illusion of being completely mobilized and utilized. Moreover, the spectacle itself is one of the richest satisfactions for the esthetic sense that the machine civilization offers to those that have no key to any other form of culture: the spectator knows the style of his favorite contestants in the way that the painter knows the characteristic line or palette of his master, and he reacts to the bowler, the pitcher, the punter, the server, the air ace, with a view, not only to his success in scoring, but to the esthetic spectacle itself. This point has been stressed in bull-fighting; but of course it applies to every form of sport. There remains, nevertheless, a conflict between the desire for a skilled exhibition and the desire for a brutal outcome: the maceration or death of one or more of the contestants.

5.   Now in the competition two elements are in conflict: chance and record-making. Chance is the sauce that stimulates the excitement of the spectator and increases his zest for gambling: whippet-racing and horse-racing are as effective in this relation as games where a greater degree of human skill is involved. But the habits of the mechanical régime are as difficult to combat in sport as in the realm of sexual behavior: hence one of the most significant elements in modern sport is the fact that an abstract interest in record-making has become one of its main preoccupations. To cut the fifth of a second off the time of running a race, to swim the English channel twenty minutes faster than another swimmer, to stay up in the air an hour longer than

one's rival did—these interests come into the competition and
turn it from a purely human contest to one in which the real opponent is the previous record: time takes the place of a visible
rival. Sometimes, as in dance marathons or flag-pole squattings,
the record goes to feats of inane endurance: the blankest and
dreariest of sub-human spectacles. With the increase in professionalized skill that accompanies this change, the element of
chance is further reduced: the sport, which was originally a
drama, becomes an exhibition. As soon as specialism reaches
this point, the whole performance is arranged as far as possible
for the end of making possible the victory of the popular favorite:
the other contestants are, so to say, thrown to the lions. Instead
of "Fair Play" the rule now becomes "Success at Any Price."
6.   Finally, in addition to the spectacle and the competition,
there comes onto the stage, further to differentiate sport from
play, the new type of popular hero, the professional player or
sportsman. He is as specialized for the vocation as a soldier or an
opera singer: he represents virility, courage, gameness, those talents in exercising and commanding the body which have so
small a part in the new mechanical regimen itself: if the hero is a
girl, her qualities must be Amazonian in character. The sports
hero represents the masculine virtues, the Mars complex, as the
popular motion picture actress or the bathing beauty contestant
represents Venus. He exhibits that complete skill to which the
amateur vainly aspires. Instead of being looked upon as a servile
and ignoble being, because of the very perfection of his physical
efforts, as the Athenians in Socrates' time looked upon the professional athletes and dancers, this new hero represents the sum-
mit of the amateur's effort, not at pleasure but at efficiency. The
hero is handsomely paid for his efforts, as well as being re-
warded by praise and publicity, and he thus further restores to
sport its connection with the very commercialized existence from
which it is supposed to provide relief—restores it and thereby
sanctifies it. The few heroes who resist this vulgariza-
tion—notably Lindbergh—fall into popular or at least into journalistic disfavor, for they are only playing the less important part
of the game. The really successful sports hero, to satisfy the
mass-demand, must be midway between a pander and a prosti-
tute.
7.   Sport, then, in this mechanized society, is no longer a
mere game empty of any reward other than the playing: it is a

profitable business: millions are invested in arenas, equipment, and players, and the maintenance of sport becomes as important as the maintenance of any other form of profit-making mechanism. And the technique of mass-sport infects other activities: scientific expeditions and geographic explorations are conducted in the manner of a speed stunt or a prize-fight—*and for the same reason*. Business or recreation or mass spectacle, sport is always a means: even when it is reduced to athletic and military exercises held with great pomp within the sports arenas, the aim is to gather a record-breaking crowd of performers and spectators, and thus testify to the success or importance of the movement that is represented. Thus sport, which began originally, perhaps, as a spontaneous reaction against the machine, has become one of the mass-duties of the machine age. It is a part of that universal regimentation of life—for the sake of private profits or nationalistic exploit—from which its excitement provides a temporary and only a superficial release. Sport has turned out, in short, to be one of the least effective reactions against the machine. There is only one other reaction less effective in its final result: the most ambitious as well as the most disastrous. I mean war.

8.   Conflict, of which war is a specialized institutional drama, is a recurrent fact in human societies: it is indeed inevitable when society has reached any degree of differentiation, because the absence of conflict would presume a unanimity that exists only in placentals between embryos and their female parents. The desire to achieve that kind of unity is one of the most patently regressive characteristics of totalitarian states and other similar attempts at tyranny in smaller groups.

9.   But war is that special form of conflict in which the aim is not to resolve the points of difference but to annihilate physically the defenders of opposing points or reduce them by force to submission. And whereas conflict is an inevitable incident in any active system of cooperation, to be welcomed just because of the salutary variations and modifications it introduces, war is plainly a specialized perversion of conflict, bequeathed perhaps by the more predatory hunting groups; and it is no more an eternal and necessary phenomenon in group life than is cannibalism or infanticide.

10.   War differs in scale, in intention, in deadliness, and in frequency with the type of society: it ranges all the way from the predominantly ritualistic warfare of many primitive societies to

the ferocious slaughters instituted from time to time by barbarian conquerors like Ghengis Khan and the systematic combats between entire nations that now occupy so much of the time and energy and attention of "advanced" and "peaceful" industrial countries. The impulses toward destruction have plainly not decreased with progress in the means: indeed there is some reason to think that our original collecting and food-gathering ancestors, before they had invented weapons to aid them in hunting, were more peaceful in habit than their more civilized descendants. As war has increased in destructiveness, the sporting element has grown smaller. Legend tells of an ancient conqueror who spurned to capture a town by surprise at night because it would be too easy and would take away the glory: today a well-organized army attampts to exterminate the enemy by artillery fire before it advances to capture the position.

11.   In almost all its manifestations, however, war indicates a throwback to an infantile psychal pattern on the part of people who can no longer stand the exacting strain of life in groups, with all the necessities for compromise, give-and-take, live-and-let-live, understanding and sympathy that such life demands, and with all the complexities of adjustment involved. They seek by the knife and the gun to unravel the social knot. But whereas national wars today are essentially collective competitions in which the battlefield takes the place of the market, the ability of war to command the loyalty and interests of the entire underlying population rests partly upon its peculiar psychological reactions: it provides an outlet and an emotional release. "Art degraded, imagination denied," as Blake says, "war governed the nations."

12.   For war is the supreme drama of a completely mechanized society; and it has an element of advantage that puts it high above all the other preparatory forms of mass-sport in which the attitudes of war are mimicked: war is real, while in all the other mass-sports there is an element of make-believe: apart from the excitements of the game and the gains or losses from gambling, it does not really matter who is victorious. In war, there is no doubt as to the reality: success may bring the reward of death just as surely as failure, and it may bring it to the remotest spectator as well as to the gladiators in the center of the vast arena of the nations.

13.   But war, for those actually engaged in combat, likewise

brings a release from the sordid motives of profit-making and self-seeking that govern the prevailing forms of business enterprise, including sport: the action has the significance of high drama. And while warfare is one of the principal sources of mechanism, and its drill and regimentation are the very pattern of old-style industrial effort, it provides, far more than the sportfield, the necessary compensations to this routine. The preparation of the soldier, the parade, the smartness and polish of the equipment and uniform, the precise movement of large bodies of men, the blare of bugles, the punctuation of drums, the rhythm of the march, and then, in actual battle itself, the final explosion of effort in the bombardment and the charge, lend an esthetic and moral grandeur to the whole performance. The death or maiming of the body gives the drama the element of a tragic sacrifice, like that which underlies so many primitive religious rituals: the effort is sanctified and intensified by the scale of the holocaust. For peoples that have lost the values of culture and can no longer respond with interest or understanding to the symbols of culture, the abandonment of the whole process and the reversion to crude faiths and non-rational dogmas, is powerfully abetted by the processes of war. If no enemy really existed, it would be necessary to create him, in order to further this development.

14.   Thus war breaks the tedium of a mechanized society and relieves it from the pettiness and prudence of its daily efforts, by concentrating to their last degree both the mechanization of the means of production and the countering vigor of desperate vital outbursts. War sanctions the utmost exhibition of the primitive at the same time that it deifies the mechanical. In modern war, the raw primitive and the clockwork mechanical are one.

15.   In view of its end products—the dead, the crippled, the insane, the devastated regions, the shattered resources, the moral corruption, the anti-social hates and hoodlumisms—war is the most disastrous outlet for the repressed impulses of society that has been devised. The evil consequences have increased in magnitude and in human distress in proportion as the actual elements of fighting have become more mechanized: the threat of chemical warfare against the civilian population as well as the military arm places in the hands of the armies of the world instruments of ruthlessness of which only the most savage con-

querors in the past would have taken advantage. The difference between the Athenians with their swords and shields fighting on the fields of Marathon, and the soldiers who faced each other with tanks, guns, flame-throwers, poison gases, and hand-grenades on the Western Front, is the difference between the ritual of the dance and the routine of the slaughter house. One is an exhibition of skill and courage with the chance of death present, the other is an exhibition of the arts of death, with the almost accidental by-product of skill and courage. But it is in death that these repressed and regimented populations have their first glimpse of effective life; and the cult of death is a sign of their throwback to the corrupt primitive.

16.   As a back-fire against mechanism, war, even more than mass-sport, has increased the area of the conflagration without stemming its advance. Still, as long as the machine remains an absolute, war will represent for this society the sum of its values and compensations: for war brings people back to the earth, makes them face the battle with the elements, unleashes the brute forces of their own nature, releases the normal restraints of social life, and sanctions a return to the primitive in thought and feeling, even as it further sanctions infantility in the blind personal obedience it exacts, like that of the archetypal father with the archetypal son, which divests the latter of the need of behaving like a responsible and autonomous personality. Savagery, which we have associated with the not-yet-civilized, is equally a reversionary mode that arises with the mechanically over-civilized. Sometimes the mechanism against which reaction takes place is a compulsive morality or social regimentation: in the case of Western peoples it is the too-closely regimented environment we associate with the machine. War, like a neurosis, is the destructive solution of an unbearable tension and conflict between organic impulses and the code and circumstances that keep one from satisfying them.

17.   This destructive union of the mechanized and the savage primitive is the alternative to a mature, humanized culture capable of directing the machine to the enhancement of communal and personal life. If our life were an organic whole this split and this perversion would not be possible, for the order we have embodied in machines would be more completely exemplified in our personal life, and the primitive impulses, which we have diverted or repressed by excessive preoccupation with mechani-

cal devices, would have natural outlets in their appropriate cultural forms. Until we begin to achieve this culture, however, war will probably remain the constant shadow of the machine: the wars of national armies, the wars of gangs, the wars of classes: beneath all, the incessant preparation by drill and propaganda towards these wars. A society that has lost its life values will tend to make a religion of death and build up a cult around its worship—a religion not less grateful because it satisfies the mounting number of paranoiacs and sadists such a disrupted society necessarily produces.

QUESTIONS

1. Mumford states one of his major assumptions in paragraph 2: "the demand for sadistic exploits and finally for blood is characteristic of civilizations that are losing their grip. . . ." How does he establish or defend this assumption? How does it underlie his definition of mass-sport?

2. How does Mumford's analysis of mass man in a mechanical civilization give further support to his definition? How broad is the definition? Does it include activities not usually thought to be sports?

3. What assumptions does Mumford make about man and his needs in his analysis of the elements of sport in paragraph 4?

4. How does the definition of mass-sport provide the basis of the distinction between chance and record-breaking in paragraph 6?

5. If the major assumption (stated in paragraph 2) is taken as the major premise of the discussion, what are the minor premise and conclusion?

6. Does Mumford defend the assumption that conflict is "a recurrent fact in human societies"? Does he defend the assumption in paragraph 9 that war is not "an eternal and necessary phenomenon"?

7. Not only is conflict a "recurrent fact," it is also a phenomenon that exists apart from the good reasons nations go to war (or say they do): "If no enemy really existed, it would be necessary to create him, in order to further this development" (paragraph 13). What kind of analysis (economic, psychological, historical, and so on) does Mumford employ to establish this assumption? Does he appeal to our common experience and recognition of its truth?

8. What indications are there in paragraphs 8–17 that Mumford considers his assumptions as "given" in the argument? What conclusions does he derive from them in paragraphs 16 and 17, and in particular from the final statement in paragraph 15?

9. How basic to these conclusions are his earlier comments on mass-sport? Is he saying that war is a mass-sport?

WRITING ASSIGNMENTS

Analyze a major sport to determine the extent to which it supports Mumford's analysis. If you disagree with his conclusion, indicate your assumptions and defend them; if you agree, indicate your reasons for agreement.

Compare and contrast Mumford's assumptions and conclusions about modern war with those of Mencken.

Theodore Roszak
THE HUMAN ENVIRONMENT

1.   There exists a rock-solid consensus in urban-industrial society as to what is the proper measure of our progress beyond the primitive. It is the degree to which the environment we inhabit becomes more artificial, either by way of eliminating the original given by nature or by way of the predictive anticipation and control of natural forces. To be sure, the human environment must always have a touch of the artificial about it. One might almost say that the living space of human beings is destined to be "naturally artifical" to the extent that they spontaneously surround themselves with artifacts and institutions and with cautious, customary deliberations about their future. Human beings invent and plan and imaginatively embroider—and the result is culture, a buffer zone of the man-made and man-construed which it is as proper for humanity to inhabit as it is for plant and animal to reside in their sphere of tropisms and reflexes and instinctive responses. But in acknowledging the cultural capacity of human beings, we must not ignore the fact that there *is* a natural environment—the world of wind and wave, beast and flower, sun and stars—and that preindustrial people lived for millennia in close company with that world, striving to harmonize the things and thoughts of their own making with its non-human forces. Circadian and seasonal rhythms were the first clock peo-

THE HUMAN ENVIRONMENT: Originally published as "The Urban-Industrial Imperative" from the book *Where the Wasteland Ends* by Theodore Roszak, Doubleday & Company, Inc. Copyright © 1972 by Theodore Roszak. Reprinted by permission of Doubleday & Company, Inc.

ple knew, and it was by co-ordinating these fluid organic cycles with their own physiological tempos that they timed their activities. What they ate, they had killed or cultivated with their own hands, staining them with the blood or dirt of the effort. They learned from the flora and fauna of their surroundings, conversed with them, worshiped them, and sacrificed to them. They were convinced that their fate was bound up intimately with these non-human friends and foes, and in their culture they made place for them, honoring their ways.

2.   It would be impossible to exaggerate how important to the evolution of human consciousness this prolonged intimacy between the human and non-human was, though it is not an easy realization to recapture beyond the purely verbal-cerebral level. Unhappily, this poor, devitalized word "nature" which we must use to speak of the non-human world has lost its force by coming to mean for us an objectified realm of miscellaneous physical things and events which is outside of and other than us. We tend, for example, to think of "nature poetry" as poems that speak of daffodils or sunsets, a single possible subject matter among many, and at this point rather an outmoded one because largely irrelevant to the life of modern urban society. We forget that nature is, quite simply, the universal continuum, ourselves inextricably included; it is that which mothered us into existence, which will outsurvive us, and from which we have learned (if we still remember the lesson) our destiny. It is the mirror of our identity. Any cultural goods we produce which sunder themselves from this traditional, lively connection with the non-human, any thinking we do which isolates itself from, or pits itself against the natural environment is—strictly speaking—a delusion, and a very sick one. Not only because it will lack ecological intelligence, but because, more critically still, it will lack psychological completeness. It will be ignorant of the greatest truth mankind learned from its ancient intimacy with nature: the reality of spiritual being.[. . .]

3.   Until well into the industrial period, the natural environment—that which was neither humanly made nor controlled—was never far removed from the routine round of mankind's daily life. Throughout much of the civilized past, even those who lived in that most humanly regulated of abodes, the city, knew that not far beyond the town limits untamed wilderness and forest held possession. The town walls of medieval Europe may

have been a fair defense against the wolf; but they were useless against the plague-bearing rat, who could, even in the time of the high Renaissance in Italy, panic urban populations into mass exodus and bring great cities to a standstill. Within the city itself, until the very recent advent of modern sanitation, the tenor of life preserved much of the noisome earthiness of the rural village—to a degree that would be intolerable even in many American ghettos today. The grime and stench of animals filled the streets; the fetor of sickness, death, and human wastes was never absent. Imperial Rome, equipped with better sanitary engineering than many eighteenth-century European cities, still dumped its dead in *carnaria* just beyond the city wall. In Dr. Johnson's London, one might happen upon the decaying bodies of starved paupers in cellars and garrets; in English industrial towns until well into the nineteenth century, pigs continued to be the major street cleaners. In the New York of that day cattle were still being driven through the business district to be publicly butchered, and—in an incident no further back than 1844—a citizen out for a walk along the Bowery was gored to death by an angry bull escaped from the herd.

4.   We take legitimate pride in whatever success we have had in eliminating such crudity and unpleasantness from our midst. But we forget that, while these afflictions freely interpenetrated life even in the shelter of the city, they served as constant, if often harsh reminders to people of their dependence upon forces of nature they could never hope to subjugate. At this existential boundary, where human self-sufficiency gave way before the indomitable and inscrutable power of the non-human environment, men and women discovered that experience of psychic contingency which they attributed to the presence of the sacred. The embrace of nature may often have been rough, even murderous, as when nature assumed the formidable aspect of Mother Kali; but it was nonetheless an embrace. Locked within it, mankind found a sense of the human limits which precluded both arrogance and that dispiriting conviction of cosmic absurdity which haunts contemporary culture.

5.   In our time, the opportunity to live a life completely enveloped by the man-made and man-controlled has increased rapidly and enormously. We are in the way of suffering what can justly be called a cataclysm of urbanization. It was only in 1850 that England, the first industrial society, became as much as 50

per cent urban. Today, nearly 40 per cent of the world as a whole lives in urban areas; in another fifteen years, the figure will rise to over 50 per cent. In another fifty years, very nearly 100 per cent of the global population will be living in cities of over one million, with the largest megalopolitan complexes totaling well above one billion residents. These supercities will merely be the integrated versions of what we today call "urban sprawl": a Bosnywash stretching from Boston through New York and Philadelphia to Washington; a San Difranangeles running down the Pacific coast from San Francisco to San Diego.

6.   Such headlong urban concentration, it should be clear, has nothing to do with industrial necessity and little to do with population pressure. Industrial plant, no longer anchored to inflexible, bulky steam power, could easily and with great advantage be decentralized nowadays. And the rapid urbanization of many countries in Asia, Africa, and Latin America is happening at the cost of crippling depopulation in village and rural areas still quite capable of supporting life at a higher level than is possible in the shantytowns that encircle Calcutta or Lima or Stanleyville. One could in fact make an excellent case that rapid, massive urbanization in both the developed and underdeveloped societies is extremely anti-functional—though few economists have troubled to do so. Both those who make decisions about the course of history and the millions who are their trusting publics have simply accepted urbanism as, inevitably, a key measure of development—like it or not. They have mistaken a style of life for a necessity of life. That is why urbanism must be treated, with industrialism, as a separate and parallel force in what we call the modernization of the world. The building of megalopolitan complexes is no longer a derivative of industrialization, but an imperative in its own right, because only the urban showcase serves to display the industrial pattern of life, its products and values, with maximum visibility and intimidating eminence. It is the stage on which we have chosen to enact the drama of our time; it is our collective mindscape physically embodied. The supercity alone guarantees the utmost in artificiality, which is the unquestioned goal of progress.

7.   Already in the western world and Japan millions of city-dwellers and suburbanites have grown accustomed to an almost hermetically sealed and sanitized pattern of living in which very little of their experience ever impinges on non-human phenom-

ena. For those of us born to such an existence, it is all but impossible to believe that anything is any longer beyond human adjustment, domination, and improvement. That is the lesson in vanity the city teaches us every moment of every day. For on all sides we see, hear, and smell the evidence of human supremacy over nature—right down to the noise and odor and irritants that foul the air around us. Like Narcissus, modern men and women take pride in seeing themselves—their products, their planning—reflected in all that they behold. The more artifice, the more progress; the more progress, the more security. We press our technological imperialism forward against the natural environment until we reach the point at which it comes as startling and not entirely credible news to our urban masses to be told by anxious ecologists that their survival has anything whatever to do with air, water, soil, plant, or animal.

8.   Is it any wonder that they find these ecological forebodings the most difficult of all scientific expertise to accept? How much of their environment do most city-dwellers ever see and use in the raw? Remarkably little, compared to the overwhelming amount that comes to them pre-packaged, arranged, purified, remodeled, and, according to all the most reliable reports, *enriched.* How easily we forget that behind the technical membrane that mediates our life-needs, there *is* ultimately a world not of our making and upon which we must draw for sustenance. The air conditioner must still rely upon a respirable atmosphere; the chlorinated, fluoridated, piped-in water supply must still connect with potable lakes and rivers; the neatly displayed cans, jars, and cartons in the supermarket must still be filled with the nutritive fruits of the earth and the edible flesh of its animals.

9.   I can recall still the day my daughter first realized that the meat we ate at home was the flesh of slaughtered animals. She was then eight and a half years old, city born and bred, and only learned the terrible truth when she visited her first European butcher shop. There she saw the unmistakable carcasses of cattle, pigs, sheep, and poultry openly displayed. The connection dawned upon her as a brutal shock; and as much of a shock to me to realize that she had not until then known such a basic fact of life. But then, how could she? In America, she had known meat only as something we bought at the supermarket frozen, neatly carved, and plastic-wrapped. Not a hoof or a claw or a bloody pelt in sight. These chunks of food simply emerged from

a screened-off back room of the store where the gore and guts were hidden from view. She knew the meat "came from" animals; but her thought was that animals *gave* meat the way cows *gave* milk.

10.   The incident was as instructive for me as it was for my daughter. It made me vividly aware of how remote we can become from the resources of our daily life. With the result that we grow hopelessly stupid about our relations with the natural environment. We live off land and forests, animals, plants, and minerals; but what do we know of their ecological necessities or the integrity of their being? How can we, in our ignorance, make responsible decisions about resources we can only recognize and name when they arrive to us at the end of a long line of processing?

11.   Yet even if we were to trace our life-needs back to their ostensible origin, we would finally be confronted with insurmountable barriers of artificiality which screen off basic nature as much from those who raise and produce our food as from ourselves—so determined have we become to subordinate the natural environment. Agriculture today is largely a species of industrial mass production worked up off a soil that is little more than a chemical blotter. Increasingly, the business is swallowed up by conglomerate companies which clearly have no love or knowledge of farmcraft, but only perceive the land and its produce as so many profit and loss statistics in their ledgers. The fruits and vegetables themselves have already been predesigned to the commercial specifications of a food research industry that dictates the color, shape, size, taste, and aroma of every last grape and pea. The researchers know the natural product will be unacceptable to the eyes and palates of consumers who have learned from books, advertising copy, and canned goods what food is *supposed* to look and taste like. Our eggs are pumped out of carefully dieted battery hens that never see the light of day. Our meat comes to us from factory farms where immobilized, fast-fatted cattle and pigs are fed by the time clock and scientifically tranquilized to hold down the often violent anxiety that comes of lifelong close confinement. These beasts we eat are all but a fabricated counterfeit; we do not even grant them the dignity of setting foot in the open air once in a lifetime. For after all, what difference does *their* dignity make to *us*? Meat is meat, isn't it?

12.   Not only does the artificial environment blind us to the

paramount facts of our ecology, but we become convinced that there are human substitutes for everything we exhaust or contaminate. The scientists can manufacture vitamins and wonder drugs, can they not? They can spin cloth and building materials out of pure chemicals. Then surely, if need be, they can conjure sunshine, fresh air, clean water, nutritious foods out of their magic test tubes . . . or discover ways to cure us of the ailments that follow from their absence. Have they not already promised us programmed genetics and surgical immortality by way of major organ transplants? "We cannot duplicate God's work," a medical researcher quoted in *Newsweek* (April 24, 1967) tells us, "but we can come very close."

13.   To lament the expanding empire of urban-industrialism is one of the oldest and seemingly most useless preoccupations of social criticism. Since Rousseau and the Romantics, hostility toward the artificial environment has run through our culture like a soft, lyrical counterpoint to the swelling cacophony of the machine.[. . .] Yet what chance of success can the Romantic critique enjoy as long as the gains—both material and moral—of increased artificiality are so widely and spontaneously felt to outweigh the costs? Even such imponderable values as creativity, dignity, and heroism have become inseparably wedded in the popular imagination with our power to boss nature about and to surround ourselves with the products of advanced technology. We have come to believe that mankind is never so essentially human as when it is cast in the role of *homo faber*. It is upon inventing the machine, Buckminster Fuller tells us, that "man . . . began for the first time to really employ his intellect in the most important way." And J. Bronowski echoes the sentiment: "that is where the human mind realized itself most fully: in the cities that stand at the peak of technical achievement in their time. That is where great men flower . . . ."

QUESTIONS

1. Roszak is concerned with a premise of urban-industrial society that has led, in his view, to confused thinking about the environment; he states this premise in paragraph 1. What is the premise, and how does Roszak indicate that it is accepted without question?
2. How is this premise shown in paragraph 6 to account for depopulation in many parts of the world and for the rise of the supercity?

3. What other consequences are shown to proceed from this premise? How is it restated in paragraph 7 and later in the essay?
4. Roszak's attitude toward and criticism of the premise constitute the thesis of the essay. Where is the thesis first stated, and how is it restated in the course of the essay?
5. Roszak makes assumptions of his own—assumptions that he regards as self-evident, needing illustration but not proof. One of these, in paragraph 2, is that "nature is, quite simply, the universal continuum, ourselves inextricably included." What conclusions does he draw, based on this assumption, later in the essay?
6. Another assumption—introduced in paragraph 13—may be reworded: The Romantic critique has little or no chance of success as long as the gains of artificiality are widely and spontaneously felt to outweigh the costs. And it can be paraphrased in even fewer words: People will not recognize the costs of the artificial environment until they no longer consider its benefits necessities. How are the costs and benefits illustrated in the course of the essay?

WRITING ASSIGNMENT

Discuss other attitudes and practices in our society that might be traced to the assumptions Roszak criticizes. If you disagree with his assumptions or conclusions, explain why you do.

Jacques Maritain
THE AIMS OF EDUCATION

1.   Man is a person, who holds himself in hand by his intelligence and his will. He does not merely exist as a physical being. There is in him a richer and nobler existence; he has spiritual superexistence through knowledge and love. He is thus, in some way, a whole, not merely a part; he is a universe unto himself, a microcosm in which the great universe in its entirety can be encompassed through knowledge. And through love he can give himself freely to beings who are to him, as it were, other selves; and for this relationship no equivalent can be found in the physical world.

THE AIMS OF EDUCATION: From *Education at the Crossroads*. Reprinted by permission of Yale University Press. Selection title by editor.

2.   If we seek the prime root of all this, we are led to the acknowledgment of the full philosophical reality of that concept of the soul, so variegated in its connotations, which Aristotle described as the first principle of life in any organism and viewed as endowed with supramaterial intellect in man, and which Christianity revealed as the dwelling place of God and as made for eternal life. In the flesh and bones of man there exists a soul which is a spirit and which has a greater value than the whole physical universe. Dependent though he may be upon the slightest accidents of matter, the human person exists by virtue of the existence of his soul, which dominates time and death. It is the spirit which is the root of personality.

3.   The notion of personality thus involves that of wholeness and independence. To say that a man is a person is to say that in the depth of his being he is more a whole than a part and more independent than servile. It is this mystery of our nature which religious thought designates when it says that the person is the image of God. A person possesses absolute dignity because he is in direct relationship with the realm of being, truth, goodness, and beauty, and with God, and it is only with these that he can arrive at his complete fulfillment. His spiritual fatherland consists of the entire order of things which have absolute value, and which reflect, in some manner, a divine Absolute superior to the world and which have a power of attraction toward this Absolute.

4.   Now it should be pointed out that personality is only one aspect or one pole of the human being. The other pole is—to speak the Aristotelian language—individuality, whose prime root is matter. The same man, the same entire man who is, in one sense, a person or a whole made independent by his spiritual soul, is also, in another sense, a material individual, a fragment of a species, a part of the physical universe, a single dot in the immense network of forces and influences, cosmic, ethnic, historic, whose laws we must obey. His very humanity is the humanity of an animal, living by sense and instinct as well as by reason. Thus man is "a horizon in which two worlds meet." Here we face that classical distinction between the *ego* and the *self* which both Hindu and Christian philosophies have emphasized, though with quite diverse connotations.[. . .]

5.   I should like to observe now that a kind of animal training, which deals with psychophysical habits, conditioned re-

flexes, sense-memorization, etc., undoubtedly plays its part in education: it refers to material individuality, or to what is not specifically human in man. But education is not animal training. The education of man is a human awakening.

6.   Thus what is of most importance in educators themselves is a respect for the soul as well as for the body of the child, the sense of his innermost essence and his internal resources, and a sort of sacred and loving attention to his mysterious identity, which is a hidden thing that no techniques can reach. And what matters most in the educational enterprise is a perpetual appeal to intelligence and free will in the young. Such an appeal, fittingly proportioned to age and circumstances, can and should begin with the first educational steps. Each field of training, each school activity—physical training as well as elementary reading or the rudiments of childhood etiquette and morals—can be intrinsically improved and can outstrip its own immediate practical value through being *humanized* in this way by understanding. Nothing should be required of the child without an explanation and without making sure that the child has understood.

7.   We may now define in a more precise manner the aim of education. It is to guide man in the evolving dynamism through which he shapes himself as a human person—armed with knowledge, strength of judgment, and moral virtues—while at the same time conveying to him the spiritual heritage of the nation and the civilization in which he is involved, and preserving in this way the century-old achievements of generations. The utilitarian aspect of education—which enables the youth to get a job and make a living—must surely not be disregarded, for the children of man are not made for aristocratic leisure. But this practical aim is best provided by the general human capacities developed. And the ulterior specialized training which may be required must never imperil the essential aim of education.

QUESTIONS

1. Like Roszak, Maritain regards man as part of a whole, but he differs somewhat in his definition and assumptions. How much more encompassing is his conception of the whole? What other differences do you note?

2. Maritain looks to Aristotle and to Christianity for a statement of his conception, not for proof of it. What conclusions does he reach

about what is "specifically human in man" through his statement of
assumptions in paragraphs 2 and 3?

3. How does the statement "The education of man is a human awakening" serve as the major premise in the deductive argument developed in paragraph 7? This premise can be reworded to satisfy the
form of the deductive syllogism: Whatever awakens the specifically
human in man contributes to his education. The minor premise will
state what it is that is awakened. What other conclusions about the
aims of education depend on this major premise?

4. The study of English language and literature, modern languages,
Greek and Roman language and literature, philosophy, and sometimes history and archeology are generally referred to as the "humanities." Maritain helps us to understand why the word continues
to be important to teachers in these fields and how the word might
be used to characterize all kinds of education. How might chemistry
or economics be considered a humanistic experience?

WRITING ASSIGNMENT

Show how your assumptions about yourself as a person help to shape
your attitudes toward the courses you are taking now or underlie your
view of your high-school education.

Andrew Hacker
THE ILLUSION OF INDIVIDUALITY

1.   Among the more widespread postwar preoccupations
has been the growing impersonality of life in America. While the
major causes will turn on each commentator's disposition, most
agree that rootlessness, alienation, and a crisis of identity characterize the time. Confused over goals and values, and no longer
capable of establishing meaningful relationships with one another, Americans find themselves powerless and frustrated appendages in an age of dehumanized institutions.

2.   My interest in this chapter will be to inquire why criticism of this sort has evoked such a strong response. One reason
is that these commentaries depict much that is true about post-

war America. Mass production, mass consumption, and the mass media; specialization, secularization, and suburbanization; the growth of government, of corporate capitalism, and of messianic militarism—these are all clear and present conditions having deep-seated effects on the attitudes of Americans. However, the social structure and economic development of any society leave a mark on the character of its citizens. What is different here is the intensity of concern over the status and predicament of "the individual."

3.   While philosophers have been locating "the individual" at the center of their systems for several centuries, it is only recently that this emphasis has entered the vernacular. When a society's population consists mainly of peasants or proletarians, only a small minority can voice the theory of individuality. However, most Americans, now liberated from the confines of rural bondage and industrial exploitation, have embraced an outlook that was once the property of an elite few. Thus, today virtually everyone looks upon himself as an "individual." For with new occupations, enhanced education, and liberation from constricting surroundings, people formulate new conceptions of themselves and their hitherto hidden potentialities. Not only do more Americans expect more out of life, but they are also more sensitive to forces pronounced harmful to their newly discovered capacities.

4.   Assertions of individuality, while ideologically understandable, form the basic myth of American democracy. More Americans have attained new jobs, more schooling, and a greater exposure to the variety of what life has to offer. Nevertheless, in major attributes they remain essentially the same sort of people as were their peasant and proletarian forebears. This is to suggest not only that their new conceptions of self have no factual basis— for it would be difficult to show that the materials of which Americans are made have undergone a marked improvement—but also that the average person cannot be expected to live up to the standards he now sets for himself. Moreover, most of the sensations of injustice about which citizens complain arise from overinflated hopes concerning what an ordinary person may experience throughout his life.

5.   But because assumptions are not examined, even the most sophisticated commentaries take the view that in more salutary circumstances American men and women would reveal ca-

pacity for outlooks and accomplishments they have not yet achieved. Current attitudes and behavior are seen as corrupted crudescences: for contemporary humanity has been distorted by institutions and imperatives resulting from either accidents of history or the intrigues of those who profit from a maldistribution of power. Were these constrictions to be removed, "the individual"—every man and woman—could ascend to a level of life where their potentialities for a creative existence would reach a full flowering.

6.   But the problem with discussions of human "potentialities" is that no facts support the arguments. The historical record may be used to demonstrate man's inherent good nature, his tendency toward evil, or some mixture of these and other attributes. Equally authoritative evidence can be cited to demonstrate that he has the reason and intelligence to control his destiny, or that he has always drifted in a chartless sea. Indeed, the historical record is irrelevant: for mankind's capabilities have hardly had an opportunity for realization in any society the world has known. Thus, the release of potentialities remains a hope for the future rather than an extrapolation from past performance.

7.   One can only speculate, therefore, about what may reasonably be expected from the people who comprise our present society. Here is an automobile salesman in New Jersey, there a television repairman in Alabama; here is a black teenager in Chicago, there a housewife in suburban San Diego. What capabilities lie dormant in them?

8.   Honest observation indicates that on the whole these Americans—and millions like them—are not extraordinarily intelligent, not terribly ambitious, and tend chiefly to be wrapped up in themselves. But suppose that they were somehow released from the thralldom of salesmanship and racial prejudice, from the destructive life of the slums and the dull domesticity of the suburbs—supposing all this, can it be conceived that such people as these, even given the most encouraging conditions, would display some inherent "individuality"? For it may be that assumptions about unfathomed potentialities are only a myth—an illusion that persists because any serious investigation of its premises may prove hazardous to a nation at a difficult stage in its history.

9.   Most people are ordinary. And ordinary people are ordi-

nary, regardless of the time or society or setting in which they live. Moreover, ordinary people are relatively unintelligent, incapable of abstraction or imagination, lacking any special qualities of talent or creativity. They are for the most part without drive or perseverance; easily discouraged, they prefer the paths of security. Whether slave or serf or sweated worker, most people in the past have displayed these traits. And most who inhabit the present, whether scientist or suburbanite or sophisticate, continue to manifest these tendencies.

10.   This is the human condition. One need not invoke theology, nor is it necessary to assert that man is a creature of evil and tainted with sin. I simply argue that in any society all save an exceptional few will lack the capacity for attainments that transcend the mediocre.

11.   Quite obviously words such as these can carry unpleasant implications. However, allusions to differentials in human talents need not originate in pseudo-genetic doctrines or ideologies intended to flatter members of a particular class, race or nationality. What I mean is that most people—white as well as black, rich no less than poor—are not terribly clever or creative or venturesome. Yet, despite these disclaimers, the mere mention of mediocrity raises problems for democratic rhetoric. Indeed, of all the world's peoples, Americans have the greatest difficulty in facing the fact that human beings can be subjected to qualitative judgments.

12.   Hence the emphasis on "excellence"—a quality Americans are prepared to discover in more people and places than was ever thought possible. While competition often compels the ranking of individuals, this does not discourage the concept that the achievements and products of excellence may be attained by virtually everyone.* To inform an American that he has limited intelligence or a sinewless character can only be construed as an insult. Not only does the democratic spirit make it difficult for one person to pass judgment on another; an accompanying presumption is that everyone carries the capacity for excelling in at least several areas of life.

---

* To be sure, many middle-class Americans enjoy dilating on the moral and intellectual shortcomings of whole categories of citizens they deem their inferiors. And by the same token not a few Caucasians find it difficult to discover potentialities in persons more darkly hued than themselves. Yet, despite the standards they set for others, such individuals attribute quite flattering qualities and accomplishments to members of their own race and class. Perhaps, then, it would be more accurate to say that it is *within* their own races and classes that Americans display their magnanimity toward one another's capacities.

13.   The ideology of individuality—and I purposely use this term—is of comparatively recent origin. Until the last generation or so, the emphasis was on "individualism," and the connotations were almost exclusively economic. Moreover, this doctrine was quite straightforward in its intentions: to exalt the entrepreneur and encourage the quest for profit. Hence the qualities it celebrated: a willingness to put aside current earnings and defer gratifications; a readiness to risk these savings in an enterprise of one's own creation; and the determination to make that enterprise succeed by hard work, native wit, and the seizing of opportunities. For all these requisites, those who succeeded were hardly exemplary figures by contemporary standards. Rough-hewn and self-centered, they displayed a bare minimum of moral awareness and eschewed any notions of social responsibility. Patronizing the arts and supporting civic causes earned esteem in certain circles, but such activities were by no means expected by the individualist ethic. One could achieve that status simply by building or enlarging an enterprise that surpassed and outlasted the efforts of others.

14.   Current assumptions require that expressions of individuality be more than economic. However, any attempt to extend an ideology of this sort to non-economic areas encounters serious difficulties. For, while success in entrepreneurial individualism lay solely in how much money a self-made man might amass, no methods have been devised for assessing or identifying qualities unsusceptible to monetary measurement. What one person will see as a genuine philosophical talent, another will perceive as exhibitionism or eccentricity. Where some will detect a statesmanlike courage, others will find opportunism and expediency. (Certainly not all departures from convention can be construed as evidence of praiseworthy qualities. Why else has the term "neurotic" become so common?) Because of the impossibility of agreeing on its attributes, the democratic resolution has been to bestow candidacy for individuality on everyone.

15.   Clashes over definitions fail to impress middle-class Americans, who remain persuaded that with just a little more effort and some added insight they may discover their true selves. Thus the growing commitment to education, and the conviction that with schooling can come not only worldly success but also an awareness of one's own potentialities. Yet the majority content themselves with unexamined assumptions: one is that what

happens in classrooms has an influence on subsequent behavior. Yet, on the whole, the educational process has surprisingly little effect in determining how people will finally shape their lives. Apart from technical training, what education imparts is chiefly a set of perceptions through which the world may be seen, plus a vocabulary for describing that vista. The process may occasionally instill values or induce feelings of guilt, although this is far rarer than most would like to believe. And while there can be no denying that augmented schooling can awaken both a consciousness of style and a sophistication of manner, these are chiefly lessons in how to make the most of prevailing conditions.

16.   Certainly the overwhelming majority of college graduates—presumably the class from which the most should be expected—show little in their lives which can reasonably be called individuality. Despite their exposure to higher education and their heightened awareness of life's options, they nevertheless take paths of least resistance when faced with critical decisions throughout their lives. What their education gives them is the ability to rationalize these choices: a series of verbal strategies for justifying their actions to others and for making peace with themselves.*

17.   Neither the information in a person's head nor the values in his conscience have much to do with his behavior. The principal determinant of human action stems from the fact that most people lack the courage to take chances. Learning lessons of right conduct has become an academic exercise; but conversations of this sort are incapable of instilling the self-confidence needed to pursue even the most noble principles. Americans who have experienced higher education find themselves especially vulnerable because society offers them an array of ascending opportunities—on the condition that they conform to the codes set by those who bestow the material rewards and symbols

---

* What about the liberal-arts curriculum, which a growing number of Americans elect to study? Quite clearly, most students still go to college to secure credentials for the status and occupations of middle-class careers. Even so, a rising proportion of undergraduates evidence genuine eagerness for a critical understanding of themselves and their world. During these years of suspended animation they can be a real pleasure to teach: their eyes are opened; they ask interesting and important questions; they begin to abandon the cautionary maxims that hitherto held their minds in check.

However, this is an interlude in their lives. For the years of liberal learning cannot extend into the time when careers must be chosen and bargains struck with the arbiters of promotion. This is one reason why professors show little enthusiasm for meeting those students later on. For minds that were once inquiring have now settled into place; and the verbal skills learned in the liberal arts are deployed to defend compromises and accommodations.

of success. In short, the college graduate, more than others, has a great deal to gain by being the sort of person others want him to be. And in this situation all talk of inculcating individuality has little meaning.* The one trait America's educational institutions cannot teach is personal courage, and the one quality they cannot abscind is human weakness. Considering the prizes held out to those educated for future success, it should not be surprising that so many strike the bargains they do.

18.   Even if the United States could end poverty and bigotry, diffuse its pyramids of power, and suppress its imperial tendencies, there is no reason to believe that such a society would contain a greater quotient of talented people. For talent has always been, and will always be, a scarce commodity.

19.   Recall for a moment the classical literature of Utopia: portrayals of a benign future where the authors have caused the pressures of contemporary life to disappear. But then take a closer look at the characters who inhabit these idyllic communities. While they are polite, sensible, and socially responsible, most also emerge as very ordinary and unprepossessing people. Even the creators of Utopia, free to devise any manner of population, avoided creating societies of philosophers, artists, and heroes. Perhaps they realized that even in Utopian circumstances the majority of citizens would remain unexceptional. (They may also have suspected that too many talents would strain the community structure.) And in so doing most Utopians have been eminently realistic: their aim has been to make men happy rather than to elevate their aptitudes.

20.   In the past, ordinary people thought of themselves in unpretentious terms, acknowledging their limitations and accepting stations relatively consonant with their capacities. But the emergence of individuality has changed self-conceptions, creating discontents of a sort that were unlikely to occur to men and

---

* It is, of course, easy enough to solve the problem simply by debasing the coinage of individuality. Anyone who wishes to discover uniqueness in every member of a community can achieve this end by inflating small talents and marginal distinctions: this woman has a unique recipe for angel cake, that housewife knits her husband's neckties; this man rides to work on a bicycle, that one collects old circus posters; he plays a fine game of golf, she set a shorthand speed record, and they vacationed on a barge canal. Perhaps something is gained in telling the orthodox that they are unconventional, by persuading the weak that they are creatures of courage. Such fictions may obviate the endemic envy of the average and impart a veneer of romance to lackluster lives. Certainly most of those choosing to congratulate everyman on his individuality understand that they tell gentle lies. Perhaps no great harm results from these exercises, except that they encourage the unexceptional to believe that all avocations are of equal quality.

women of earlier eras. Once persuaded that he is an "individual" entitled to realize his assumed potentialities, a citizen will diagnose himself as suffering quite impressive afflictions.

21.   The intensity with which Americans now explore their egos arises from the conviction that even an average personality is a deep and unparalleled mechanism. Whether psychoanalytic or existential in emphasis, people take pleasure in examining the quality of their "relationships" and achieving an "insight" into their own internal functioning. The heightened concern over sex derives in no small measure from a search for one's "real self" and attempts to find realization through close contact with another person. Hence also the stress on individual "powerlessness," and the constrictions that large institutions impose on self-discovery and self-development. While these terms of discourse are not of recent invention, their employment by so large a part of society is certainly new. Alienation, powerlessness, and crises of identity come into being only if citizens decide to invest their personalities with potentialities ripe for liberation. As soon as people make such decisions about themselves, regulations once taken for granted appear as oppressive instruments of government and society.

22.   Thus, most of those who describe themselves as "alienated" lack any credentials for so tragic a predicament. Given the unexceptional quality and character of the vast majority of Americans, it should be apparent that, however painful the problems they encounter, little is gained by inflating their troubles to traumatic proportions. The average college student—or factory worker or welfare recipient—may indeed feel pushed around, robbed of dignity, or consigned to a status incommensurate with his talents. But to call him "alienated" assumes that if he were liberated from constraints that now annoy him, he would emerge as a different person. To be sure, millions of Americans live at a subsistence level, while others face arbitrary and irrational discriminations throughout their lives. The grievance of such persons is that they have been deprived of experiences enjoyed by people really no different from themselves. To say that you wish to enjoy amenities now available to others ought to be a sufficient argument for eliminating inequality. Considering the behavior of those who have achieved such privileges, the claim that sharing these enjoyments will enhance one's humanity remains a most precarious proposition.

23.   The notion that modern society thwarts self-discovery, compelling people to don masks and distort their true personalities, carries a series of parallel assumptions. However, the fact that so many Americans have become absorbed with asking "Who am I?" need not be construed as evidence of a nationwide "identity crisis." On the contrary, it shows that citizens now feel entitled to give their personal problems philosophical connotations. Self-indulgence of this sort merely indicates that Americans have expanded their vocabularies: it does not mean that these self-estimates have much to do with reality.

24.   To ask "Who am I?" is really rather presumptuous. In actual fact, people may still be summed up largely by the roles they fill in society—housewife or husband, soldier or salesman, student or scientist—and by the qualities others ascribe to them: a person "is" black or blind, fat or feminine, indolent or efficient. No one likes being "identified" as simply a fat salesman or a black housewife, and of course the list of a person's roles and characteristics can be extended, but it remains an inventory of attributes externally imposed. Quite clearly many Americans prefer to believe that beneath all the labels lies a unique and identifiable self. Unfortunately for them, the "Who am I?" question can never be answered except in inventoried terms. But the fact that people persist in asking it shows how a little learning can disrupt sensibilities and produce crises unknown in less literate days.

25.   Nor should society be blamed for these problems, particularly those afflicting members of the middle class who complain about restrictions imposed by their communities and careers. It is quite disingenuous to maintain that society forces anyone to be or become anything at all. A person still has the freedom to decide whether or not he will compromise with the world of rewards. If he wishes the comfort and security available to those who join this game, then he will be required to follow certain rules. Those opting for "success" will of course have to adjust to occupational and organizational imperatives. But no one is compelled to enter this gamut. If an individual elects to live an anonymous and unexposed life, if he chooses to stand apart from competitive pressures, then his personality will be left alone. American society has plenty of such places; of course the jobs they offer tend to be uninteresting and poorly paid. Many people obviously want the best of both worlds: material and social success and the freedom to indulge their idiosyncrasies.

But it is difficult to muster sympathy for those who complain about the costs of competition. A society that distributes the good things of life with an uneven hand should require some sacrifice of those who reap its rewards.*

26.　Anxieties over problems such as "alienation" and "identity" will continue to preoccupy Americans, for each year more people develop a heightened sense of their own importance. Feelings of isolation and injustice, of powerlessness and oppression, will become more exacerbated among all classes as people expand the enjoyments they consider their due. A people so impressed with their entitlements cannot be expected to revert to simpler settings, to codes and conventions that would prevent the ills they now say they suffer. Skeptical toward all authority and made restive by an encapsulated existence, Americans have divested themselves of the attitudes required for a more commonplace contentment.

27.　The difficulty is that, for all their verbal facility, the great majority of Americans are basically no different from their forebears who lived with a minimum of self-created dilemmas. As contemporary citizens have no higher an endowment of quality or character than did their less literate predecessors, it remains only to say that pursuit of an ephemeral individuality will certainly increase their frustrations. It is a symptom of our age that people invest themselves with grand attributes, even though they lack the talent or perseverance to realize potentialities they have convinced themselves they have. Hence the need for the illusion of individuality. For this fragile myth is the only support that remains for uncertain spirits in their quest for self-respect.

QUESTIONS

1. Establishing the premises on which arguments are built is often more important than the conclusions reached—particularly when the argu-

---

* If I may digress for a moment, I would like to apply this general observation to a quite different question: Who is to be held responsible for wartime atrocities? Every soldier can plead that he was simply following orders, in which case only a single national leader can ultimately be blamed. However, an alternative answer would divide any military force into those who apply for or accept promotions, and those who don't. Individuals who seek or accept elevation above the rank of conscript in effect give their consent to the regime and its works. In taking the rewards it offers, they become tacit participants and acquiesce in its acts. No one has to accept promotion; no private soldier is penalized for choosing to remain a private. Hence, guilt for war crimes should be ascribed to everyone, from corporal to field marshal, who elects to succeed under the regime. Having opted to do as well as they could in the system, such persons cannot complain if they are held as consenting members and hence answerable for its atrocities.

ment is over that broad and elusive term "human nature." Arguments over the proper definition and role of education inevitably deal with statements like the following:

> A sound philosophy in general suggests that men are rational, moral, and spiritual beings and that the improvement of men means the fullest development of their rational, moral, and spiritual powers. All men have these powers, and all men should develop them to the fullest extent.—Robert Maynard Hutchins, "The Basis of Education"

> The modern secular way of life is not suited to the real nature of men. For it withholds from them that discipline of their own impulses which is indispensable to their health and their happiness.—Walter Lippmann, "An Image of Man for Liberal Democracy"

Notice that in these statements no qualification about kinds of men are made. Does Hacker make comparable assertions about *all* men?

2. What assumptions about men or human nature is Hacker attacking? Does he reject them because they contradict his observations of what men are or because they contradict other self-evident assumptions?

3. What evidence or support does Hacker provide for his statements on "ordinary" people in the whole essay? To what extent would he agree with the statements of Hutchins and Lippmann quoted above?

4. Note these statements in paragraph 9:

> Most people are ordinary. And ordinary people are ordinary, regardless of the time or society or setting in which they live. Moreover, ordinary people are relatively unintelligent, incapable of abstraction or imagination, lacking any special qualities of talent or creativity.

How is this basic view related to middle-class Americans in paragraph 15. If the major premise is the statement "Most people are ordinary," what are the minor premise and the conclusion as indicated in paragraph 15?

5. How does Hacker derive "the fact"—discussed in paragraph 17—that "most people lack the courage to take chances." Considering his earlier statements about men, does Hacker assume that the reader will consider the statement self-evident?

6. Hacker grants that a number of definitions of individuality are possible. How does he seek to persuade his reader that the usual definition—discussed in the footnote to paragraph 17—is misleading or inadequate?

7. What is the principle of division in the footnote to paragraph 25? Are you persuaded by Hacker's reasoning?

8. Does Hacker assert or imply what the goals of education ought to be? Or is his purpose in writing merely to analyze the current situation without making recommendations?

WRITING ASSIGNMENTS

Indicate the extent to which Hacker would agree with the assumptions and conclusions of Krutch and Newman.

Indicate the extent of your agreement with Hacker through an estimate of the "individuality" of your fellow students in high school or college.

Argue whether a soldier ought to be held responsible for "wartime atrocities" if he were ordered by a superior to perform them. Be careful to distinguish your assumptions from your conclusion.

Basing your reasoning on Hacker's statements, discuss how you think he would regard the admissions policy and aims of your college as stated in its catalog.

Herbert J. Muller
THE "RELEVANCE" OF THE "HUMANITIES"

1.   Needless to say, I am sure that I am a good humanist. Since my interests have long been focused on contemporary issues, and no less when I was dealing with the uses of the past, I took for granted that they were clearly relevant too. Thus in a recent seminar in political philosophy, centered on the issues of democracy, I started for the sake of historical perspective with some study of freedom in the ancient world—a major item in my professional stock in trade. One day an impatient student suddenly launched a harangue on the terrific problems looming up, such as the population explosion, the prospects that millions of people are going to starve to death; and here we were way back in ancient Greece, reading Plato's *Republic*. Patiently I explained that while I shared his concern over these problems we could not tailor the whole curriculum to the present emergency, we had to try to get down to basic principles, and we needed some perspec-

THE "RELEVANCE" OF THE "HUMANITIES": Reprinted from *The American Scholar*, Volume 40, Number 1, Winter, 170–71. Copyright © 1970 by the United Chapters of Phi Beta Kappa. By permission of the publishers. The first half of the essay is omitted here.

tive in order to size up both our current crises and our traditions
and living beliefs, or simply as a means of keeping our heads.
For the long run, historical perspective was indispensable to any
hopes of wisdom.

2.   Yet even as I made this sensible answer, I felt pretty academic. I stick to this kind of wisdom, or am stuck with it; but is
it the best wisdom for aroused students at this time? Specifically,
are the perspectives got from the political thought of the little
Greek *polis* really of much help in understanding our massive
technological society? As for the *Republic,* it is relevant because of
Plato's concern with basic issues, such as the nature of a "just"
society, his principle of rule by an elite, and his critique of democracy; but even apart from his dubious model of a just society—serviceable neither for ancient Athens nor for us—the
terms of his argument are hardly applicable to the political problems of America, a radically different experiment in democracy
on an immensely larger scale. So too with the "tragic sense" of
history I have long dwelt on, with much stress on basic incon-
gruities, ambiguities, ironies and paradoxes. It seems to me
clearly essential to a proper understanding of not only the past
but also our situation today, and as essential to hopes of wisdom.
But this can become too easy a habit, or lead to an aloof, tired
kind of wisdom; and again I cannot be confident that it is the
best kind for students much concerned about the state of
America and wanting to be "involved" or "committed." It will
not do to tell them that the human condition has always been
tragic, for they see evils that are quite unnecessary, clearly reme-
diable. The immediate relevance of a sense of the tragic dignity
of human history may be chiefly a disheartening consciousness
of how little such dignity there is in our disastrous war in Vietnam, and in the grievous failures on the domestic front.

3.   Or "wisdom" may be too highfalutin a word. While we
naturally tend to be too confident that we both possess it and impart it, we cannot in any case hope to turn out a generation of
wise men. Enough if we meet the simple need for more intelligence: an informed, critical intelligence, with a proper concern for human values, which can then be brought to bear on our
social and political problems. This, however, is substantially
what aroused students have been demanding of us. Repelled by
the ruling values of our society, they are questioning the relevance of our own values to the "real" world—a world full of

urgent problems. Hence I have had second thoughts, too, about the broader traditional objectives that I have been pleased to share.

4.   One traditional objective has been to turn out "cultivated," "well-rounded" men. These are clearly admirable types, especially needed in a technological society, which, we must hope, still finds enough professional room for them. We must acknowledge that we have not been doing too well by this objective because of the intensive specialization, but we must also wonder whether our society does provide enough room for such men. Students preparing to follow us into the academic profession can expect to find a suitable niche (although now with increasing difficulties because of an overproduction of Ph.D.'s), but what about the many more students who are going out into the world? What kind of "culture" do they need? Much of what marked the cultivated man in the past may be of little service to them except for conversational purposes when not on the job. Even breadth of interest and outlook, which I like to stress because I specialize in this kind of thing, may help little—unless such interest is concentrated on contemporary problems.

5.   The same is true of a related objective, going back to Aristotle, that has become popular of late—education for a wise use of leisure. This might seem to be eminently relevant in a society that promises increasing abundance and leisure. It is most obviously needed, however, by technical or vocational students, who are least likely to get it or want it. It can also be interpreted as a tacit admission that the humanities have little other real use today. In any case, the aroused students are not thinking about the uses of leisure. They don't want merely the comfortable berth that satisfies most vocational students. They want challenging work, opportunities to be of use to their society, or to do something about the abuses of its wealth and power. Not being a career counselor, I can only hope they find such work. The immediate question remains: Can the humanities do more to prepare them for it?

6.   As a possible answer, I could suggest a kind of course that I have ventured, one on the impact of modern technology on society and culture. No subject is more important today; it is the locus of all problems of human values, a means of making value judgments more concrete and clearly relevant; and I have been pleased to find that students from many different departments

rise to it enthusiastically. But for the purposes of a humanities curriculum, it raises obvious practical difficulties. It does not fit clearly into any of the departments, and it calls for more knowledge of the sciences and technology than most teachers of the humanities have. However desirable it may be that they have such knowledge, it cannot reasonably be expected of them in our professionalized world, any more than I can be expected to master linguistics, mathematics or symbolic logic. Moreover, my growing concern with the abuses of our fabulous, fearful technology, which makes me suspect I am becoming obsessed by them, also makes me appreciate more fully the conventional values of detachment, even a *right* to irrelevance amid the clamor of our day. Just because students are so much concerned about contemporary issues, they may the more enjoy some respite from them and know better the deep, lasting satisfaction of intimate acquaintance with the great works of the past.

7.   In short, I am still up in the air. Dissatisfied with my own teaching, I am no more satisfied with this effort at soul-searching. My belief that almost any subject can be made relevant enough not only leaves unanswered the question of how best to do so but might suggest that any old program will do, might encourage the addition of still more miscellaneous courses to a humanities curriculum whose traditional aim has been described as a quest for order and meaning. Knowing of no ideal curriculum, I conclude by merely amplifying a few of the questions I have raised.

8.   What we need, President Theodore Hesburgh of Notre Dame has said, apropos of the student unrest, is "a rebirth of academic, civic, and political leadership—a sharing of those youthful ideals and dreams, whether they are impossible or not." Why a *re*birth? It follows that the universities have not been providing such leadership or nourishing such idealism. I suppose the humanities cannot be expected to provide leadership in either our technological society or the multiversities it has spawned; but what about idealism? Although we of course can't simply "teach" it, I wonder how much our practice has tended to nourish any but academic ideals, not vitally related to our students' quest of freedom, justice and significance in a society that once upon a time was dedicated to ideal propositions. At least, we must question the traditional assumption of a "transfer of learning"—the assumption that exposure to humanistic learning

necessarily induces humane, civil attitudes. Not only is it difficult to detect such attitudes in many a learned article, but we must remember that the many Doctors of Letters in Germany who supported Hitler included Dr. Goebbels.

9.   Accordingly, we might reconsider the common assumption that political interests are not the business of the humanities. Such interests were accepted as a matter of course in the old classical education, whose avowed aims included the education of man as a political animal, a responsible citizen, fit to be a leader in his society. Although in America political leaders now come chiefly out of business, law and machine politics, and are served by specialists trained in the social sciences, it is still habitually said that one aim of a liberal education is to turn out good citizens. What, then, does it take to be a good citizen today? To my mind, it need not mean dedication to political activity, or constant readiness to march in demonstrations, and it cannot mean a lot of desirable things, such as a full comprehension of economic problems. But surely it should at least mean a live concern with human values, an awareness that political issues come down to moral issues, and some ability to size up leaders, to distinguish honest thought from campaign rhetoric or blah-blah—matters that are very much our business.

10.   Above all, we must ask the most obvious but most difficult question: What are the basic needs of our students today, other than their immediate professional needs? We must try to answer it with something like our traditional authority, inasmuch as almost all students still share our assumption that they need teachers. But in view of all the fashionable talk about the virtues of "dialogue," we might try as well to listen more to what they think they need. At this point the troubles begin again. Students have many different ideas about their needs, some of them still conventional, the rest sometimes superficial, immature or unrealistic. We can't just let them concentrate on doing whatever they think is their thing if we want to restore order, purpose or even relevance to a fragmented curriculum. In particular we run into the militants addicted to lawlessness, violence and contempt for the indispensable academic ideal of free, reasonable and civil discourse. Some of the young radicals further confuse the issues because they are not really interested in improving the humanities curriculum, but rather in starting a revolution—an "impossible dream" that we cannot share with them even if we

feel the need of radical change, since they have no mass support, least of all from the workers.

11.   Yet most of the discontented students have reasonable ideas about their needs. They are not simply rebelling against either the past or our authority, but in effect are asking us to earn our authority by making the past more meaningful in the "real" world—a world that in some ways they know better than we do. They grew up in the affluent society, know more intimately the common hollowness of its living values that we generalize about fro·n an academic distance. Liable to the draft, sometimes exposed to the brutalities of the police, they may have a keener sense of social injustice, and of crisis too. Likewise they may suffer more from feelings of the randomness, aimlessness and meaninglessness of modern life that we take judicious note of in lectures, comfortably sustained by our conviction that we ourselves have high aims. They may really feel that life in America today is a tale told by an idiot, signifying nothing.

12.   In any case, they will inherit all the messes created by their elders in a technological society; so they force another question more pressing than ever before, the relevance of education to the future. I have read that the humanities in particular encourage dreaming about the future, but on the record of our century, I doubt it. In the popular journals, visions of the future come chiefly from technicians and scientists, and too often they are simply naïve visions of all kinds of new wonders. Serious efforts at forecasting, such as those by the Commission on the Year 2000, make it plain that we cannot educate students for a known future, but only for one that will be still fuller of problems because of the fantastic pace of technological development. What do teachers of the humanities have to contribute to such enterprises? Although not qualified as forecasters, they at least have something to say about the most important consideration, the question of what America *ought* to do with its fabulous technology. They can promote criticism of the actual uses of this technology, the trends toward something like Aldous Huxley's Brave New World. And on this score, too, they might give more heed to students' notions about their needs. "The best informed, the most intelligent, and the most idealistic" generation in our history constitutes our best hope for the future, which in any case they will have to bear the brunt of.

13.   So let us consider, lastly, the question Roger Shattuck asked of teachers of the humanities: "Are we the Establishment

or the Underground?" The answer, as I see it, is that we are both: an Establishment because of common scholarly and pedagogical tendencies, and a vested interest in hanging on to our professional privileges; and an Underground in an ambiguous sense, as a haven for molelike research but also as a source of subversive ideas. There is plenty of potential dynamite in our curriculum. While most apparent in courses on the modern world, it can be found, too, in many other courses, such as American literature and history, political philosophy, and ethics. Above all, it is implicit in the sonorous generalities about the aims of the humanities. Taken seriously, these aims can constitute an indictment of a society that does not welcome criticism of the American way of life.

14.   Thus, if the humanities indeed make people more "humane," our students might be more repelled by the barbarous inhumanity of our war in Vietnam. If the humanities further our understanding "of such enduring values as justice, freedom, virtue, beauty, and truth" (to cite one of the generalities), students might grow more indignant over all the injustice, hypocrisy and falsity accepted in the American way. If they "help men to live more fully and creatively and to expand their dignity, self-direction, and freedom," students might grow still more aware of all the obstacles to full, free personal development in our society, including its universities. Or if we simply awaken them to the values of beauty and to the importance of aesthetic judgments in any consideration of "the quality of American life"—a phrase no less meaningful because it has become a cliché—they might be appalled by the national insensitivity to ugliness, the commercial blight on the landscape of what used to be called God's own country.

15.   Then we must realize that we are headed for more trouble. Insofar as we satisfy our aroused students we will incur more of the growing public hostility to the universities; we cannot satisfy both them and all the Americans who resent them. Whatever our choice, we cannot hope to play it safe as either an Establishment or an Underground, since all the signs are that more troubles are sure to come. However good or bad the good old days, they are gone forever.

QUESTIONS

1. Muller builds to the point-at-issue, stated at the beginning of paragraph 2. How does the episode in paragraph 1 help to focus his con-

sideration on current attitudes toward education and current issues in American life?

2. How does Muller *restate* the point-at-issue through a consideration of *objections* to traditional ideas of education in paragraphs 4 and 5?

3. Does Muller reject these traditional ideas or enlarge and redefine them or show that they continue to have a limited relevance or application to current problems? What does his answer to the question— "Are we the Establishment or the Underground?"—show?

4. Muller's discussion illustrates a special kind of deductive essay: the search for common grounds or assumptions on which different groups or classes (here teachers and their students) can unite. The rhetorical strategy employed seeks primarily to defuse tensions and persuade the opponent that good will exists on both sides. How does Muller seek to persuade his readers that they do share common assumptions and that good will does exist? Is he directly concerned in the essay with the dangers of confrontation in current public debates?

WRITING ASSIGNMENTS

The second part of Muller's essay printed here may be analyzed according to the traditional pattern cited earlier (see page 255). Paragraphs 1–3 constitute an introduction to the discussion that follows, appealing to the interest of the reader and stating the point-at-issue and a thesis; paragraphs 4–5 constitute a narrative, reviewing traditional ideas of education. Analyze paragraphs 6–15 to distinguish the confirmation (the argument in support of the "relevance" of the humanities) from the refutation of the charges of irrelevance. Then analyze the rhetoric of the essay in light of the comment in question 4 above.

Discuss what you understand to be Muller's ideal of education, and compare it with Maritain's.

INDUCTIVE REASONING

Halldor Laxness
MANKILLING IS THE KING'S GAME

1.   When as a youngster I went to a Jesuit school (Osterley, London, 1923–24) I learned this: "Mankilling is the King's game."
2.   I forgot to ask who wrote it; it sounds Shakespearean. To me it had a homely strain. From my Old Norse textbook back in Iceland I had become familiar with battle poetry rooted in searobber experience and the warlike spirit of petty Scandinavian kings, the so-called scaldic poetry. This heroic literature from the turn of the first millennium, two hundred fifty years plus or minus, is not to be confused with the Edda poetry, which never describes a battle and is exclusively legendary and mythological and probably of a younger date.
3.   Although this scaldic poetry is high-class poetry in its own right, it has never been as popular as the Eddas. It is relatively voluminous; the Copenhagen-Christiania edition from the Icelandic vellum is more than twelve hundred double-columned pages in quarto. If you fastened the poems together end to end this poetry would be almost a mile long. Most of it is composed by Icelandic scalds (poets or bards) either itinerant or engaged as house poets of kings and pirates.
4.   This is a poetry of grim beauty composed by happy warriors in the most intricate of meters. It is considered by encyclopedists to contain some of the most beautiful verses inspired by fighting in any age and any nation. Modern battle descriptions, including death rolls (anemic impersonal body counts; Hill No. this or that) make pale reading to Icelanders compared to the scaldic accounts of the famous battles of yore in which a great hero is dying a formidable death in almost every verse and battle is praised as the acme of human existence, war as the consummate glory of man.
5.   This poetry is very particular about light and color in a

battle, and about the right hour of day to fight one. The hour
before daybreak is all right because it lends to the crimson of liquid blood a nice admixture of an azure sky and the silvery grey of
a fading moon. Most good battles take place at dawn when you
may behold the blue of your naked steel reddened by your
worthy enemy's blood in perfect juxtaposition with the golden
radiance of the rising sun. You delight in the frolics of blue colliding edges, accompanied by that seething din which this poetry holds to be characteristic of lethal wounds. Spears are singing and skulls crack with a thundering sound. The "flower of the
wound" is one of the beautiful names given to a sword.

6.   A battle is the "divine service," or mass, of swords; it
also is the fun of swords, a happy bout of carnage, a kill spree. In
all the poems the names of places where famous battles were
fought are given; so are the names of chieftains and prominent
heroes. A single poem might record a few dozen battles; one
mentions fifty. Battles and heroes may or may not have their origin in reality. But you are left in the dark why all these battles
were fought. The question seems never to have arisen. For all
you know they might have been fought for fun, maybe not for
fun of those who were actually slain, but for the many others
who were supposed to hear the story and learn the poem. It is
significant that a scaldic poem never misses one elaborate passage of big joy, that is the joy of the hungry raven and the eagle
and the swift-moving wolves amidst the fresh-reeking carrion of
the battlefield. At times you might think the only idea of all the
wars was to produce plenty of "warm prey" for empty-
stomached scavengers.

7.   In the Norse war poetry you will note that a battle story
never stands as a substitute, symbol or *exemplum* for anything
outside itself; it never tries to put over on you any moral or give
you tips about how to change the world for the better or save it.
Evidently these poets were living in a perfect world.

8.   To them war is the real thing; moreover, it is the thing of
which it is always real fun to hear the news, the game of games,
the Super Olympics of which other Olympics are a substitute or a
symbol.

9.   The situation has not changed much since scaldic times;
anything to do with war still makes good copy. As our ancestors,
we have the feeling that war is always with us, a *casus belli* is
always round the corner. There are always plenty of facile "be-

causes." You open a war with someone because you think he is weaker than you or because he is your equal or you fear that he is stronger than you—all equally natural and legitimate arguments in favor of declaring war: let us go ahead and kill them! If you are afraid of being killed yourself, you are a scoundrel and a coward.

10.   Matching the "Shakespearean" phrase about war as the game of kings, "war as a man's glory" is the unadulterated moral of our good old Icelandic classics. In modern times there are notions about wars being caused by people having different ideas, diverging *Weltanschauungen,* colliding philosophical, economic or theological theories, or not agreeing on the interpretation of Bible phrases and suchlike.

11.   This conception does not get much support from serious scrutiny of human history or natural history in general, of which wars are part and parcel. Ask Dr. Konrad Lorenz or, say, the American ethnologist Robert Ardrey. To me these notions have the flavor of modern cant, a sham moralism ascribing sublime motives to war-making in order to excuse war. In the pre-Christian and even the medieval North we never seem to have had such dear moralizing aunts who did not know that war is supreme fun for everybody except the man who is being shot at, and maybe his mother. There is a widely held opinion among scholars, supported by established fact, that our old war poetry was memorized by old women and recited by them in the process of putting children to sleep.

12.   In our Western cultures male adulthood means being ripe for a kill spree. This is called conscription age. Nice people say war is all right as long as only young men are sent off to die honorably on the battlefield, but think it is immoral to kill girls, old men and kids. Why?

13.   In this case, as so often in ethnology, we do not have the rationale. Some enlightening stories about this thing may be read in fairy tales, mythology and poetry, even in the Bible: Saul killed one thousand, David killed ten thousand. Prophets and scientists, students of this syndrome, have several explanations about why only young men should be shot, but not girls, etc., but each one of their conclusions is disputed by the next bunch of experts.

14.   Looking at the matter from the outside, for instance from the Moon, which might be as good a place for wisdom as

any (or Iceland, for that matter), war looks like the fulfillment of a pact between two partners of mutually executing each other's young men. In recent years there have been symptoms, even forebodings, of a conceivable reverse in the situation. If wonderful young men with the future in their lustering eyes should take over one of these days as they threaten to do, let us pray they are not going to march us old devils off to die honorably in some far-away hell of which you don't even know the name, still less the number of the hill on the top of which you are going to be killed.

15.   A famous scaldic poem ends on this bit of moral: "Why should a boy be nearer to death than other boys although he be placed in the front rank in a battle?" (Fate decides the issue.) "Many a man has led a long life of grumbling although he never was eaten by an eagle at a spree of swords. It is said to be hard work to raise the spirits of a coward: the heart of a coward is a useless thing to him." But this bit does not take us far either; these might just as well be the maxims of a desperado.

16.   There is nothing that seems to stop a dedicated man-killer. Hitler and Stalin had their sprees all right and it is for the next generation of suckers to understand and forgive. The question remains open from one generation to the next what was the reason for this and that war, or did war come first and reason as the runner-up or vice versa: the old dispute about hen and egg.

17.   Then there is the question who was the better man, Hitler or Stalin: who represented the just cause; whose was the more sympathetic side? It is almost safe to say now that they were both very good buffoons. Many would say that Hitler was the greater buffoon though. But Stalin was a very good buffoon too. If their greatness be measured in body count as that of other mankiller kings on record, they are both great. Doubtless, both are passable stuff for that rather inane fiction called World History. Even a moralist would be hard put to decide who was representing the good side and who the bad side. A computer would have a hard time solving it. It depends on your own bias. And there you are. The Soviet Socialism of one and National Socialism of the other, yes, but who stood for Revolution and the revolution of what; and who was on the side of Reaction—to what?

18.   When you travel in the East you sometimes see lepers sitting crosswise on the sidewalks sticking out at you their rottening limbs proudly, hatefully, defyingly, as if saying: "We are

holy. We alone belong to God." To leprosy there is only one side, the side of leprosy. There you have a circumscription of war as good as any: War is the leprosy of the human soul. As in leprosy, there is only one side in war, the side of war.

DISCUSSION: INDUCTIVE REASONING

Induction means deriving generalizations from particular instances. More strictly defined, an inductive argument is one in which the conclusion refers to something not included in the premises. Inductive arguments are neither valid nor invalid; they are characterized as being more or less probable depending on the strength of the premises in proportion to the conclusion. The stronger, or more inclusive, the premises are in relation to the conclusion, or the more restricted the conclusion is in relation to the premises, the more probable is the inductive argument.

In some circumstances, when the generalization is made about a limited class, the induction can be perfect: each member of my college class enjoyed reading *Hamlet*. But most inductions deal with classes containing a large, if not unlimited, number of members—a number too great to survey. It would be impossible to determine whether all college students have enjoyed reading *Hamlet;* it would be difficult to determine whether all living college students have enjoyed reading it. Thus the problem in induction is to choose particular instances that we can say are truly representative of the class about which the generalization is made. To say that all people have enjoyed *Hamlet* since its first performance and publication is preposterous.

But we often make similar statements that do not seem preposterous to us: small towns are safe places to live; the Irish have short tempers; New Yorkers are rude; children who watch television are fast learners. To establish these inductions we must show that the particular small towns or the New Yorkers we have encountered do represent their class—that there are no special circumstances that would account for the quality cited. The New Yorkers cited may have been observed on a crowded, stalled bus on a hot day.

An inductive argument is considered only probable because of the difficulty of guaranteeing a perfectly random or representative sample. A special kind of inductive argument, argument by analogy in which similarities between entities or situations are taken to imply other similarities, is probable for other reasons. If identical twins wear the same clothes, enjoy the same films and music, play the same sports, have the same hobbies, and are both training to be nurses, their respective friends probably will resemble one another. The greater the number of points of similarity, the stronger the probability of this conclusion. But these points of similarity—particulars in the process of generalization—must be relevant to the conclusion and lend strength to it. They do not, for example, establish that the twins have the same friends or always will have the same kind.

The points of dissimilarity must not weaken the conclusion. If, in seeking a job as a shoe salesman, I argue that my three years as an army drill sergeant fit me for the job, I will have to show that certain indispensable skills are common to both jobs and that certain differences in situation or dissimilarities are relatively insignificant (customers can walk out of the store: recruits cannot walk off the parade ground). Dissimilarities may increase the strength of an argument, too. If I argue that fifty former army drill sergeants are now successful shoe salesmen and that I should be hired for this reason, my argument will be strengthened if the sergeants *differ* in age, background, experience in selling, and any other relevant characteristics.

In general a limited conclusion may be drawn from a limited analogy if the points of similarity are clearly specified (or at least agreed on), if there is agreement on the relevance of the factors considered, and if inferences are drawn from these points only. If these limits are not observed, the analogy may be considered false. Many people will accept the notion that "anything goes" in advertising because, they are told, the world of buying and selling is a jungle in which only the "fit" survive. The shoe salesman who thinks of himself as a "tiger" may discover that the deceived buyer (unlike the tiger's dinner) is permitted to learn from his mistakes.

Cause-and-effect reasoning, on which analogy often depends, is also capable of reaching probable—sometimes highly probable—but not absolutely certain conclusions. We may think (on the basis of repeated efforts) that we know the conditions sufficient to produce a perfect soufflé—until we try to make one in a city at a high elevation, and the soufflé fails to rise. This limitation on cause-and-effect reasoning applies to the various kinds considered earlier (see pages 89–90).

Here, briefly described, are a few of the more common errors in reasoning:

Post hoc, ergo propter hoc ("after this, therefore because of this"): the mistaken assumption that one event is the cause of a second event merely because it precedes it. Temporal sequence is not sufficient for causation. People who are convinced that nuclear explosions have changed the weather merely because they occurred before these supposed changes (a sudden increase in tornado activity, for example) make this error. If air pollution does heat the earth, it must do so for an observable reason other than temporal sequence.

Begging the question: If I propose to argue that the "useless custom of tipping for service should be abolished because it no longer has a purpose," I have assumed as proven—by calling the custom "useless"—what I am seeking to prove.

Arguing in a circle: This is a form of question begging. "Nice girls don't chew gum because that is something no nice girl would do." "People who use the double negative and *ain't* speak bad English. Good English is logical and refined. By logical and refined I mean avoiding illiterate constructions like the double negative and *ain't.*" The issue that should be argued is the test of literacy; the meaning of *refined* and *logical* with respect to language should be examined as well.

Non sequitur ("it does not follow"): If I assert that I am a Democrat or Republican because my father is, I am assuming, without saying so, that fathers know best. Without this explicit premise the second part of the statement does not obviously or clearly follow from the first. The hidden premise may have been suppressed because, once stated, it shows the statement to be questionable or unsound.

Ignoratio elenchi ("irrelevant conclusion"): If the point-at-issue is whether private insurance companies or a federal agency should operate a national health-insurance plan, the argument that national health insurance is needed now is an irrelevant consideration.

Argumentum ad hominem: attacking the man rather than the issue— for example, arguing that a proposal for national health insurance is unsound because its proponents are in the pay of special interest groups. In other circumstances, the character of the proponents (as in an election campaign) may be the specific issue.

Argumentum ad populum: appealing to popular prejudices, patriotic feeling, and the like to gain support for or to attack an issue—Jefferson or Lincoln would have favored national health insurance or opposed it.

Either-or hypothesis: setting up two alternatives—for example, private insurance plans or national health insurance—and not allowing for other possible plans or solutions to the problem. Such reasoning may be highly emotional and even threatening: either we disarm completely or we face total nuclear annihilation.

Hasty generalization: forming judgments on the basis of insufficient evidence or special cases—for example, arguing that people over seventy should be denied licenses to drive because an extraordinary number of old people were involved in traffic accidents during a particular winter. The argument might be worth considering if the behavior of the old people involved in the accidents could be shown to be typical. Other relevant evidence should be considered: an extraordinary number of drivers between sixteen and eighteen might have been involved in such accidents; indeed, the severity of the winter might account for an extraordinary number of traffic accidents involving men and women of all ages. It may be added that judgments and generalizations of any sort should be tested by any exceptions that we can think of or that are brought to our attention; the statement "the exception proves the rule" means that the generalization must be able to explain *all* apparent exceptions to it.

QUESTIONS

1. At the conclusion of the essay Laxness states, "War is the leprosy of the human soul." The choice of words here suggests that he considers war a tragic phenomenon. Does he state or imply earlier in the essay that war is to be regarded in this light?
2. Is Laxness suggesting that wars happen because men enjoy killing? Or does he leave the reason for war unstated?
3. Is Laxness suggesting that we must accept the inevitability of war?
4. This informal discussion begins not with a theoretical statement about man and war, but with an account of what war *meant* to ancient Scandinavian kings. The discussion thus is inductive to the extent that it draws a conclusion from recorded experiences of war. Is this account the basis for his rejection of the ideas about men mentioned in paragraph 10? Or is Laxness making value judgments in paragraphs 11–17 unsupported by evidence?
5. What is illogical about the following statements?
   a. We should know the rules of grammar because we have inherited them from the past.
   b. More people than you would guess accept his proposal.
   c. Teddy Roosevelt would have supported a responsible fiscal policy that ended deficit spending.
   d. It has been more or less shown that intellectuals tend to be radicals or reactionaries.
   e. My dog obeys my commands; he understands everything I say.
   f. That there is a law against counterfeiting proves that counterfeiting is not only illegal but immoral.
   g. Juvenile delinquency was not a serious social problem before the Second World War; obviously the Second World War caused the juvenile delinquency of the postwar years.
   h. Mercy killing is wrong because one should not take human life.
   i. Eighteen-year-olds are too young to vote. The numerous teenagers arrested in recent disturbances testify to their immaturity.
   j. Alcoholism is caused by the inability to stay away from intoxicating beverages.
   k. He will make a good shop foreman because he ran his father's country store for a month.
   l. A fountain pen is a writing implement that uses ink.
   m. The reason the law should be passed is that it exists in every other state.

n. I do not like classical music because I like jazz.

o. We can never discover the intentions of a novelist because the motives of a writer can never be fully known; for this reason we cannot understand his novels.

p. The government should liberalize tax credit for plant expansion and improvement of tools. A healthy economy depends on continued business expansion.

q. Fatcat stockholders and oil lobbyists have always supported high tariffs and restrictive quotas. They are fighting a new bill that proposes lowering tariffs on West European oil imports.

WRITING ASSIGNMENTS

Indicate the extent to which Laxness would agree with Mencken or Mumford in their assumptions and conclusions about war.

Analyze the tone of the essay, indicating those points at which the tone is modified or altered markedly. Account for these changes through analysis of the build-up of ideas in the whole essay.

Brooks Atkinson
THE WARFARE IN THE FOREST
IS NOT WANTON

1. After thirty-five years the forest in Spruce Notch is tall and sturdy. It began during the Depression when work gangs planted thousands of tiny seedlings in abandoned pastures on Richmond Peak in the northern Catskills. Nothing spectacular has happened there since; the forest has been left undisturbed.

2. But now we have a large spread of Norway spruces a foot thick at the butt and 40 or 50 feet high. Their crowns look like thousands of dark crosses reaching into the sky.

3. The forest is a good place in which to prowl in search of wildlife. But also in search of ideas. For the inescapable fact is that the world of civilized America does not have such a clean record. Since the seedlings were planted the nation has fought three catastrophic wars, in one of which the killing of combatants

and the innocent continues. During the lifetime of the forest 350,000 Americans have died on foreign battlefields.

4.   Inside America civilized life is no finer. A President, a Senator, a man of God have been assassinated. Citizens are murdered in the streets. Riots, armed assaults, looting, burning, outbursts of hatred have increased to the point where they have become commonplace.

5.   Life in civilized America is out of control. Nothing is out of control in the forest. Everything complies with the instinct for survival—which is the law and order of the woods.

6.   Although the forest looks peaceful it supports incessant warfare, most of which is hidden and silent. For thirty-five years the strong have been subduing the weak. The blueberries that once flourished on the mountain have been destroyed. All the trees are individuals, as all human beings are individuals; and every tree poses a threat to every other tree. The competition is so fierce that you can hardly penetrate some of the thickets where the lower branches of neighboring trees are interlocked in a blind competition for survival.

7.   Nor is the wildlife benign. A red-tailed hawk lived there last summer—slowly circling in the sky and occasionally drawing attention to himself by screaming. He survived on mice, squirrels, chipmunks and small birds. A barred owl lives somewhere in the depth of the woods. He hoots in midmorning as well as at sunrise to register his authority. He also is a killer. Killing is a fundamental part of the process. The nuthatches kill insects in the bark. The woodpeckers dig insects out. The thrushes eat beetles and caterpillars.

8.   But in the forest, killing is not wanton or malicious. It is for survival. Among birds of equal size most of the warfare consists of sham battles in which they go through the motions of warfare until one withdraws. Usually neither bird gets hurt.

9.   Nor is the warfare between trees vindictive. Although the spruces predominate they do not practice segregation. On both sides of Lost Lane, which used to be a dirt road, maples, beeches, ashes, aspens and a few red oaks live, and green curtains of wild grapes cover the wild cherry trees. In the depths of the forest there are a few glades where the spruces stand aside and birches stretch and grow. The forest is a web of intangible tensions. But they are never out of control. Although they are wild they are not savage as they are in civilized life.

10.   For the tensions are absorbed in the process of growth, and the clusters of large cones on the Norway spruces are certificates to a good future. The forest gives an external impression of discipline and pleasure. Occasionally the pleasure is rapturously stated. Soon after sunrise one morning last summer when the period of bird song was nearly over, a solitary rose-breasted grosbeak sat on the top of a tall spruce and sang with great resonance and beauty. He flew a few rods to another tree and continued singing: then to another tree where he poured out his matin again, and so on for a half hour. There was no practical motive that I was aware of.

11.   After thirty-five uneventful years the spruces have created an environment in which a grosbeak is content, and this one said so gloriously. It was a better sound than the explosion of bombs, the scream of the wounded, the crash of broken glass, the crackle of burning buildings, the shriek of the police siren.

12.   The forest conducts its affairs with less rancor and malevolence than civilized America.

QUESTIONS

1. One sometimes hears the argument that violence is natural to man, since man is a part of a warring natural world. How does Atkinson implicitly reject this analogy? More specifically, what are the points of dissimilarity between the world of the forest and the world of man?
2. How might the world of the forest be used to argue that competition in the world of man need not be destructive of some of those competing—as the argument that only the "fit" survive in the world of business implies?
3. How does Atkinson increase the probability of his argument through the details he marshals in support of it?

WRITING ASSIGNMENT

Each of the following statements suggests an analogy. Write on one of them, discussing points of similarity and dissimilarity and using this discussion to argue a thesis.
a. The family is a small nation.
b. The nation is a large family.
c. College examinations are sporting events.

Edward Jay Epstein
NETWORK NEWS: THE MIRROR ANALOGY

1.   David Brinkley, in an N.B.C. News special entitled "From Here to the Seventies," reiterated a description of television news that is frequently offered by television newsmen:

> What television did in the sixties was to show the American people to the American people. . . . It did show the people places and things they had not seen before. Some they liked, and some they did not. It was not that television produced or created any of it.

In this view, television news does no more than mirror reality. Thus, Leonard Goldenson, the chairman of the board of A.B.C., testified before the National Commission on the Causes and Prevention of Violence that complaints of news distortion were brought about by the fact that "Americans are reluctant to accept the images reflected by the mirror we have held up to our society." Robert D. Kasmire, a vice-president of N.B.C., told the commission, "There is no doubt that television is, to a large degree, a mirror of our society. It is also a mirror of public attitudes and preferences." The president of N.B.C., Julian Goodman, told the commission, "In short, the medium is blamed for the message." Dr. Frank Stanton, vice-chairman and former president of C.B.S., testifying before a House committee, said, "What the media do is to hold a mirror up to society and try to report it as faithfully as possible." Elmer Lower, the president of A.B.C. News, has described television news as "the television mirror that reflects . . . across oceans and mountains," and added, "Let us open the doors of the parliaments everywhere to the electronic mirrors." The imagery has been picked up by critics of television, too. Jack Gould, formerly of the *Times,* wrote of television's coverage of racial riots, "Congress, one would hope, would not conduct an examination of a mirror because of the disquieting images that it beholds."

2.   The mirror analogy has considerable descriptive power, but it also leads to a number of serious misconceptions about the

medium. The notion of a "mirror of society" implies that everything of significance that happens will be reflected on television news. Network news organizations, however, far from being ubiquitous and all-seeing, are limited newsgathering operations, which depend on camera crews based in only a few major cities for most of their national stories. Some network executives have advanced the idea that network news is the product of coverage by hundreds of affiliated stations, but the affiliates' contribution to the network news programs actually is very small. Most network news stories are assigned in advance to network news crews and correspondents, and in many cases whether or not an event is covered depends on where it occurs and the availability of network crews.

3.   The mirror analogy also suggests immediacy: events are reflected instantaneously, as in a mirror. This notion of immediate reporting is reinforced by the way people in television news depict the process to the public. News executives sometimes say that, given the immediacy of television, the network organization has little opportunity to intervene in news decisions. Reuven Frank once declared, on a television program about television, "News coverage generally happens too fast for anything like that to take place." But does it? Though it is true that elements of certain events, such as space exploration and political conventions, are broadcast live, virtually all of the regular newscasts, except for the commentator's "lead-ins" and "tags" to the news stories, are prerecorded on videotape or else on film, which must be transported, processed, edited, and projected before it can be seen. Some film stories are delayed from one day to two weeks, because of certain organizational needs and policies. Reuven Frank more or less outlined these policies on "prepared," or delayed, news in a memorandum he wrote when he was executive producer of N.B.C.'s nightly news program. "Except for those rare days when other material becomes available," he wrote, "the gap will be filled by planned and prepared film stories, and we are assuming the availability of two each night." These "longer pieces," he continued, were to be "planned, executed over a longer period of time than spot news, usable and relevant any time within, say, two weeks rather than that day, receptive to the more sophisticated techniques of production and editing, but journalism withal." The reason for delaying filmed stories, a network vice-president has explained, is that "it gives the producer

more control over his program." First, it gives the producer control of the budget, since shipping the film by plane, though it might mean a delay of a day or two, is considerably less expensive than transmitting the film electronically by satellite or A.T. & T. lines. Second, and perhaps more important, it gives the producer control over the content of the individual stories, since it affords him an opportunity to screen the film and, if necessary, re-edit it. Eliminating the delay, the same vice-president suggested, could have the effect of reducing network news to a mere "chronicler of events" and forcing it "out of the business of making meaningful comment." Moreover, the delay provides a reserve of stories that can be used to give the program "variety" and "pacing."

4.   In filming delayed stories, newsmen are expected to eliminate any elements of the unexpected, so as not to destroy the illusion of immediacy. This becomes especially important when it is likely that the unusual developments will be reported in other media and thus date the story. A case in point is an N.B.C. News story about the inauguration of a high-speed train service between Montreal and Toronto. While the N.B.C. crew was filming the turbotrain during its inaugural run to Toronto, it collided with—and "sliced in half," as one newspaper put it—a meat trailer-truck, and then suffered a complete mechanical breakdown on the return trip. Persistent "performance flaws" and subsequent breakdowns eventually led to a temporary suspension of the service. None of these accidents and aberrations were included in the filmed story broadcast two weeks later on the N.B.C evening news. David Brinkley, keeping to the original story, written before the event, introduced the film by saying, "The only high-speed train now running in North America has just begun in Canada." Four and a half minutes of shots of the streamlined train followed, and the narration suggested that this foreshadowed the future of transportation, since Canada's "new turbo just might shake [American] lethargy" in developing such trains. (The announcement of the suspension of the service, almost two weeks later, was not carried on the program.) This practice of "preparing" stories also has affected the coverage of more serious subjects—for instance, many of the filmed stories about the Vietnam war were delayed for several days. It was possible to transmit war films to the United States in one day by using the satellite relay, but the cost was considerable at the

height of the war—more than three thousand dollars for a ten-minute transmission, as opposed to twenty or thirty dollars for shipping the same film by plane. And, with the exception of momentous battles, such as the Tet offensive, virtually all of the network film was sent by plane. To avoid the possibility of having the delayed footage dated by newspaper accounts, network correspondents were instructed to report on the routine and continuous aspects of the war rather than unexpected developments, according to a former N.B.C. Saigon bureau manager.

5.   The mirror analogy, in addition, obscures the component of "will"—of initiative in producing feature stories and of decisions made in advance to cover or not to cover certain types of events. A mirror makes no decisions; it simply reflects what takes place in front of it. But considerable initiative was displayed in the feature story with which David Brinkley closed N.B.C.'s evening news program on the same night he told the public that news was not "produced or created." Brinkley reported:

> A vastly popular hit song through most of the summer and fall is called "Ruby, Don't Take Your Love to Town." It's been high on the best-seller list, sung by Kenny Rogers and the First Edition. But it's more than a pop song; it's a social document, a comment on our times, and on the war. It is the lament of a Vietnam veteran, returned home gravely wounded, confined to his bed, lying there listening as his wife goes out at night leaving him, because the war has left him unable to move. Well, what the song says, and its wide popularity in this country, may tell more about the ordinary American's view of the Vietnam war than all the Gallup Polls combined, and here is the song, set to film.

6.   A three-minute film followed, supposedly illustrating the song. It showed the room of a crippled veteran, complete with pills, medicines, photographs, and "Ruby's" belongings. Interspersed with scenes of the room were scenes having to do with the Vietnam war—flamethrowers, helicopters, tanks, and casualties, and Presidents Eisenhower, Kennedy, Johnson, and Nixon—all combined in a montage. The illustration of the pop song was, of course, pure invention. The "veteran's room" was a set in Los Angeles, rented for the occasion. All the props were selected, the field producer explained to me later, "to create an

atmosphere of futility and absurdity." A few seconds of battle scenes, intercut into the story "to show what the veteran was thinking as his wife left him," were culled from ten years of stock film footage, according to the producer. And, of course, the song itself was a work of the imagination. In its total effect, such a feature story may, as Brinkley claimed, have accurately captured "the ordinary American's view of the Vietnam war," but this one obviously required a number of decisions on the part of the producer and commentator. First, a song had to be selected from literally hundreds of popular ballads that could be identified as "a comment on our times." Second, the song, once selected, could have been used to illuminate the news in a number of entirely different ways, and not only as an index of public opinion on Vietnam. Third, a decision had to be made on what type of film would be used in the montage to show the veteran's thoughts; scenes of enemy atrocities would have fit the lyrics just as easily as the scenes of American bombing attacks that were actually used. Finally, the selection of props to "create an atmosphere" also offered a great deal of leeway.

7.   When the question of their responsibility is raised, the networks freely acknowledge that their coverage of events can be controlled by advance decisions, or policy. For example, an N.B.C. staff lawyer informed the Federal Communications Commission that during the Democratic National Convention in Chicago in 1968 "special directives" were issued to N.B.C. news personnel that "no demonstrations were to be telecast live, no mobile units were to be dispatched until an event had actually occurred, and demonstrations or violent confrontations were not to be telecast until properly evaluated." Reuven Frank, explaining why few of the early demonstrations or "provocations" in Chicago were broadcast, wrote, in *Television Quarterly*, "Up until the serious violence, it was our conscious policy to avoid covering too much of the activities of demonstrators lest we fall into the trap of doing their advertising for them." C.B.S. had a similar policy during the Convention. Richard Salant, the president of C.B.S. News, told the National Commission on the Causes and Prevention of Violence, "We have a policy about live coverage of disorders and potential disorders. . . . The policy is that we will not provide such live coverage except in extraordinary circumstances."

8.   Policy can determine not only whether or not a subject is

shown on television but also, if it is shown, how it is depicted. At a time when American ground troops were still involved in the Vietnam war, Av Westin, executive producer of the A.B.C. Evening News, wrote to correspondents, "I have asked our Vietnam staff to alter the focus of their coverage from combat pieces to interpretive ones, pegged to the eventual pull-out of the American forces. This point should be stressed for all hands." In a Telex to A.B.C. News's Saigon bureau, Westin informed news personnel of the kind of specific stories he expected that altered focus to produce:

> I think the time has come to shift some of our focus from the battlefield, or more specifically American military involvement with the enemy, to themes and stories which can be grouped under the general heading: We Are On Our Way Out of Vietnam. . . . To be more specific, a series of story ideas suggest themselves.

9.   The list of suggested stories included such topics as black marketeering ("Find us that Oriental Sidney Greenstreet, the export-import entrepreneur," the Telex suggested), a replaced province chief ("Is the new man doing any better than his corrupt and inefficient predecessor?"), political opposition ("Could you single out a representative opposition leader . . . and do a story centered about him? Preferably we would like to know about the most active opposition leader"), medical care for civilians ("Does the granddaughter sleep under the old man's hospital bed, scrounge food for him, etc?"), and the treatment of ex-Vietcong. After Westin made these suggestions, a radical change from combat stories to "We Are On Our Way Out" stories ensued in A.B.C.'s coverage of the Vietnam war.

10.   A somewhat similar decision was reached at N.B.C. after President Johnson announced a halt in the bombing of North Vietnam. The executive producer of the nightly news program told the news staff that the "story" now was the negotiations, not the fighting, and although combat footage was sent to New York from Saigon virtually every day for two months following the decision, almost none of it was used. Yet, as it turned out, the end of United States participation in the war was actually more than four years off.

11.   Policy decisions of this kind can also affect the depiction of domestic events in important ways. During the riots that

followed the assassination of Martin Luther King, N.B.C. News apparently decided to minimize the extent of the violence—which was considerable—in New York City. An N.B.C. memorandum on riot coverage says that "Robert Northshield, executive producer of the Huntley-Brinkley Report, told us that he made an effort to use the minimum amount of riot footage following the assassination of King." The correspondent who narrated the story told me subsequently that he was aware of the "rioting" and the "tense situation" in the black community but that the producer had decided before he edited the story that it should emphasize the restoration of peace rather than continued violence (and the correspondent agreed). The producer later said that it was his responsibility to "evaluate all the information, including the social context" of a news event and then "decide how it should be presented." In evaluating such a story, he said, it must be decided whether the violence is "isolated incidents" or a "general trend." The point here is not the journalistic soundness or the social value of such policy decisions but simply that they exist, and that television news is something more than a mirror.

12.   Some television executives, while admitting the weakness of the mirror analogy, maintain that decisions in network news are shaped less by organizational needs and expectations than by the independent judgment of "professionals." They argue that television newsmen, as professionals, are in some ways analogous to doctors and scientists, who take their values from the standards and code of their profession rather than from any organization employing them. Doctors and scientists are given a good deal of latitude, if not complete autonomy, by their administrators, because the presumption is that they have a virtual monopoly of knowledge in their special fields. Television journalists, however, have no such claim to a monopoly of knowledge in their work. Consequently, interventions by the producer or by assistant producers in decisions on how to play the news are the rule rather than the exception. Television newsmen sometimes explain these interventions by saying that all the members of news organizations, whether they are executives, producers, or correspondents, share certain concepts of what constitutes news and will conform to these concepts rather than simply serving the interests of the organization that employs them. The trouble with applying this formulation of "profes-

sionalism" to television newsmen is that the various members of news organizations necessarily have different responsibilities and values. Executives are responsible for seeing to it that the product of the news division meets its budget and the expectations of the network; producers are responsible for seeing to it that their programs conform to budget, quality, and policy guidelines; correspondents and other newsmen are responsible only for their own work on individual stories. These different sets of responsibilities necessarily create tensions between the correspondents, with their basic news values, and the executives, whose values are predominantly organization values.

13.   Network news operations do provide opportunities for initiative and idiosyncratic judgments on the part of correspondents, editors, and producers. But over the long run such an organization must rely heavily on a set of internal rules and stable expectations. Although operating rules may not predetermine any particular stories, they do define general characteristics of network news, such as the length of film reports (whether three minutes or thirty minutes long, say), the amount of time and money available for individual film reports (which, in turn, may define the "depth" of news coverage), the areas that are covered most heavily (which might be said to delineate the geography of news), the models for dealing with controversy (whether the "dialectical" model, in which two sides are presented together with a synthesis, or the "thesis" model, which tries to prove that one side is correct), the ratio of "prepared" or delayed news to immediate news, and the general categories that are given preference by producers. And it is these general characteristics, proceeding from the structure and the needs of the organization—not the choice of one story rather than another—that give network news an over-all consistency.

QUESTIONS

1. In how many ways does television news resemble a mirror, according to television news executives? How are these ways stated?
2. What is Epstein's objection to the mirror analogy? Does he accept any point of similarity between the mirror and the news show?
3. How does Epstein employ the mirror analogy not only to tell us about the conception of television news but also to criticize that conception? Is his criticism implicit throughout the discussion?

4. Does he reject the analogy between television news commentators and doctors and scientists?

5. Does he attribute motives to the television news executives or merely analyze what they do?

WRITING ASSIGNMENTS

Take notes on the order of news stories in a single half-hour evening news program and consider whether a pattern emerges. For example, are the less serious stories saved for the middle or the end, or are they interspersed with the more serious ones? Does the news commentator express an attitude toward the story being reported?

Discuss whether, in your opinion, commentators should take stands on the news and the issues they report.

Jane Jacobs
SPECIOUS "CAUSES" OF CITY GROWTH

1.   The mouth of the Connecticut River, the largest river of New England, is so fine a site for a depot city that had a major city grown there, we may be sure it would have been accounted for in the geography textbooks by its location at the river mouth. But in reality, this site has brought forth only the little settlements of Lyme and Old Saybrook. At the time Washington was designated to be the capital of the young United States, Americans seem almost universally to have believed that because it was to be the capital, it was destined to become a great commercial and industrial city too, a London, Paris or Rome. But cities simply cannot be "explained" by their locations or other given resources. Their existence as cities and the sources of their growth lie within themselves, in the processes and growth systems that go on within them. Cities are not ordained; they are wholly existential. To say that a city grew "because" it was located at a good site for trading is, in view of what we can see in the real world, absurd. Few resources in this world are more common than good

SPECIOUS "CAUSES" OF CITY GROWTH: From *The Economy of Cities*, by Jane Jacobs. Copyright © 1969 by Jane Jacobs. Reprinted by permission of Random House, Inc. Selection title by editor.

sites for trading but most of the settlements that form at these good sites do not become cities. Among the best natural harbors in Britain, for example, are those belonging to the settlements of Ipswich, Yarmouth, King's Lynn, Sunderland, South Shields, Lossiemouth, Shoreham, Stornoway and Greenock.

2.   Many and many a name on the map of the United States tells of a fine trading location and high hopes: Centropolis, Central City, Center Junction, Centerton, Centralia, Center Port, Centerport, Centreport. . . . Mark Twain, in *Life on the Mississippi*, tells how the people of Hannibal expected their settlement to grow automatically into a city when the railroad came through, and then were baffled when most of the trains went right by, as the riverboats had done before them. Many cities engaging in enormous trade occupy notably inferior trading sites. Tokyo and Los Angeles are examples. A senator from Maine—a state with many fine harbors but no very consequential cities—once told the people of Los Angeles, "You have made a big mistake in the location of your city." He was annoyed because Los Angeles, in the 1920s, was lobbying for Federal funds to build itself a port. "You should have put it at some point where a harbor already exists," he scolded, "instead of calling on the U.S. government to give you something which nature has refused!"

3.   Even for a settlement to have become an important depot does not insure its subsequent growth as a city. Sag Harbor at the eastern end of Long Island (a mangificient depot site), and Portsmouth, North Carolina (where now not even the mailboat stops), commanding Pamlico Sound with its extensive waterways penetrating the interior, were sufficiently important soon after the American Revolution to be sites of customs stations. Plymouth, at the time of Queen Elizabeth I, was a more important port—although not a more important commercial and industrial city—than London. Many depots established by colonial powers in Latin America and Africa have not grown further as cities. But colonial depots are not always inert; Hong Kong has become one of the world's great industrial and commercial cities.

4.   We are all taught in school that New York grew so rapidly after 1825 "because" of the Erie Canal. Did it really? Then why not Jersey City? Jersey City had as good an access to the Erie Canal and the Atlantic Ocean as Manhattan did. It also had the added advantage of being on the mainland. Alexander Hamilton, observing the start of Manhattan's rapid development and

growth (beginning soon after the close of the American Revolution), and shrewdly noting that Jersey City had an even more advantageous location, buoyantly predicted that Jersey City would
become "the metropolis of the world." In the quarter century
before the canal opened, New York—which had been relatively
stagnant throughout the colonial period—was developing new
goods and services so rapidly that by 1824 it had already outdis-
tanced Philadelphia, formerly the chief manufacturing city of the
country, in the number of its factories and the varieties of its
manufactured goods, although not yet in their total value. Development and growth processes were going on in New York that
cannot be accounted for, retroactively, by the canal. To be sure,
New York's high rate of development work put the canal to
heavy use after it was built. But lesser cities found no such potent magic in the canals they built in emulation of New York.

5.   The great capitals of modern Europe did not become
great cities because they were the capitals. Cause and effect ran
the other way. Paris was at first no more the seat of the French
kings than were the sites of half a dozen other royal residences.
Indeed, until the twelfth century, Orléans, another center of
trade, was more imposing than Paris as a seat of king and court
and as a cultural and educational center too. Paris became the
genuine capital only after it had already become the largest (and
economically the most diversified) commercial and industrial city
of the kingdom. Berlin was not even the capital of its province—
Brandenburg was—until after it had become the largest, and economically the most diversified, commercial and industrial city in
Prussian territory. London was neither de facto nor formally the
capital of England—Winchester was the secular capital and Can-
terbury the ecclesiastical capital—until the eleventh century
when, London having already become the largest (and economically the most diversified) commercial and industrial center of the
kingdom, it became de facto capital and then, gradually, the formal capital. In the ancient city-states and empires, the cities were
capitals because they were large and strong enough to export
their city governments, first to the hinterlands beyond the home
territory and then frequently farther, and were handsomely paid
for their rule. Thus Rome's government first governed only
Rome, but ultimately government became Rome's chief export
work—in principle, much like other local goods and services becoming exports.

6.   A settlement to which the work of government is given

as its chief or initial export work may become a great city. Constantinople did. But it is more common for small settlements that are selected arbitrarily as capitals to develop no other appreciable economic reasons for being. Washington, Ottawa, The Hague, New Delhi and Canberra are examples; probably Brasilia will prove to be another. Many provincial or state capitals are thoroughly inert towns or stagnated little cities. A capital with government work as its initial or chief export work has much in common, economically, with a company town.

7.   In the case of some cities, no given advantage can be found to "explain" their existence in a specious way. All that Birmingham seems to have had, to begin with, was a good supply of drinking water—no novelty in Renaissance England. Alcaeus made the point in 600 B.C. when he wrote of the cities of Greece, "Not houses finely roofed nor the stones of walls well built nor canals nor dockyards make the city, but men able to use their opportunity."

QUESTIONS

1. Jacobs shows that it is mistaken to assume that a port city or capital city became great owing to its geographical location and potentiality for development—an obvious assumption when we observe the natural resources of cities like Hong Kong and San Francisco. But does she state or imply that a superior location is a necessary condition of development—that is, a condition "in whose absence the event cannot occur" (see page 89)—though not a sufficient condition, one "in whose presence the event must occur"?
2. Does she state or imply that strong economic activity is a necessary condition of city growth?
3. Given her statement in paragraph 1 that cities are "wholly existential," is she likely to be concerned with the sufficient condition of city growth? How would she distinguish between specious and real causes?
4. How does she indicate that her concern is with probabilities only? What degree of probability does she claim for her analysis of particular city growth?

WRITING ASSIGNMENT

Indicate what you take to be the necessary conditions of the following ideas or situations. Indicate also whether the sum of these is sufficient to explain the idea or situation.

a. ideal performance in examinations
b. enduring friendship
c. ideal recreation

Norman Cousins
WHO KILLED BENNY PARET?

1.   Sometime about 1935 or 1936 I had an interview with Mike Jacobs, the prize-fight promoter. I was a fledgling newspaper reporter at that time; my beat was education, but during the vacation season I found myself on varied assignments, all the way from ship news to sports reporting. In this way I found myself sitting opposite the most powerful figure in the boxing world.

2.   There was nothing spectacular in Mr. Jacobs's manner or appearance; but when he spoke about prize fights, he was no longer a bland little man but a colossus who sounded the way Napoleon must have sounded when he reviewed a battle. You knew you were listening to Number One. His saying something made it true.

3.   We discussed what to him was the only important element in successful promoting—how to please the crowd. So far as he was concerned, there was no mystery to it. You put killers in the ring and the people filled your arena. You hire boxing artists—men who are adroit at feinting, parrying, weaving, jabbing, and dancing, but who don't pack dynamite in their fists— and you wind up counting your empty seats. So you searched for the killers and sluggers and maulers—fellows who could hit with the force of a baseball bat.

4.   I asked Mr. Jacobs if he was speaking literally when he said people came out to see the killer.

5.   "They don't come out to see a tea party," he said evenly. "They come out to see the knockout. They come out to see a man hurt. If they think anything else, they're kidding themselves."

6.   Recently a young man by the name of Benny Paret was killed in the ring. The killing was seen by millions; it was on

television. In the twelfth round he was hit hard in the head several times, went down, was counted out, and never came out of the coma.

7.   The Paret fight produced a flurry of investigations. Governor Rockefeller was shocked by what happened and appointed a committee to assess the responsibility. The New York State Boxing Commission decided to find out what was wrong. The District Attorney's office expressed its concern. One question that was solemnly studied in all three probes concerned the action of the referee. Did he act in time to stop the fight? Another question had to do with the role of the examining doctors who certified the physical fitness of the fighters before the bout. Still another question involved Mr. Paret's manager; did he rush his boy into the fight without adequate time to recuperate from the previous one?

8.   In short, the investigators looked into every possible cause except the real one. Benny Paret was killed because the human fist delivers enough impact, when directed against the head, to produce a massive hemorrhage in the brain. The human brain is the most delicate and complex mechanism in all creation. It has a lacework of millions of highly fragile nerve connections. Nature attempts to protect this exquisitely intricate machinery by encasing it in a hard shell. Fortunately, the shell is thick enough to withstand a great deal of pounding. Nature, however, can protect man against everything except man himself. Not every blow to the head will kill a man—but there is always the risk of concussion and damage to the brain. A prize fighter may be able to survive even repeated brain concussions and go on fighting, but the damage to his brain may be permanent.

9.   In any event, it is futile to investigate the referee's role and seek to determine whether he should have intervened to stop the fight earlier. This is not where the primary responsibility lies. The primary responsibility lies with the people who pay to see a man hurt. The referee who stops a fight too soon from the crowd's viewpoint can expect to be booed. The crowd wants the knockout; it wants to see a man stretched out on the canvas. This is the supreme moment in boxing. It is nonsense to talk about prize fighting as a test of boxing skills. No crowd was ever brought to its feet screaming and cheering at the sight of two men beautifully dodging and weaving out of each other's jabs. The time the crowd comes alive is when a man is hit hard over

the heart or the head, when his mouthpiece flies out, when blood squirts out of his nose or eyes, when he wobbles under the attack and his pursuer continues to smash at him with poleax impact.
10.   Don't blame it on the referee. Don't even blame it on the fight managers. Put the blame where it belongs—on the prevailing mores that regard prize fighting as a perfectly proper enterprise and vehicle of entertainment. No one doubts that many people enjoy prize fighting and will miss it if it should be thrown out. And that is precisely the point.

QUESTIONS

1. Cousins distinguishes between the immediate or proximate and the mediate or remote causes of Paret's death. What does he show to be the immediate cause, and why can this cause be stated with virtual certainty?
2. Cousins is concerned chiefly with the mediate cause of Paret's death. How is this concern basic to his purpose in writing the essay? What are the chief indications of that purpose?
3. How would a different purpose have required Cousins to focus instead on the immediate cause?
4. How does Cousins establish the mediate cause? Is his evidence statistical—based on a sample of statements of boxing fans? Is it theoretical—based on a discussion of "human nature"? Is he concerned with the psychology of the crowd or the sociology of boxing? Is his analysis of the event intended to offer a complete explanation?

WRITING ASSIGNMENT

Analyze the appeals of a mass-sport like pro football or hockey to determine the extent of the appeal to violent emotions.

Diana Trilling
EASY RIDER AND ITS CRITICS

1.   Bernard Shaw's *Quintessence of Ibsenism* was first presented in 1892 as a lecture to the Fabian Society in London.

Shaw's justification for bringing the theater into discussion with
people chiefly engaged in government, politics, economics, and
the law was his belief that the drama has a significant influence
upon the individual life and the life of society. "Art," Shaw
wrote, but he was speaking primarily of the theater, "should
refine our sense of character and conduct, of justice and sympathy, greatly heightening our self-knowledge, self-control, precision of action, and considerateness, and making us intolerant of
baseness, cruelty, injustice, and intellectual superficiality and
vulgarity." A formulation like this was possible eighty years ago
as it of course no longer is; today, its language must seem to
verge on quaintness. We nevertheless recognize that Shaw is
voicing a conviction which in transmuted form is still very much
alive for us. Certainly it is some such appreciation of the high
moral function of the theater that warrants our appeals for government support of the stage and makes the basis of our contempt for the philistine and commercial theater.
2.   And his statement of the high purpose of the dramatic
art makes plain why Shaw found it appropriate to talk about
Ibsen to a group of people whose first commitment was to political and social improvement. For if it is the purpose of the theater
to instruct us in character and conscience, then clearly all men of
character and conscience, all persons devoted to the public good,
should be informed of the way in which the theater is discharg-
ing, or might discharge, this important duty.
3.   There can be no question that were Shaw addressing
himself to present-day affairs he would put the film under quite
as strict scrutiny as the stage, or even stricter, and not merely
because the movies reach so much wider an audience than stage
plays but also because he would be bound to respond to the
special force of the visual as compared to the predominantly verbal medium. Indeed, I have only a most formal hesitation in bor-
rowing his authority for the opinion that no art now exerts more
moral influence than the films, and that for the present generation, and particularly among our best-educated young people, more than personal character is being formed by our film-
makers: a culture, a society, even a polity.
4.   It is as an exemplification of this power of moral and
social instruction that I wish to discuss *Easy Rider*. But perhaps I
should first say what I mean by instruction in this context. I do
not mean overt pedagogy, and I do not even mean what the

famous director Jean-Luc Godard presumably had in mind when he was speaking at Harvard recently about his film *See You at Mao,* and said, "The movie is like a blackboard. A revolutionary movie can show how the arms struggle may be done." *Easy Rider* is not at all a film of this order. Although it is highly tendentious, it wears the mask of disengagement: its atmosphere, in fact, is that of a pastoral. Its method is that of implication and suggestion rather than that of assertion. Its notable achievement lies in its ability to communicate states of feeling: it is through its skill in the creation of emotion and mood that it does its work of persuasion.

5.   An air of purposive mystification, a sense of the existence of tensions which are perhaps made the more significant by never being named, is established from the start of the film. *Easy Rider* opens with its two main characters, Wyatt, played by Peter Fonda, and Billy, played by Dennis Hopper, having crossed the border from California into Mexico to do business with a Mexican peasant. Both the young men are long-haired, one of them bearded, and both wear clothes which, like their style of hair, at once authenticate their dedication to freedom. Both are riding simple motorbikes. It is of some importance, I think, that Fonda and Hopper are the leading actors in a film which they wrote together, with some unspecified assistance from Terry Southern, and which Hopper directed. *Easy Rider* represents an unusually direct statement on the part of its authors: there are no paid "stars" to intervene between them and us, no interposition of an alien personality or will.

6.   The business on which Wyatt and Billy have crossed to Mexico is the purchase of heroin. At least, we conclude it is heroin although it could of course be cocaine—it is a white powder and the two men sniff it. Apparently the purchase is satisfactory, because they then go on to their next rendezvous: a chauffeur-driven Rolls-Royce meets them at what seems to be the edge of an airfield, and a sallow and sleazy man of about forty— we notice that he is close-shaven and wears city clothes—gets out and takes their supply of drugs, in exchange for which he gives Wyatt and Billy a wad of money which they will later stash away in their bikes. Before this unalluring character drives off and out of the film, he takes his own revitalizing snort of the powder he has purchased. Although he is doing precisely what the two young men had done just a moment before, his use of the heroin

is made to seem ugly and furtive whereas theirs has been presented as an exercise in connoiseurship—apparently with dope as with sex it is the style of the agent which makes for the moral meaning of the act.

7.   As a first gain from the sale of the heroin, the simple motorbikes on which Wyatt and Billy were riding at the start of the picture are replaced by a pair of the biggest, flashiest, most expensive motorcycles ever to fill the male American heart with envy. It is on these splendid vehicles—Fonda-Wyatt's is decorated with a splash of American flag—that the two men now begin their beautiful journey from California to near New Orleans, where their trip will be suddenly and violently cut off. It is a handsome travelogue, this West to East tour of the Southwestern United States. And we are no doubt the more moved by the loveliness and variety of the country because it is offered to us as the stage on which two people already certified as heroes of dissidence are about to act out their fate. Too, this is an America whose purity has not been polluted. The landscape of *Easy Rider* would seem to have known no human desecration other than the building of the highways which Wyatt and Billy ride—they pass no cars, no buses, no billboards or roadside stands or motels. When there is any form of human encounter, which is rare, it is played for its symbolic meaning.

8.   Thus, the two young riders stop at a lone ranch for repairs on one of the motorcycles. The rancher is shoeing a horse, and in his barn the wheel on which the camera fixes its editorializing gaze is that of a wagon. But even the farm itself is something of an anomaly in Fonda and Hopper's vision of the American West: we have been shown no other such instances of human enterprise. And indeed, the rancher inhabits a boundless universe; the land is his as far as the eye can see—what the film appears to be asking us is why, in an America this big and empty, we crowd as we do in our cities. He receives the two strangers at his table and within his family in the kind of openness and trust which consorts with the freedom and openness of the life he lives. His wife serves him in sweet docility, surrounds him with the happy-faced children she breeds for him. In a brief colloquy over their meal—in the idyllic imagination of *Easy Rider* farmers eat their meals at picnic tables set outdoors—Wyatt inquires whether all this vast spread belongs to the farmer, and he receives his host's assurance that it does. It is a

good life to live, is Fonda-Wyatt's comment, and it is of course
our response as well.

9.   A counterpoint to this scene is provided very little later
in the film when Wyatt and Billy, once again on the road, pick up
a traveler—his style is not unlike their own—who takes them to
his rural commune. Until now, *Easy Rider* has engaged in considerable conscious evasion: it has not told us where its two main
characters come from or where they are going, what drug they
have trafficked in or what use they plan to make of the money
they earned by its sale, or, for that matter, what in their previous
personal or social experience has brought them to their present
condition. But now the film becomes not so much mystifying as
surrealist. The commune contains some thirty or more young
people and a few small children who all live together in what is
no doubt meant to represent an entire goodness and harmony,
each pursuing his concern. Playacting appears to be one of the
group occupations: we see bits of miming in the manner of the
guerrilla theater and even a rude outdoor stage. There is also a
prayer scene similar to the Thanksgiving devotions in *Alice's Restaurant*; I took it, perhaps wrongly, to be an appeal for rain to
water the crops—for it is a gentle point of this commune
sequence that these young people would wish to grow their food
but do not know how, their unnatural modern upbringings having cut them off from the vital springs of life: dazed but intent,
they stamp barefoot upon the unharrowed, even unplowed,
ground on which they have dropped the seed. Drugs are not
mentioned; for one viewer, they were nevertheless omnipresent
in the appearance and behavior of the members of the commune.
There is a moment when the camera circles the group, moving
slowly from one vacant-eyed face to the next: they are the faces of
madness, of a perhaps irremediable break with reality, or so they
looked to me, but I am afraid that what I saw was not necessarily
what the makers of the film intended. Before Wyatt and Billy
again take to the road, they have an innocent naked romp in a
nearby stream with two of the commune girls.

10.   The beautiful journey resumes. At the end of each day's
run Wyatt and Billy camp at the roadside. We do not discover
them buying or preparing their food, washing themselves or
their clothes, or even actually building the fires over which they
sit at night, quietly smoking their pot, quietly getting stoned.
The inessentials of life have been eliminated to reveal life's es-

sential joyous simplicity—obviously the two men supply each
other with the kind of companionship in which marijuana is said
to make its happiest effect: at any rate, they laugh together for no
apparent reason. And if there is any doubt in the viewer's mind
as to what it is that provides this nightly relaxation, it is nicely
dispelled when the two men offer a cigarette to a drunk they
have picked up who refuses it in terror—hasn't he, he asks,
enough trouble already with the booze? Wyatt can reassure him:
this anodyne has no devil in it as whiskey does.

11.   The new member of what now becomes a trio of riders
had joined them in the jail of his Southern town where he was
sleeping off a binge. Riding into the town, Wyatt and Billy had
playfully got entangled in a parade and been arrested. After a
night in jail, the third young man, an ACLU lawyer, arranges for
their release. Gentle, liberal, idealistic, he is the defeated son of
the big man of the town, whose power is to be withstood only by
drinking—the symbol of the son's remembrance of joy is a football helmet cherished since boyhood. Wearing his helmet, he
hops a ride with his new friends: he is bound for a brothel in
New Orleans. At a modest restaurant the trio attracts the attention of the sheriff and some cronies of his who mobilize a quick
brutal hatred of the hippie outsiders; that night, as the three men
sleep at the roadside, the sheriff and his people sneak up on
them—they manage to kill only the local lawyer. Just as the
sheriff stands for American xenophobia and violence, the lawyer
represents, we must suppose, the soft liberal underbelly of
American establishment. Well-meaning but misguided, he is
first to succumb to a repressive social authority with which he
had attempted to live and even deal, blind to its implacable enmity.

12.   The pop music which functions as a kind of Greek chorus to the mounting doom of *Easy Rider* carries much of the
emotion with which Wyatt and Billy receive the death of their
new friend. They now undertake to complete his journey for
him, and they go to the brothel in New Orleans, where they join
up with two young prostitutes—but not sexually, only in com-
radeship. The four go together to the Mardi Gras, then continue
the day in a cemetery where they get high on pot and liquor. By
the time Wyatt distributes the LSD he has in his pocket, the girls
are too intoxicated to care what they are taking. The inhabitable
world vanishes from the screen: as in one of Dr. Leary's psyche-

387

ıtions, the film now is given over to describing the tes induced in Wyatt, Billy, and the two girls by the watch them writhe among the gravestones, suffering the ently joyous agony of their self-willed release from the limitations of our reality-bound consciousness. When one of the girls takes off her clothes, no one has use for her naked body: with the help of drugs Wyatt and Billy have transcended more than our society, more even than their minds: their bodies. *Easy Rider* celebrates not only a pretechnological but also a presexual, or at least a pregenital, world.

13. But they have not transcended death. The acid trip over, the other journey across an America which once was, and presumably might still be, must once more begin. The two men get but a short distance beyond New Orleans, however, when they are overtaken on the deserted road and shot down, in coldest blood. Whether it is the same sheriff of their previous encounter or a counterpart who commits the murder, I am uncertain. But it cannot matter. What matters is that we have been shown vigilante America at work, out to destroy whatever loves freedom and is different from itself. The film ends in a bloody dawn, with Wyatt's and Billy's smashed bodies lying in the road. We understand that their murderers will go unapprehended.

14. This is, I think, a fair synopsis of *Easy Rider,* though not uncharged with my adverse feelings about the film. But it is necessary for me to make plain that although, while I was in the theater, I was aware of weighty reservations on the score of its moral content—they were provoked from the very start of the picture, by the sale of the heroin—I was also considerably seduced by it. It is not difficult for me to identify my seducer—ironically, it was America. I say ironically because, even apart from the fact that the point of the film is its attack upon America for failure to fulfill its promise to us, the America of *Easy Rider* is largely a pictorial illusion. The landscape it spreads out for us is mythic—I had almost said epic—in its lack of industrialization, of technology, even of population: I daresay there are still sections of the Southwest where one can travel big distances without seeing a billboard or a hamburger stand and where such farms as there are exist in isolation, but I doubt that one can travel from California almost all the way to New Orleans on main highways that are this totally bare of other humans and vehicles. And yet no other film that I can recall has so poignantly reminded me of the beautiful heritage we have in this country. It was the American land

which seduced me in *Easy Rider*—and this would seem to suggest
that I too, like the makers of the film, am caught in the dream of a
country unscathed by modernity.

15.   But the longing for unravished land is obviously not a
new emotion for Americans. It appears in our literature even
before the existence of what can properly be described as a technological society, in the work of Cooper, Thoreau, Whitman, and
of course Mark Twain—when Huck Finn lit out for the territory
he too, even in his time, was trying to escape the restrictions of
civilized modern life; and in our more recent literature it has
played a decisive part in the imagination of Hemingway. For all
of these men the unspoiled forests, prairies, mountains, and
rivers of America make not only the setting for their quest of
freedom but also the actual condition by means of which they
discover their wholeness and worth as human beings. *Easy Rider*
leans heavily upon the charm and authority of this literary tradition. But the unravished countryside which makes the landscape
of its dream of the free life has, in fact, no integral relation to the
film's representation of freedom—it is nothing *but* landscape. Its
beauty is used, or misused, to validate the only freedom of which
Fonda and Hopper have any genuine conception, that which is
imputed to the drug experience. It is a first and basic dishonesty
of *Easy Rider,* that is, that it proposes more than a kinship, actually an equivalence, or at least an interdependence, between the
fulfillment which may be sought by moving beyond the frontiers
of civilization and the gratifications which are sought in extending the frontiers of consciousness by the use of drugs.

16.   But a dishonesty of this dimension requires other de-
ceptions to sustain it. The search for a new frontier beyond
which life will have retained its old innocence is, to be sure, recurrent in American literature, but we know it is not our sole
American dream, nor ever has been: there has always gone along
with our nostalgia for the fair and innocent land another dream,
that of F. Scott Fitzgerald's Gatsby—the American dream of happiness through power and wealth. This was the conqueror's
dream, and today we direct our sternest disapproval to those
who submit themselves to it. Wyatt and Billy are so clearly presented to us as the very antithesis and negation of the predator's
America that when at the end of *Easy Rider* they are destroyed by
the forces of darkness, we are meant to feel that more than individual lives have been wiped out: virtue itself has been defeated.

17.   Gatsby, we recall, tried to buy his transcendence over

limiting social circumstance by bootlegging: Fitzgerald conceals from us no part of Gatsby's moral implication in this way of getting rich. Wyatt and Billy try to buy their transcendence over limiting social circumstance by trafficking in drugs, but they are made to bear no moral responsibility for *their* way of getting rich—unless we were perhaps to argue that their death at the end of the film is a punishment for wrong-doing, in which case *Easy Rider* would have to be accused of having vested its moral authority in cold-blooded murders. The transaction in heroin is indeed embedded in moral obfuscation. We see the expensive white powder being given to the man in the Rolls-Royce, we never see to whom he gives it other than himself: we are never shown, say, the schoolchildren in Los Angeles who will become our newest statistics in heroin addiction and death. Certainly nothing in the film suggests that the money with which Wyatt and Billy undertake to escape this tainted world of ours is itself tainted—the sale of the heroin behind them, Wyatt and Billy represent the film's appeal on behalf of America's lost purity.

18.   And just as the filthy business in which the heroes of *Easy Rider* make their wad is somehow disinfected by the presumed decency of their intentions in life, just so their recourse to heroin and LSD is somehow obscured by the innocent pleasure they have from marijuana. In general, the enlightened public now makes a distinction between marijuana and the other drugs which have come into wide use. In fact, the argument, not that all drugs should be legalized in order to take them out of the sphere of criminality, but that marijuana should be legal because it is harmless, rests on the belief that the use of marijuana is a quite separate activity from the use of "real" drugs. The evidence of *Easy Rider*, however, is against such a distinction. For Wyatt and Billy pot seems to be the basic daily fare which makes life supportable for them between their adventures with more potent medicines. We see the two men sniff heroin only once, at the start of the film; their practiced performance with it nevertheless makes us fairly sure that this is not an initial experience. Similarly, their composure after their bad acid trip suggests that this is not their first excursion in LSD. It is difficult to see how the young filmgoers who chiefly make up the audiences of *Easy Rider* can fail to conclude from the example of Wyatt and Billy that the sniffing of heroin and the taking of LSD are simply alternative to smoking pot, or, at least, that the taking of these more drastic

drugs can be slipped in and out of at will, between joints, dreary medical injunction to the contrary notwithstanding.

19.   Nor can we place more confidence in the social-economic import of *Easy Rider* than in its moral instruction. The film implies that spiritual freedom depends upon an escape from technology, and it gives us the happy rancher in example. In his barn a horse is being shod, and we are shown the wheel of a wagon—there is no farm machinery, there are no farmhands, and the rancher's sons are too young to help him. Apparently we are to believe that it requires only one man plus a horse and wagon to put a great tract of land under cultivation. We could perhaps accept a simplification of this sort as merely an aesthetic concentration, were it not for the extreme social and political disingenuousness of the film as a whole, including, as a prime instance, its assumption that one has only, like Wyatt or Billy, to be the target of evil forces within our corrupt society to be oneself wiped clean of all corruption. This curious assumption of course established itself in American liberal thought in the McCarthy period, when one had only to be the object of McCarthy's malignity to be warranted as forever blameless.

20.   As in a traditional Western, *Easy Rider* divides the world into the good and the bad guys. But what gives *Easy Rider* its chic is its definition of good guys and bad in the sentimental terms which are at present being sanctified by left-wing thought: good guys want to be left in peace to live out their lives of natural freedom, bad guys want to impose their way of being upon others. In the revolution of the seventies the contending social forces are, of course, no longer labor and capital. They are the passively virtuous and the actively wicked. In *Easy Rider* the proletariat, with its auspicious place in history and its decisive role in determining the fate of mankind, is transformed into a pair of mindless cop-outs (not to say criminals) for whom there is neither past nor future, imagination, curiosity, desire. Symbols of what we are to suppose is the idealism and aspiration of this revolutionary day, Wyatt and Billy lack the energy to create anything, comment on anything, feel anything except the mute pleasure of each other's company.

21.   But the muteness of *Easy Rider* not only accurately represents the anti-intellectualism of the contemporary revolution, it is also essential to the myth-making impulse of the film. By this I mean, simply, that were *Easy Rider* more verbal, more given to

the exposition of its ideas, it would be more accessible to the skeptical intellect. For example, the pivotal point of the film, or at any rate what many viewers have taken to be its moral climax, depends upon our interpretation of a sudden statement by Wyatt—the statement consists of three words. Wyatt and Billy are once again about to hit the road after their acid trip, and Billy murmurs something about their having made it. To this Wyatt replies, "We blew it." This utterance might perhaps indicate that Wyatt thinks their journey has failed in its spiritual intention, or it might even suggest—which is not too different—that Wyatt has come to recognize his moral responsibility for the drug transaction. But nothing in the film supports such interpretations, and I am myself inclined to believe that the ambiguousness of the statement is a deviousness, and that it was formulated to allow the viewer to draw from it whatever moral conclusion would make him most comfortable. By staying with so few words and refusing to explicate Wyatt's summary assessment of his and Billy's quest, the authors of *Easy Rider* concur in an adverse moral judgment of the central characters of the film, if that is how we prefer it. But at the same time they protect the central figures of the film against adverse judgment so that they can be retained as examples of innocent victimization. And it is as examples of innocent victimization that Wyatt and Billy of course enter the pantheon of contemporary heroic dissent.

22.   Here, then, are some of the lessons taught in this popular film, and an enticing brew of the fashionable, the false, and the pernicious they are. How are we to respond to such an offering? Surely not by legal censorship, which in America doesn't even raise questions of the control of moral and social ideas, only of what may be thought pornographic or obscene, and which in countries where it does treat such questions necessarily operates to suppress anything which challenges the assumptions of the official culture. But the rejection of censorship implies that we put our faith in moral and social intelligence either as exercised by the artists themselves or by those who receive their work.

23.   It is a piety of our art-loving culture that between moral and social intelligence and artistic intelligence there is an inevitable congruence. *Easy Rider* is demonstration that this is not so. As an instance of the art of film-making, it is much to be praised: it is well played and well directed, imaginative, adroit, visually pleasing, and undoubtedly fulfills the intentions of its authors.

But these positive qualities not only co-exist with grave deficiencies of moral and social intelligence; they give authority to the film's false view of the moral and social life. If *Easy Rider* were less attractive as a piece of film-making, we would not need to be concerned about its influence. It therefore rests with us who receive the film to exercise the moral and social discrimination which the authors show themselves unable to exercise. In particular, this responsibility devolves, I think, upon those whose work it is to tell us how well the theater is fulfilling its high mission of instructing us in character and conscience: the critics.

24. It is my sense that more than any other group within the critical profession the film critics have the public's attention—for instance, less than a week after the warm critical welcome that was given the film *Z*, it was impossible to get a seat in the theater at eleven o'clock in the morning. I was out of the country when *Easy Rider* opened; but from the reviews I have since retrieved I have the impression, certainly not of general unqualified approval—only Penelope Gilliat of the *New Yorker* would seem to have given it that—but of a response in which any critical unease engendered by the film was always eventually, and effectually, buried in the reviewer's need to concur in what was taken to be its invaluable social message: it was as if Fonda's and Hopper's observation of Middle America's hatred of anything different from itself and of the American capacity for mindless violence constituted an insight of such freshness and magnitude as to render paltry or carping any adverse judgment the critic might be moved to make on the film's validity as a document of American life. Except for Paul Schrader in the Los Angeles *Free Press*, who boldly ridiculed *Easy Rider* for its indulgence in stale left-wing ritualisms—and it is worth noting that with the publication of this review Mr. Schrader's connection with the paper was terminated—even critics who, like Richard Schickel in *Life*, spoke of the air of self-congratulation in which Wyatt and Billy have their being, or, like Joseph Morgenstern in *Newsweek*, mocked the sententiousness of the film, raised these objections in a context of appreciation.

25. And even Mr. Schrader went but half the course. Although he did indeed firmly denounce the nondimensional politics of *Easy Rider*, he mentioned not at all the means by which Wyatt and Billy financed their journey. The oversight, however, little distinguishes his reception of the film from that of the other

reviewers. To be sure, Vincent Canby of the *New York Times* wrote: "After all, Wyatt and Billy, the heroin pushers, may be the same kind of casual murderers as the southern red necks." Stanley Kauffmann of the *New Republic* wrote: "In cold factual terms, Fonda and Hopper are pretty low types—experienced drug-peddlers, criminal vagabonds. . . ." And Joseph Morgenstern, again in *Newsweek*, wrote: "Neither of these two riders . . . is conspicuously innocent. They've gotten the money for their odyssey by pushing dope." But these comments, which at least announce disapprobation of drug-trading, are curiously brief, unreverberant—they scarcely describe a rousing opposition to the film's own bland acceptance of drug-dealing—while the other reviews I have read fail to make even this small obeisance to the moral occasion. For Dan Wakefield, writing in this magazine, the drug in which Wyatt and Billy traffic is cocaine—he is positive in the identification. And extensively and eloquently outraged as Mr. Wakefield is by the bad treatment hippies receive at the hands of their fellow-citizens, he finds it possible to concentrate the whole of his judgment of Wyatt and Billy's drug transaction into a single sentence of narration: "The two hippies . . . make a highly profitable sale of some cocaine they score in Mexico to a sinister-looking connection in Los Angeles, and with the money stashed in the red-white-and-blue Stars-and-Stripes painted fuel tank of Wyatt's motorcycle, they take off east for New Orleans. . . ." In fact, later in his piece Mr. Wakefield makes explicit his faith in the two central characters of *Easy Rider* as figures of virtue: "Why," he inquires, "the needless death and destruction of these fairly innocuous, generally pleasant, and harmless young men?" But it is left to Miss Gilliat of the *New Yorker* to bring the moral and social-political concerns of the film into most reassuring accord with each other. Of Wyatt and Billy she writes: "By smuggling dope across the frontier and selling it to a gum-chewing young capitalist disguised as a fellow-hippie, they make enough money to live life their own way." With a stroke of the pen, that is, Miss Gilliat certifies the heroes of *Easy Rider* as proper symbols of the lost freedom and decency of American life: they are genuine hippies rather than capitalists disguised as hippies, and they do not chew gum.

26.   We are accustomed, of course, to the reluctance of our critics to submit to rigorous examination any political or social idea which offers itself as enlightened dissidence. It is indeed by

its accessibility to whatever is opposed to established values or whatever may be regarded as innovative thought that criticism defends itself against the imputation of academicism and brings itself into the full current of strenuous contemporary life. Are we to conclude, then, from Mr. Wakefield's or Miss Gilliat's unperturbed acceptance of drug-dealing and from the self-effacing comments upon this enterprise on the part even of the critics who oppose it that drug use has made good its claim to radical-ideological status?

27.   I do not think so. I think, rather, that what we are seeing in the less than satisfactory response of the critics to *Easy Rider* is their obedience to the modern injunction against moralizing about art. Quoting from Shaw, I said that the language in which Shaw described the function of the theater could only sound quaint to our contemporary ears. I meant that such outright moralizing puts us in mind of a culture in which there could be good firm working formulations of right and wrong and in which there were wise men, teachers, whose job it was to guide us through the few possible areas of doubt. Obviously, our sense of our own times is just the opposite of this. So extreme, in fact, is our awareness of the absence of such rules and of the lack of such persons, and of the consequent need for each one of us to improvise his own morality, that we have all but lost sight of the dynamics of culture. We forget that codes for the guidance of our moral lives are constantly being proposed for us by the culture.

28.   In the fashioning of these codes the artists—especially, nowadays, artists in the popular media—have a primary role. But the role of the critics is far from negligible. It is the critics who are supposed to warn us not to be seduced by art and who are delegated to ask questions about the reliability and feasibility and worth of the codes which are being offered us. Theirs is always, if you will, a moralizing function. It is today, when they seem to be most moved to forget this responsibility, that they are perhaps most to be recalled to it.

QUESTIONS

1. What are the necessary conditions of good critics as Diana Trilling defines them in paragraphs 1, 27, and 28? Is she proposing a complete definition of the good critic—that is, does she state the sufficient condition?

2. How does her analysis of *Easy Rider* and its implications help to establish the need for good criticism? How does she defend that need, particularly in her comment on censorship in paragraph 22?

3. What is her precise attitude toward the drug-culture and the use of marijuana? What is the point of her statement in paragraph 18 that attitudes toward drugs are shaped by their use?

4. Is her point that the movie proposes an inconsistent and confused view of Wyatt and Billy or that the view is a consistent, but pernicious one—approving values and conduct that deserve to be condemned? Does she state or imply that the critics quoted are themselves inconsistent and confused?

5. The author uses *Easy Rider* and its critics to make a general point about American culture. What is that point, and how is it introduced, stated, and restated in the course of the essay?

6. The analysis is inductive to the extent that it generalizes from particulars of American culture: a popular movie and critical responses to it. How does the author establish that these are typical enough of certain phenomena of American life to provide probable evidence for her conclusion?

7. The following statements are *effects* of causes identified in the whole essay:

> But what gives *Easy Rider* its chic is its definition of good guys and bad in the sentimental terms which are at present being sanctified by left-wing thought: good guys want to be left in peace to live out their lives of natural freedom, bad guys want to impose their way of being upon others. (paragraph 20)

> But the muteness of *Easy Rider* not only accurately represents the anti-intellectualism of the contemporary revolution, it is also essential to the myth-making impulse of the film. (paragraph 21)

How are the causes established in the whole essay? How are key words like *sentimental* and *anti-intellectualism* defined by example?

WRITING ASSIGNMENTS

Compare reviews of a controversial film like *Easy Rider* to determine the values on which the judgments are made.

Write a review of a recent film, analyzing the values that govern the depiction of character and action. Indicate clearly the basis of your admiration or dislike of the film.

PERSUASION

Archibald Cox
FOR FREEDOM OF SPEECH

1.   My name is Archibald Cox. I beseech you to let me say a
few words in the name of the President and Fellows of this university on behalf of freedom of speech. For if this meeting is
disrupted—hateful as some of us may find it—then liberty will
have died a little and those guilty of the disruption will have
done inestimable damage to the causes of humanity and peace.

2.   Men and women whose views aroused strong emotions—loved by some and hated by others—have always been
allowed to speak at Harvard—Fidel Castro, the late Malcolm X,
George Wallace, William Kunstler, and others. Last year, in this
very building, speeches were made for physical obstruction of
university activities. Harvard gave a platform to all these
speakers, even those calling for her destruction. No one in the
community tried to silence them, despite intense opposition.

3.   The reason is plain, and it applies here tonight. Freedom
of speech is indivisible. You cannot deny it to one man and save
it for others. Over and over again the test of our dedication to
liberty is our willingness to allow the expression of ideas we
hate. If those ideas are lies, the remedy is more speech and more
debate, so that men will learn the truth—speech like the teach-in
here a few weeks ago. To clap down or shout down a speaker on
the ground that his ideas are dangerous or that he is telling a lie
is to license all others to silence the speakers and suppress the
publications with which they disagree. Suppose that speech is
suppressed here tonight. Have you confidence that all who follow
the example will be as morally right as they suppose themselves
to be? History is filled with examples of the cruelty inflicted by
men who set out to suppress ideas in the conviction of their own
moral righteousness. This time those who have talked of disruption have a moral purpose, and may indeed be right in their

FOR FREEDOM OF SPEECH: Reprinted by permission of the author.

goals and objectives. But will others be equally right when they resort to the same tactics? The price of liberty to speak the truth as each of us sees it is permitting others the same freedom.

4.   Disruptive tactics seem to say, "We are scared to let others speak for fear that the listeners will believe them and not us." Disruptive tactics, even by noise alone, start us on the road to more and more disruption, and then to violence and more violence, because each group will come prepared the next time with greater numbers and ready to use a little more force until in the end, as in Hitler's Germany, all that counts is brute power.

5.   And so I cling to the hope that those of you who started to prevent the speakers from being heard will desist. You have the power to disrupt the meeting, I am quite sure. The disciplinary action that will surely follow is not likely to deter you. But I hope that your good sense and courage in doing what's right will cause you to change your minds—to refrain from doing grievous and perhaps irretrievable harm to liberty.

6.   Answer what is said here with more teach-ins and more truth, but let the speakers be heard.

DISCUSSION: PERSUASION

How we choose to present our ideas depends on our purpose in writing or speaking. The demands of exposition and persuasion are not the same. In exposition, we are guided by the need to make our ideas clear to the audience we have in mind. In persuasion, we are guided not only by the need for clarity but by the need to present our ideas in the most convincing way. There are occasions when the need to persuade an audience quickly makes a brief but clear statement of assumptions imperative. An address to a jury allows a more leisured or extended statement of assumptions as well as an account of pertinent experiences. Socrates, in his "apology" to the jury that sentenced him to death, dealt at length with the charges against him in light of the principles by which he had lived.

   Classical orators were concerned with defining the occasion of their speeches as a preliminary to organizing them. The rhetoric of the law courts (forensic rhetoric) usually required an extended narrative or review of the facts of the case and an extended confirmation and refutation, since the defendant would want to establish the facts of his presumed innocence and to attack the charges made. In eulogies and funeral orations (ceremonial rhetoric) the narrative, or account of a great man's deeds, might be the center of the oration and the refutation dispensed with altogether (it would be inappropriate in a funeral oration to defend the virtues of the dead man or to refute charges against him). Mark Antony's funeral oration, in Shakespeare's *Julius Caesar*, begins as a ceremonial oration and ends as an indictment of Brutus and his fellow conspirators; Antony is concerned ostensibly with praising the dead Caesar. Actually, he turns this praise into an accusation of Caesar's murderers. The repetition of "But Brutus is an honorable man" implies that the real issue is the character of Caesar's assailant—the very point-at-issue on which Brutus had defended himself in his previous statement to the assembled Romans. In the rhetoric of law-making bodies (deliberative rhetoric) narrative, confirmation, and refutation are employed for other purposes: the narrative may constitute a review of grievances that require a remedy in legislation; the confirmation, a defense of proposed legislation; refutation, an answer to objections raised against the legislation.

These points add up to one important point: no choices can be made in paragraph development, sentence structure, diction, and the general ordering of ideas until the writer has defined his purpose and decided what audience he wishes to reach. And the act of writing has this advantage: new choices can be made if the original ones prove to be ineffective. Revision means something more than catching spelling and grammatical errors: it involves thinking and rethinking an essay in light of what the writer discovers he wants to say—and in the most effective way.

QUESTIONS

1. The occasion of Archibald Cox's statement was a teach-in on Vietnam at Harvard University on March 26, 1971, sponsored by the Young Republicans and Young Americans for Freedom. In the course of this brief statement, Cox reviews events of the past pertinent to the attitudes and behavior of the people seeking to disrupt the meeting. What information does he provide about these past events?
2. Cox combines confirmation with refutation. What is his chief argument in favor of freedom of speech? How does he anticipate objections to his argument and deal with them in the course of his statement?
3. How does the occasion shape the argument—its length, its defense of basic assumptions (or the absence of a defense), the direct appeal to the audience?
4. How theoretical is this defense of freedom of speech? Is Cox concerned with the theoretical necessity of free speech or with the practical consequences of denying it, or perhaps with both?

WRITING ASSIGNMENT

Analyze the rhetoric of a classic statement of free speech or liberty to determine the audience to which it was directed, the use of the elements of the oration, and the appeals of the speaker (to the good will of the audience, for the respect of his opinion and character, to immediate as well as mediate consequences). Milton's *Areopagitica,* Thoreau's *Civil Disobedience,* Alexander Solzhenitsyn's letter of November 12, 1969 to the Soviet Writers' Union, or Plato's *Apology* would be suitable for analysis.

Vine Deloria, Jr.
THE GRANDFATHERS OF OUR COUNTRY

1.   The little children stare at a picture of George of the blue eyes and white hair and seek a connection between that apparition and the statement "Father of Our Country." Seek no further, little brown-eyed, brown-skinned ones. George *is* the father of your country.

2.   But George and Company did not spring full-blown from Hydra's head—although Indians sometimes wonder. Someone had to prepare the way for them. Someone had to help them get rid of the French. If George Washington is the father of this country because he defeated the English, then logic impels one to conclude that the men of the Iroquois are the grandfathers of this country.

3.   George, prior to 1776, was a foreigner in America. He was an Englishman by birth and allegiance. The English, from the time they planted themselves on this shore until 1759, were waging a desperate struggle with the French for control of the North American continent. It is an established fact (at least in Indian country) that the English could not have succeeded in ousting the French if they had not had the assistance of the Iroquois Confederacy.

4.   The league of the Iroquois was composed of six tribes: the Mohawks, the Oneidas, the Onondagas, the Cayugas, the Senecas and the Tuscarora. Actually, the Iroquois were fighting

the French without the aid of the British during the 1680's and the 1690's—and doing a pretty good job of it. Thus, it may be said that the Iroquois kept the French at bay until the English were strong enough to fight alongside the Confederacy.

5.   In 1754, what is called in American history books "The French and Indian War" (conveniently ignoring the fact that the Iroquois sided with the English—George and Company) broke out. In the first major action of that war, Washington and his Virginian militiamen were forced to surrender to the Indians and their French allies. He went back for help. A year later he and his militiamen returned, accompanied by the English general Edward Braddock and 2500 British regulars. Once again the Indians and their French allies taught the British some New World military tactics.

6.   It wasn't until the English obtained the good offices of the Delaware chief, Tedyuskung (whose tribes were under the protection of the Iroquois Confederacy), and a Moravian missionary, that the English were able to negotiate a peace treaty with the Indian allies of the French, and thereby secure peace on that front.

7.   The Iroquois played an even greater role in the French and English War when the theater of action was in their own country. Alvin M. Josephy, Jr., in his book, *The Indian Heritage of America*, writes: ". . . [the Iroquois] gave both direct and indirect aid to the British. Their geographical position lay athwart the principal routes connecting eastern Canada with the French positions in the Ohio Valley and Louisiana, and this fact hobbled French strategy, movements and command. At the same time, the Iroquois controlled the water routes leading from the St. Lawrence to the heart of the English colonies, and when the French tried to use them, some of the Iroquois joined the British forces in halting them. An important British victory was won at Fort William Henry, near Lake George, when a Mohawk sachem named Hendrick (of all things), responding to an appeal from his friend, Sir William Johnson, England's agent among the Iroquois, led several hundred warriors in helping the British turn back a French invasion force."

8.   The Iroquois, being of unforked tongue, maintained their loyalty to the English long after George and Company had turned their red coats in for blue. Four of the six tribes sided with the English in the Revolutionary War. (Two remained neu-

tral.) The colonists had to call in their old enemy, the French, and other Indian tribes to defeat the Iroquois and the English.

9.   However, the Iroquois got their oar in when it came to laying the philosophical foundations of the new country of America. Ben Franklin noted in 1754 that, "It would be a strange thing if six capital nations of ignorant savages [???] should be capable of forming a scheme for such a union, and be able to execute it in such a manner as that it has subsisted ages and appears indissoluble; and yet that a like union should be impracticable for ten or a dozen English colonies, to whom it is more necessary and must be more advantageous, and who cannot be supposed to want an equal understanding of their interests."

10.   Josephy writes again: "In time, the structure of the league had an indirect influence not only on the union of the colonies, but on the government of the US as it was constituted in 1789. In such forms as the methods by which Congressional, Senate and House conferees work out bills in compromise sessions, for instance, one may recognize similarities to the ways in which the Iroquois league functioned."

11.   Thus, little brown-eyed, brown-skinned ones, don't worry: One way or another Americans have an Iroquois Indian in their ancestry.

QUESTIONS

1. Is this essay directed solely to the little children, or above their heads to another kind of reader, or perhaps *only* to that reader?
2. Deloria might be talking to adult readers as if they were little children. Does the tone of the essay support this possibility? Is it mocking?
3. As in all persuasive writing, Deloria has chosen a strategy by which to reach his audience. How would you characterize it? How effective do you find it in relation to the purpose of the essay?
4. Unlike Cox, Deloria does not make a direct appeal to his reader—that is, he does not appeal directly for understanding or tolerance. Given his purpose and the strategy he adopts, why would a direct appeal be inappropriate?

WRITING ASSIGNMENT

Use a strategy like Deloria's to realize a similar purpose. Write to a specific audience, though you need not name or identify that audience in your essay.

Bayard Rustin
THE PREMISE OF THE STEREOTYPE

1.   The resort to stereotype is the first refuge and chief strategy of the bigot. Though this is a matter that ought to concern everyone, it should be of particular concern to Negroes. For their lives, as far back as we can remember, have been made nightmares by one kind of bigotry or another.

2.   This urge to stereotype groups and deal with them accordingly is an evil urge. Its birthplace is in that sinister back room of the mind where plots and schemes are hatched for the persecution and oppression of other human beings.

3.   It comes out of many things, but chiefly out of a failure or refusal to do the kind of tough, patient thinking that is required of difficult problems of relationship. It comes, as well, out of a desire to establish one's own sense of humanity and worth upon the ruins of someone else's. Nobody knows this, or should know it, better than Negroes and Jews.

4.   Bigots have, for almost every day we have spent out of Africa or out of Palestine, invented a whole catalogue of Negro and Jewish characteristics, invested these characteristics with inferior or undesirable values, and, on the basis of these fantasies, have engaged in the most brutal and systematic persecution.

5.   It seems to me, therefore, that it would be one of the great tragedies of Negro and Jewish experience in a hostile civilization if the time should come when either group begins using against the other the same weapon which the white majorities of the West used for centuries to crush and deny them their sense of humanity.

6.   All of which is to say that we ought all to be disturbed by a climate of mutual hostility that is building up among certain segments of the Negro and Jewish communities in the ghettos.

7.   Jewish leaders know this and are speaking to the Jewish conscience about it. So far as Negroes are concerned, let me say that one of the more unprofitable strategies we could ever adopt is now to join in history's oldest and most shameful witch hunt,

anti-Semitism. This attitude, though not typical of most Negro communities, is gaining considerable strength in the ghetto. It sees the Jew as the chief and only exploiter of the ghetto, blames the ghetto on him, and seems to suggest that anything Jews do is inherent in the idea of their Jewishness.

8.   I believe, though, that this attitude has two aspects—one entirely innocent of anti-Semitic animus. The first is that the Negro, in responding justifiably to bitterness and frustration, blames the plight of the ghetto on any visible reminder or representative of white America. . . .

9.   Since in Harlem Jews happen to be the most immediate reminders of white American oppression, they naturally inherit the wrath of black frustration. And I don't believe that the Negroes who attack out of this attitude are interested in the subtleties of ethnic, cultural, and religious distinction, or that they would find any such distinction emotionally or intellectually useful.

10.   It is the other aspect of the attitude that is more dangerous, that is consciously anti-Semitic, and that mischievously separates Jews from other white Americans and uses against them the old stereotypes of anti-Semitic slander and persecution. It is outrageous to blame Harlem on Jewishness. Harlem is no more the product of Jewishness than was American slavery and the subsequent century of Negro oppression in this country.

11.   In the ghetto everybody gets a piece of the action: those who are Jews and those who are Christians; those who are white and those who are black; those who run the numbers and those who operate the churches; those—black and white—who own tenements and those—black and white—who own businesses.

12.   Harlem is exploited by American greed. Even those who are now stirring up militant anti-Semitic resentments are exploiting the ghetto—the ghetto's mentality, its frustration, and its need to believe anything that brings it a degree of psychological comfort.

13.   The Jews are no more angels than we are—there are some real grounds for conflict and contention between us as minority groups—but it is nonsense to divert attention from who it is that really oppresses Negroes in the ghetto. Ultimately the real oppressor is white American immorality and indifference, and we will be letting off the real oppressor too easily if we now concentrate our fulminations against a few Jews in the ghetto.

14.   The premise of the stereotype is that everything that a man does defines his particular racial and ethnic morality. The people who say that about Jews are the same people who say it about Negroes. If we are now willing to believe what that doctrine says about Jews, then are we not obligated to endorse what it says about us?

15.   I agree with James Baldwin entirely. I agree with him that we should "do something unprecedented: to create ourselves without finding it necessary to create an enemy . . . the nature of the enemy is history; the nature of the enemy is power; and what every black man, boy, woman, girl is struggling to achieve is some sense of himself or herself which this history and this power have done everything conceivable to destroy."

16.   To engage in anti-Semitism is to engage in self-destruction—man's most tragic state.

QUESTIONS

1. Rustin deals with a specific point-at-issue—the attitude of the Harlem black to the Jewish businessman and landlord—but he addresses certain larger issues also. What are these issues?
2. These larger issues are a means—a strategy—of persuasion. Rustin might have appealed to the sense of fair play—another strategy—but he does not. Is the strategy he adopts more effective, in your opinion, and would an appeal to fair play have been ineffective?
3. Has Rustin sought to shame his reader? Is his tone accusing or conciliatory? Could the issue be treated in a satirical manner?

WRITING ASSIGNMENT

Rustin states: "The premise of the stereotype is that everything that a man does defines his particular racial and ethnic morality." Show how the "premise of the stereotype" can be used to deal unfairly with another minority, social or ethnic: women in public life, women in business, college students, the Irish, the Italians, the Poles.

INTERPRETATION
OF EVIDENCE

Walter Houghton
THE VICTORIAN WOMAN

1.   Of the three conceptions of woman current in the Victorian period, the best known is that of the submissive wife whose whole excuse for being was to love, honor, obey—and amuse—her lord and master, and to manage his household and bring up his children. In that role her character and her life were completely distinct from his:

> Man for the field and woman for the hearth;
> Man for the sword, and for the needle she;
> Man with the head, and woman with the heart;
> Man to command, and woman to obey;
> All else confusion.

Against that conservative view, spoken by the Prince's father in Tennyson's poem,[1] the Princess Ida represents the most advanced thought. She is the "new woman," in revolt against her legal and social bondage (and against the boredom of life in homes where servants and nurses now do all the household chores), and demanding equal rights with men: the same education, the same suffrage, the same opportunity for professional and political careers. Ida's passionate oration closes with a prophecy which Tennyson hardly imagined would come true:

> Everywhere
> Two heads in council, two beside the hearth,
> Two in the tangled business of the world,
> Two in the liberal offices of life,

THE VICTORIAN WOMAN: From *The Victorian Frame of Mind, 1830–1870* (Yale University Press, 1957). Reprinted by permission of the publisher. Selection title by editor.

[1] *The Princess* (1847), Pt. V, lines 437–41. See John Killham, *Tennyson and "The Princess": Reflections of an Age* (London, 1958) for an illuminating account of the whole question.

> Two plummets dropt for one to sound the abyss
> Of science and the secrets of the mind;
> Musician, painter, sculptor, critic, more.[2]

Between these two poles there was a middle position entirely characteristic of the time in its mediation between conservative and radical thinking. By all means let us remove the legal disabilities and give "more breadth of culture"; but higher education is unwise, the vote is dubious, and professional careers are dangerous. For after all woman is *not* man; she has her own nature and function in life, not inferior to his but entirely different; and the only test to apply to the "woman question" is simply, "Does this study or this activity help or injure her womanhood?" That is Tennyson's stand, expounded by the Prince and Ida at the close of the poem. Together they

> Will clear away the parasitic forms
> That seem to keep her up but drag her down—
> Will leave her space to burgeon out of all
> Within her—let her make herself her own
> To give or keep, to live and learn and be
> All that not harms distinctive womanhood.
> For woman is not undevelopt man,
> But diverse.

Let be with the proud watchword of "equal,"

> seeing either sex alone
> Is half itself, and in true marriage lies
> Nor equal, nor unequal. Each fulfils
> Defect in each.[3]

2.   What is meant by "distinctive womanhood" and what defect in man the woman should fulfill are only implied by Tennyson. The answers are spelled out in Ruskin's important lecture "Of Queens' Gardens" in 1865. There he begins by rejecting the notion both that woman is "the shadow and attendant image of her lord, owing him a thoughtless and servile obedience," and that she has a feminine mission and feminine rights that entitle her to a career in the world like man's. Her true function is to

---

[2] Ibid., Pt. II, lines 155–61. Amy Cruse, *The Victorians and Their Reading*, chap. 16, gives a good sketch of "The New Woman," with many illustrations from contemporary literature.

[3] *The Princess*, Pt. VII, lines 253–60, 283–6.

guide and uplift her more worldly and intellectual mate: "His intellect is for speculation and invention; his energy for adventure, for war, and for conquest, wherever war is just, wherever conquest necessary. But the woman's power is for rule, not for battle,—and her intellect is not for invention or creation, but for sweet ordering, arrangement, and decision." Although this lofty theory had been gaining ground through the 1850's, Ruskin is aware that he is challenging the ordinary assumptions of male superiority and command. He marshals his evidence. In Shakespeare and Scott, in Dante and Homer, women are "infallibly faithful and wise counsellors"; and by their virtue and wisdom men are redeemed from weakness or vice. Then, with their role defined, he proceeds at once to his description of the home, since it is women so conceived who make it a temple and a school of virtue. The more reason, therefore, to keep it a walled garden. While the man in his rough work must encounter all peril and trial, and often be subdued or misled, and always hardened, "he guards the woman from all this; within his house, as ruled by her, unless she herself has sought it, need enter no danger, no temptation, no cause of error or offence." [4]

3.   This woman worship, as it came to be called in the sixties, was as much indebted to the need for fresh sources of moral inspiration as it was to Romanticism in general. In a sketch by Lancelot Smith, the hero of Kingsley's *Yeast* (made, it should be noted, when his only bible was Bacon), Woman was portrayed walking across a desert, the half-risen sun at her back and a cross in her right hand, "emblem of self-sacrifice." In the foreground were scattered groups of men. As they caught sight of this "new and divine ideal of her sex,"

> the scholar dropt his book, the miser his gold, the savage his weapons; even in the visage of the half-slumbering sot some nobler recollection seemed wistfully to struggle into life. . . . The sage . . . watched with a thoughtful smile that preacher more mighty than himself. A youth, decked out in the most fantastic fopperies of the middle age, stood with clasped

---

[4] "Of Queens' Gardens," sec. 68 in *Works*, *18*, 111–22. With the last remark cf. George Eliot in "Amos Barton," *Scenes of Clerical Life, 1,* chap. 7, p. 85: "A loving woman's world lies within the four walls of her own home; and it is only through her husband that she is in any electric communication with the world beyond." In *Silas Marner* the bad habits of Godfrey and Dunstan Cass are attributed mainly to their growing up in a home without a mother (chap. 3, pp. 30–1), and Godfrey longs to marry Nancy Lammeter because she "would make home lovely" and help him conquer his weakness of will (chap. 3, pp. 39–41)—which is exactly what she does effect after the marriage (chap. 17, pp. 207–8).

hands and brimming eyes, as remorse and pleasure struggled in his face; and as he looked, the fierce sensual features seemed to melt, and his flesh came again to him like the flesh of a little child.

The drawing is entitled "Triumph of Woman." [5] Other writers emphasized a more specific mission in more mundane terms: to counteract the debasing influence on religion as well as morals of a masculine life preoccupied with worldly goods and wordly ambitions. Mrs. Sara Ellis, whose *Daughters of England, Wives of England,* and *Women of England* were standard manuals, brought that argument to bear directly on the "Behaviour to Husbands." Since the life of men, especially businessmen, is tending, she said, to lower and degrade the mind, to make its aims purely material, and to encourage a selfish concern for one's own interests, a wife should be supremely solicitous for the advancement of her husband's intellectual, moral, and spiritual nature. She should be "a companion who will raise the tone of his mind from . . . low anxieties, and vulgar cares" and will "lead his thoughts to expatiate or repose on those subjects which convey a feeling of identity with a higher state of existence beyond this present life." [6] Indeed, the moral elevation of man became so closely identified with this feminine duty that a moralist like Baldwin Brown in his sermons called *The Home Life* was ready to blame women for the deterioration of men under the hardening influence of business. They have themselves succumbed to mean desires for money and family position; or they have been seduced by the ridiculous phantom of woman's rights when their true power, the birthright they would sell for a mess of pottage, is the "power to love, to serve, to save." But many, thank God, are still faithful to their trust: "I know women whose hearts are an unfailing fountain of courage and inspiration to the hard-pressed man, who but for

---

[5] Chap. 10, pp. 148–50. Kingsley was one of the leading exponents (along with Ruskin, Tennyson, Patmore, and—more moderately—George Eliot) of this view of woman. See his statement in 1870 (*Letters and Memories, 2,* 283: unabridged ed., *2,* 330): He will continue, he says, "to set forth in every book I write (as I have done for twenty-five years) woman as the teacher, the natural and therefore divine guide, purifier, inspirer of the man."

This woman worship was not, of course, universal. It is less likely to be found among "earnest" Victorians than "enthusiastic" Victorians. It is conspicuously absent from Macaulay, Carlyle, Trollope, and both the Arnolds, and from Mill as a general principle (Mrs. Taylor is a very special case!). In "Emancipation—Black and White," (1865), *Science and Education,* pp. 68–9, Huxley protested against "the new woman-worship which so many sentimentalists and some philosophers are desirous of setting up."

[6] *The Wives of England. Their Relative Duties, Domestic Influence, and Social Obligations* (London, 1843), pp. 99–100.

them must be worsted in life's battle . . . and who send forth
husband or brother each morning with new strength for his conflict, armed, as the lady armed her knight of old, with a shield
which he may not stain in any unseemly conflicts, and a sword
which he dares only use against the enemies of truth, righteousness and God." Like the hero, the angel in the house serves, or
should serve, to preserve and quicken the moral idealism so
badly needed in an age of selfish greed and fierce competition.[7]
4.   This accounts (as Brown's remark would suggest) for
the wide hostility to her emancipation. Feminist claims to intellectual equality with man and to the same education and professional opportunity were attacked by liberals—let alone conservatives; partly, no doubt, to forestall competition, but much more
to prevent what they honestly believed would mean the irrepara-
ble loss of a vital moral influence. Lancelot Smith is the more
eager to assert his mental superiority over Argemone, the
heroine of *Yeast* (who imagined there was no intellectual difference between the sexes), and at the same time to look up to
her "as infallible and inspired" on all "questions of morality, of
taste, of feeling," because he longs to teach her "where her true
kingdom lay,—that the heart, and not the brain, enshrines the
priceless pearl of womanhood." [8] Even a perfectly commonplace
writer like Edwin Hood calls a chapter of *The Age and Its Architects* "Woman the Reformer" and begins by announcing: "The
hope of society is in woman! The hope of the age is in woman!
On her depends mainly the righting of wrongs, the correcting of
sins, and the success of all missions," and goes on, therefore, to
condemn the utterly mistaken tendency now growing up to encourage women to enter professional and political careers.[9] All
this is touched with melodramatic and sentimental exaggeration,
but many intelligent women—George Eliot, Mrs. Humphry
Ward, Mrs. Lynn Linton, Beatrice Potter Webb, for example—
viewed with uneasiness or apprehension any emancipation of
their sex which would weaken its moral influence by distracting
attention to the outside world or by coarsening the feminine nature itself.[10]

[7] Brown, pp. 23–5.

[8] Chap. 10, pp. 143–5.

[9] Pages 393, 400. The particular sins woman is to correct (pp. 393–4)—revolution, prostitu-
tion, and atheism—are major anxieties of the period.

[10] The main document is "An Appeal against Female Suffrage," *The Nineteenth Century*, 25
(1889), 781–8, signed by about 100 women, including Mrs. T. H. Huxley, Mrs. Leslie Stephen,

5. However conceived, the Victorian woman was not Venus, nor was meant to be. If it was only the feminists who rejected love—and often dressed accordingly—their more conservative sisters were not exactly objects of desire. Their sexual attraction was kept under wraps, many and voluminous. To employ it, except obliquely, was to run the risk of being considered "fast." Victorian ideas about sex were—very Victorian.

BIBLIOGRAPHY

Brown, James Baldwin. *The Home Life: in the Light of Its Divine Idea* (1866). New York, 1967.
Cross, J. W. *George Eliot's Life as Related in Her Letters and Journals.* 3 vols. New York, 1885. Vols. 22–24 of her *Works*.
Cruse, Amy. *The Victorians and Their Reading.* Boston and New York, 1935.
Eliot, George. *Works,* Illustrated Cabinet Edition, 24 vols. New York, n.d.
Ellis, Sara. *The Wives of England, Their Relative Duties, Domestic Influence, and Social Obligations.* London, 1843.
Hood, Edwin P. *The Age and Its Architects. Ten Chapters on the English People, in Relation to the Times* (1850). London, 1852.
Huxley, Thomas Henry. *Science and Education. Essays* (1893). New York, 1898.
Killham, John. *Tennyson and "The Princess": Reflections of an Age.* London, 1958.
Kingsley, Charles. *His Letters, and Memories of His Life,* ed. by his wife (1879), 2 vols. New York, 1900 ["abridged edition"]
———. *Works,* 28 vols. London, 1880–85.
———. *Yeast. A Problem* (1851), in *Works,* Vol. 2.
Ruskin, John. *Works,* 39 vols. ed. E. T. Cook and A. D. O. Wedderburn. London, 1902–12.
Tennyson, Alfred Lord. *The Poetic and Dramatic Works,* ed. W. J. Rolfe. Boston and New York, 1898.
Beatrice Webb. *My Apprenticeship* (1926). London and New York, 1950.

DISCUSSION: INTERPRETATION OF EVIDENCE

The kind of evidence a writer presents depends on whether his approach in the essay is chiefly inductive or deductive. If he assumes that his major ideas are "given" and will be accepted as such, he will select explanatory and illustrative material to remind the reader of what he already knows and to provide a background of ideas. If he intends to establish the probability of his ideas, he will present explanations and arguments to clarify and support them. Whether his reasoning is chiefly inductive or deductive, the writer's evidence will represent his own point of view. However, he will also select a variety of examples to show that other people in different circumstances could arrive at the same conclusion.

The effective presentation of evidence depends on its organization: if it is disordered, the most convincing evidence will persuade few peo-

Mrs. Matthew Arnold, Mrs. Walter Bagehot, and Mrs. Arnold Toynbee, as well as all of those cited in the text except George Eliot. For her, see Cross' *Life, 3,* 346, in his summary of her character and ideas. There is an account of this "Appeal" by Beatrice Webb, *My Apprenticeship,* pp. 302–4.

ple. The principle of order will depend on the nature of the subject and the thesis—some points and examples must be presented in chronological order—as well as on the audience.

In choosing evidence it is important to distinguish between primary and secondary sources—between first-hand accounts by participants or observers, and later reports and interpretations. Primary evidence must be sifted for differing versions of an event and for distinctive viewpoints that color the reporting. More than ten years after the assassination of President Kennedy, authorities disagree on what to consider evidence and on what alleged eyewitnesses heard or saw. Determining the reliability of certain eyewitness accounts is one of the writer's major difficulties; the motives of witnesses can obviously affect the report of events and their interpretation. A German general's account of the Normandy invasion, in a dispatch to Hitler, is certain to be different from the account of an American general witnessing the same events. Secondary sources may help the writer determine what is factual and accurate in interpreting primary sources, but these secondary sources also must be used with caution since later writers often shape evidence to fit a particular view of man or history. Primary and secondary sources supplement each other as means to arriving at the truth about a subject. As in all inductive investigations, the truth can be probable and never certain, but a careful sifting and comparison of evidence can increase that probability considerably.

QUESTIONS

1. What kinds of primary evidence does Houghton draw on?
2. What would have been lost if Houghton had drawn his evidence solely from poems and novels of the Victorian age? Could an accurate portrayal of the American woman be drawn from contemporary films or magazine fiction?
3. What information is reserved for the footnotes? Is it of less weight or significance than the information of the text?
4. Why does Houghton believe that the desire to preserve "the angel in the house" is a sufficient explanation for widespread hostility toward emancipation? Why is it important to cite the views of women like George Eliot and Beatrice Potter Webb?
5. How does the concluding comment on sexual attraction (developed in the succeeding section of Houghton's book) support the thesis of this section?

WRITING ASSIGNMENTS

Use magazine advertisements to draw a conclusion about qualities generally taken to be ideal in housewives. Be careful to note differences that suggest divergent views.

Compare the fathers, teenagers, or high-school or college students in various television advertisements or shows to determine whether they are stereotyped.

Use primary and secondary sources to determine how closely the fictional character in a work listed below corresponds to the historical person:

a. Stalin, in Solzhenitsyn's *The First Circle*
b. Hitler, in Richard Hughes's *The Fox in the Attic*
c. Franklin or Eleanor Roosevelt, in Dore Schary's *Sunrise at Campobello*
d. Winston S. Churchill, in Rolf Hochhuth's *Soldiers*

Elizabeth Janeway
FEMININE STEREOTYPES:
THE SHREW AND THE WITCH

A whistling maid and a crowing hen
Are neither fit for gods nor men.
OLD SAYING

It became the custom, when cows aborted, swine took fever, crops failed, floods rose and people perished, to look around for a witch. It has been a matter for much modern bewilderment that the guilt was almost always laid at the door of some lonely, poor and wretched old woman, hitherto submerged in humdrum insignificance. The explanation suggested by the witchcraft of West Africa is that the old woman voluntarily asserted and insisted upon her guilt. . . . In Africa . . . a witch spontaneously declares that it is she who killed every kinsman whose death she can recall, who ate all the dead infants, who blighted the dead cocoa-trees and engineered all the lorry-accidents.—M. J. Field, *Search for Security* [1]

1.   There must have been witches since time began. Shrewish wives and henpecked husbands appeared as soon as the in-

[1] M. J. Field, *Search for Security* (London: Faber and Faber, 1960), pages 36, 39.

stitution of marriage did, and fairy tales tell us that ogres and evil stepmothers were haunting figures before history was written. Dr. Field and other anthropologists report that witch cults still flourish today. All these creatures are aberrant types, deviates from expected roles. No wonder they persist, for there are always people who can't fit the patterns prescribed by any society, no matter how lenient.

2.   An interesting suggestion comes from Dr. Robert Jay Lifton, the social psychologist, whose knowledge of the Far East we have called on before. Lifton's study of China since the Second World War and the Communist take-over indicates "a sudden emergence in often exaggerated form of psychological tendencies previously suppressed by social custom." He believes that this "release phenomenon," producing a proliferation of deviant types, follows unexpected social upsets.[2] In other words, when aberrant roles are commonly seen, we may take it as a hint to look for profound social change. More and more individuals are finding it impossible to fit into the old sanctioned patterns.

3.   Among women in China, says Lifton, the suppressed psychological tendencies which are now being acted out take the form of "displays of assertion and unwavering ideological aggressiveness." They are encountered not only among the female cadres of the Communist party, but also "in Chinese women who were still operating primarily within their families at a time when the society surrounding those families was literally falling apart." This outbreak of shrewishness was at least as startling in China as here, for the docile and pleasing woman was the expected, desired norm in the Orient as well as in the West.

4.   It is Lifton's hypothesis that " 'the shrew,' whenever she appears in significant numbers, whether in China or Elizabethan England, is a specific product of social breakdown." We may add to these epochs that of our own stressful frontier society, which gave birth to such nineteenth-century militants as Carrie Nation, and we should not forget those vengeful *tricoteuses* of the French Terror, knitting away at the foot of the guillotine.

5.   But the very fact that the shrew appears so promptly when shifting social circumstances call for changes in role behavior should warn us that she does not represent a true alternative to the old feminine role. As we have noted time and again,

[2] Robert Jay Lifton, ed., *The Woman in America* (Boston: Houghton Mifflin Company, 1965), page 41.

roles develop out of relationships, and it takes time for this to happen. Role behavior expressive of the action appropriate to a new relationship isn't understandable until it's been acted out, accepted and absorbed both by the role-player and the other people who are part of the changed situation. As these new styles of living appear, they combine character traits in new patterns, they open channels of expression here and they free frozen talents there. They are truly creative: one couldn't imagine them until the altered situation has called them forth.

6.   Thus we can see how the growing strength of the new middle class at the end of the medieval era contributed to the blossoming of abilities which produced the Renaissance. Not only did the rising bourgeoisie channel economic vitality into the community, it also brought forth new men to challenge the old orthodoxies of thought and conduct, and a new mood of hope and daring very different from the endemic melancholia which Huizinga found so characteristic of the period he examined in *The Waning of the Middle Ages.*[3] No doubt the intimacy of personal connection which the new sort of home and the new small family produced had a part to play in this changed character structure.

7.   We don't see this sort of new creation in the shrew. She is, rather, a negative caricature of the compliant, pleasing woman. As we know, there are two sides to a role: what the role-player does, and what the role-others understand him to be doing. *It is easier for each side to do the opposite of what was done before than to create something new.* Consider it first from the woman's side: overnight responsibility is thrust on someone who has been trained to leave action to others. The role she knows best will no longer serve her. With no one to please or beguile into acting for her, she must act for herself. In turning away from her old role, she reverses it in a total looking-glass shift to its opposite, with the idea that if the old ways won't work, she'll get as far from them as she can.

8.   In the background is the long indoctrination she has had to assure her that women will lose their ability to please men if they act independently. Now she must act independently. What is more natural, then, than to assume that she will not please men and to let the whole exercise go by the board? Under the

---

[3] Johan Huizinga, *The Waning of the Middle Ages* (London: Edward Arnold, 1924).

strain of making decisions and learning to manage for herself in man's world, it is likely that she will happily dispense with any social efforts that don't seem necessary, and that old methods of charming and persuading will be the first to go into the discard, for they have clearly lost their usefulness.

9.   But this is a reversal and not a creation. The shrew's behavior expresses the same message as does that of the compliant woman: pleasing goes with dependence and subordination. Being no longer subordinate, being charged with responsibility and forced to act, the shrew accepts, and indeed may enjoy, the fact that she doesn't please her former superiors. As we all remember, Shakespeare's recipe for turning an Elizabethan shrew back into a pleasing woman was to reverse the reversal. He gave Kate a dominant male to take the possibility of action out of her hands, and she learned soon enough how to please him. If her role had really been a new creation, with its own vitality, it would not have been so easily overthrown.

10.   As for the other participants involved in the relationship, we can understand their contribution to the negative role of shrew easily enough if we consider that what is happening is what they have always feared. The myth of female power is supplanting the myth of female weakness. The negative role of shrew is one they *expected* to surface, if that happened. Again, there is nothing for them to learn *de novo*, there is simply the opposite of what had been expected in the past.

11.   The role of shrew, then, represents what happens when the ritual actor of the title part in the myth of female weakness takes the first step away from her traditional role, and it appears more forcefully when this step is sudden because external circumstances make it necessary. A forced change like this may call forth new energies as hitherto passive subordinates rise to the occasion, but it does not allow creativity to develop a new role. Negative roles are reactions, not actions. The unpleasing face of the shrew has had no time to learn a new expression, it merely reacts away from the mask of necessary pleasing it had worn for so long. If her behavior is rough and insensitive, it is because she has had to abandon the old virtues of the courtier which she knew so well: to please, to yield, to charm and to be docile. No one has taught her the prince's virtues of honor, generosity and panache. We know from Freud how close opposites lie to each other within our minds, and the shrew is the opposite

counterpart of the feminine woman produced by the traditional role.

12.   Of course throughout history there have been women who broke out of the feminine stereotype and got away with it, exceptional women who were allowed to be exceptional and were still admired. When we come to examine these cases, however, we find that one way or another these women who departed from the female role *took on another.* Their behavior was comprehensible because it could be identified with some other familiar pattern. The alternative role they made theirs did not have to be specifically feminine as long as it wasn't exclusively masculine. It was enough for the new role to be recognizable so that the player could be defined and some sort of prediction made about what behavior could be expected. Once this is possible, the player ceases to be a frightening deviate.

13.   Thus Joan of Arc could be assigned to the role of saint, moved by God through the voices she heard, and so not herself responsible for donning armor and leading the French to victory on the battlefield. Her English enemies and captors did not dispute her supernatural powers. They simply claimed that these were evil, not holy, and burned her as a witch, assigning her, for political purposes, to a negative role. It was ineffective in the long run, and Joan figures in social consciousness today as saint and martyr. Elizabeth the First of England and Catherine the Great of Russia were queens, women who ruled. The role of ruler could be accepted as taking precedence over the role of woman in the public mind particularly because each woman was a successful ruler. Each of them, too, had a keen public relations sense and consciously played to the nation. Their much publicized favorites also let the public know that if they were unfeminine, they were not unfemale: though the queens did not play woman's submissive role, they did not overtly deviate from it as did Christina of Sweden, who suffered for it. Even so, the feminine Mary of Scotland, unsuccessful as a ruler, has always been more popular than her rival.

14.   Victoria, of course, was the Queen as Wife. In her era, Florence Nightingale suppressed the open display of her considerable administrative talents and figured in the public mind as The Lady with the Lamp, nurse and healer. Madame Curie could also be seen in the role of nurturing woman whose work would contribute to healing the sick. What's more, she worked with her

husband and not alone. And so on. Even Eleanor Roosevelt, who
was hated and mocked at first view for the "unpleasing" qualities attributed to her, came in the end to be loved and esteemed
when she had aged into the recognizable role of slightly eccentric
great-aunt-to-the-world and lady of the manor with a concern for
the poor.

15.   These role-breakers make one thing clear: it is possible
to move away from one stereotype with impunity, if there is
shelter near another. If one doesn't find an alternative, the negative role which shadows the traditional role will take over. Sometimes, as with the shrew, the role-player may invite this to happen, but the other people involved will see that it does in any
case. For these role-others expect to be guided by the role-player.
If his behavior deviates from the expected pattern, they may find
it simply funny at first, but if it persists they move from bewilderment to hostility. They cannot predict what this role-breaker
is going to do, specifically what he is going to do *to them.* Bad
enough; but beyond it there is a further complication: they do
not know what is expected *of them.*

16.   For roles are reciprocal. The principal player not only
communicates the significance of what he is doing, he evokes the
proper responses from the others involved with him. When the
actions of the central figure become confusing, what are the other
participants to do? Their first reaction, we have noted, is to
laugh—if the deviation is minor and does not touch them too
clearly. In fact, one of the great sources of humor is inappropriate
action by a role-player. Probably humor has the specific social
value of enabling this sort of minor deviation to be accepted and
"laughed off," so that the tenor of life continues. To laugh at an
action implies that it happened "in play" and needn't be taken
seriously, and therefore that one isn't involved oneself. That
saves the other members of the relationship from anxiety, and it
also allows the entrance into the situation of "play" in another
sense—flexibility and permissible deviation from a norm. This,
in turn, permits a degree of change in the role which is accept-
able because it isn't demanding and therefore isn't frightening. When a situation is only "funny ha-ha," as the children
say, it isn't "funny peculiar." [4]

17.   But if the inappropriate action becomes too strange or

---

[4] For a discussion of the play factor in culture, see Johan Huizinga, *Homo Ludens* (Boston:
The Beacon Press, 1955).

cuts too close to the bone, it ceases to be funny. Then the role-others feel themselves threatened from without by the possibilities of what the deviant may make happen. Worse, they feel threatened from within by the fear of falling into inappropriate actions themselves, for they have lost any certainty as to what their own behavior should be. This intimate difficulty is even more menacing than the threat of unpredictable conduct on the part of the mold-breaker. *That* might just possibly be ignored, but what one does oneself, one is responsible for and may be shamed for. One cannot ignore one's own inability to act properly, one's ignorance of what to do next. The role-breaker threatens the order of the universe not just by his own challenge to it, but by disturbing the accustomed connection with this order which is felt by other people. Suppose one becomes identified with this challenge? Strangeness becomes more than external. It invades one's own inner citadel, and it is this which is unforgivable.

18.   Faced with this threat to their own inner stability, the confused participants in a relationship menaced by a role-breaker reach out for some explanation of his conduct, some guide to their own proper behavior in this unwarranted situation. What is he doing, and how are they to treat him? Being frightened, they want to separate themselves from the troublemaker and hold him at a distance. The means they find at hand is to call up the negative, shadow role, the opposite of the expected one. Thus, the pleasing woman, the public ideal of wife and lover, is shadowed by the shrew. Such a woman is seen not as trying to do something new, but as failing to do something old: so the feminists are told over and over that they are losing their ability to please.

19.   The dominant male is also shadowed by a negative role. In his case it is not a reversal of the traditional pattern, but an exaggeration of it. What is feared in every negative role is willful, uninhibited, antisocial power, an ego on the loose and uncontained by social obligations to others. In the case of women, this means a reversal of behavior from docility to dominance. For men, it means the increase of the dominance they wield already until their power grows so great that they are answerable to no one. The shadow role of the dominant male is the ogre.

20.   We have witnessed a near-perfect illustration of this shift from the traditional to the negative role in our own time. During his second term in office the public personality of President Lyn-

don Johnson underwent a remarkable transformation. Johnson had always been seen as a powerful and dominating character, but now his behavior became so obtrusive that it began to over-shadow, in the eyes of the public, all that he had actually ac-complished. His energy and his ambition had helped him to achieve a great deal, but now the "can-do" man began to do too much. He was breaking out of the relationship which must bind the President to the public, and he was ceasing to make what he was doing explicable. This came through as willfulness and in-sensitivity. The public began to feel that they could not safely predict his behavior. His actions seemed extreme. But not only did he appear unable to retreat from them, he did not even seem to recognize that they could be assessed as strange or unjustified.

21.   Uneasily his constituents felt that he was leaving them behind, leaving them out of his calculations and moving past the proper activity of the dominant male into its negative role. Of course there were objective political reasons for the switch, but they do not explain the speed with which it took place. From being "Big Daddy," a figure of authority who could be under-stood though not loved, Johnson passed into being the shadow behind Big Daddy, which (as the fairy stories make clear) is the ogre who eats the young. No doubt Johnson himself changed very little, at least until he began to sense the change in the way people felt toward him. But public opinion changed quickly and profoundly because the expected role of President was violated and the ruler could no longer evoke the necessary reciprocity from those who were ruled. In their eyes all vestige of a father figure who respected their rights and their being had vanished. The result was an extraordinarily fast reversal from positive to negative in Johnson's image. This is evidence of the close tie be-tween the negative image and the threat of unlimited power. Once Johnson announced that he would not run again for the Presidency, his popularity began to return; and when he was fi-nally out of office, his aura of mythic menace disappeared en-tirely. Even some who had attacked him most bitterly grew rather nostalgic over the outsize gesture and rhetoric that had worried them before. Which should remind us that political fac-tors are impossible to gauge except at the moment when the emotions they awake are actually in being. This is why the "science" of poll-taking founders so often on unexpected reefs.

22.   The most familiar negative role of all is the witch. If the

shrew is the opposite and shadow of the ideal pleasing woman, the witch is the shadow and opposite of the loving mother. Here too it is the power that is feared, but in this case it is magic power. It is easy to see why if we think again of the early mother-child relationship from the point of view of the child. The mother's power to give or to withhold comfort seems magical to the child, because he experiences it long before he can understand the whys and wherefores of the gift or the denial. It antedates language and logic. The child learns to trust and to love the huge creature who comes and goes, gives and denies, and changes the world around him before he and she have any words with which to communicate. Things happen magically, in mysterious ways. The witch retains the magical power of the woman who can effect these mysterious changes, but she has forfeited the trust of her partner-child. Joan of Arc thus was accused of witchcraft by the English because they couldn't deny her power, for she had beaten them in the field, but they couldn't permit themselves to think that such a defeat by a woman was normal. It had to be magical.

23. The witch, in short, is the bad mother—or, rather, the mother who seems to the child to be bad, for every child must be frustrated and left wailing by his mother at some point, since his desires begin by being total and what he really wants is omnipotence. Because the mother-child duality begins before any sort of behavior can be expected or any explanations offered, every thwarted child has had a glimpse of the witch behind the beloved face of his mother: this figure is really universal. She turns up everywhere, in any number of forms. The witch who caught Hansel and Gretel is (in psychological terms) the mother who might punish them for running away. The West African witch cited by M. J. Field in the quotation at the head of this chapter, spoke of "eating all the dead infants." In Chicago only the other day (so to speak) Bruno Bettelheim found that one of the schizophrenic children he was treating "was convinced that her mother wanted to bake her in the oven and eat her," just as Hansel's witch was planning to bake him.[5] A nursing child, we might remember, "eats" its mother. Anger and fear of the mother, dating back to those early days, might well bring forth the idea that the guilty child may expect a reversal of the process: it will be

[5] Bruno Bettelheim, *The Empty Fortress* (New York: The Free Press, 1967), page 71.

eaten by the witch-mother. Among the Pueblo Indians, a cure for any disease which the patient believes to be caused by witchcraft is for the sick man or woman to be adopted into another clan. This effectively provides him with *a new mother* and breaks the link with the old one, now turned into a witch.

24.   These negative roles are all associated with the abuse of power and, as Lifton suggests, with social change, for we often find that social change permits and increases this abuse: when traditional hierarchies break down, power is no longer bound by customary limits. The breakdown calls for new approaches—that is, for new roles—and at the same time it makes it harder for people to understand what the central role-player is trying to do: custom no longer helps to explain his actions. Lifton noted the appearance of the shrew in modern China and in Elizabethan England. The latter period was one in which we also find another deviant type, the witch, on the rise. Hugh Trevor-Roper, the English historian, has recently documented a recrudescence of the witch craze in the 1560s, at a time when religious wars were turning Europe upside down.[6] The witch hunts which became so frequent then lasted well into the seventeenth century and, as we all remember, reached as far as Salem, Massachusetts.

25.   In India today social change continues to produce witches. There is a section of Mysore where irrigation has recently been introduced. With it has come a sudden prevalence of witches. The increase in the quantity and the variety of agricultural products has brought this backward region into a money economy and women have overnight become moneylenders. In the past, such few advances of credit as were made came from rich landholders to their clients, were long-term, and were hedged about with traditional safeguards which prevented the ruin of the borrowers. The new women moneylenders, however, are not inhibited by such considerations, and they are often hard and demanding. Their driven clients tend to react by accusing them of witchcraft.

26.   For these women are violating the role expected of them. The anthropologist who reports the case, Scarlett Epstein, remarks that they are not only being condemned for their greed, but that "such a condemnation is a reaffirmation of the traditional social structure in which women did not enter the field of

---

[6] Hugh Trevor-Roper, "The Witch Craze," *Encounter* (London, May and June 1967).

money lending. . . . The ideal peasant woman . . . was a woman who worked hard on the lands of her husband and in the house, who bore many children, particularly many sons, and who was obedient to her husband . . . and generous to his kin." Summing up, Dr. Epstein adds, "A sociological function of witch beliefs widely recognized in anthropological literature is their tendency to support the system of values and thus to sustain the social structure." [7] In other words, negative roles work to support the order of the universe just as positive roles do. The latter are promises, the former threats.

27.   Dr. Field's work in West Africa reveals another aspect of the witch role: the acceptance by the woman of the role. Social change has been endemic for a generation in this part of the world. Dr. Field is both an anthropologist and a practicing psychiatrist, who first went to Ghana in the 1930s and returned in 1955 to practice there. She is thus familiar both with the colonial period and with the effect of independence on the population. Aside from these political changes, both of which broke old tribal patterns, economic change has had repercussions.

28.   In her practice, Dr. Field finds a regular tendency among women who are suffering from depression—that is, from an overwhelming sense of failure and weakness in their real lives—to accuse themselves of witchcraft, often including the murder of their children. They may fear this identification and struggle against it, and yet accept it because it seems to offer the only possible explanation for the course of their lives. Any identification, it seems, is better than the baffling confusion of not knowing where one is or what is to happen next. In addition, of course, the witch role permits the woman to imagine that she can exercise some sort of power, even if it is evil power; and no doubt it recalls the time when, as the mother of young children, she really did enjoy power. Thus, in her need for some understanding of, and control over, the world, she accepts and even courts (while still fearing) the dark role that shadows the mother role which once was hers.

29.   The ease with which these negative roles appear suggests that roles have a cohesive internal strength. A questioned role doesn't simply disappear, it flips over into its opposite, with the character traits reversed but holding together in

[7] Scarlett Epstein, "A Sociological Analysis of Witch Beliefs," in *Magic, Witchcraft and Curing*, John Middleton, ed. (New York: The Natural History Press), page 144.

the same old way. It seems that even when the social context surrounding it begins to crack and to fade, a role will struggle to endure and to reproduce the same sort of relationship in which it was first conceived. The reciprocal action which the role commemorates and calls for worked once; perhaps it can be put to a new use.

30.   What I am saying here is more than "habits are hard to break." So they are, and anyone who has learned a pattern of behavior will tend to persist in it, like Pavlov's dogs. But roles are, by definition, more than individual in their scope. They involve other people. They reflect the working of the social system and the influence of the cultural ambience. They express significance and invoke reaction: "If I do this, the right thing for you to do is that. If my attitude is thus and so, yours should respond in this fashion. This is a serious matter. That is a joke." Their persistence reaches beyond the role-player and affects those who are involved with him. Once these others have been taught what to expect from the player of a certain role, they will expect such behavior from other players of roles that are similar, and they will know how to behave in return. The self-sustaining momentum of a role, therefore, makes it a conservative force, but as long as it contains any social utility, it will also be a shaping force.

31.   Thus, social upheavals are more apt to widen or narrow the utility of any role and to put it to work in new ways than they are to destroy it entirely. Woman's traditional triple role instructs girls in how to get on in the world by pleasing men, how to care for children and how to manage a household. How important each segment of the role is depends partly on the personality of each woman, partly on the people around her and partly on the current social situation. If we take an overall look at the situation today, we see that each segment of woman's role is affected differently. Pleasing men may be less important for more career women than it used to be, but it is still a valuable capability. Caring for young children is, in America, a larger part of a woman's life, for a limited time, than it is almost anywhere else. [. . . T]he two-generation family and the lack of servants put young mothers in sole charge of pre-school children more than 90 percent of the time, apparently a unique situation. Managing a household otherwise, however, has declined spectacularly as a socially useful skill, even with servants almost nonexistent. Nowadays one buys in a shop things that were made at home only a

generation or two ago, and food is processed so completely that cooking has ceased to be a necessity and become a leisure art.

32.   This decline in the economic value of woman's traditional role has, in fact, drawn a great deal of significance and reward out of it. When a household was in part a factory, women were in touch with society and its demands at home almost as much as their husbands were abroad, and more than many women with jobs in business are now. When Solomon described "the virtuous woman" in the last chapter of Proverbs, he set the limits of her activity very wide indeed. She was no housebound creature, but instead one who "seeketh wool and flax, and worketh willingly with her hands. She is like the merchants' ships; she bringeth her food from afar. She riseth while it is yet night, and giveth food to her household and a portion to her maidens. She considereth a field and buyeth it; with the fruit of her hands she planteth a vineyard. . . . She perceiveth that her merchandise is good; her candle goeth not out by night. She layeth her hands to the spindle and her hands hold the distaff. . . . She maketh herself coverings of tapestry. . . .She maketh fine linen and selleth it, and delivereth girdles unto the merchant. . . . She openeth her mouth in wisdom, and in her tongue is the law of kindness. . . . Give her of the fruit of her hands, and let her own works praise her in the gates."

33.   Entrepreneur, trader, investor in land, manufacturer of many sorts of salable merchandise, capable of opening her mouth in wisdom and commanding respect for her opinions, here is the picture of a woman whose role made her an active member of the community, whose work had a fundamental objective value that was clear to all, and whose energies and talents could be used to the full. Nor was such activity thought to make her family suffer: "Her children rise up and call her blessed; her husband also, and he praiseth her." If this is woman's traditional role, it is being played today not by suburban housewives, but by the manager of a middle-sized business or the mayor of a small city. And yet the *idea* of a limiting traditional role is still piously invoked to keep women in their place "at home." It is a very different kind of home, however, from the busy community Solomon described, or even the reduced single-family unit of the nineteenth century which still possessed considerable economic utility.

34.   What we have now is a discontinuity between the idea of what a role should include and involve and its actual contem-

porary content and usefulness. Getting rid of the role, however, is not the answer; or it is very, very seldom the answer, and getting rid of roles altogether is impossible. For human behavior is patterned by learning and playing roles, just as animal behavior is patterned by instinct. In fact, some ethologists are coming to believe that animal behavior, too, is learned, in part at least, and not entirely a matter of instinct. Even in the animal kingdom, that is, situations and relationships affect behavior. As for us, at any rate, to recall Talcott Parsons' words once more, we do not know who we are without roles, nor who other people are.

35.   But if we don't we are lost in a world of strangers. The English theoretical analyst, R. D. Laing, believes that it is just this sort of confusion which induces schizophrenic splits: "Interpersonal action which tends to confuse or mystify . . ." he writes, "makes it difficult for the one person to know 'who' he is, 'who' the other is, and what is the situation they are 'in.' He does not know 'where he is' anymore." [8] Behavior, that is, has got to fit some accepted pattern, or it will not communicate sensibly with those others with whom we live from the day of our birth to the day of our death. No single action means anything at all until it can be seen as part of a language of conduct that is understood in a social system, just as no single sound means anything until its hearers know what language the speaker is using. By patterning behavior so that it is comprehensible, roles keep society coherent.

36.   This being so, the continuing concern of any society must be to avoid freezing behavior into roles that were appropriate to past situations, but have now lost so much of their utility that they invite misunderstanding, both from the role-player who may find himself forced into attitudes that don't suit him and from the other members of the relationship. As Laing remarks, "Those who deceive themselves are obliged to deceive others. It is impossible for me to maintain a false picture of myself unless I falsify your picture of yourself and of me [that is, the picture of the relationship]. I must disparage you if you are genuine, accuse you of being a phoney when you comply with what I want, say you are selfish if you go your own way, ridicule you for being immature if you try to be unselfish, and so on. The person caught within such a muddle doesn't know whether he is

[8] Ronald D. Laing, *Self and Others* (New York: Pantheon Books, 1969), page 122.

coming or going. In these circumstances what we call psychosis may be a desperate effort to hold on to something. It is not surprising that the something may be what we call 'delusions.' '' [9]

37.   A changing society tends to negate old roles, and so to falsify them. Since we cannot make and unmake them quickly, we must accept the necessity of changing them, or else our common language of behavior will lose its relevance. The enormous advantage that human beings have over the rest of the animal kingdom is the flexibility which our command of languages—of words, but also of behavior—gives us. We can keep in touch with new needs and with each other. The conservatism of a going system tugs us one way, the demands of new conditions tug us another. In order to continue to speak to each other, we shall have to coin new words and learn to accept and understand new ways of acting.

38.   The position of women is one of the areas of contemporary life in which new demands are being strongly felt. Woman's role as conceived in the past was a means of channeling activities, some of which have become outmoded, within relationships which are changing their structures. The orthodox pattern is taking on an air of absurdity and exaggeration: of falseness. Still revered by some, it is bitterly attacked by others; Alexander Portnoy's view of the mother role, for example, could hardly be more negative.* His mother's approach to the role was hated and feared. One reason is that it doesn't work any longer. It is not what society needs.

39.   But because some aspects of woman's role still incline women to obsolescent behavior, we can see before our eyes the way that social tradition and present social needs struggle together until new life styles emerge. Woman's role is a good laboratory example to examine, because it has been the scene of such a struggle long enough for us to note effects and not simply beginnings. Here, roles are changing and even some of the mythology surrounding them has been shifted and replaced.

---

[9] *Ibid.,* pages 124–25.

* The hero of Philip Roth's 1967 novel, *Portnoy's Complaint,* says of his mother: "What radar on her! And this is *before* radar! The energy on her! The thoroughness! For mistakes she checked my sums; for holes, my socks; for dirt, my nails, my neck, every seam and crease of my body."[Ed.]

QUESTIONS

1. Elizabeth Janeway draws on her observations of people, certainly, in developing her theory of role playing; but that theory is—like all theories we hold—influenced, and perhaps even shaped, by books. These constitute the secondary sources that she cites throughout the discussion; they serve as a kind of expert witness—a way of establishing the probability of the argument. How many kinds of evidence—historical, psychological, sociological, and so on—does she provide?

2. She draws on familiar historical examples (Joan of Arc, Eleanor Roosevelt) as well as on contemporary history to make her points. How does she fit these examples to her audience? How would you characterize that audience? Is she writing for the general reader, or perhaps exclusively for women?

3. How broad the generalizations we make depends on the range and solidity of evidence we can muster for them. Does Elizabeth Janeway offer generalizations about men or women or role-playing for which she presents no evidence? Must she defend all of her assumptions?

4. Primary evidence would consist of first-hand accounts, personal testimonies, quotations from letters and journals, and the like. For which of her ideas would it be difficult to provide primary evidence of this sort? What kind of evidence can be provided for them?

5. Must the shrew be explained before we can understand the witch—or is the order of ideas determined by what the author believes is the more persuasive example or consideration?

WRITING ASSIGNMENT

Discuss your agreement or disagreement with any of the ideas in the essay by analyzing role-playing you have observed.

THEMATIC TABLE OF CONTENTS

INDEX OF AUTHORS AND TOPICS